SMALL WARS PERMITTING
Dispatches from Foreign Lands

CHRISTINA LAMB

HarperPress
An Imprint of HarperCollins*Publishers*

Harper*Press*
An imprint of HarperCollins*Publishers*
77–85 Fulham Palace Road,
Hammersmith, London W6 8JB
www.harpercollins.co.uk

Published by Harper*Press* in 2008

1

A catalogue record for this book
is available from the British Library

ISBN 978-0-00-725689-1

Typeset in Minion

Printed and bound in Great Britain by Clays Ltd, St Ives plc

Mixed Sources
Product group from well-managed
forests and other controlled sources
www.fsc.org Cert no. SW-COC-1806
© 1996 Forest Stewardship Council

FSC is a non-profit international organisation established to promote the
responsible management of the world's forests. Products carrying the FSC
label are independently certified to assure consumers that they come
from forests that are managed to meet the social, economic and
ecological needs of present and future generations.

Find out more about HarperCollins and the environment at
www.harpercollins.co.uk/green

In memory of Wais Faizi,
and all the many people like him all over
the world on whom we journalists depend

Contents

Prologue: The Plane to Kish Island 1

Where It Began: Invitation to a Wedding 7

How Many Wars Have You Covered? 27

Death of a General 49

The Last Happy Nation 67

Dictators and Dinghies: Journeys in Latin America 93

The Rise and Fall of Fernando Collor 107

The Tarantula Crossing the Street 121

Love Intervenes 143

To the City of Gold – via Baghdad 149

You Never Know When You Might Need a Wailer 169

Yes, I Was a Cynic until I Met Her – Diana 179

A Zanzibari Wedding 185

Tea with Pinochet 191

A Day Trip to Lagos – the Sad Story of Damilola Taylor 197

A Short Arrest in the Ivory Coast 209

9/11 – Back to Where It Started 223

All Roads Lead to Pakistan 243

War in Iraq with a Dolphin-tamer 255

The Last Summer in Baghdad 279

Saddam Stole Our Water   297
An Afghan Asks Why   307
The Madness of Mugabe   309
Where's bin Laden?   331
'Have You Ever Used a Pistol?'   351
'It was what we feared, but dared not to happen'   367
PS In Memoriam   381

Acknowledgements   385
Index of Articles   388

'Goodbye,' said the fox to the Little Prince. 'And now here is my secret, a very simple secret: It is only with the heart that one can rightly see; what is essential is invisible to the eye.'

ANTOINE DE SAINT-EXUPÉRY

Prologue:
The Plane to Kish Island

Here is a typical morning in my life. It happens to be Sunday, 2 July 2006 and it is the day of my son's seventh birthday party.

I arrived back on a plane early this morning from Afghanistan. At Heathrow I am one of the lucky people greeted by a name board: for the first time ever my newspaper has arranged a car to pick me up. London has a grey hung-over gloom and St George's flags droop forlornly from windows. The driver tells me that England was knocked out of the World Cup by Portugal the night before. Penalties, of course: I needn't ask.

After dropping off my bags at home along with some Starbucks croissants from the airport, and drinking my first decent cup of tea in a month, we drive to Sainsbury's to buy ham and sliced bread. I have to make ham sandwiches for twenty 7-year-olds.

I make twice as many as anyone will eat, buttering slice after slice of bread with great purpose. Then I take them and a cool box of drinks to nearby Palewell Park where we are having a football party.

Some of the children at the party are pointing at me and whispering. They have seen me on the news or the front page of the *Sunday Times* that morning and know that four days ago I was almost killed by Taliban – the 'baddies' I hear one of them explain.

My mother is there, looking shocked, though I had phoned from Heathrow to warn her before she bought the paper. My husband, who is Portuguese, has said nothing.

This, after all, is what I do.

It is a sunny afternoon and I throw myself into arranging children's drinks and ice creams and acting supremely unbothered. I want to keep hugging the blue-eyed birthday boy who I thought I would never see again but I know he will regard that as 'embarrassment-making'. My phone beeps insistently with text messages – a bizarre mix of horrified concern from those who have seen the story in the paper and jokes about the state of my marriage after the Portugal–England match from those who haven't.

My jeans and long printed smock are covering cuts, bruises, burns and thorns that I will still be picking out in six months. Some of them are infected and in a few days I will go to a local GP who will say, 'You have been in the wars,' and I will laugh and let him assume I fell off my bike into a thorn bush.

I have spent twenty years living on the edge. I have been pinned down by Russian tanks in a trench in Kandahar, narrowly missed a brick that smashed through my car windscreen on the West Bank, navigated through roadblocks manned by red-eyed drug-crazed boys with Kalashnikovs in West Africa, been kidnapped in the middle of the night by Pakistani intelligence, survived car crashes and emer-gency landings in planes held together by tape, and come under sniper fire in Iraq. All around me people have died. My life, I believe, is charmed.

Now I have come as close as possible to being killed. The British paratroopers with whom I was ambushed were so convinced we were about to be 'rolled up' that they talked of saving their last bullets for themselves. In that ditch surrounded on all sides by Taliban with mortars, RPGs (rocket-propelled grenades) and Kalashnikovs, for the first time I really believed I would die. And I swore if I ever got out I would never go back.

Two months later, I will grab the bag with my flak jacket, helmet, medical kit and satellite phone and be back on a plane to Afghanistan.

Why do it? Every day I run away from that question.

I am not an alcoholic, a heroin addict, or from a broken home. I am a mother of a gorgeous curly-haired boy, wife of a loving husband, daughter of devoted parents, part of a close circle of friends…I have no excuses.

I could tell you it's a search for truth. A hope that by exposing the evils and injustices of the world I can help make it a better place. Sadly, the pen is not that mighty or else the likes of Mugabe would not still be in power.

I could tell you that when I was a child I loved to read the poems of Robert Louis Stevenson and turn the sheets hanging on the washing line into doors on to faraway places. One of our neighbours had an apple tree that served just as well as Stevenson's cherry tree for climbing up and looking 'abroad on foreign lands'.

I could tell you that I felt suffocated by suburbia, living in a place called Carshalton Beeches where the only excitement was to go 'up the wine bar' or 'down the pub'. Adventure was missing the last train from London and having to take a series of night buses from Trafalgar Square.

I could tell you that I adored Hemingway and wanted to run with the bulls in Spain, watch big game among the green hills of Africa (though not hunt it), drink mojitos in bars in old Havana and find love behind the lines.

I could tell you that once you see others die and evils such as boys turned into killing machines with AK-47s, or families forced to bury stick-limbed girls because they could not afford HIV drugs, one's own life becomes pretty insignificant.

I could tell you that there is nothing more thrilling than getting on a plane to somewhere you have never been, particularly with a name like Bujumbura or Cochabamba. That used to be true but these days endless security queues have spoiled the magic of airports.

Maybe the truth lies in Dubai Terminal 2. That's where you go to catch planes to the bad places. The destination board reads Kabul, Baghdad, Mogadishu and the airlines have names you've never heard of like Chelyabinsk Airlines, Don Airlines, Kam Air, Ossetia, Mahan Air and Samara Airlines. These are airlines so dodgy that they are not allowed to land at the proper airport. Many, like Ariana Afghan Airlines or Reem Air of Kyrgyzstan, are on a list banning them from European airspace and describing them as 'flying coffins'. Their planes are old Tupolevs bought second or third hand from Aeroflot or Air India.

The name, Terminal 2, makes it sound as if it is attached to the main airport but in fact it lies a half-hour's taxi ride away. It seems in another country entirely to that gleaming glass temple to capitalism where Arabs in white *dishdash* and sunburnt passengers in shorts and miniskirts shop for Rolex watches and Fendi handbags and buy $100 lottery tickets to win a Jaguar X-type.

At Terminal 2 there is just one shop and people stock up on Mars Bars, tampons and biscuits, for they don't know what will be available at the other end. Mostly they are bounty hunters, Afghan money-changers, aid workers, private security guards and journalists. Instead of smart shiny suitcases they have battered kitbags and rucksacks, black plastic crates of survival equipment, or, in the case of the Afghans, large cloth bundles. The ones with briefcases are consultants, being paid thousands of dollars for something called 'capacity building', but they will get on a special United Nations plane. Sometimes there are dead bodies being flown back from comfortable exile to be buried in harsh homelands.

Most people have grimly resigned expressions, particularly if like me they are flying Ariana. For the airlines of Terminal 2 departure times mean nothing and it is common to turn up day after day before a plane finally arrives. Besides we all know that the Ariana pilots prefer staying in Dubai to piloting their 'coffins' back to a destroyed country. We debate with those holding Kam tickets whether it's safer to fly with an airline that has already crashed or one that always seems about to crash. Passengers that make a fuss and try to find non-existent airline representatives are exposed as newcomers.

Some might be committed do-gooders; others are only doing it for money. 'George Bush has paid off thousands of mortgages,' says a Scottish ex-para on his way to be a $1,000-a-day security consultant in Afghanistan after a long stint in Iraq.

But there are a few that have a look on their face that I recognise. It's a sort of suburban restlessness. Not in a grass-is-always-greener kind of way: but a search for adventure.

These are the people whose eyes light up when they see the name Kish appear on the destination board. Where is that? Kish Island in Iran, someone tells me. It sounds intriguing. I know I will try to go there. It will mean flying Kish Air which last crashed two years ago.

Biographers of Alexander the Great used the Greek word *pothos* to describe his endless yearning to be somewhere else, whether it was to cross the Danube, go to the oracle of Ammon, sail the ocean, see the Persian Gulf or untie the legendary knot at Gordium.

I liked that description. But then I read that the longing for something unattainable expressed by *pothos* could also signify a desire to die. For *pothos* is also the name for delphiniums, the flowers that Greeks traditionally placed on someone's tomb.

I never set out to be brave or daring or intrepid or any of those labels often attached to the title 'war correspondent'. What I wanted to be is a storyteller. I have been lucky enough to live in countries in Asia, Latin America, Africa, the Middle East and Europe at a time of huge upheaval when the world was adjusting from the cold war to a whole new war of terrorist attacks and suicide bombs.

To me the real story in war is not the bang-bang but the lives of those trying to survive behind the lines. Working for a weekly paper has given me the luxury of time to be able to go behind the lines where other reporters don't and tell the stories of the forgotten. Sometimes the story behind the article is more interesting than what appeared on the printed page, and where that is so I have tried to include it.

This book then is not an attempt to answer the question why, but a record of what I have seen as it is. It is a mixture of memories, articles and impressions jotted in notebooks and diaries. These are my places of hope and despair.

London, October 2007

Where It Began:
Invitation to a Wedding

Pakistan 1987–1989

I am lying in bed in Karachi. The air is damp and sticky and I am breathing in the headachy smell of jasmine. White and crimson petals are falling over me. Bollywood film stars, politicians and khans are flitting around like shadow dancers. Delicate henna flowers and blossoms twist across both sides of my hands and over my feet, and fireworks explode into showers of red and white stars in the sky.

It is very hot. Several times in the night I had to put my sheet under the cold water tap to cool myself down.

In and out of consciousness I drift, peacock colours flashing before my eyes. At the edges of my slumber I am dimly aware of a man shouting and drumming. The sound is growing louder and louder and my henna-painted palms itch until I can resist no longer. I open the curtains and blink at the yellow morning sun over Clifton beach, a sun that at 8 a.m. is already blurred round the edges and throbbing ominously. On the seafront is a tattered monkey in a red fez, banging a drum while its owner jerks a chain round its neck to make it dance. Beyond, a line of camels bobs slowly up and down along the sand and a group of women in long baggy pyjamas are dipping their toes in the Arabian Sea.

It is day three of the wedding celebrations of Benazir Bhutto and my life has just changed for ever.

Only a few days earlier I was in drizzly Birmingham, blinking back tears as I drove round and round Spaghetti Junction in my electric-blue Morris Marina. I was trying to find the turn-off for the Bullring, the

most depressing shopping centre in Britain, a hulk of concrete in a web of ring roads. Inside, most of the shops were either closed down or closing down and two local firemen were trying to beat the world record for the number of days wearing gas masks. I was interviewing them for Central TV where I was a trainee reporter. Once the camera-man, sound man and sparks (lights man) had all arrived (separately, so as to each claim mileage allowance), we got under way. The report was supposed to be funny, the firemen's answers distorted by their masks. However, it was so cold that the camera battery kept seizing up, forcing us to start all over again. By the fifth take even the firemen were looking bored.

Actually that was a good day. As the most junior person in the Central newsroom, I often spent mornings going through the tabloids checking out stories in our patch and discovering half were not true. Worst of all were the door-knocks. Our area encompassed both the M1 and M6 motorways where young people were often killed in drink-driving accidents and there was nothing harder than knocking on the doors of their families and asking for a photo.

So it is that on that December morning in 1987 when I look out on Clifton beach, a huge grin spreads across my face. Later that day, I walk along the promenade to the green-domed shrine to Abdullah Shah Ghazi, an eighth-century mystic regarded as Karachi's patron saint. There, I pay a few rupees to a man with a scrawny parakeet for it to pick me tarot cards. 'You will be back within a year,' he predicts. I manage to get through to the international operator and make a reverse-charge call to the *Financial Times* in London. They put me through to something called Copy where a very nice lady tells me not to speak so fast. It is my first report as a foreign correspondent.

Bhutto the bride
Financial Times, 19 December 1987

THERE'S A STORY going round Karachi at the moment of a wedding so successful that the gifts had to be carried away in trucks. But over the past few weeks gold cards have been landing on doormats around the world inviting people to a wedding destined to outdo them all.

Invitations to the public reception are in such demand that fortunes have been made forging them, while one man in Punjab set himself alight because he could not afford the train fare.

The five-star hotels are full; the tailors are working day and night to create visions in spun gold. Like a huge Christmas tree, 70 Clifton Road is festooned with lights. Inside, preparations and festivities have been under way all week. For this is no ordinary wedding. The lights are red, white and green – the colours of the Pakistan People's Party (PPP). And Pinkie, as the bride is affectionately known, is more familiar as Benazir Bhutto, leader of the opposition People's Party and daughter of Zulfikar Ali Bhutto, the former Prime Minister hanged in 1979.

Inside the women's quarters, the pressure is intense. Weddings are a matter of face here and families will go without food and spend much of their lives in debt to give their daughters a good send-off. The average wage is £50 a month, yet parents spend £100 a time on gold-threaded dresses for the bride's trousseau that will probably end life as cushion covers.

Benazir's landed family is far from poor and her husband-to-be is from one of the twenty-two families which once owned two-thirds of Pakistan. He has already given her a heart-shaped ring of diamonds and sapphires and sends her roses every day. But the would-be prime minister is locked in a battle with an array of aunties dismayed at her refusal to accept the traditional trousseau from the groom's family. Instead of the twenty-one to fifty-one sets of clothes usually presented to the bride, Benazir has set the limit at two. As for the gold bangles that brides are supposed to wear all the way up each arm from wrist to elbow, she says she will wear glass. When Auntie Behjat complains this will bring shame on the family, Benazir protests, 'I am a leader, I must set an example to my people.' For once her voice is ignored. Every day more and more presents arrive at the gate: embroidered shawls, platters of sweets, fruits and almonds dipped in silver and gold.

Benazir is a fanatical perfectionist and her assistants are well aware that the eyes of the world are focused on their efforts. But, they complain, she will keep slipping out to the office when traditionally she should spend this week in purdah – behind a veil and inside four walls and wearing yellow clothes and no make-up so as not to attract the evil eye. 'I don't have time for this,' she protests.

Every few minutes another gaggle of cousins arrives from New York, Tehran, London or Bombay, prompting hysterical scenes. This is the first time in years that the entire Bhutto clan has been together (less an errant sister-in-law facing trial in France and Benazir's estranged brother Murtaza wanted in Pakistan for hijacking a PIA plane). Some have risked imprisonment by returning.

Between frantic sewing and talking and preparation of sweetmeats, the time is spent singing and dancing. The girls have been practising for weeks, singing of the bride's beauty and the groom's weaknesses, ready for competition with the groom's family at Thursday's *mehndi* or henna celebration. 'On my beloved's forehead his hair is shining. Bring, bring, bring the henna which will colour my beloved's hands,' they sing. Already there are many hoarse voices. And laughter too, when less traditional lines are added like 'You must agree that Benazir will serve the nation.' Every so often the merrymaking is stopped abruptly by a power cut. These prompt speculation that the military dictator

General Zia, who hanged Benazir's father, is reasserting his authority.

A multi-coloured marquee has been erected in the garden between the palms and mango trees. Bowers of jasmine and roses lead to a silver tinsel-bedecked stage. On top of this is a mother-of-pearl bench – the wedding stage where Benazir will sit next to Asif and say yes three times to become a married woman. A mirror will then be held in front of them so they can see each other as partners for the first time while sugar is ground over their heads so their lives will be sweet.

Are they in love? I wonder. It was an arranged marriage – Benazir's press statement announcing her engagement began less than enthusiastically: 'Conscious of my religious obligations and duty to my family, I am pleased to proceed with the marriage proposal accepted by my mother.'

But everyone tells me that in arranged marriages you learn to love each other. 'It's better because you go in with no preconceptions or expectations,' say her friends Yasmin, Sanam and Laleh. All her aunties tell me how pleased they are that 'Bibi' is finally settling down.

The morning before the main celebrations is devoted to beautification. Underneath Mr Bhutto's powerful portrait, groups of brightly swathed girls sit chattering for hours while intricate henna designs are painstakingly etched on their hands and feet and aromatic oils massaged into their skin. Upstairs Benazir is undergoing the painful process of having all her body hair removed, but there are no screams to be heard above the din down here – this after all is a bride who has endured years in detention by a military regime, including ten months in solitary confinement in Sukkur jail.

The police stationed outside number 70 raise their eyes at all the commotion, unable to see a way of extracting baksheesh from the situation. On my first few visits my car was followed in a way Inspector Clouseau would have appreciated but they have given up trying to keep track.

For once, though, politics seem forgotten. Even the orange-seller on the corner, usually anxious to explain how the 'CIA devils' are destroying the country, is obsessed by the wedding. Rumours abound about who is and who is not coming. David Owen has accepted, and Colonel Gaddafi was never invited, despite stories in the Urdu press that he declined because of domestic problems and has sent a six-seater Cessna as a gift. Benazir assures me she's seen no sign of it.

Of course being Benazir, you couldn't expect the political to stay out of the wedding altogether. Ten thousand people – many of them PPP workers – are already camped out at the Lyari grounds where a stage and massive speakers have been erected for a public ceremony that has the sound of a party rally to me.

Weddings are a time when personality clashes are put aside. Rival leaders of the Movement for the Restoration of Democracy and former leading members of the PPP are here, though no generals have been invited. Many non-political alliances will be forged over the next few days as eagle-eyed aunts and mothers look out for suitable catches. Being tall, fair and holding a British passport qualifies me for many of their shortlists, but unfortunately I cannot claim to be particularly 'domestically well versed' and, gin and tonic in hand, I am certainly not a good Muslim…

I had spent the previous summer as an intern on the foreign desk of the *Financial Times* and knew that more than anything I wanted to be a foreign correspondent.

The camel corps they called them. Occasionally they would waft in with the smell of the desert or tang of the sea, dressed in crumpled linen suits, their tanned faces making the people in the office look washed-out and grey. They covered wars, revolutions and insurgencies, and spoke on the phone in exotic languages. They were glamorous, rugged, the skin round their eyes all wrinkled from the sun, and they carried battered leather satchels full of notes and foreign newspapers.

They were all men and to me they were like gods.

The FT in those days was more grandly housed in Bracken House (now a Japanese bank) opposite St Paul's at the tail end of Fleet Street. It had two neighbouring watering holes – Balls Brothers and the Dolphin – to one of which the gods would sometimes take me. They would order champagne by the bottle which impressed me greatly, and I hung on to their every word. Far from pronouncing on important world issues of the day, mostly they would grouch about the foreign desk rewriting their copy or not giving it its due prominence. How could they complain? They had dream jobs.

Occasionally some news event would happen in their part of the world and the phone would ring in the bar. Whoever's region it was would curse, return to the office, hammer out some words on the typewriter, throw the copy into a wire basket then be back in the bar for another 'El Stiffo'.

I didn't understand when people did any real work or how the newspaper came out, but I wanted that life.

One day I too got to toss a carbon-copied sheet in the basket and see my words magically appear in the next day's newspaper. Jurek Martin, the foreign editor, had been due to attend a lunch of South Asian politicians. At the last minute he could not go and looked around for someone to send in his place. I was always talking about India where I had spent the previous summer and written a thesis on Kashmir, and through his thick glasses his gaze lighted upon me. At the lunch I sat next to a gentle-voiced man called Bashir from the Pakistan People's Party – Benazir Bhutto's party – and he asked me if I would like to interview her. Of course I said yes. She had just announced her engagement and was sitting serenely in her Kensington flat, surrounded by lava lamps and cellophane-wrapped bouquets. The resulting interview was my first big article in a national paper and it would decide my destiny.

Throughout my teenage years I had yearned for adventure. My parents had moved from gritty, council estate Morden to leafy Carshalton Beeches so I could go to one of England's last state grammar schools. Nonsuch High School for Girls liked to boast it had only two rules – Consideration to Others and Always Walk on the Right – but whatever I did I broke them. I was always running along corridors or walking on the wrong side or alerting classmates to flashers by the top field which bordered on to a park. So bored was I that I wrote bloodthirsty stories to shock my teachers and kidnapped the headmistress's special chair, sending a ransom note demanding 40 million Green Shield stamps or a limb would be amputated every hour. I was endlessly in detention.

Kept after school writing lines, I would gaze out of the window conjuring up far-off worlds.

I suppose it didn't help that I spent most of my teens trapped inside a body brace. A visit to the hospital for a broken little finger led to a general check which revealed that I had scoliosis, curvature of the spine. I was lucky – the Boston brace made of foam-lined plastic had just been invented and was far less uncomfortable and obtrusive than the old Milwaukee, a leather-and-iron contraption with chin pad. Even so, for an adolescent girl starting to be conscious of her appearance, wearing a back brace twenty-three hours a day was not easy. From the ages of 13 to 18 my life revolved around hospitals where men in white coats scratched their heads as they applied compasses and protractors to X-rays of my contorted spine. The only good part was getting out of hockey.

Despite the school I missed and the trouble I got into when I was there, I was lucky enough to win a place at Oxford. No one in my family had ever been to university and I applied to University College on the basis that it was on the high street between a bank and a pub. Oxford seemed terribly elitist and I hadn't thought I wanted to go until, driving home from the interview with my dad, I looked back through the gap in the Chilterns and saw the sun setting over the dreaming spires.

At Oxford the world seemed full of possibility. Being dragged along by a friend to a cheese and wine party hosted by the university newspaper *Cherwell* eventually led to me becoming editor. I loathed the smell of the Dyson Perrins organic labs and swapped chemistry for PPE – philosophy, politics and economics. My mum was horrified, unable to imagine what kind of job might require a knowledge of Descartes or Kant. She was not reassured when she saw me writing essays on topics such as 'Can Sheep Have Religious Beliefs?' and 'Can a Geranium Have a Point of View?'

After graduating, my summer at the FT was followed by a job at Central TV. I was one of two trainees, both female, in a newsroom full of male reporters and editors. Most of them had worked their way up through local newspapers and radio and were not at all keen on the idea of graduate trainees, particularly ones from Oxford who smoked white-tipped Cartier cigarettes. My fellow trainee Ronke was a glamorous single mother who had already spent a few years in local radio and we eyed each other like tomcats marking out territory before ending up best friends.

I had only been there a few months when the large gold-inscribed invitation to Benazir's wedding landed on my mat.

After that introduction to Pakistan I knew I could not go back to my job covering local news in Birmingham. I went to see the FT and got a vague agreement that they would rent me a Tandy word processor and pay for whatever they published. I bought a bucket-shop flight to Lahore and packed everything I imagined I would need to be a foreign correspondent, including a tape of Mahler's Fifth, a jumbo bag of wine gums, a lucky pink rabbit and a bottle of Chanel No. 5 that my boyfriend's mum had got at trade price. I could hardly carry the suitcase.

The foreign editors I had spoken to in London had all expressed more interest in Russian-occupied Afghanistan than Pakistan, so I headed for the border town of Peshawar in Pakistan's North-West Frontier Province. The place names alone promised Kipling-like adventure. In my case was a copy of *Kim* and I liked the idea of following in the footsteps of the little boy who had been sitting drumming his heels astride the Zamzamma gun on the Lahore Mall when a yellow-faced lama in a dingy robe appeared and lured him to the Frontier region.

A minibus service called the Flying Coach plied up and down the Grand Trunk Road from Rawalpindi to Peshawar and I was the only foreigner on board. Green parakeets were flying back home in their droves and the dusk-time sky was streaked with apricot and purple as we turned off by Peshawar fort and arrived in the Old City. Immediately I was surrounded by people trying to sell me everything from Chinese hairgrips to onyx chess sets. It was here, among the leaning wood-framed houses and narrow alleys piled high with spices and brass pots, that Mahbub Ali, the wily horse trader, entrusted Kim with secret letters revealing the plots of Central Asian emirs.

I had my own pack of letters from a Pakistani friend in London but no idea where I was going so let a rickshaw take me to Greens Hotel. This turned out to be where the arms dealers hung out. My first night there someone tried to sell me a multi-barrel rocket launcher. My small room was already inhabited by shiny brown cockroaches and the mattress was so thin that the broken springs jabbed into my skinny frame. But out of the window I could see the dark serrated ridges of the Khyber Pass silhouetted against the sky and that was all that mattered.

Everything in Pakistan seemed to be about who you knew. My unpromising-looking letters from London would open all sorts of doors. One of them led to me being befriended by the Arbabs, a family so well connected they even had roads named after them. The old man Fateh Khan Arbab told me bloodcurdling stories about the Pathan tribes and their Pashtunwali honour code that gave protection to strangers, whoever they might be, and demanded an eye for an eye for any offence. It was he who arranged for me to go and spend a day with a tribal chief in his fort on the Khyber Pass. I took my friend Tanya who was visiting me on holiday from her high-powered advertising job.

Malik Nadyer Khan Afridi was a small dapper man in his fifties wearing an oversize overcoat and astrakhan hat and carrying a large black furled umbrella. He looked like someone's harmless grandfather, or at least would have done were it not for the seven Kalashnikov-toting heavies who followed him everywhere. In fact he was chief of the Zakakhels, a sub-tribe of the Afridis, guardians of the Khyber Pass. So renowned are they for their ferocity that it was said during colonial times that if you found a snake and an Afridi in your bedroom you should kill the Afridi first.

'Foreigners are not allowed beyond this point,' reads the sign as one passes between the two stone turrets of the Khyber Gate. Behind us we left the green plains of Peshawar, and ahead lay a dry stony land in washed-out hues of grey and beige. The pass is about twenty-five miles long and it took a while to climb in my little blue Suzuki car, weighed down by two sulky Pathan tribal guards, in long black tunics and clutching Kalashnikovs, squashed into the back seat. Just as in Kipling's day, Peshawar still had a deputy commissioner and he had only granted us a permit on condition we took the guards for our protection. I had picked up enough Pashto to realise they were discussing how much two healthy young Englishwomen would fetch on the open market.

The way starts wide and flat, bounded by low stony hills, then snakes up to the British-built Shahgai Fort, now home to the Khyber Rifles, where visitors to this day are still greeted by bagpipers. From there it plunges down through a gorge so narrow that at times the cliff walls overhead almost seem to touch. Small stone forts dot the mountain tops and the cliff walls are decorated with pennants from regiments that have served in the Khyber Rifles. Along the valley bottom were concrete 'dragon's teeth' laid down in World War II by the British fearing a German tank invasion of the subcontinent.

For it was the history, more than the scenery, that stirred the blood. Images crowded my head of armies of conquerors such as Alexander the Great, Genghis Khan, Tamerlane and Babur, the first Mogul Emperor, with their cavalcades of elephants or camels. All had marched through this pass seeking the great prize of India. Each had to fight with the Afridis.

This was also the land of the Great Game, where British officers played the tribes off against each other, and Russia and Britain vied for control of India. The British first marched up the Khyber Pass in 1839, on their way to the first Anglo-Afghan war, which was to end in disaster three years later with the massacre of every soldier save the lone Dr William Brydon, spared to tell the story. They returned in 1878 and again were forced by the Afghans to withdraw. Each time, they lost hundreds of men fighting their way through the Afridi-held Khyber territory.

We saw no women on the way up and all the men we passed were armed. I wondered if their taste for British blood had dulled over the years.

We were starving by the time we got to the fort and devoured the plates of yellow cake and spicy samosas that were brought out, washed down with warm Russian champagne served in pint glasses. Then two men appeared with skewers the length of swords bearing roasted pieces of freshly slaughtered sheep.

After we had eaten our fill the *malik* rang a little bell. 'Now we will have lunch,' he said.

Tanya and I looked at each other in horror. He led us through to a wood-panelled room with a long table laden with plates of food.

'If I have to eat any more, I'll cry!' hissed Tanya.

I was unsympathetic. The *malik*'s eyes glinted pistol-grey as he bit into the skewered lamb and bloody juices ran down his chin.

'We'll have to eat it or he'll kill us,' I replied.

I had been in Pakistan long enough by then to be adept at playing with food and taking many small helpings. But Tanya was seated alongside the *malik* with no place to hide her plate, on to which he piled more and more. The conversation moved on to Afghanistan; his tribe, like many Pathans, was split along both sides of the border. Afghanistan's then President Najibullah was known as the Ox for his strength, but the *malik* was disparaging. 'He used to clean my shoes,' he said. But he waxed lyrical about the country which he described as a land of milk and honey where pomegranates shone like giant rubies and peaches grew to the size of footballs.

'I would love to go there,' said Tanya.

'Why not?' he replied.

Why not? Well, there was the small matter of its being under Soviet occupation.

Not a problem. He rang his little bell to summon some gunmen.

Woozy from our second bottle of Russian champagne, we piled into his jeep and drove though Landikotal bazaar where men in shacks either side of the road were selling opium in goatskins. The sudden putter of machine-gun fire made us jump.

'What are they doing?' asked Tanya.

'Shooting each other,' replied one of the *malik*'s henchmen.

Finally we got to the Afghan border at Torkham and its long-abandoned Customs house. Two hours later it was blown up by a Scud missile. We would tell everyone afterwards we had a narrow escape.

Smuggler's paradise
Financial Times, 3 September 1988

Khyber Pass

LAST WEEK I HAD DINNER with a smuggler. The directions, which sounded bizarre, were precise: the sixth fort on the left after the English grammar school for young ladies, halfway up the Khyber Pass.

As I waited for the huge door to open and swallow me up, I could not help noticing the anti-aircraft gun mounted on one of the four watchtowers. Over warm Russian champagne, my host explained that his family had a long-standing feud with another tribe since his cousin had abducted one of their women. The score on revenge killings was now four all.

It seemed reasonable. Only that morning, my friend Amjad, the regional manager of an agricultural credit bank, had told me about the difficulties of ensuring that field officers were not posted to areas where they might be shot as part of a feud.

Feuds and smuggling are a way of life in the tribal areas of Pakistan's North-West Frontier Province, but the spillover of sophisticated weaponry and Soviet booty from Afghanistan has heightened the stakes. My smuggler friend complained wistfully: 'It was far more fun in the old days when enemies often had to be stalked for years with a Lee-Enfield. Now, with Kalashnikovs and rocket launchers, whole families can be wiped out in minutes.'

Often, they are. Shootouts in which eight to ten people are killed rate only an inside paragraph in the local press.

He insisted that 'an eye for an eye' was an 'excellent' system. The previous week he had burned down his best friend's fort after the man's son had stolen a car. Now the son had apologised and my friend was helping him rebuild it.

It is not just for security reasons that tribal smugglers like my host dwell in forts. Inside the high mud walls were piles of Soviet refrigerators and microwaves, smuggled from Kabul.

Prices of smuggled Russian goods have undercut the once-popular Japanese items by so much that these are now rarely seen in Pakistan's bazaars. Few homes are without a Soviet air conditioner. And despite the Islamic prohibition on alcohol, a roaring trade is done in the Russian vodka known fondly as 'Gorbachev'.

In the smugglers' bazaar just outside Peshawar, you can buy anything from Chinese toilet paper to Bulgarian beer, Scotch whisky to Mothercare baby lotion, Black Sea caviar to Marks & Spencer mumsy knickers. Indeed, smuggling has become a complex business. No longer can a self-respecting operator rely on a few mules laden with Afghan cigarettes. These days, garishly painted government trucks fight it out on the highway between Kabul and Peshawar, piled high with all sorts of luxury goods.

Several resistance commanders inside Afghanistan have struck deals with the Kabul regime not to block off the road so that they can continue to levy 'taxes' on such vehicles. And some of the heaviest infighting between resistance groups has been on the main route between Kabul and the Soviet Union, which each group wants to control so it can hijack trucks full of goodies destined for Russian officers in the capital.

Similarly, many of the weapons given to Afghan commanders are sold off in frontier arms markets en route.

Aid organisations such as the United Nations High Commission for Refugees (UNHCR) take smuggling so seriously they are hesitant about sending mules to Afghanistan to replace the estimated half a million oxen killed there in the war. Last year, a consignment of Texas mules intended to be used by the Afghan resistance fighters were swapped for

scrawnier Pakistani specimens long before reaching their destination.

It is not always easy being a smuggler despite the high returns – my friend would not deal in anything that gave him less than a 500 per cent profit. Ironically, his main complaint is over the widespread corruption, which means he must pay many bribes. As a practising Muslim with a weakness for alcohol, he claims most of his countrymen are hypocrites. 'Ten years ago,' he says, 'each village had a tiny mosque with a handful of people praying. Now, there are mosques everywhere full of prostrate people, yet corruption is far worse.'

A sizeable portion of the smuggler's takings is earmarked for Customs officials who turn a blind eye. Being a Customs man has become highly lucrative; in a recent survey at Karachi University, the majority of students listed it as their most sought-after career.

The other major consideration for aspiring smugglers is the difficulty in turning black money into white. My host has, among other things, an estate in the United States, a yacht in the south of France and a Swiss bank account. If he gets stuck with too much cash,

he legitimises some by buying winning government lottery tickets at
several times their surrender value.

Pakistan was an astonishingly hospitable place where it was easy to get
passed on from one friend to another, catching a lift from one or
sleeping on cushions on the floor of another. Like this, I managed to
travel all the way south to the old city of Mojendaro then far north up
the Karakoram Highway for the world's highest polo match between
Chitral and Gilgit, up among the peaks of the Hindu Kush. I camped
on a green plateau between two lakes that for much of the year is cut
off by snow.

But its most intriguing place lay at its western extreme. Baluchistan
was Pakistan's most backward province, bordering Afghanistan and
Iran and stretching down to the Arabian Sea. It was a strange toffee-
colour land of arid desert and rugged mountains that roasted in
summer and shivered in snowy winters, and where men with black-
rimmed eyes and jewel-studded high-heeled sandals walked hand in
hand in the bazaar. Foreigners rarely went there, though I did once see
one of those double-decker overland buses that had come all the way
from Marble Arch.

Although it was one and a half times the size of England,
Baluchistan had just 4 million people and had been completely
neglected until the Russian invasion of neighbouring Afghanistan in
1979 made it strategically important.

Not only was it huge and hard to defend but extremely tribal. In
years to come it would be the perfect sanctuary for Taliban launching
raids across the border into Helmand and Kandahar.

Where medieval ways die hard
Financial Times, 5 August 1989

THE 14-YEAR-OLD BOY looked a bit confused by it all. A week earlier,
he had been sitting in uniform in his public school reciting English

verbs. Now, bedecked with shawls and an elaborate headdress, he was sitting on a gaily decorated stage and being crowned sardar, the most powerful man in the 20,000-strong Tareen tribe.

Tribal chiefs in flowing turbans whose daring raids on the British had made them his childhood heroes had arrived from all over Baluchistan for the coronation. Most agreed the boy would be the last of the sardars. His grandfather had died the previous week and his father, in delicate health, passed the title to his oldest son. From now on Mohammad Qaddafi Khan Tareen will control the destinies of the 20,000 Tareens. On his say they live, die, prosper or starve.

The celebratory lunch for a mere 5,000 resembled the court of Henry VIII with row upon row of chiefs sitting cross-legged and munching great hunks of meat, tossing the bones carelessly over their shoulders. Some 172 sheep and 18 cows had been slaughtered for the occasion and an entire room was piled high with 10,000 pieces of naan, flat unleavened bread.

There may be no more such occasions. Each of Baluchistan's tribes is ruled by a sardar whose authority until recently was rarely questioned. But with development bringing roads and exposure to the outside world, the sardars seem to be losing power. 'We are becoming figureheads like the Queen of England,' said one. They will not go without a fight, though.

The heyday of the sardars was during the days of the Raj. When the British took over the region in 1846 they followed a policy known as 'masterly inactivity'. This meant dividing it into settled areas that were British-governed; an independent state known as Kalat ruled by a khan; and tribal zones which British administrators were forbidden to enter. But the tribes relied on continually looting and raiding the settled areas, knowing the British were powerless to follow them.

Matters came to a head in 1867 when 1,500 armed raiders struck at the frontier district of Dera Ghazi Khan in Punjab. Britain's Deputy Commissioner there, Robert Sandemann, raised a force of local tribesmen and drove them off, killing 120 and taking 200 prisoners. Later he concluded a treaty under which the sardars promised not to raid his district. To discourage looting he provided the tribesmen with employment. By 1877 inter-tribal warfare had almost stopped.

After Indian independence in 1947, the Baluch – along with the Khan of Kalat – were reluctant to become part of the newly created Pakistan. But, in 1948, the army moved in to 'persuade' them. At first they were allowed to keep their old tribal ways but, in 1958, President Ayub ordered the surrender of unlicensed firearms.

The furious Baluch, feeling their identity under threat, refused to give up the weapons that are part of their dress, and revolted. Many sardars were imprisoned. There was a second rebellion from 1973–7; some 80,000 Pakistani soldiers were sent in, razing villages, while the Baluch People's Liberation Front attacked army convoys. Leaders of the rebels were arrested and thousands were killed. After General Zia imposed martial law in1977, the jailed leaders were released and went into exile.

All that changed with the Soviet invasion of Afghanistan. With Baluchistan's strategic location between Iran, Afghanistan and the Arabian Sea, the West feared a Russian push, supported by disgruntled tribesmen, and began pouring so much aid into the province that, by last year, it amounted to $1,000 per head. According to a top Baluch official: 'All usual restrictions were relaxed to give us far more aid than we could absorb. We could not provide enough proposals but the World Bank even gave $40 million for irrigation schemes they have never seen.'

But leading sardars were determined to prevent the spread of education and communications, knowing that bringing their tribesmen into contact with the outside world could weaken their base further. Even today in these areas, a radio is a novelty and inhabitants are governed by medieval laws. Criminals are tried by walking across burning coals; if their feet burn, they are guilty.

The tribal system is weakening nonetheless and more and more sardars are realising that the only way to retain support is to bring in development themselves. Perhaps the most progressive are the Magsis, whose area – like 64 per cent of Baluchistan – is still under tribal laws, with no police or government.

In the 1930s, the Magsi chief made education compulsory and built the area's first school, imposing jail sentences on fathers who failed to send their sons there. According to Tariq Magsi, one of the present sardar's family: 'Now, there are more educated Magsis than uneducated. Many have gone abroad, there are 25,000 working in the Gulf, and many have government jobs.'

Even in the Magsi lands, however, tribal customs still reign supreme. Tariq Magsi says the big problem is killings caused by feuds over women, land, guns and cattle. Blood must be avenged by blood – if the offender is absent, then his nearest relation is slain; if he is from a different tribe, then a section of that tribe must be killed. With the influx of sophisticated arms from Afghanistan, there can be hundreds of deaths.

Most influential of all the sardars is Nawab Bugti* who is known as the Tiger of the Baluch. With his striking demeanour and white handlebar moustache, he has been described as looking like Sean Connery playing a tribal chief. An Oxford graduate, he talks in a clipped public school accent quite matter-of-factly about killing his first man at the age of 12. 'Two years ago,' he said, 'I sorted out a feud

* A new armed struggle was launched by the Baluch in 2004 and Bugti was shot dead by the Pakistan army in August 2006.

in which 250 people had died in thirty years and people kept cutting each other's ears off.'

Today, even he has come round to allowing developments that he blocked in the past. The discovery of Asia's largest gas field at Sui, in the Bugti area, brought money into the district, making the tribesmen less bound to old allegiances. But when the government tried to carry out a development programme, the bulldozers were seized and the workers chased out of the province. Nawab Bugti takes the line that if there is any development to be done, he is the one to do it.

Although tribesmen still fall at their feet and rush to touch the hems of their shirts, today's generation of sardars has little desire to return to the ways of the past when they were mini-gods. Now they are more likely to be watching Michael Jackson videos and eating French fries than slaying foes in the mountains. 'We are the pragmatic sardars,' says one.

———————————

I had long dreamt of writing a novel, always scribbling ideas in notebooks, thinking once I had saved up enough money from my articles, I would rent a garret somewhere. But in Pakistan it had become clear to me that real life was often far stranger than fiction. Everyone I met seemed to have a story. Besides, I was growing addicted to journalism.

How Many Wars Have You Covered?

Afghanistan 1988–1990

Oh for a hero!
Financial Times, 9 July 1988

THE PHONE CALL warning me to be ready came in the dead of night in the Pakistani town of Quetta. I had booked a trip into Afghanistan with 'Resistance Tours Limited', one of seven Peshawar-based mujahideen groups to offer the ultimate war-zone trekking trips for journalists, soldiers of fortune, and public schoolboys eager for adventure.

Several nail-biting hours after slipping into my Afghan disguise and packing a rucksack as instructed, my guide arrived. The jeep was impossibly full of elaborately turbaned Kalashnikov-wielding mujahideen, who could have stepped out of a Hollywood rent-a-crew.

Dressed as an Afghan refugee in a huge shroud they call a burqa, I thought I could not go wrong. My guide thought differently. Clicking his tongue, he pointed out my pink socks and newish sneakers peering out from beneath my walking tent. Quickly I swapped them for a pair of old flip-flops. This time I passed inspection, and was solemnly presented with my Mujahideen Survival Kit – a packet containing a few boiled sweets, some oral dehydration powders, a small plaster and two antibiotic pills.

Inside the burqa, life was reduced to a series of bumps in the road and fragments of passing scenery seen through a small embroidered grille which seemed to correspond more with my nose than my eyes. As dawn broke it was already 40°C and, for eight hours, I was enclosed inside the most effective sauna I have ever experienced.

After travelling all day, we reached our guesthouse, a mud-baked fort piled high with Kalashnikovs and Stinger missiles, used as a staging post from which commanders deep inside Afghanistan receive reinforcements. We soon got into the spirit of things, dribbling greasy goat stew as we struggled to remember which hand one is supposed to eat with and which is for less savoury purposes. After dinner, during which fellow journalists compared insurgencies they had known, it was war games. As strategy was discussed, using matchboxes and an ashtray made from the cover of a Stinger, it became clear that no one had a clue quite what we were to do. I began to understand why, in nine years, the mujahideen had been unable to capture a major town.

The next morning, dressed as a mujahid in baggy shirt and trousers and flat Chitrali cap of prickly wool, I was raring to go. My fellow muj, however, seemed reluctant to move. A strangely effeminate fighting force, they sat around preening themselves in the pocket mirrors that seem an essential part of their uniform, drawing on eyeliner and fixing down their moustaches with Nivea.

Eventually, some of them were persuaded to take us to the outskirts of the town of Spin Boldak – although only after we had agreed to hire a taxi.

The last thing I expected to find in Afghanistan was a taxi service, although it came complete with six Kalashnikov-toting bodyguards. It also had something called a Computer Laser Disco that emitted flashing lights at not quite the same speed as the discordant music.

When the road ran out, I was given a mule. I have never got on with mules and their ilk since a donkey bit me at an early age at a circus. This particular mule was laden with Kalashnikovs, rocket launchers and mortars, and so was hardly a comfortable ride. Finally, somewhat bruised, we reached the next staging post.

We were supposed to depart the next morning at 6 a.m. At 8.15, I awoke to find myself surrounded by still-sleeping muj, who did not

want to move. All sorts of excuses were proffered – the route was mined, they were tired, and finally, incredibly, that they might get hurt. Eventually, I shamed them into leaving. Grudgingly, we were taken up a few hills from where, with the aid of high-powered binoculars, I could just make out Spin Boldak, where a few guerrillas were firing on a tank.

Back at base, more reporters had arrived. There was even a television camera, so the guerrillas felt compelled to lay something on. We were taken to a launch pad where they shot several rockets after borrowing a journalist's penknife to cut off the end of the detonator. We all took pictures and looked suitably impressed and the television reporter did a dramatic piece to camera.

I returned to Quetta, relieved to have suffered nothing worse than a sunburnt nose, but knowing I had seen little of the real war where heroes – not media stars – are made.

———————————

'How many wars have you covered?' drawled the American with the sunburnt face and a web of lines around his eyes. A row of men in those war-correspondent khaki vests with multiple pockets slowly spun round on their bar stools to look the newcomer wearily up and down.

'None,' I replied, smiling nervously, and watched most of them spin back to their Johnnie Walkers and cigarettes. I noticed that some of the khaki backs had dried bloodstains and one appeared to have a bullet hole.

It was my first introduction to the American Club in Peshawar.

As the only place in town where you could drink alcohol, sooner or later most foreigners in Peshawar ended up in the American Club. It was a squat two-storey building in a compound of trees and flowers in University Town, the area where almost all the aid agencies were based – as was a certain Osama bin Laden, though in those days none of us had heard of him. The club's clientele was basically spies, aid workers, journalists, diplomats and soldiers of fortune. Many of the Americans were Vietnam veterans and still bore the grudge. As they often reminded us, the US had lost 58,000 men in Vietnam and they seemed determined that the Russians would lose as many in Afghanistan (they lost 15,000).

Over cheeseburgers or sloppy joes, we listened and laughed to a pot-bellied twinkle-eyed American called Steve Masty strum his guitar and sing songs like the 'Burqa Boogaloo' or 'Disco Pir', poking fun at the mujahideen. But woe betide anyone that dared criticise them in print. The American Club was lorded over by a clique of right-wing American journalists led by Kurt Lohbeck of CBS and his girlfriend Anne Hurd of the Mercy Fund who saw this war strictly in black and white. The Afghans were the good guys, noble warriors fighting solely to liberate their country from the evil commie invaders. Anyone who wrote otherwise was labelled a communist and ostracised from the club.

On one level it was easy to portray the war in Afghanistan as a David-and-Goliath struggle – these men from the mountains in rope sandals with old Lee-Enfield rifles, ranged against one of the most powerful armies on earth. Like many British before me, I was captivated by the proud-faced Afghans who I found to be impressive, brave, and the most hospitable people I had ever met.

But I soon learnt it was not so simple. The Afghans may not have had tanks or planes but they did have Stingers and blowpipes and billions of dollars in the CIA's biggest ever covert operation. Their leaders were living in luxury houses and many had property overseas. The money-making potential was enormous.

Psst...Wanna buy a tank?
Time magazine, 9 January 1989

SOME COUNTRIES WILL do just about anything to buy a hot tank – in this case a Soviet T-62 model equipped with the latest laser range-finding gear. The French dispatched a few video cameras as a token of their interest. The West Germans, more pragmatically, proffered mine-sweeping equipment. A third country maintained its anonymity by sending a Swiss middleman, impeccably coiffed and dressed in a double-breasted suit, to barter over dishes of mutton in the Pakistani frontier city of Peshawar, where Afghan mujahideen occasionally stroll the dusty streets with AK-47 rifles slung over their shoulders. In the end, though, the discreet Swiss lost out to representatives of a West European member of NATO, who weighed in with the highest of the bids – a cash offer of $135,000.

The tank was the most spectacular commodity at auction in Peshawar, the venue for a brisk trade in all kinds of Soviet war materiel in the waning phases of the Afghan war. In Peshawar, an AK-47 sells for about $1,000, while an anti-aircraft gun can bring anywhere from $3,200 to $5,350. A Soviet jeep goes for $16,000.

The sought-after T-62 was not the latest Soviet model, but its range-finding equipment made it a notable prize. It was captured outside Kandahar by a unit of the Afghan National Liberation Front, one of the smaller members of the seven-party resistance alliance. As soon as news of the prize leaked through the intelligence grapevine, the unit's commander was inundated with importuning messages and presents from interested embassies in the Pakistani capital of Islamabad.

For the commander, the T-62 represented not only a source of extra funds but also an opportunity to gain greater tactical independence. Most of the weapons support for the Afghan resistance comes from the US, and is funnelled through Inter-Services Intelligence, Pakistan's military intelligence agency. All too often, the mujahideen believe, ISI uses its control over equipment and purse-strings to insist that the guerrillas conduct operations of greater interest to Pakistan than to the resistance. In July, for example, the mujahideen were forced to fight the pro-government forces of tribal leader Ismat Muslim at Spin Boldak near Kandahar. They suffered heavy losses and failed to achieve their objective. But when the mujahideen baulk at ISI's requests, the arms pipeline can dry up. Consequently, guerrilla leaders are always looking for alternative means to keep their military effort going.

Bringing a tank to market is a complicated affair. Driving the T-62 from Kandahar to the Pakistani border took twelve days – travelling initially by night to avoid attack by Soviet aircraft – while a contingent of guards walked alongside to ward off potential hijackers. Once across the frontier, the tank was hidden in a tribal enclave in Baluchistan while the sales negotiations took place. Well-armed tribal members stood guard to prevent the weapon's seizure by ISI, which a year ago successfully liberated from the guerrillas another highly coveted bit of war booty, an armoured personnel carrier.

Once the deal was struck, the tank was covered with a tarpaulin, loaded on a flatbed truck and hauled to a Karachi warehouse. The commander then turned over the tank, leaving the buyer the task of getting the behemoth out of Pakistan.

When all his accomplices were finally paid off and bribes were delivered to the many people in authority who kept silent about the deal, the Afghan commander was left with about $80,000. For the hardscrabble fighters, that sum translated into a prized measure of independence. For this particular English-speaking commander, it was then time to get back to the fighting – but not before buying an airline ticket for a brief respite in Hawaii. The arms business, Afghan-style, is hard work.

———————

I celebrated my twenty-second birthday in a kebab shop in Peshawar's old Storytellers' Bazaar with flat chapli kebabs followed by yellow cake with a candle on top. When my friends asked what I most wanted to do afterwards, options being limited in Peshawar, I said, 'drive a rickshaw'.

A rickshaw driver was duly waylaid and his tuk-tuk appropriated for a suitable fee and we spent a hilarious hour careering in and out of the alleys of the bazaar scattering Pathans horrified to see a foreign woman at the wheel. Afterwards we went for a moonlit swim in the pool of the Pearl Continental, or PC as we called it, where proper correspondents with expense accounts stayed.

There were other things to celebrate that night: 15 May 1988 marked the start of the withdrawal of the Red Army that had occupied Afghanistan since Boxing Day 1979. The supply of Stinger missiles which could down Soviet planes had turned the war around. For the mujahideen who had humiliated the largest army on earth, these were the glory days before jihad became a dirty word.

Like most journalists in Peshawar I spent much of my time going back and forth across the border into Afghanistan. 'Going inside', we called it. When you were out you spent all your time attempting to get in, and once in, living in caves on stale bread and trying to avoid landmines and bombs, you desperately wanted to be out.

By foot, donkey or motorbike we would slog across the jagged mountains, terrified of stepping on a mine or being spotted by a Soviet MiG. We were scared too of the Arabs who had come to join the jihad and just across the border in Jaji had set up a menacing-looking camp entered through a crevice in the rocks. Sometimes I would be disguised in a burqa, even provided a small child for authenticity; sometimes as a muj, swathed in shawls and my face darkened with a mixture of dirt and potassium permanganate.

Even when you got in, Afghanistan, like all guerrilla wars, was not an easy conflict to cover. I was convinced that one of the reasons the Soviets found the mujahideen so hard to defeat was that they were impossible to predict because they themselves had no idea what they were going to do next. The Afghan capacity for exaggeration is legendary. I would constantly arrive in places after a long journey for them to claim I had just missed a battle or them shooting down a Russian helicopter earlier that morning. Strangely there would be no sign of wreckage.

You might be away for weeks and then not get a story. I made eleven trips across the border yet only on four did I see any real action. These were the days before satellite phones so even if something did happen there was no possibility of filing from inside Afghanistan; it would have to wait for the return to Pakistan and the hated PCO or Public Call Office and a bribe for the telex operator.

For those correspondents coming in especially on assignment from London or New York, the idea of all that risk, hardship and expense for no return was unthinkable and they would invariably emerge with tales of a major attack. Mostly the mujahideen took them to Khost, which was reasonably easy to get to. Those of us that lived there would laugh as we saw yet another dramatic article appear on the 'Battle for Khost'.

As later became public, some TV crews did not even bother going in to Afghanistan but filmed rockets firing from the Pakistan side. There was no marked border and both sides looked the same. Others weaved in material shot inside by brave freelance cameramen like Rory Peck, Peter Jouvenal and Vaughan Smith, many of whom were former soldiers.

The Afghans were often complicit. Pakistan intelligence (ISI), through which US aid was funnelled, had divided the resistance into seven groups, following the British model of divide and rule, and would withhold arms supplies from any not in favour. ISI officers laughed at the Americans' gullibility as they directed most of the CIA funds into the hands of Gulbuddin Hekmatyar who made no secret of his hatred of the US.

Most media-savvy were Jamiat, led by Professor Rabbani, and National Islamic Front of Afghanistan (NIFA), led by the Gilani family. Some of the Gilani boys had lived in Chelsea and we called them the 'Gucci muj' for their designer combats and gold pens fashioned from AK-47 bullets.

If it is true, as Martha Gellhorn said, that you only fall in love with one war, then mine was undoubtedly Afghanistan. I would find myself drawn back again and again. To this day I still wear on my wedding finger a ring of yellow gold studded with tiny coloured jewels given to me by a proud Afghan tribesman.

Never had I met people with such passion for their country. For me England was just somewhere I happened to be born and I could easily imagine living in Spain, Italy or Brazil. But for my Afghan friends, who would regale me with stories of the exquisitely perfumed flowers, the mouthwatering fruit, the word-spinning poets, their dusty broken land was the most beautiful country on earth.

Inevitably, all of us living in Peshawar developed allegiances. Some journalists only ever travelled with Ahmed Shah Massoud, the charismatic Tajik known as the Lion of the Panjshir; others like me hung out with the Pashtuns. My favourite commander was Abdul Haq, a young Kabul commander who had lost his foot stepping on a landmine and told stories of how he had watched it fly up in the air. Over bowls of pink ice cream, he would tease me: 'You're a girl. Girls don't go to war.'

One of the smallest and least influential parties was that of Professor Sibghatullah Mojadidi. Its spokesman was a young man called Hamid Karzai, with whom I shared a love of Keats and Tennyson poems and

Cadbury's chocolate. He was a Popolzai, one of the royal tribes of Kandahar, and would talk to me late into the night about the tribes and his beloved homeland, where he said forty different kinds of grapes

grew. He complained that very few journalists made the journey to
Kandahar and determined he would take me there.

Jihad on stale bread and mud crabs
Financial Times, 17 September 1988

Kandahar

ABDUL WASIE is an 18-year-old Afghan guerrilla who has been
fighting since the age of 15 to free his country from Soviet occupation.
Clutching a powerful heavy-calibre rifle, he was the first of 100 young
mujahideen to pass under a copy of the Koran last Tuesday night before
risking his life in a daring operation to destroy a military post in the
centre of Kandahar. President Najibullah's Afghan government forces
have been in control of this city in south-west Afghanistan since the
departure of Soviet troops last month.

The raid was important for the Afghan resistance; it proved they
can, at will, break through the government defences and strike at the
heart of key cities. Kandahar is the most important city after Kabul, the
land of Afghanistan's first king and a place which the Najibullah regime
is desperate to hold.

Guerrillas fighting to dislodge government forces from Kandahar
are nicknamed 'Texans' because of their loud-mouthed and abusive
behaviour. But they were unusually silent as they gathered at the city
perimeter on foot, bicycles and motorcycles – anything larger is swiftly
detected and destroyed by government forces.

The group comprised mujahideen allied to five of the seven
resistance parties based in the Pakistani border town of Peshawar. But
these parties have little relevance in Kandahar where strategy is decided
by tribal councils.

Our move into the city centre began at dusk. The men were tense –
government reconnaissance planes had buzzed overhead all day and
heavy shelling was under way in the southern area of Malajat, whose
inhabitants have fled, leaving the area inhabited only by resistance
fighters.

In single file we tiptoed barefoot past military posts – often so near that conversations inside were clearly audible. Rocket launchers, Kalashnikovs and machine guns were clasped tightly – even the slightest metallic click would alert the guards.

The target was next to the Governor's office in Kabul bazaar, once a famous wood market, in the city centre. The Russians long ago felled the pines lining Kandahar's streets to prevent their use as cover, and bulldozed the bazaar to construct a wide highway connecting the government security posts which bisect the city. Only the shop backs remain, giving the appearance of a walled road.

At 2.20 a.m. the city shook as all the guerrilla groups fired off their weapons simultaneously, filling the air with choking dust and flames. Within ten minutes their ammunition was spent, the post knocked out and the guerrillas were racing away silently through the streets.

The government forces, caught on the hop by the first such attack on a post in the city centre, reacted slowly and then indiscriminately; bullets and mortar fire rained down on civilian homes while the mujahideen escaped unharmed, scrambling over the dried-up irrigation ditches. To my horror, they then stopped just outside the city to catch up on the evening prayers they had forgone earlier.

This hit-and-run operation in the heart of the city marked a change in resistance strategy for Kandahar, the scene of some of the bitterest fighting during the nine-year war against the Soviet occupation and its puppet regime in Kabul. Until now the mujahideen have launched mortar attacks and fought from outside the city.

The plains surrounding Kandahar resemble the set of a war film, criss-crossed with muddy trenches, scattered with burnt-out tanks and rotting bones. This style of fighting was partly forced on the resistance commanders by the open nature of the terrain, which is unsuitable for guerrilla tactics, unlike the mountains to the north and east. The wheat fields give some cover and the fighters move around by motorbike, me clinging on the back trying not to lose my turban which kept unwinding.

Mullah Mohammad, deputy commander of the largest guerrilla front in the region, is dismissive of what he calls 'the war of technology' under way elsewhere in Afghanistan. The Soviet-trained government forces invariably win such missile contests, their precision far outranking the guerrillas', who often have no idea of range, relying on a sort of third-time-lucky principle. Nonetheless, the accuracy of guerrillas in the Kabul area has improved immeasurably in recent months and they have scored important hits on the airport, the Soviet lifeline.

According to Mullah Mohammad the arrival of the US ground-to-air Stinger missile last year has made the guerrillas far less vulnerable to air attack, previously their main hazard on the plains. Although one Stinger was recently swapped for a prisoner, Kandahar mujahideen still have in reserve six of the resistance's original fifty.

Mullah Mohammad claims that the mujahideen could 'take Kandahar tomorrow' if they wished. Since the Soviet troops pulled out of the city in mid-August, the 10,000-strong resistance forces have gained control of all but the city centre, the heavily defended airport fourteen miles south-east, and a few posts to the east.

Of the three defence rings round Kandahar, the outermost has been destroyed and the innermost evacuated by government forces who have moved out to strengthen the second belt. It was to prove that the remaining ring could be penetrated that Tuesday's operation was undertaken.

Trenches had been prepared for an all-out attack on Kandahar. But fearing just such an attempt, the government sent in 6,000 fresh troops, boosting their forces to around 20,000. A tribal council of resistance commanders decided that an assault would inflict too many civilian casualties in the city centre.

A raid launched from the trenches on the airport last week resulted in the men being pinned down in the muddy water for two days by Russian tanks. Mujahideen morale had also been shaken by an attack on Arghandab, an orchard area north of Kandahar, where taking a small post had cost 200 dead and caused 50,000 civilians to flee. The fruit crop on which Arghandab depends for its livelihood was almost completely destroyed.

Dad Mohammed, another of the regional commanders, says: 'None of us wanted the attack but one of the political parties sent money to pay people to fight. I do not call that jihad [holy war].'

Such conflict over strategy between commanders in the field and the parties in exile is symptomatic of a growing rift. The so-called Peshawar leaders believe impressive victories are necessary to prove their worth, whereas field commanders, often reliant on local goodwill for supplies and shelter, are reluctant to risk further civilian lives and property. Instead of full-scale attacks, the field commanders are opting for sieges and hit-and-run attacks.

They have started laying siege to Kandahar, gradually replacing the civilian population with guerrillas and cutting off supply routes to the government forces. The resistance controls important sections of the highways to Kabul and Herat, lining each side with a wall of burnt-out tanks. Since the Russians left, no government convoy has been able to reach the city.

The only remaining supply route is from the airport and the guerrillas have dug trenches close to the road and worked under it through flood pipes. Even this strategy has aroused civilian resentment because it has resulted in scarcities and rising prices.

Many mujahideen do not relish another winter living on stale bread and mud crabs from the trenches and the truth is that both sides in the local conflict would like it to end.

The Governor of Kandahar has approached nationalist forces and

tribal leaders to negotiate a surrender. But they will only agree if the air force also surrenders and hands over the airport to the guerrillas, which seems unlikely.

The war in Kandahar will probably continue for many months, with the guerrillas continuing their attempts to demoralise and destabilise the government forces with more attacks in the heart of the city like Tuesday night's.

―――――――――――

Years later the Mullahs' Front would become the Taliban with Mullah Mohammad as deputy leader to Mullah Omar. For a while Hamid Karzai was their chief fund-raiser though he would later prefer to forget that.

It was generally assumed that the communist regime in Kabul had no support and once the Russians had left, the mujahideen would simply sweep in and take over. The American embassy in Islamabad held weekly briefings, known as sit-reps, where we would be told of all the many Afghan government posts that had been captured by the resistance. One day I added them all up and discovered that in Jalalabad alone they had taken five times as many as actually existed. The US envoy in Islamabad, Peter Tomsen, talked of 'riding into free Kabul on the back of a muj tank'.

But when the last Russian soldier crossed the Oxus on 15 February 1989, far from the war being over, it was about to get a whole lot messier. Yet almost overnight, the world lost interest. Diplomats, spies, aid workers and journalists packed up and left. I was shocked.

So angry was General Hamid Gul, the ISI chief, that he called me in for a rare briefing in an office dominated by a map of Afghanistan. 'The West thinks they can use these fundamentalists as cannon fodder and abandon them,' he raged. 'They were all right to win the war but not to run the future Afghanistan. Well, we will not allow that and I tell you this will come back to haunt them.'

With the Russians all gone, the mujahideen were under growing pressure to capture a city. It was clear that this would have to be Jalalabad as that was logistically easiest, just fifty-seven miles from

Peshawar. We all knew that ISI had drawn up a plan. One day I was in Islamabad when I got a call from an Afghan friend. 'It's starting tonight,' he said.

I grabbed the small khaki rucksack I always kept ready. It contained little more than a toothbrush, a spare pair of socks, water bottle, notebook and pens. Back in those days I did not see the need for sun cream, moisturiser, medical kits, coffee sachets or cereal bars. Then I jumped in my small blue Suzuki car to drive up the Grand Trunk Road, impatiently weaving in and out of the jingle trucks and camel-drawn wagons.

I run the gauntlet of fear to siege city
Daily Express, 17 March 1989

LUCKILY, I could not guess at the nightmare that lay ahead of me.

The safest way to reach a war front, I reasoned, was by ambulance. There is no shortage of them trundling the dusty roads to Jalalabad, where the mujahideen are now dug in for the bitterest bloodiest fighting yet of this endless Afghanistan war.

The ambulances go up empty and come screaming back with the bloodied, shattered bodies of the hundreds of resistance fighters who have long since overflowed the Peshawar hospital.

I was given the choice of two vehicles – one a dented pick-up truck, the other a battered van covered with mud and branches as camouflage. I chose the van. It was a good choice.

Had I ridden in the pick-up, I would not have survived the next six hours.

I was dressed in pyjama-like Afghan garb behind which I hoped to disguise my blonde hair and green eyes. I added a woollen hat and shawl and dirtied my face for good measure. My companions were five young guerrillas, with two Kalashnikov rifles and an unlimited supply of hashish and a tape recorder. On this, for hours on end, they played Eurotrash disco music from a group called C. C. Catch.

Journalists are not only barred from heading towards Jalalabad by Pakistani border guards but any mujahideen who take them in now face heavy fines. As the border approached, floor cushions were removed and I was bundled into their place and covered with blood-stained sheets and blankets reeking of Dettol.

I was dozing, partly anaesthetised by the fumes, when they shook me awake. 'We're in Afghanistan!' said Shisha.

The road, pockmarked with shell holes, was packed on our side with truckloads of mujahideen waving guns and chanting, 'Allahu Akbar!' – God is great.

Coming the other way was a stream of refugees, mainly women and children, clutching small bundles of possessions. The women wailed. Many had lost children in the rush to escape, and husbands in the war.

The plan had been to take Jalalabad within two days, reinforcing mujahideen claims to be in control of 90 per cent of the country and providing a city in which to base a provisional government pending the fall of Kabul.

Initial fighting was successful with the muj quickly capturing several key posts, including Samarkhel, headquarters of the Kabul regime's 11th Division, where half-eaten meals lay as evidence of the suddenness of departure. Three dead Afghan soldiers lay splayed in the field face down, shot as they tried to flee their post.

Commander Noor Haq, from the National Islamic Front of Afghanistan's guerrilla forces, which spearheaded the attack, said: 'The regime just fell back and left.'

He kicked one of the dead bodies over and took a red ID book from the dead man's pocket, which he presented to me.

It was on the road just ahead of Samarkhel that we heard the first rumble of bombing. Sher Ali picked up a clutch of bullets from the floor. 'See,' he grinned. 'That was last time. An ambush.' He pointed to a string of holes across the rear door.

No one was grinning a second later. The drone of planes suddenly got much louder. A jet had dipped low and was coming straight at us.

'Cut!' screamed someone as the ambulance slowed to a halt. The earth vibrated as we scrambled clear and threw ourselves down the slope at the roadside.

But the other ambulance kept going. There followed an eerie moment of silence punctuated by a dog whining. Then, as if in slow motion, we watched the pick-up explode in a single vivid orange burst of light.

I was unable to speak, as I waited for some sign of life. When the planes had gone, we rushed to the burning wreckage. The occupants – two male nurses and a doctor, all Afghans – were dead.

After ten years of war, Afghans show a cold indifference to death. My companions shrugged over the victims, straightened their bodies out and left them beside the road.

Then, we turned back. It was too dangerous, I was told. 'Of course it is, it's a war!' I replied. 'Aren't you supposed to collect the wounded?' But my words fell on deaf ears. Ten miles further on at a mujahideen staging post, they told me to get out. But the next day, they promised, they would be back.

I spent the night surrounded by twenty soldiers in the *hujra*, or men's council room, of what was probably once a beautiful mansion but was now a ruin.

In the circumstances, I slept well on the floor. But the next day I was worried. Were my companions fundamentalists eager to dispose of a western infidel?

They plainly had no intention of going to war and were amused by my plight. As I scanned the horizon for my missing ambulance, they burst into gales of laughter.

By extraordinary good fortune, I recognised the commander of a truckload of men who had pulled in on their way to the front. We had met in Peshawar. Realising the hopelessness of my position, he promised I could go with them.

Their destination was Jalalabad airport, a few kilometres outside the city, where one of the bloodiest battles was now raging.

Control of Jalalabad is a major prize for both sides. It lies across the main highway to Kabul. It must be taken if Kabul is to fall; it must be held if the regime of President Najibullah is to survive.

Although Samarkhel fell quickly, the airport and the gates to the city have proved much harder to penetrate. The regime has sent in reinforcements from Kabul, including the elite presidential guards, and started intensive bombing.

We drove to a thick wood just outside the perimeter of the airfield and the men took up posts at Position BM12, a rocket-launching site protected by tree cover. Around us, scattered through the wood, were apparently more than 600 guerrillas. Behind them were several tanks – captured earlier in the fray but apparently abandoned. 'We cannot drive them,' my commander admitted.

Our rocket battery began unleashing sporadic bursts of fire. They say 5,000 rockets have been launched in the bid to take this city.

Occasionally there was a cheering charge up to the fence. But heavy fire drove them back each time, casualties staggering from the ranks. My commander says 500 men have been lost in the past week. Civilian casualties are thought to be much higher.

Mujahideen leaders broadcast loudspeaker warnings to civilians to leave. Shah Zaman, spokesman for Pakistan's Afghan Refugee Commission, said 18,000 refugees had arrived in one week, the biggest evacuation of the war. But many had died in strafing attacks along the way and thousands more are trapped in the ruins of what was once known as Afghanistan's 'garden city'.

'At the end of the day we may be left in control of a pile of rubble,' one commander told me. 'But there can be no going back.'

I was one of only two journalists to get into the battle at the start and I was horrified by what I had seen. So were the stalwarts of the American Club when they saw my story plastered across not just the *Daily Express* but the front page of the FT and *Time* magazine. This was not the accepted line. My membership was suspended.

It didn't really matter. Much as I enjoyed the camaraderie and jokes of my fellow hacks, I already knew that when it came to work I didn't want to be part of the pack. I spent most evenings with Pakistani and Afghan friends, squatting on the ground eating greasy mutton stew and rice with my hands, entranced by their Kiplingesque stories about tribes and feuds.

I never went back into Afghanistan with the mujahideen after Jalalabad. Although I had seen fighters getting killed on my previous trips, that battle was the first time I witnessed mass deaths of civilians.

I couldn't get out of my head the beseeching faces of women along the roadside with injured children who had thought I was a nurse. Back in the cold light of Peshawar I could not believe I had just driven past them in my rush to get to the front line. It was the ugliest thing I had ever done and made me realise just what an ugly thing war is. When I phoned in to dictate my copy, the *Express*'s gentlemanly foreign editor John Ellison must have thought I had overdone the vodka because I kept giggling; in those days no one talked of post-traumatic stress disorder.

Mostly I was angry and disillusioned, watching the Afghans turn on each other. Pakistan's manipulation through ISI had become more and more open. During the battle for Jalalabad I had seen an ISI officer, Colonel Imam, directing operations and heard one of the commanders, Rahim Wardak, ask him bitterly: 'How can you who have never won a war dare give orders to we who have never lost one?'

A *shura* (council) held in Rawalpindi to form an interim government collapsed within forty minutes, unsurprisingly after all those years of ISI stoking division. General Gul's men then locked the more than 400 Afghan delegates inside the Haji complex and tried to force them to choose a government headed by one of ISI's pet fundamentalists – either Abdul Sayyaf or Gulbuddin Hekmatyar.

One day I got a call from Benon Sevan, the bear-like UN envoy who shuttled back and forth between Kabul and the Holiday Inn in Islamabad. He had persuaded President Najibullah to grant visas to some journalists who had covered the war from the other side. My name was on the list.

It was scary landing in Kabul. The Afghan capital nestles deep inside the Hindu Kush and the old Antonov seemed almost to touch the mountains as it circled. As we dropped down in a corkscrew landing, flares of white potassium exploded all around us to deter mujahideen rockets. The hills were covered in square mud-baked houses and it seemed like a place drained of colour. 'Even in summer it's a city of grey,' I wrote in my diary.

The airport building had been recently rocketed, the glass blown out, and we did not hang around. But to my surprise Kabul was pretty intact. Life seemed to be going on much as usual. The streets were busy with yellow taxis and people selling second-hand clothes and birds in wooden cages. Somehow, from Peshawar, I had imagined it as a place in suspension.

The Hotel Kabul where we stayed was a dark, depressing place, its grimness not helped by the knowledge that the US Ambassador Adolph Dubs had been murdered in one of the rooms ten years earlier. There was little food apart from eggs and hard naan bread. The telephones did not work and copy had to be sent back by telex. The telex operator had just one arm and, even more alarmingly, doubled as the hotel driver, his one black-gloved hand switching back and forth from steering wheel to gear stick.

Now when I look at some of my photographs from that trip and compare it to the Kabul of today, it is hard to believe it is the same place.

Westernised women dread return to a veiled existence
Financial Times, 23 June 1989

IT COULD BE any western university campus. Brightly dressed girls in tight miniskirts or jeans and baggy T-shirts proclaiming 'I'm Not with This Idiot' sit in the sun, licking ice creams and discussing everything from their favourite Indian film stars to politics. Western rock music blares from a portable stereo.

A group of literature students are discussing Fariba's newly blonde hair. 'If Gulbuddin comes to power he'll cut it all off and lock you up,' jokes one.

The laughter is a little hollow. Women such as these, at Kabul University, seem a different species from the Afghan women who, as refugees in Pakistan, are forced by threats from the more fundamentalist Afghan resistance parties – such as that of Gulbuddin Hekmatyar – to hide themselves in burqas, unsightly, tent-like garments with only a small grille for vision, commonly known as shuttlecocks. This is when they are allowed out on the streets at all. Some, who have dared work as teachers, have had acid thrown in their faces.

The women of Kabul University are not the only ones fearful that if the extreme fundamentalists among the mujahideen take power they will be forced to stay at home, abandoning their ambitions and modern lifestyles for what they call 'Gulbuddin's medieval fortress'.

In a government flat, Wajia, a well-known singer, strums her guitar and, between puffs of her cigarette, says she will have to leave the country if Gulbuddin comes.

Women's fears about a fundamentalist regime surfaced last summer when the mujahideen announced the Constitution of their government in exile, stating that women must be kept in purdah. Headlines across the US screamed, 'Mujahideen Will Force Women Behind the Veil' – something of an embarrassment for Washington, which has spent more than $2 billion (£1.3 billion) funding the resistance since Soviet forces entered Afghanistan in 1979 – the main portion going to the fundamentalists.

Not a single woman was invited to the 400-member *shura* (council), held in Pakistan in February, to choose a government. A good many of the seven resistance leaders say they would not want women to vote if elections were held.

President Najibullah, meanwhile, has tried to win over women, giving them places in his administration and creating a special 600-member women's militia. Nadya, a 20-year-old cadet, has just returned from

Jalalabad, where she says she fired rockets on mujahideen. 'We women have become a force to reckon with and will not let Gulbuddin here.'

Women have become vitally important to the economy, with 1.5 million men of Afghanistan's pre-war population of 15 million killed in the ten years of fighting and many more rendered incapable of work through injury. Most staff at Afghan factories are women and, when the refugees return, reconstruction could again fall heavily on women.

Esmatee Wardak, president of Afghanistan's women's committee, threw away her burqa in 1959 when the then King, Zahir Shah, declared them no longer compulsory for women past puberty. One of the first Afghan women to graduate, Mrs Wardak says the war has made women more assertive: 'I am a Muslim from a backward village and I will never again keep a burqa in my house. Islamic law does not require it and now there are many women like me who will fight anyone who tries to turn us back to the veil.'

However, unlike religious or ethnic groups such as Sikhs, Hindus and Hazaras who felt oppressed by the previous Pashtun rule and whom Najibullah is wooing on the basis that all groups are now treated the same, women dismiss the suggestion that the party has liberated them. There were women MPs before the war and Mrs Wardak maintains it is 'suffering and the need to be economically independent that strengthened us'.

She admits that outside the cosmopolitan city of Kabul, many rural and provincial women choose to wear burqas, but believes that with education these will be discarded.

It was Zahir Shah who gave women the vote and introduced the miniskirt to Kabul. However, women's rights is an area where Najibullah hopes to win the public relations war.

Abhorrence at the Hekmatyar speeches does not necessarily translate into support for Najibullah. Wajia looks forward to the day when she can write the songs she wants to. At the university Jumila asks: 'What is it to have equal rights under a regime which does not believe in rights?'

Death of a General

Pakistan 1988–1990

FOR ALL BENAZIR'S triumphant return to Pakistan in 1987, the country remained under military dictatorship and my first big interview was with General Zia-ul-Haq in July 1988.

It came about in a strange way. That May, General Zia had dismissed his own prime minister and announced on television that there would be party-based elections. Then a month later he held a press conference, a rare event, in a grand salon in the Aiwan e Sadr palace where he sat under a glittering chandelier and said that political parties would not be allowed to contest the elections.

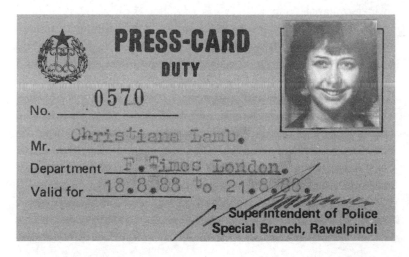

PRESS-CARD
DUTY

No. 0570

Mr. Christiana Lamb.

Department F.Times London.

Valid for 18.8.88 to 21.8.88.

Superintendent of Police
Special Branch, Rawalpindi

No one else seemed bothered by this turnaround. As usual at Pakistani press conferences, a series of journalists stood up and made legalistic points in the form of lengthy statements rather than questions. I stuck up my hand.

As a tall blonde English girl amid a sea of Pakistani men, I stood out and was handed the microphone.

'Why have you changed your mind about holding party-based elections as you said when you announced them?' I asked.

'I did not say that,' he said.

He was lying. 'Yes, you did,' I replied indignantly.

A gasp ran through the Pakistani journalists, and people either side tugged at me to sit down.

But General Zia smiled. I was wearing turquoise and yellow *shalwar kameez*, the traditional local dress of long tunic and baggy trousers, and he politely thanked me for respecting his country's culture. Then he added: 'Young lady, if you have more questions I suggest you see my military secretary afterwards to arrange an appointment.'

It was an invitation I had no intention of passing up. At the end of the press conference I went straight to Brigadier Salik and gave him my name and number. A few weeks later I found myself driving through the gates of the white-walled Army House in Rawalpindi and being led up a path through lush green lawns and beds of pink roses over which sprinklers played.

Inside, General Zia served me tea and smiled disarmingly. His eyes were deep-set and dark-ringed like a panda's; he had a twirly ringmaster's moustache; his lips were thin and his teeth big. I wondered if he had smiled as tightly when he ordered the hanging of Benazir's father along the road in Rawalpindi jail.

We talked for over an hour about everything from Afghanistan (he said he 'longed for the day' he could pray in a Kabul mosque) to the state dinner he had attended at the Élysée in Paris wearing a long black tunic and President Mitterrand had told him to take off his coat. 'I had to tell him I had nothing on underneath,' he said.

Again he denied that he had ever said he would hold party-based elections. Flourishing a copy of *The Economist*, he read a quote from a British political scientist who had said parties were not representative.

'Besides, what we have here are not parties,' he said with obvious distaste. 'They are just pressure groups. To allow them to run things would jeopardise the democratic process.'

The interview had gone well and I had some good lines, particularly his belief that the US felt they no longer needed him now the Russians were leaving Afghanistan. I drove back in haste to my cheap hotel room in G/7 (Islamabad was divided in Orwellian manner into sectors of numbers and letters starting at Zero Point). But when I switched on my recorder, the tape was blank. In my efforts to concentrate I had pressed the Play button but not Record.

What could I do? I had taken no notes. There was nothing else for it. Being a dictatorship, they too had recorded the interview. I picked up the receiver and dialled Brigadier Salik.

'There's a bit of a problem with my recording of the interview,' I said. 'I think the air conditioning has obscured some of the President's words.'

'Which bits?' he asked.

'Well, rather a lot.'

I'm sure he guessed, but shortly afterwards a man in uniform arrived bearing a copy of their transcript and a box of sweet smelling mangoes. Ever since then I have been paranoid about tape recorders.

Less than three weeks later, on 17 August, I was back in Peshawar sitting with my friend Amjad, youngest of the Arbab sons, watching the sun go down. I had been supposed to be heading into Afghanistan that day with Abdul Haq's mujahideen but the trip kept getting delayed because they were waiting for ammunition. We were finally due to leave at midnight. The trip to the outskirts of Kabul would be the longest and riskiest I had done and I was nervous. I asked Amjad if he had some Russian vodka.

He had none but reluctantly agreed to drive up the road to Barra smugglers' market. Within a few minutes he was back, empty-handed.

'You won't believe this,' he said, 'but Tariq's just told me that Zia's plane has crashed with him and all the top military aboard. They think Zia's dead.'

'Come on, if you don't want to go and get the vodka you can think of a better excuse than that,' I replied.

Then Amjad's brother Tariq, who was Mayor of Peshawar, walked in, and I realised he was serious.

I rushed into the living room and began trying to dial the international operator on their father's old Bakelite telephone. There was no direct dialling in those days. My index finger rotated the dial again and again, only to keep getting the busy tone.

I was in tears. It was the biggest story of my life, I was one of the only foreign correspondents in the country and I couldn't talk to my office. It was an hour before I got through, by which time I was in no fit state to write a story. Fortunately, the growly voice at the other end was that of Stewart Dalby, who had covered Vietnam and knew all about pressure. 'Sit down, have a drink, smoke a fag and then this is what we want from you,' he said.

So terrified was I of never getting through again that we kept the phone line open while I scribbled out my story of the death in a mysterious plane crash. It was my first front page. Inside we ran extracts from my interview three weeks earlier, which was now his last one. I remembered Zia's words that the US no longer had need of him. Pakistan was the land of conspiracy. Had he known something? But the American Ambassador had also been aboard.

When finally I had dictated the last word, Stewart told me that ITN had been calling, desperate for me to get in touch. He switched the call over and they explained that someone had set up a satellite dish on a roof in University Town and reckoned they could do a live broadcast, almost unknown in those days. That night I was on *News at Ten* just after the bongs, being interviewed by Sandy Gall and looking slightly startled.

Suddenly Pakistan was a story. Nobody knew what the army would do. Would elections go ahead or would the military once again impose martial law? I moved down to Islamabad and rented a flat near Jinnah Market.

A big story is not always a great thing for the local stringer. All the heavy-hitters arrived from London or Delhi, leaving me reduced to fixing up interviews and providing background analysis in return for lunch or dinner. One American in particular from the *Los Angeles Times* seemed to need more background than most. His name was

Mark and he had won my affection by introducing me to Oreo cookie ice cream at the American Club. One evening, I was in the middle of a bowl of ice cream and an earnest explanation about why Benazir must be allowed to stand in the elections, when he cupped my chin in his hands and placed his finger on my lips. That night we danced to 'I Got You Babe' in the fairy-lit garden of the French Club and, as he kissed me, it did not seem like Pakistan at all.

I was well aware by then that most of the Delhi correspondents who covered Asia had girls in every port and spent an inordinate amount of time covering the Philippines. But Mark had a passion about his writing that was different from his seen-it-all colleagues and he kept me amused with his telexes about my plans to smuggle myself to Kabul in the back of a cabbage truck.

Zia's funeral took place in Islamabad's vast Saudi-funded mosque, a modernistic white spaceship of a building at the foot of the green Margalla Hills. After that most of the staff reporters drifted back to their bases and my byline began reappearing. Aside from the FT and the odd 'Girl Goes to War' centre spread for the *Daily Express*, I had started working for *Time* magazine. This paid well but their fact-checkers drove me mad. 'How do you know it's fifty seven miles from Peshawar to Jalalabad?' was typical of the long line of questions awaiting me at the telex office every week.

There was no shortage of stories or people to interview. At that time, Islamabad only had one luxury hotel, the Holiday Inn. I soon found that if I spent the morning in its coffee shop, someone or other I might want to grill would appear, whether politicians, Afghan resistance leaders, Iranian clerics, Chinese arms dealers or visiting delegations from Saudi intelligence. The lobby was full of men in grey *shalwar kameez* and dark glasses – ISI agents – watching all the comings and goings.

Pakistan was five hours ahead of the UK, so I had all afternoon to write and was usually filing in the evening. Often there was 'load-shedding', which I had never heard of before but meant there was no electricity. I took to sitting on my front porch, tapping away at my Tandy in the light of my car headlamps.

To everyone's surprise the new army chief General Aslam Beg

announced that elections would go ahead as planned. The next few months sped by in a blur of noisy rallies. Most of the time I would be the only foreign woman there and I got used to pushing through crowds, elbows at right angles against all the groping hands.

Zia had scheduled elections for November because he knew Benazir was expecting a baby at that time so would be unable to campaign. But for once she had outwitted him. Knowing his spies would obtain her medical records, she had managed to have hers swapped and was actually due in September.

Her detractors were not so easily thwarted. The military intelligence put their weight behind her opponents in the Muslim League and organised them into an alliance with the main religious parties. They then airdropped leaflets showing an old photograph of Benazir's mother in a cocktail dress dancing with Gerald Ford at the White House and referring to mother and daughter as 'gangsters in bangles'.

The PPP emerged as the largest party but was still sixteen seats short of a majority. While the army dallied, Benazir's lieutenants made desperate overtures, often of a financial nature, to independents and small parties to win their support.

Meanwhile their leader held court in the sitting room of Dr Niazi, the dentist who had treated her father in jail. Receiving journalists and diplomats, her words were carefully chosen to reassure the military that she would not alter policies close to their heart, as well as occasional threats of what might happen if the people's views were ignored.

Days turned into a week, then two weeks, and editorials round the world thundered that Benazir must be allowed to form a government. On the fifteenth day, in an indication of who really pulls the strings in Pakistan, she had a meeting with General Hamid Gul, the director of ISI; tea with the US Ambassador; and dinner with the army chief. The next afternoon, official security replaced the PPP activists guarding Dr Niazi's gate. At 35, she was going to be the first female prime minister in the Muslim world.

That night there were celebrations and fireworks at Dr Niazi's house. In the street outside, supporters chanted, '*Jeay Bhutto! Bhutto zindabad! Wazir-i-azam Benazir!*' – Long live Benazir, Prime Minister Benazir! Inside gathered many of the same people who had been at the wedding. It was hard to believe that it had been less than a year earlier.

Benazir looked even more pensive that night than she had at her wedding celebrations. For power did not come without compromise. To the consternation of some of her closest advisers, she had agreed the military would still control the nuclear programme and Afghan policy. Punjab, the most populated province, was under the control of her rival, Zia's protégé Nawaz Sharif, whose family ran the country's biggest steel industry.

These were far from being the only challenges. After years of dictatorship everyone expected jobs and patronage from those now in power. I got a sense of the feudal society she had inherited one afternoon in rural Punjab.

A beast of a contest
Financial Times, 6 May 1989

PEOPLE KILL EACH other over the best buffalo contest in Gujrat's annual horse and cattle show. A dusty town in rural Punjab, Gujrat is better known for producing sports shoes and electric fans than for its bovine quality. Yet every year, come April, the nation's footwear industry grinds to a halt and local teashops shudder under the weight of conspirators plotting how to sway the judges and ensure the success of their chosen candidate.

'It's like a mafia operation,' grumbles Butt, a farmer who was persuaded by 'security considerations' to withdraw his prime beast. As in the country's elections, lines are drawn on the basis of *biradaris*, or clans. Gujrat has three main *biradaris* – Gujas, Jats and Kashmiris – each of which fields a candidate selected by practised 'spotters'.

As show day approaches, the peaceful fields around Gujrat are transformed from a rural haven straight out of Thomas Hardy to the scene of heinous crimes as rival groups go to extraordinary lengths to secure victory. 'It's a matter of honour,' explains the editor of the local newspaper. 'They start with trade-offs or bribes. If that fails they resort to grievously wounding the owner or his relations. In a close year it can be a fight to the death.'

A local police officer confirms that the crime rate 'rockets'. Oddly, the beasts themselves are rarely touched, though one year a wolf was let loose upon a particularly fine specimen.

Camel dancing and best sheep contests do not evoke such emotions. 'They are usually settled by a few wife abductions,' says the editor dismissively. He sees the buffalo show as an incentive for development, but to the onlooker it represents the worst excesses of Pakistan's feudal society. Leading landlords and industrialists lounge in comfy chairs on a rose-bedecked stage, protected from the scorching sun by colourful awnings. Hunched-shouldered waiters in skewed bow ties and crumpled white jackets proffer trays bearing china cups of milky tea topped with skin, and curling fish-paste sandwiches.

As the teams of the major feudals trot past on powerful white chargers, their riders resplendent in bright silks and jewelled turbans, the lesser landlords clap limply, seemingly oblivious to the seething mass below. For the crowds, it is perhaps the year's only entertainment, TVs being unaffordable even if they are lucky enough to have electricity, and dancing forbidden. For the area's many bonded labourers, it is probably their only day off.

The highlight of events is tent-pegging, a game similar to jousting. As expected, the team of the biggest landlord emerges victorious, its

Herculean mounts far superior to the progressively scrawnier creatures of the smaller landlords.

As with most events in Pakistan, the show has a political dimension. Local bigwigs take the opportunity to make turgid speeches, eulogising their role in upholding Islam. Using wealth and tribal connections, Gujrat's leading family won all four seats in the recent elections.

For the buffalo contest, the family has scored a further coup by attracting as principal guest Nawaz Sharif, the Chief Minister of Punjab, who in his role as high priest of patronage has come with a sackful of vote-winning goodies. Amid rousing cheers, Sharif doles out schools and hospitals.

An old man with the audacity to mount the stage is rewarded with a road to his village. Sharif's popularity rises when he upgrades a police officer for his outstanding performance in an incomprehensible game of tag wrestling played by skinny men in Speedo trunks.

'This is the politics of super-patronage,' comments a former minister. By the end of the day, Sharif's secretary is laden with sheaves of applications from people demanding postings, transfers and project approvals. Since its creation, Pakistan has become increasingly centralised. One needs to go to the top for everything.

Outside Sharif's private house in Lahore, a mini-secretariat has been built to accommodate the floods of people who arrive daily asking for help in resolving domestic disputes or minor problems that seem baffling to much of Pakistan's rural population, where literacy is less than 17 per cent.

Pakistan's new Prime Minister, Benazir Bhutto, regarded by her followers as Queen Bountiful, has even greater problems. More than 60,000 applications arrive at her secretariat daily; everywhere she goes she is mobbed by supporters waving petitions demanding jobs as recompense for their sacrifices during martial law. Under eleven and a half years of dictatorship, an awful lot of people suffered for Bhutto's People's Party, and with the Treasury coffers empty, she can satisfy few of them.

Committed to cut non-development expenditure, Bhutto already has the biggest Cabinet in Pakistan's history, and an entire battalion of advisers, known locally as the 'Under-19 team' or 'Incompetence Incorporated'.

This is not patronage politics, however. In the new government's terminology it is People's Politics. When ministers ignore their government work to spend all day arranging jobs for their voters and licences for their patrons, this is not corruption or nepotism – it is People's Government. Using the same ploy, they have renamed many of the country's schools as People's Schools, and thus claim to have created thousands of new schools.

Next year Gujrat's buffalo contest may become fair and democratic – they are considering renaming it the People's Buffalo Contest.

Pakistan might in theory have had a democratic government under Bhutto but she often complained she was 'in office but not in power'. Real power, of course, remained with the Pakistan Army, which at any moment could bring the whole thing to an end as they had done with her father.

It had never really occurred to me before to question democracy as a system. I was impressed with the Pakistani military officers I had met, many of whom were Sandhurst-trained. It was hard not to sympathise with those who argued they were a better option than some of the leading politicians who were feudal scions, used to peasants kissing the hem of their coats, and constantly switched sides to stay in power.

I got a chance to see the Pakistan Army in action when I accompanied Benazir on an incredible journey to the Siachen Glacier. The world's highest battlefield, it is a place so cold that the merest touch of metal on the skin produces instantaneous frostbite.

War on top of the world
Daily Express, 29 August 1989

FAR UP IN THE topmost reaches of the Himalayas, a war is raging on history's highest battleground. It is a war few know about, between two countries supposedly at peace.

For five years the elite forces of the Indian and Pakistani armies have

battled to control the Siachen Glacier. It is the world's most spectacular theatre of war, surrounded by icy peaks towering above 25,000 feet, including K2, the world's second-highest mountain. Its beauty masks cruelty more lethal than gunfire.

The crash reverberating across the mountains as I arrived with Pakistan's Prime Minister Benazir Bhutto to tour front-line bases at 18,000 feet made us jump.

We could see the Indian troops less than a mile away on a peak just opposite. Had they seen us? The commander of the 56th Baluch Battalion smiled wryly. It was not artillery fire but an avalanche, in which more men probably perished.

For the bravest men of the Indian and Pakistani armies have another, more deadly enemy than shelling – the weather, the killer behind eight out of every ten victims. Though neither side will release figures, officials admit there have been hundreds of deaths and thousands of casualties. Colonel Cheema, Pakistan's Junior Defence Minister, says: 'This is 95 per cent a war against nature.'

No army has ever fought in such conditions. For five years around 4,000 troops on each side have faced temperatures dropping to minus 80°C, and kept up an intermittent war while the real fight continues against the piercing cold, freezing weapons and fierce blizzards.

We were lucky, arriving on a rare clear day, the sky a brilliant blue backdrop to the dazzling peaks. It was a hazardous trip.

We left the capital Islamabad early, unnerved to be travelling in a Hercules C-130 of the type which killed Ms Bhutto's great adversary President Zia in a mysterious crash last August.

After an hour's flight, during which Bhutto caught up on paperwork with her Law Minister, we plunged between the mountains to land at Skardu.

Skardu is a conservative town where women are never seen and many crowds of men had gathered for the rare visit of a prime minister. Bhutto can never resist a crowd and had to be dragged away into the Puma helicopter to fly to Gyari, a military base at the foot of the Bilafond Glacier which connects with Siachen.

There we donned huge white padded American snowsuits and boots; only two hours earlier we had been sweating in the heat of Islamabad, which was already sizzling at dawn.

Around us huge boulders were painted with alarming slogans such as 'Kill Them All' and 'Never Surrender'.

We clambered into fragile-looking glass-bottomed helicopters. Roads have been built to the edge of the glaciers, but from that point on stores must be moved by air.

The pilot muttered his prayers and a few *Allahu Akbar*s and we were off, skimming over glaciers and skirting the side of the jagged mountains, coasting on air currents to conserve precious fuel. Lieutenant Colonel Farooq, our pilot, told us we were flying over the largest concentration of glaciers outside the polar region.

It looked like a magical Narnia world of snow and jagged ice. But the glaciers are extremely treacherous, constantly moving, pushing up rocks and boulders and creating crevasses into which men often fall, freezing to death within a minute.

Finally we touched down at Ali Brangsa. Immediately our movements became heavy. At 17,000 feet, simply talking makes one's head spin and induces nausea.

Gratefully we sucked coconut sweets proffered to keep up sugar levels. The air is so thin, with less than half normal oxygen content, that

even the fittest men must stop for three minutes' rest after every few steps. Above 14,000 feet, foot movement is so slow that to travel fifteen miles takes six days, while on the 19,000-foot glacier it takes twenty minutes to cover a hundred yards.

Before we left, Bhutto echoed all our sentiments, writing in the battalion's barely used visitors' book: 'I shall always remember this dizzying experience.'

The men of Ali Brangsa, living in bunkers decorated with nothing but religious slogans, are luckier than some of their colleagues who are alone on distant peaks, in at least having some companionship.

In their brilliant white padded suits and mirror shades, contrasting with sun-blackened skin (even the strongest sun cream gives little protection against the high levels of ultraviolet rays), the men present a strange sight, particularly when they prostrate themselves in the snow to pray.

The suits are essential – the cold can be so piercing that frostbite sets in within minutes of flesh being exposed, often resulting in amputation. For those alone on the peaks, such as the men manning Pakistan's two highest posts at more than 22,000 feet, the long isolation and confinement cause acute depression.

Says one major: 'There is nothing to do but fire and after days alone you begin to imagine targets. You need to fire to reassure yourself you are still alive.'

There are greater hazards than boredom. According to Dr Mohbashir, the battalion medic, the lack of oxygen can cause lungs almost literally to explode, filling with blood and fluid so the victim suffocates. No one stays up there for long.

Despite the extreme conditions, war is definitely going on. The difficulty of walking, let alone carrying weapons, rules out infantry campaigns, but artillery fire is frequent.

Before we arrived five shells landed and, the day before, the Indians had lobbed eleven artillery shells and five rockets which General Imran, the corps commander, says was 'light'.

After just a few hours at this altitude we were flagging, but Bhutto was still going strong, addressing troops at Gomu.

For a country so long under military rule, it was a strange role reversal to see the Prime Minister addressing the army instead of the general instructing the politicians. 'The generals and the people are one now,' said Bhutto.

The glacier war began in 1984 when Pakistan grew alarmed at seeing Siachen, which they claimed as their territory, suddenly marked on maps of India. Men were dispatched to check and found the Indians had occupied peaks of the Saltoro Range and captured 1,000 square miles. Pakistan responded by creating a special alpine commando force led by a young artillery officer Pervez Musharraf who counter-attacked two years ago, taking the Indian position at Bilafond Pass, before being beaten back.

The roots of the dispute go back to 1947 when, as the British Empire was dismantled, both Pakistan and India claimed the Muslim-dominated state of Kashmir. Pakistan managed to grab a third of Kashmir, of which Siachen is the northernmost part, before a ceasefire line was drawn in 1949.

Pakistan's attempts to take back the lost area have been unsuccessful. According to an officer, operations such as that led by Musharraf in 1987 'only proved the impossibility of conducting a war up here'.

Since Bhutto became Prime Minister in December, relations have warmed between the two traditionally hostile neighbours. Neither side can afford the glacier war and there was hope for an agreement on the issue, which Bhutto describes as a 'flashpoint' in relations. But despite the initial optimism, and a visit to Pakistan by Indian Prime Minister Rajiv Gandhi, nothing has been signed.

While visiting Siachen, Bhutto admitted: 'It seems it will be very difficult to find an agreement now before winter sets in. Everyone's dug in for the winter.'

To outsiders it seems incredible that men should expose themselves to such harsh conditions, pushing the human body to extremes, over a stretch of land no one has ever inhabited or ever could, but the men of Siachen are resolute.

The commander of Ali Brangsa explained: 'To you this may be wasteland, but to us it's our motherland.'

For all Benazir's assurances that the generals and the people were now one, it was quickly clear that the army did not feel the same way.

Most of their unease about what they referred to as the 'democratic experiment' came from the growing perception that Pakistan had never had such a corrupt government. The central figure was Benazir's husband Asif, who went from being known as Mr 10 Percent to Mr 30 Percent. As the *Financial Times* correspondent, I often met foreign businessmen who told me they were being openly asked for kickbacks to secure government contracts. 'They're about as subtle as a train wreck,' said one.

When I tried to bring this up with Benazir, her eyes narrowed angrily. I was angry with her too – how could she as a female prime minister do nothing about laws that meant in court a woman's evidence was worth half that of a man and she could not open a bank account without her husband's permission? Worst of all was the

notorious Hudood Ordinance under which, if a woman was raped, she
needed to produce four male witnesses to the penetration. If she failed
she would be imprisoned for sex outside marriage. I had visited jails in
Lahore and Rawalpindi and they were full of girls who had been raped.

In Benazir's world you were either 'with us or against us' and my
invitations to dinners at the Prime Minister's house dried up. I began
getting anonymous phone calls asking if I was being paid by the
opposition.

It wasn't long after our visit to Siachen that the army started
plotting. One afternoon, one of Benazir's key ministers stopped by at
my apartment looking flustered. He told me that a group of army
officers had been arrested to foil a coup plot. A few weeks earlier
Benazir had clumsily tried to assert her authority over the army with
an unsuccessful attempt to remove its most senior officer, Admiral
Sirohey, Chairman of the Joint Chiefs of Staff.

At the monthly meeting of the nine corps commanders, four had
openly spoken against her. Benazir cancelled all foreign trips for the
next two months. It was clearly only a matter of time before she, like
her father in 1977, woke up to be told 'the troops have come'.

I checked with a couple of other sources, who confirmed what the
minister had said, then filed my story. A few evenings later my doorbell
rang. Two men in grey *shalwar kameez* and dark glasses were standing
there. 'The chief wants to see you,' they said.

I was driven to a house in the military cantonment of Rawalpindi. I
thought it was going to be another briefing with General Gul. Instead,
I was interrogated about my activities and questioned about my 'links
with British and Soviet intelligence' and a supposed plot to bring back
the King of Afghanistan. I could not believe they were serious. I
imagined what my mum would say.

Then they presented me with a file headed 'Activities of Christina
Lamb'. It contained many of the things I had done since arriving in the
country, such as my journey to Kandahar, and some things I hadn't. I
knew that ISI obtains lists of all foreigners who board flights and check
in to hotels but there was some information that clearly could only
have been passed on by a good friend. There were also photocopies of

personal letters, which explained why my mail usually arrived opened and taped back down.

I was questioned all night and warned that it would be 'in my interests' to leave the country. Early the next morning, I was driven back to Islamabad and left dazed on a main road a short walk from my house.

When I returned to my flat it had been ransacked, and two cars and a red motorbike had appeared on the corner. These followed me most unsubtly everywhere I went. The kind Reuters correspondent Oliver Wates and his wife Rosie invited me to stay, but then he started to be trailed too and their phones tapped. Even when the commercial attaché from the embassy gave me a lift in his diplomatic car to a wedding in Peshawar, we were followed. I was determined not to be driven out of the land of mangoes and buffaloes I had so grown to love. But I had acquired some powerful enemies.

Pakistan asks FT journalist to leave
Financial Times, 21 September 1989

MS CHRISTINA LAMB, the *Financial Times* correspondent in Islamabad, was asked to leave Pakistan following the Interior Ministry's refusal to renew her visa.

The move follows objections by the Interior Ministry to the publication in the *Financial Times* of a report by Ms Lamb saying that a plot by some army officers to overthrow the government of Ms Benazir Bhutto had been foiled.

The local newspapers described me either as an Indian spy or as 'the Pamella Bordes of Pakistan,' referring to a former Miss India who had hit the headlines in the UK for simultaneous affairs with the editors of both the *Sunday Times* and the *Observer,* as well as MPs who had arranged a security pass for her for the House of Commons. One of the articles claimed I had rented room 306 of the Holiday Inn to 'entertain'. I was horrified. Not only did I always dress conservatively in *shalwar kameez* with a *dupatta* (long scarf) covering my hair, but I had been so careful of my behaviour as the only female foreign correspondent in Islamabad that I had never even let Mark visit me in my apartment.

My only consolation was that no one I knew would believe it. After all, apart from a few excellent columnists, the local papers were full of what I called 'statement journalism', reprinting press releases from politicians or army officers that they had been paid to run. But then Pakistani friends started calling me. 'We had no idea you were doing all that!' they said.

As I drove to Islamabad airport, stunned that my life as a foreign correspondent was coming to an end, I noticed freshly painted graffiti on the wall outside. 'We apologise for this democratic interruption,' it read. 'Normal martial law will be resumed shortly.'

A few months later, Benazir woke to the news that troops had surrounded ministries, TV and radio stations. That evening the President, standing flanked by the three service chiefs, announced that the government had been dismissed for 'corruption, mismanagement, and violation of the Constitution'.

The Last Happy Nation

Brazil 1990–1993

Carnival – a dance to the music of crime
Financial Times, 13 March 1993

THE ILLUMINATED CLOCK tower of Rio Central railway station told me it was 4.15 a.m. On my head I was balancing three plastic peacocks, each a metre high, and a pair of sequin-encrusted plasterboard wings sprang from my shoulders. My torso was contorted by a body stocking several sizes too small, my legs tottered on silver boots and my smile was sphincter-tight.

With my centre of gravity somewhere behind my neck, if I moved my legs an arm-piece fell off. If I waggled my arms, the headdress started to slide. As if to accentuate my discomfort, a group of wayward birds started a jarring rendition of the dawn chorus. An audience of 60,000 people awaited and the dull thud of a hangover was already pounding my temples.

I was about to compete in Rio's yearly carnival parade as one of the 4,500 dancers defending the reputation of the Mangueira samba school. And still I had not mastered the samba despite the ever more desperate efforts of Carlinhos de Jesus, my fleet-footed teacher, to make my pelvis *mais líquida,* literally 'more liquid'.

The shout went up. It was our turn. Fireworks exploded and drums thundered until the whole road shook and the air quivered with

excitement and anticipation. Our feet pawed the ground like racehorses. A man with a stick pushed us into lines and yelled, 'Move it! Open your mouth! Sing!' Then we were off, running into the glare of a thousand lights. All around in the stands was a blur of faces, people waving pink and green flags – the school's colours – and cheering 'Mangueira!'

The digital clock marking our progress moved slowly. We had seventy minutes to pass along the 540-metre-long avenue. For the first ten of them, I thought I would never make it. My throat rasped like sandpaper as, over and over, I croaked out the words of our song: *'Dessa fruta eu como até o caroço'* – 'I'll devour this mango, even the core.' Sweat poured down my face, glitter in my eyes. Suddenly, though, propelled by the energy surging from the crowd, my feet began skipping in an extraordinary way. I became part of an enormous magical opera, a wealth of feathers and glitter, of floats bearing giant golden elephants, painted zebras and fearsome warrior heads.

Carlinhos had told me that samba moves people because its rhythm is like the beat of the heart – and he was right. It was addictive; I never wanted to stop.

The parade, which stretches from dusk to dawn on two nights, is the glittering centrepiece of Carnival, the biggest, most lavish party on earth. A week-long jamboree, it involves hundreds of thousands of people and brings the whole of Brazil to a stop. But, unknown to the bedazzled tourists, the glamour and glitz hides the fact that it is funded largely by organised crime.

The sponsors of the party are the *bicheiros*, the men who run the *jogo do bicho*, or animals' game – an illegal gambling racket, whose tentacles spread through the underworld of Rio. 'Beneath the parade's beautiful face of light and art lurks a dark underside of crime, killing and urban violence,' says Maria Laura Cavalcanti, an expert on Carnival from Rio's Institute of Folklore.

It was not always so. Carnival has religious origins: the date marks the start of Lent and the name derives from the Italian *carne vale* (goodbye to meat). It began last century with European costume balls and parades for royalty, based on the Italian commedia dell'arte. At the same time, the African slaves on the sugar plantations in Brazil's north-east had their own far humbler carnival when one man would dress up as king for the day. The two fused late in the nineteenth century after abolition of the slave trade and a searing drought in the north-east sent many former slaves to Rio. The pounding samba beat was the result of a suggestion by a Portuguese named Zé Pereira that all the members of his carnival club should play their drums at the same time.

Founded in the 1920s, the first samba schools got their name because they used school grounds for their rehearsals. Today, there are sixty schools in Rio, mostly in the poorest areas after which they are named, and they have become the heart of their local communities. The fourteen top clubs, or Premier League, compete annually in the main parade. This used to be in Avenida Rio Branco, the city's main commercial thoroughfare, but in 1984 it was transferred to the Sambódromo, a purpose-built stadium designed by Oscar Niemeyer and consisting of a long cement corridor lined with tiered rows of boxes and stands.

What transformed Carnival from a somewhat ramshackle affair, with the poor scraping together their own costumes and floats, into the grandiose spectacle of today was the *bicheiros*.

The *jogo do bicho* is as old as the republic, having been launched by a nobleman called Baron João Batista Drummond to raise funds for his private zoo after the end of the Portuguese empire in 1889. The lottery – in which different animals represent different numbers – was such a success that it was copied and multiplied, going underground when gambling was declared illegal in 1946.

Despite being illegal, there are gambling points visible on almost every street corner and around 300 *bicheiros* in Rio run a network of 1,200 lotteries, employing some 40,000 people. It costs just 1,000 cruzeiros (3.5p) to bet and the game is so popular, particularly among Rio's 3 million *favela* (slum) dwellers, that it moves millions of dollars each week. No one cracks down because the police receive kickbacks, the politicians often have their campaigns funded by the *bicheiros*, and the people can dream of winning fortunes.

Bicheiros have long contributed to samba schools to gain support in the poor communities where most of their clients (and much of the electorate) live, but their patronage has become more explicit since the 1970s. The turning point was 1975 when a *bicheiro* known as Anísio hired a top carnival designer, Joãozinho Trinta, to produce a spectacular parade with huge papier-mâché animals, spinning roulette wheels and fabulous costumes for his school, Beija Flor. Since then, the *bicheiros* have thrown money at the schools in attempts to outdo each other.

In 1984, they created the Premier League, in which all but the Mangueira school are run by *bicheiros* (Mangueira has an elected president). Samba schools each spend between $1 million and $4 million on their parades, half of which is often *bicheiro* money. Such large sums mean that Carnival has become increasingly profession-alised. Schools hire directors and keep dancers and singers on fat retainers, swapping and selling them like football stars. Watched live on television by 50 million people, the splendour of the costumes and floats has superseded the importance of energy and dance skills in judging each parade.

My school, First Station of Mangueira, is one of the oldest. Its strange name comes from the fact that it was founded at Rio's first suburban railway station, back in 1924. In its fierce struggle to retain some independence, Mangueira has obtained sponsorship from companies such as Shell. But the *bicheiros* are infiltrating; they have taken one directorship already and the jaws of the big-timers who do not yet control a school are snapping at the door. The last-but-one president was assassinated and rumour has it that drug money is rife.

This year, a series of misfortunes suggested that Mangueira could keep out the *bicheiros* no longer. Already-scarce funds were frozen last month when a judge ruled in favour of a woman who claimed that Mangueira had stolen her song. Rehearsals were cancelled and fierce squabbles broke out. Dona Neuma, the school's 70-year-old First Lady and daughter of one of the founders, attacked the 'new administration' and said she would not parade for the first time in sixty-four years. Roberto Firminho, the president, retorted furiously that 'the old lady should retire and stay at home with her mouth shut'. The case was, however, resolved a week before Carnival and Dona Neuma relented.

Four weeks before the big night I visited the *barracão*, the school's centre of preparations. The enormous concrete hangar, with a corrugated-iron roof and a pink gate, was guarded to prevent rivals taking a sneak preview. Inside, the air reeked of carpenters' glue, and hammers were banging and drills whirring everywhere. Disembodied papier-mâché figures and limbs lay discarded on the floor: here a cow's head, there a count's leg. It seemed they could never be ready on time and the workforce was buzzing with talk about other schools' sumptuous special effects.

Roberto Firminho sauntered out to greet me. Rubbing his moustache, he claimed everything was under control. 'It's always like this,' he smiled, unconvincingly.

He was right, though. The week before Carnival, the *barracão* had been transformed into a magical kingdom of medieval castles, French drawing rooms complete with marble columns, green brocade, gilded mirrors and chandeliers, Portuguese galleons on a silver sea, ten-foot-high elephants, and zebras dancing around an enormous African warrior head.

A man with a clipboard of pencil sketches was barking orders at a hundred people working round the clock on ten floats, scurrying up and down ladders with hammers and paint brushes, creating marvels from foam, fibreglass, wire and paints of myriad colours. Ilvamar Magalhães is the *carnavalesco*, the man who creates the Mangueira 'look'. Having chosen this year's mango theme almost a year ago, he buried himself in libraries to discover how the fruit came to Brazil and to design the floats and costumes (known as *fantasias*) to tell the story.

Carnival is an enormous industry, bigger in Rio now even than shipbuilding. Preparations for the big week provide permanent employment for 80,000 people, including musicians, architects, carpenters, electricians and sculptors. Samba schools are the main breeding ground for musicians and dancers, who spend the rest of the year giving demonstrations. Some of the painters in the *barracão* are well-known artists.

Parade day dawned cloudy and rain-laden but could not dampen the general glee. Inflation of 30 per cent a month and searing recession were forgotten as society figures and slum-dwellers mingled, worry lines falling from faces before my eyes. Walking towards the lights of the Sambadrome through a warren of tiny streets littered with beer cans and feathers and sequins from costumes, Cosmi Tudo, a drummer from Mangueira – resplendent in white silk tunic and gold turban and unrecognisable as a construction worker – said: 'We're poor and no one notices us but, for one day of the year, we're kings.'

As we watched the other schools parade, our spirits soared. Surely, we said, the Mangueira song is catchier, its floats prettier. We laughed cattily as Salgueiro's flag-bearer slipped, someone lost a hat, and a dancer from Estácio fainted. On and on went the processions of warriors, Indians, voluptuous women in rhinestoned bikini bottoms (their breasts splendidly naked and surely silicone-enhanced), cavemen under showers, giant insects, mermaids, and older women whirling in hooped skirts held up with hosepipes.

We marvelled at the giant steamships of Salgueiro and the gadgetry of Mocidade with its flying model helicopter, lasers and video screens. It seemed an incredible waste in such a poor country for so much luxury to be created for just one night and then thrown away, but Trinta explained: 'Intellectuals idealise poverty but the masses don't. They want luxury.'

Finally, it was our turn as the last school of the second night, the pink glow of dawn visible already over the lights of the *favelas*. The roar of the audience sent us into ecstasy – except for five breath-stopping minutes when the mast of our Portuguese *caravela* got stuck under the television tower. Afterwards, Magalhães was jubilant: 'It's definitely our best since 1987 [the last time the school won].'

Convinced we had come second, the results announced the following afternoon were a huge disappointment: Mangueira was a dismal fifth and Salgueira had clinched its first victory in seventeen years, scoring top marks in all categories from choreography to floats, story, costumes and music. A devastated Firminho said the school would appear at the champions' parade for the top five schools wearing black headbands. He complained: 'Some judges always try to appease the most powerful.' Dona Neuma was more philosophical: 'Mangueira has been parading for sixty-eight years. We're used to such results. I cry.'

Over at Salgueira, it seemed the celebrations would never stop. King of it all, in a white suit and banana grin, was Waldemir Garcia, known as Miro – a *bicheiro* who describes himself as a farmer. Only a week earlier, he had been in court – bracketed by heavily armed security guards in dark glasses – facing charges for drug trafficking and running gangs.

It's every aspiring foreign correspondent's dream when the foreign editor calls you in to his glass box and asks: 'Where in the world would you like to go?' In the late 1980s no other newspaper had as many overseas bureaux as the FT and on the foreign editor's wall there was a huge map of the world dotted with coloured pins to represent them all. Red for staff, blue for super-stringers, and yellow for stringers. I was being promoted from yellow to blue, which meant I would get a fixed salary and my own office and secretary.

It was December 1989 and I had little doubt about where I wanted to be. I had had war and now I wanted revolution. The Berlin Wall had just fallen and the only place for a reporter, it seemed to me, was Eastern Europe where people were taking to the streets and communist regimes were toppling like dominoes.

I had grown up on the Cold War and nuclear bunkers, Brezhnev of the bushy eyebrows and talk of détente. One of my school friends was Polish and her father regularly disappeared to smuggle bibles across the Iron Curtain. When we were lined up in the school playground to check that our heels covered a fifty-pence piece, we often talked about what we would do if the Russians dropped a nuclear bomb. The end of the world seemed a distinct possibility: at home in the evenings we all watched *Survivors*, the programme about people who had come through a mysterious plague and were having to rebuild civilisation all over again.

The foreign editor agreed he would send me to Budapest and introduced me to the paper's Eastern Europe editor, John Lloyd, who was one of my heroes.

That afternoon I went to Foyles and bought books on the Hungarian Revolution and the Prague Spring. Then I went to one of my favourite places in London, the Albanian record shop in Covent Garden, where men in long macs exchanged whispered messages amid busts of Enver Hoxha.

Instead of Afghans in rope sandals shooting at each other with Kalashnikovs, it was going to be a whole new world of spies, intellectuals and long evenings downing schnapps with revolutionaries while gypsy violins played in the background.

A few days later the editor, Geoff Owen, called me in. 'I want you to be our new Brazil correspondent,' he said. I looked at him in astonishment. I'd never been to Latin America in my life. All I knew about Brazil was coffee, Carnival and football. I couldn't remember the last time I'd read a story from there in a newspaper.

The editor was of athletic build and had once played tennis at Wimbledon. He was an awkward man who never looked you in the face. He admitted he'd never been to Brazil either. 'I think São Paulo is a bit like Milan,' he mumbled.

It turned out that the Eastern European correspondent, who had been Vienna-based for twelve years without much happening and spoke all the languages, had undergone a sudden change of heart about leaving. I wasn't surprised. Who would not want to stay amid such turmoil?

I went back to Foyles and swapped Milan Kundera, Václav Havel and Ivan Klíma for Gabriel García Márquez, Mario Vargas Llosa, Pablo Neruda and Jorge Amado.

From the moment I stepped off the plane in Rio de Janeiro, clutching the requisite chest X-ray to prove I wasn't bringing TB into the country, I adored it. Warm soft ocean air caressed my cheeks and I breathed in the red pepper smell of *flamboyante* trees, mixed with a sweet scent I later learnt was from the alcohol on which many of the cars ran instead of petrol.

The drive along the sea to Ipanema where I was staying was dreamlike. I'd never seen anywhere so beautiful in my life. The road followed the bay, curving round and round in inlets dotted with phallus-shaped granite mountains that were draped in lush greenery like something from lost worlds. On the left was the Sugarloaf with its two cable cars dangling from wires running up and down. On the right was the Corcovado, the hunchback-shaped hill topped with a towering Christ figure, arms outstretched as if blessing the city.

In 1502, when the Portuguese fleet sailed into Guanabara Bay for the first time, they were stunned by its beauty. The twisting inlets apparently confused the chief pilot Amerigo Vespucci into thinking it was a river mouth. As it was 1 January, he named it Rio de Janeiro – January River. Now, 488 years on, despite the proliferation of apartment blocks along the seafront and *favelas*, or shantytowns, up and down the hills, it seemed just as spectacular.

My first afternoon, on a road leading to the beach, I found the Garota de Ipanema or Girl from Ipanema bar where Vinícius de Moraes and Tom Jobim wrote their famous song on a napkin. Over a chilled beer, I watched the bronzed bodies, swinging hair and hips, 'tall and tanned and young and lovely', like Heloísa Pinheiro who had inspired the words back in the 1960s. These were the *cariocas* – the word means natives of Rio, though for me it would soon come to mean a state of mind. I thought I had never seen such beautiful people, nor so scantily clad. It could not have been more different from Peshawar.

On the corner was a juice bar, O Rei dos Sucos (the King of Juices), where people were ordering mixtures from lists of fruits I'd never heard of. In those days back home, pineapple still came in tins and even kiwi fruit were yet to appear on supermarket shelves. Aside from mango, passion fruit, papaya and star-fruit, there were guava, cashew and jackfruit and Amazonian fruits which had no translation like *açaí, acerola, bacuri* and *cupuaçu.*

I walked down to the sea and wandered to Copacabana along pavements fashioned in wave designs from black-and-white mosaics. Every few blocks stood a digital clock that switched between the time and, far more interestingly, the temperature. One informed me it was 38°C (later I would see them reach 46°C). At a kiosk, I bought a green coconut from a pile and watched the man hack off the top with a machete and insert a straw so I could sip the cool cloudy water. I felt like I'd gone to heaven.

My office was in downtown Avenida Rio Branco. Every day, after a shot of *cafezinho* and a hot crunchy bread roll at the counter of a street café, I would drive along the bay. Beach and sea were on one side; on the other, park and mountains. Rare was the morning it did not dawn sunny. Even when it was rainy the sky was the pearly grey of piano sonatas (though occasionally there would be tremendous tropical downpours when the traffic would come to a halt and mudslides would wash down the hills, carrying hundreds of shacks in their wake). There were never those endless dark drizzly days of England. Whatever kind of mood I left my house in, it was impossible not to be smiling by the end of that journey to work. Federico Fellini had called Brazil the Last Happy Nation. I decided then and there it would never have a revolution.

With the 'Girl from Ipanema' playing in my head, I rented a flat right on the seafront – Avenida Atlântica. But then I was invited to dinner by a professor who helped Chilean political prisoners find refuge. She had fallen in love with one and was moving with him abroad so needed someone – preferably female and foreign – to rent her apartment. It was just under the Sugarloaf in a little enclave called Urca, on Avenida São Sebastião, the oldest street in Rio. The apartment was uninspiring from the outside, reached by steps going down to the basement rather like Don Giovanni disappearing into hell. Once inside, however, it opened out on to a spectacular terrace overlooking Flamengo beach and the Corcovado, where I would lie in my hammock and watch the sun go down and the stars of the Southern Cross appear. Just round the corner, at the foot of the Sugarloaf, was a little beach, Praia Vermelha. By its side was a walk through one of the only surviving strips of Atlantic rainforest where if you were lucky you could see golden lion tamarinds.

My office also had a fabulous view, looking out from the twentieth floor over Guanabara Bay. Sometimes it would be torture to stay there working. Rio is a city where even bank clerks wear shorts; never had I met people whose life so revolved around the beach. So it was a joy to discover public phones on the beach – the *orelhão* – or Big Ears. This was before the era of mobile phones. The time difference – Rio was five hours behind London – meant I had to file my copy by lunchtime (not easy in a land where even Central Bank officials often did not start till eleven). Then in the afternoon I could go to the beach, phoning in to check or update.

'The line's bad today,' the sub-editors would say. 'It sounds as though you're speaking through the sea.'

'Yes, the lines are terrible,' I would agree, wondering what they would say if they knew it actually *was* the sea.

The beach is the bottom line – Copacabana beach
Financial Times, 18 July 1992

FOR THE FIRST twenty-five years of my life I lived under the misguided impression that beaches were fun but limited places where one went to toast one's body and unwind with the latest paperback before returning to London the colour of a walnut, to the envy of one's pallid friends.

Then I moved to Rio de Janeiro and discovered Copacabana, perhaps the world's most famous beach, which this week celebrates its hundredth anniversary. The subject of numerous songs, the name of bars the world over, the birthplace of bossa nova and even the inspiration for a Walt Disney character, Copacabana may be a little shabby these days but remains as exotic as ever and the soul of Brazil.

A sweeping crescent of white sand lashed by the Atlantic and backed by craggy hills (nowadays scattered with slums) between a military fort and Sugarloaf Mountain, Copacabana is more than a beach, it is a way of life. Seething with activity almost twenty-four hours a day, its four kilometres of sand act as Brazil's best singles bar, open-air nursery, sports field, aerobics studio, concert venue, the Rio equivalent of housewives' coffee mornings and even the setting for business deals, as well as home to some of Rio's many down-and-outs.

My first encounter with the Copacabana phenomenon can only be described as brutal. I had rented a seafront apartment, thrilled by the realisation of a lifetime dream of being gently awoken by the sound of crashing waves. Day One I realised my mistake. Barely had morning broken when I was jolted awake by the ear-splitting twanging of something called an *elétrico* parked outside my window – a lorry stacked with amplifiers blasting rock music that sent shudders through my apartment.

Pulling on a few clothes (beachwear in Rio can only be described as minimalist), I ventured outside. For as far as I could see the beach was swarming with people – not simply lying in deckchairs or on towels reading books or sun-worshipping, but all involved in some form of activity.

These were not tourists. Most foreigners have been frightened off Rio by the tales of pickpocketing and 'dragnet' operations in which bands of street children armed with knives and shards of glass sweep the beach clean of wallets, sunglasses and even sneakers. Instead they were almost all *cariocas* – natives of Rio – at play in the city's largest backyard.

Two years on, I remain astounded by the same daily display. In a bustling scene, a series of bronzed musclemen, surfboards under arm, scatter small children flying bird kites, as they rush into the water to 'catch' the next wave. Curvaceous women in scarlet lipstick and dental-floss bikinis strut along the shore. Everyone is an enviable shade of brown – here skin cancer are dirty words and telling a Brazilian it is fashionable to be pale could result in an unfortunate incident.

Revelling in air filled with laughter and the aroma of salt and coconut oil, wrinkled old people lower their sagging bodies into the shallows. Groups of beer-guzzling and pot-smoking teenagers squat in the sand puzzling the meaning of life. Spiritualist groups ceremoniously place small offerings of quails' eggs and empty perfume bottles on mounds of sand or cast roses and lipsticks to the waves to please the vain goddess of the sea.

Activity reaches a peak at weekends. True *cariocas* even have a 'beach address' where they can always be found on Saturday mornings. In among everything hawkers wind their way selling 'natural' sandwiches, foam biscuits, suntan oil and green coconuts. Even the police wear bermudas.

At the top of the beach loud cheers emanate from the vigorous volleyball and football matches under way. Exercise bars have been erected from which grunting athletes practise monkey-like swings. There is so much activity that some years ago the authorities had to widen the beach through a landfill and install floodlights so that play could continue into the night, when the beach becomes the preserve of prostitutes clad only in G-strings and open jackets, baring all to passing motorists.

Most bizarre of all is the assortment of people standing with one leg in the air or jerking their arms skywards as they jog in what could be mistaken for audition time for Monty Python's Ministry of Silly Walks. All this in the name of beauty. Brazilians are big on body culture – not for nothing is Rio's main bikini shop called Bum Bum.

Across the city, gymnasiums pound morning to night with people preparing their body for display on the beach – there are more than forty studios in Copacabana alone. I tried one for a time with the aim of keeping fit rather than sculpturing my backside, but the teacher was relentless. 'Bottoms are not for sitting on, girls!' she shouted, if we dared let up on the fight for the perfect buttocks. 'They are for showing off.'

If one is more impatient, or simply a lost cause, there is always plastic surgery. Rio has 500 registered plastic surgery clinics and the number one op is not the nose job but the bottom tuck – perceptible only by suspiciously firm peach-shaped buttocks with narrow scars in the centre, often covered by tattoos.

But Copacabana beach is not just for the body beautiful or those who can afford to cheat. Long gone are the days when it was an essential stop for Hollywood stars. Black-tie balls at the Copa, as the Copacabana Palace Hotel is known, attended by such notaries as John F. Kennedy, Eva Perón, Charles de Gaulle and Gene Kelly, are a distant memory.

Under Brazilian law beaches are public goods which cannot be fenced off and, since Rio's populist Governor arranged bus routes direct to Copacabana from the poor northern slums, its beach is no longer the preserve of the middle class.

It is the one facility accessible to all in the world's most inequitable society. Many Brazilian sociologists believe the beach is why, in spite of lurching from crisis to crisis in which the poor become poorer, the country experiences little social unrest.

———————————

Days were for the beach, but my evenings were spent in smoky bars listening to bossa nova that ran up and down my spine like massage and drinking *caipirinhas*, a wicked concoction of crushed lime, sugar and ice with *cachaça* – sugar-cane spirit. Best of all was going to hear Tom Jobim sat at the piano with a bottle of whisky and a cigarette to fuel his gravelly voice.

Never had I been to such a hedonistic place. Yet it was also mystical. On Friday nights, I would often come across little offerings on street corners of quails' eggs, candles and perfume bottles to appease the 'devils of the crossroads'. And on New Year's Eve, the whole of Rio, it seemed, would dress in white and head to Copacabana beach to throw gladioli into the waves to Iemanjá, the goddess of the sea. If your flower was carried out to sea it meant a good year, so most of us waded quite far before throwing them.

Iemanjá, the sea goddess, cast some of her magic over me that first year and, being in Rio and 25, I fell in love. He was a surf-mad banker called Claudio who accompanied his boss to my office for a meeting, carrying a suitcase, and stayed in my life for the next three years. He lived in São Paulo but was a *carioca* by birth and heart. He loathed São Paulo and every Friday jumped on the *ponte aérea* – the air shuttle between the cities – and came running down the steps to my flat. Sometimes we would go and visit his grandmother in Ipanema. She lived in one of Rio's few remaining old houses, squeezed by apartment blocks either side, and resolutely refused the entreaties of developers with big chequebooks. Her husband had been an admiral and she had travelled with him to London. Every so often she would shout out 'Piccadilly' or 'Buckingham' as she remembered the names of the places they had seen.

One Saturday we drove out of town as we often did, beyond the crowds, to our favourite beach of Grumari. On the way back we stopped at the Pôr do Sol bar to watch the sunset over *caipirinhas* and shells of spiced crabmeat. I could think of nowhere in the world I would rather be and when Claudio asked me to marry him as the sun swelled red and disappeared beyond the edge of the sea, I was accepting Rio as much as him. The following week he presented me with a ring, a delicate wave of gold and diamonds, as we dined on langoustines in champagne at the Copa.

But it was not all wonderful. The *morros* or hills that give Rio its unique topography were gradually being occupied by drug barons. Rio was the world's murder capital and crime was so rife that the police chief warned people not to stop at red traffic lights at night for fear of hold-ups. Friends of mine had been tied up in their homes by robbers; my own apartment had been broken into, and I had been held up in my car three times at knife-point or with a shard of glass wielded by *pivetes* or street kids. But I carried little cash and had no expensive jewellery to worry about (I used to laugh at the women taking their gold out from hiding places once inside the lift going up to a penthouse party). Anyway, it seemed a fair price to pay for all that beauty.

There was one aspect of life in Rio I knew I would never get used to. Every morning when I arrived at my office downtown, there would be little bundles in the doorways. After a while I discovered they had names and faces. These were children, some of the thousands – some say millions – of street kids who roam Brazil's cities. Sometimes they would be sniffing glue from shoemakers' tins or out of Coke bottles for a high and to dampen their hunger. Most *cariocas* just step over them as if they were insects. Some areas like Ipanema had even erected iron railings round the parks to stop the children going in.

The first year I lived in Rio, Amnesty International ran a series of advertisements: 'Brazil has found a new way of taking its children off the streets – killing them.'

Why Rio is murdering its children
Marie Claire, June 1991

IN LARGO DA CARIOCA, a square in the old centre of Rio de Janeiro, a pile of bodies starts to squirm as the whirr of rubbish trucks rouses the city from its slumber. Ten small boys sleeping on top of a hot-air vent above the Rio Metro stir uneasily, fearing another, similar noise – that of the body truck making its daily rounds, collecting the corpses of those murdered in the night.

It might be famed as the city of Carnival, beaches and dental-floss bikinis, but Rio is also one of the most violent cities in the world. In just one month – April 1989 – there were 500 killings. Many of the dead were children. These deaths are not just the result of ordinary crime. Death squads pick up and kill the street kids who so upset the tourists and the businesses dependent on tourism. Many of the squads are run by policemen who have no shame about their methods of cleaning up the streets. Their victims often have no families, no history, no names, no rights: like the 10-year-old boy in a parka jacket found dead with six bullets in his head and neck last September in the Niteroi area of Rio. He was tortured for more than half an hour by the two hooded men who had kidnapped him. His pleading voice was heard throughout the neighbourhood, but no one came to help. His last words were: 'Mother, mother, they are going to kill me! For the love of God, don't let them do this to me! I am only a child.'

The approach of footsteps awakens Alex, a cheeky lad in a faded yellow T-shirt, torn black shorts and rubber sandals. He sizes me up in an adult way to see if I am a threat or an opportunity though he looks much younger than the 13 years he claims to be. He has lived hand to mouth on the streets since he was left in Largo da Carioca by a mother who could no longer feed him. Alex thinks he has been there two years, but time has little meaning in his daily battle for survival.

To Alex and the small gang of boys on the air vent, home is the few square feet of cracked concrete pavement in Largo da Carioca. They are just 10 of an estimated 7 million children living abandoned on Brazil's streets – victims of the most unequal distribution of a nation's wealth in the world. Most of them are black and come from the *favelas* (slums), in which a third of Rio's 6 million population lives. Their parents tend to be migrants from the poor north-east of Brazil who have moved to the city in search of work only to end up in shacks cobbled from cardboard and plastic sheeting that wash away in mudslides. Ignorance, as much as religious abhorrence of contraception, results in families of four, five or more, too many to feed. (Sometimes whole families live on the street. On Sundays they turn the commercial centre into a massive laundry, hanging out their washing across the smart streets.)

The children are sent out to work at an age when they should be learning their times tables. Many end up stealing, mugging, picking pockets or prostituting themselves. Others work for Rio's narcotics traffickers, starting off as lookouts or 'airplanes', tipping off the drug lords when a rival or the cops approach. Later they might graduate to working as guards, often ending up addicted themselves.

Alex's day usually begins with a kick in the ribs from a worker at the fast-food restaurant outside which he sleeps. On a good day they might give him a bit of food; if not, he will forage in the rubbish bins, beg from a customer or steal from a bakery. Sometimes one of the others in his gang will have enough to share.

Like many of his fellows, Alex began by trying to scrape a living cleaning shoes and selling peanuts. But unable to afford the polish and nuts, he started scavenging rubbish. It is a marked contrast to the high life of Copacabana and Ipanema, where apartments sell for more than a million dollars. Brazil has no state welfare system to which the boys can turn, and many of his fellows end up picking pockets as the only way they can support themselves.

Often, it is the police who introduce the children into the crime for which they pay with their lives. Alex began by looking out for what he calls a *boi*, Portuguese for cow and street slang for an easy mugging. He then moved on to shoplifting. Once he started he found himself caught in a web from which he says he could not escape now even if he wished. He explains: 'The police ask us to steal for them. I used to take just food and clothes for myself, but six months ago a military policeman grabbed me and demanded I steal him two watches. Then his demands got bigger. If I refuse he will kill me. Every time he asks for more he taps the gun on his hip.' He showed me vivid bruises on his scrawny upper arm where the policeman had grabbed him.

It is common in Rio for children to work for the police. The kids guarding cars outside the Scala nightclub in the fashionable area of Leblon during Carnival balls have to give half their meagre earnings to local police. On Copacabana beach, bands of children terrorise tourists. At traffic lights they threaten motorists with knives or broken glass if handbags and jewellery are not handed over. They operate in front of police guard boxes. Each member of Alex's gang has tales to tell of carrying out crime for the police and of what happens to those who refuse.

One of Alex's companions told me the story of his 13-year-old girlfriend. Like an estimated 500,000 other street girls, she had turned to prostitution to survive. 'We were caught fucking by this military policeman, a real swaggering character. He called us names, then he smashed me to the ground with his pistol and said to her, "I'll show you a real penis." Then he took her. I haven't seen her since.' He thinks she must be working for that policeman now.

Girls make up about 10 per cent of Brazil's street children. Rita, aged 14, has doe eyes and hips that roll as if she is dancing a perpetual samba. She left home because her drunken father sexually abused her, and sex is the only way she knows to make a living. She sells her body for a hot meal or a night in a dingy hotel and considers Aids 'just part of the scene'. Girls like Rita need protection even from other street children, so they form their own gangs and pimp for each other. And they have children themselves: the mother of baby Marcio is 14, and his cradle is a cardboard box. She is proud to have someone to look after, proud to be able to get enough money to feed him, but she will not

open the cloth he is wrapped in. She does not want me to see the sores on his skin.

Alex's gang functions as friend, mother, brother and teacher. They search for nits in each other's hair while we speak. Today, Paulo, the leader of the group, dishes out the bread and ham I have brought them for breakfast with impeccable democracy, giving what is left to one of the many other groups of small bodies huddled in the square. Chewing on the food, they seem no different from kids the world over, gossiping about girls and planning raids. But the girls they chat about are under-age prostitutes, subject to sexual abuse from their fellow street children too, and the raids that they plan are not cowboys and Indians games but real attacks with knives.

Alex, Paulo and the rest do not question their lives; they see no further than surviving the day. Fourteen-year-old Paulo has already escaped one attempt on his life. He shows me a raised scar near his knee where a bullet grazed him. One night he was foraging in the streets when a station wagon slowed down and a hand pulled him inside. 'We all live in fear of the sound of an engine slowing or a car approaching. We sleep with our eyes open.' Dumped in a gutter and shot at, Paulo was one of the lucky ones. He survived. He knows 'heaps' who weren't so lucky.

Suddenly the breakfast chatter ceases. A military policeman is pacing alongside our group, glaring. No doubt he has a 'request'. For me to stay any longer would endanger Paulo, Alex and their comrades. As I leave they scuttle off towards the cathedral, where they hope to get a warm meal or a wash under a trickle of tap water.

Social workers estimate that at least one child a day is murdered on the streets of Rio and far more endure torture such as burning with cigarettes and electric shocks to their genitals. Accurate figures are almost impossible to obtain. These children have no birth certificates, and those who survive or witness such acts are afraid to speak out.

By compiling figures from newspaper reports, the privately funded Institute of Social and Economic Analysis (IBASE) found that last year 457 children were killed by death squads in just three Brazilian cities. Those, they emphasise, are just the cases reported. Herbert de Souza, head of IBASE, says he cried when, at the first meeting of the National Streetchildren's Movement, a group of children stretched a ribbon listing the names of all their dead companions around a sports hall. He says: 'This is worse than anything that happened under twenty-one years of military rule.' Those twenty-one years ended in 1985, leaving weakened civil institutions and a climate of impunity and violent lawlessness. Some of the police involved in killing children are the same who were torturing people during the military years.

Bodies turn up floating in the filthy rivers or buried in makeshift cemeteries. Killings and torture are so frequent that a daily newspaper was launched last year called *O Povo*, categorising page after page of crimes in gory detail.

A large proportion of the victims are from Baixada Fluminense, a slum on the outskirts of Rio. Wolmer do Nascimento, the local coordinator for the National Streetchildren's Movement, runs a day centre in the Duque de Caxias area of Baixada – perhaps the most violent part of Rio. He says that in addition to one or two children being murdered each day, there is also everyday abuse. Marcio, one of the children at the centre, complains: 'The police take our food and grind it under their heels. They call us whores and vermin.'

Inside the centre is a huge white board painted with red letters. On it are listed 106 names of murdered children, ranging in age from 5 months to 17 years. Most of the victims are male and between 14 and 17; all were killed during 1987 and 1988. Since then, says Wolmer, the situation has worsened. After receiving death threats, he started living under police protection in order to draw public attention to his cause. He estimates that between ten and fifteen of these death squads are now operating in Baixada alone. 'Everyone knows who they are but no one dares speak,' he says.

Many social action groups, like the National Streetchildren's Movement, grew up in response to Héctor Babenco's film *Pixote*, released in 1980, which portrayed the tragic life of a 10-year-old slum boy in São Paulo, Brazil's largest city. The 12-year-old boy who was picked from Baixada to play the title role did not see his own life improve. He turned to crime; three years ago he was reported assassinated by military police.

International attention was focused on the issue when the killings spread to wealthy suburbs. As the lure of dollars attracted the children to tourist areas, tourism dropped off, falling by around 50 per cent in the past two years. It was this threat to Rio's economic mainstay that prompted hoteliers and restaurant owners to encourage 'the most brutal form of social control by people who think of street kids as lice, and killing them as cleansing the streets', as Maria Teresa Freire, who runs a charity called Children's Crusade, describes it.

On 1 May 1989 the strangled body of a 9-year-old called Nico was found in a wealthy Ipanema street. A card beside the small corpse read: 'I killed you because you weren't studying or building your future. The government shouldn't allow the city's streets to fill up with brats.' It was this that made Freddie Marques, now press officer for the National Streetchildren's Movement, decide to devote his life to helping the children. He himself has a baby by a street girl with whom he lived for four years, before she was lured back on to the streets. He explains: 'It's not just a matter of giving money. The kids need to be given values and respect. The attitudes of Brazil's main economic players have to change. Maybe these children do look black and dirty, but they are not dogs or pests, they are Brazil's future.'

Unfortunately, Freddie and the few who think like him barely scratch the surface of the problem. The safe houses and day centres run by the Church and social organisations in Rio can cater for only a few hundred.

Paulo Faustino runs República dos Meninos (the Boys' Republic), a safe house where up to forty boys learn to integrate with society. He arranges for them to get legitimate work, explains their rights and sends them to school. He says: 'The idea is for them to learn self-respect. But the real problem is for society outside to learn a social conscience. The people of Rio cannot wear jewellery in the streets or have car radios, they must have countless door and window locks and wear plastic watches. Yet, rather than trying to understand why this is so and pressurising the state, they blame the children.'

At the root of the problem lies a federal government that appears to have little interest in 18 million of Brazil's children living in subhuman conditions, and the fact that only 25 per cent of its 63 million under-eighteens finish primary school. Alceni Guerra, the Minister for Children, recently said in an interview, 'It's Rio's problem.' The participation of police in atrocities has been repeatedly claimed and proven by judicial investigation (police were identified by surviving victims and witnesses), and the Rio state government set up a commission of inquiry into death squads in 1983, yet witness intimidation and murder make prosecution almost impossible.

Amnesty International's report last year did not mince its words. It stated: 'Hundreds of children are being assassinated by death squads and tortured by police in various Brazilian cities, in some cases to clean the roads.' The government recently announced an investigation into the involvement of Rio businessmen in the financing of death squads. But, says Freddie Marques, using a common Brazilian expression, 'This is *para inglês ver* – just for the English to see.'

Many of the people enjoying Rio's high life are oblivious to the killings and have grown accustomed to seeing small bundles in the road or stepping over them on the way to work or to a restaurant. Others condone the deaths of those whom they regard as a nuisance. The head of Rio's Shopkeepers' Association, Silvio Cunha, told Rádio Nacional, a Brazilian radio station: 'When a *pivetinho* [slang for street child] is killed, this is doing society a favour. What is being killed is not a child but a small bandit. Children are what live with people in homes.'

Now, a second generation of street children is emerging – those actually born on the street, often looked after by sisters or brothers, themselves aged 10 or less, or, like Marcio, by teenage single mothers. With no identity papers and no education it is hard to see how they will ever escape from the vicious circle into which they were born. And because those who should be preventing or solving the crimes are actually committing them, the morals of the celebrated city have become so topsy-turvy that killing children seems to have become accepted. Freddie Marques believes that the only hope for Rio's under-age victims is external pressure. He pleads: 'The western world is worried about ecology and Brazil destroying the Amazon, but surely the death of a child means more than the death of a tree?'

Two years after I wrote this report, the baroque-fronted Candelária church that I passed every morning, a block away from my office, was the scene of a horrendous massacre. Around seventy children were sleeping huddled in the doorway when, at midnight on 23 July 1993, several police cars drove by and started shooting at them. Eight were killed, many more wounded.

When I arrived the next morning all that remained were two pairs of torn canvas plimsolls with no laces and a grubby, bloodstained blanket. Someone had erected a makeshift wooden cross. But most office workers were walking past without stopping.

I liked the Candelária church. It was said to have been built with the money of a group of Spanish sailors whose ship, the *Candelária*, had almost sunk during a tempest at sea at the beginning of the seventeenth century. In the midst of the storm they had vowed to pay for a chapel if they survived.

I didn't like passing it any more. It seemed to symbolise Brazil not caring.

Back home it was summer and there was not much news and the killing of the Candelária children led to an international outcry. A few days after the massacre, three policemen were taken into custody. They had been identified as the gunmen by Wagner dos Santos, a 22-year-old veteran of the streets of Rio and one of the survivors of the massacre. 'I will never forget that night even if I live 100 years – they must pay for what they did,' he said as he recovered from two bullet wounds.

Brazil actually had some of the most advanced child protection legislation in the world. Yet, according to the police's own records, 320 children had been murdered in Rio in the first six months of 1993 – more than in the whole of 1991. Aid agencies estimated that between two and four children were being killed in the city by death squads every night.

The problem was that the very people responsible for preventing crime were themselves involved. Paulo Melo, a former street kid who had become a member of the state assembly, told me: 'Rarely does an extermination gang not contain a policeman. Everyone knows who the murderers are and where to find them, but people are scared to give evidence.'

More chilling still was the public support for the killings. I listened in disbelief on my car radio after the massacre, when the overwhelming majority of people calling a phone-in on CBN national radio approved of the killings.

Outside the church, a man who identified himself only as Jorge, told me: 'These children have been sent where they belong. We should kill them all.' But another man, Ronofri Cabral, a worker from Petrobras, the state oil company, who had brought his 12-year-old son to the site, said: 'This all comes down to the failure of the state to provide a decent wage. What we should ask is why children, many of whom have families, are living in the streets without food, clothing or shelter.'

The rising international pressure forced Brazil's President Itamar Franco to go himself to Rio to monitor investigations. A grumpy Victor Meldrew character with a shock of white hair and a baffled expression, he turned the blame on the developed world. 'The poverty and misery that exists here is often caused by the industrialised countries, which place obstacles in the way of our search for science and technology,' he complained.

That was not the end of the story.

Five officers were accused of the massacre. One of them, Maurício da Conceicão, died during a shoot-out as he was about to be arrested in 1994. Two, Marcos Emmanuel and Nelson Cunha, were handed life sentences. Two others were acquitted, including one who Wagner dos Santos said had shot him in the face.

A social worker later tracked the fate of the sixty-two children who survived the attack. He found that thirty-nine of them had either been killed by police or on the streets.

One of the survivors was Sandro Rosa do Nascimento. He later became famous for hijacking a bus on 12 June 2000 – the Brazilian equivalent of Valentine's Day – in an incident that was made into a film, *Omnibus 174*. Sandro had boarded the 174 armed with a .38-calibre revolver, intending to rob the passengers. But a passenger somehow signalled to a police vehicle, prompting the police to intercept the bus.

With nowhere to run, Sandro took the ten passengers as hostages. The bus was soon surrounded by police and TV news cameras, broadcasting live. The driver escaped through the window. Sandro at first reassured the passengers, the police, the television crews and their viewers that he did not intend to kill anyone. However, as the hours passed, he grew agitated and began screaming out of the window to the cameras a litany of compaints about the injustices of Brazilian society and its failure to treat homeless people as humans. 'You pigs can't terrorise me now!' he yelled at the police. 'Didn't you kill my friends at Candelária? I was there!'

The stand-off lasted for more than four hours as police and SWAT teams were prevented from intervening by politicians reluctant to provoke a bloodbath on national television. By the time Sandro finally exited the bus at 6.50 p.m., some 35 million Brazilians were glued to their screens – a quarter of the population. Both he and a teacher he used as a human shield were killed in the ensuing gun battle.

Rio continues as violent as ever, so much so that in February 2007 a group of human rights activists started a website called Rio Body Count. It was modelled on the Iraq Body Count, which monitors deaths in the insurgency. Rio had no suicide bombs but within a week its body count was eighty-eight. A third of the dead were children.

Dictators and Dinghies: Journeys in Latin America

The strange case of the Bolivian Navy
Financial Times, 11 September 1993

Lake Titicaca

CAPTAIN LUIS ARANDA is the proud commander of the Fleet of the Fourth Base of the Bolivian Navy. But the only ships at his command are those he makes at home from matchsticks, along with a motley flotilla of five small metal ferry and patrol boats that are gently rusting in the waters of Lake Titicaca. Aranda's 150-strong division spends most of its time raising chickens and cultivating prize tomatoes. The reason: Bolivia may have a navy, but it has no sea.

Bolivia has been landlocked since losing the War of the Pacific against Chile in 1879. Its capital La Paz is the world's highest at 12,000 feet and the only place I have ever stayed where the list of numbers by the hotel phone includes 'Dial 0 for Oxygen'. But from the moment one steps off the plane it is evident that neither the rarefied air nor the passage of years have served to quell passions.

A tiled plaque across an entire wall of the airport asserts that 'Bolivia Is a Maritime Nation'. Taxicab windows all bear bright-coloured stickers proclaiming, 'The Sea Belongs to Us – to Recapture It Is Our Duty.' Newspaper editorials rail almost daily at Chile's mulishness in refusing to relinquish the land that blocks Bolivia from the Pacific coast.

El Mar Boliviano is a primary school set textbook crammed with pictures of crashing waves described as 'our sea'. Statues in otherwise sleepy town centres depict demonic Bolivians bayoneting hapless Chileans above the inscription: 'What once was ours will again be.'

'We're the only landlocked nation in the world' is a frequent complaint from locals, blaming Bolivia's glaring poverty on its lack of coastline. They close their ears if one points out other examples of prosperous sea-less nations such as Switzerland or Austria.

Bolivia is certainly one of the world's most unfortunate or misguided nations. Once the second-largest country in Latin America, it has lost territory to almost all its neighbours in wars. But it is the loss of the sea that really rankles. At every international conference Bolivia raises the issue, demanding its land back, and Chile always replies no. On 23 March every year a Day of the Sea is held to mourn the loss, and thirty years ago the navy was re-established to show that Bolivia would never yield.

A smart ten-storey building is headquarters to the high command of the 8,000-strong navy and its tiny fleet. On the top floor sits the commander-in-chief himself, Admiral Miguel Alvarez. Surrounded by pictures of ships on the high seas, he booms: 'The sea is in the soul, spirit and heart of every Bolivian. Every one.'

Admiral Alvarez believes that with the end of the cold war it is time to solve territorial disputes such as that between Bolivia and Chile. 'We have great hopes from the new world order and will raise this issue at every forum until we get a satisfactory resolution reintegrating the land which, by historic, geographic and legal right, belongs to this country.'

He thinks Britain should take a lead in this process, claiming that British merchants in Chile, seeing the value of nitrates in Bolivia, inspired and funded the Chilean invasion of the Bolivian port of Antofagasta. Apparently, during Queen Victoria's reign, maps of the region were printed in Britain omitting Bolivia altogether – clear proof, he says, of conspiracy.

According to the story, the problem began when the British Ambassador back in the 1860s declined a bowl of *chicha*, local fermented wine, from the then President Mariano Melgarejo. Some say it was because he didn't care for it; others that he objected to the President's insistence that the diplomatic corps drink from the same bowl as his favourite horse Holofernes, a regular guest at palace banquets.

The Ambassador's punishment was to drink an entire barrel of chocolate, then to be led, facing backwards, astride a donkey through the main street of La Paz. He was sent back to London.

Queen Victoria's initial reaction is alleged to have been 'send in the navy!' On being told that Bolivia was a landlocked country, she reputedly asked for a map of South America, drew a cross through Bolivia and declared furiously: 'Bolivia doesn't exist.'

This must be an apocryphal story since Bolivia had not then lost its coastline. Whatever the truth of the matter, as Admiral Alvarez waits for Britain to get its act together, he sees nothing incongruous about being commander-in-chief of a navy which has no sea. He does, however, admit a certain envy for neighbouring maritime nations such as Argentina, Peru and Brazil, on whose goodwill he relies to allow his forces to practise their seafaring skills. Only the luckiest Bolivian naval cadets get to go to sea once a year.

Out at the fourth naval base of Tiquina on Lake Titicaca, Captain Aranda says his men are ready to take to the high seas at any time. While they are waiting for that great day, the Bolivian Navy is giving a useful lesson to the rest of the world in how to utilise an idle military. Captain Aranda's men patrol the lake looking for Sendero Luminoso guerrillas in hiding from Peru, and his colleagues in the Amazonian naval bases chase narco-traffickers.

But most of the time the men of the fourth base are engaged in raising chickens, growing vegetables and planting trees to replace those removed by locals. 'Perhaps you might think it a little strange to see a navy growing vegetables,' says the captain as he shows off a splendid selection of lettuces and tomatoes, 'but armed forces should adapt to the necessities of the situation. It's our duty to contribute to the development as well as the defence of the country.'

The missing children of Argentina
Marie Claire, May 1992

Buenos Aires

Ten-year-old Marie Jose Lavalle Lemos was watching Disney cartoons at a friend's house in the small Argentine town of Mar del Plata when the local judge arrived and escorted her to his office. Teresa Gonzalez de Ruben, the police sergeant she knew as Mummy, was waiting there. 'Your mummy has something to tell you,' said Judge Juan Ramos Padilla.

Marie Jose was told that the people she had always called Mummy and Daddy were not her parents. She had been born in a concentration camp, not a local hospital. Her real parents were victims of the systematic repression inflicted by the military regime that lasted from 1976 until 1983. They were imprisoned and killed: two of the thousands of Argentinians who are referred to as '*desaparecidos*' or 'the Disappeared', eradicated because of their opposition to the regime. Their corpses were disposed of in secret dumping grounds, all records of their fate destroyed. The woman who had brought Marie Jose up and registered her as her own daughter had been a guard in the camp and may even have been responsible for the torture and death of her natural mother and father.

Known as *niños desaparecidos*, hundreds of children were also abducted with their parents, or their mothers were kidnapped during pregnancy and kept alive just until they gave birth. Some of the children were adopted by childless couples who were unaware of their origins; more chillingly, others like Marie Jose were adopted by the very officers who had tortured or even murdered their parents.

Marie Jose remembers the three days following the painful revelations at Judge Padilla's office as a void; everything she thought was true was not. 'I didn't know who I was any more.' She was taken to hospital for a blood test then put up in a local hotel while the results were scrutinised. On the third morning the results came through, revealing with 99.88 per cent certainty that she was the lost daughter of Monica and Gustavo Antonio Lavalle, who were abducted in July 1977 while students at Buenos Aires University and later killed.

While for Marie Jose the discovery of her true origins threw her life into turmoil, for her maternal grandmother Haydee Vallino Lemos it was the joyful culmination of a long search. Haydee worked closely with an organisation called the Grandmothers of the Plaza de Mayo, formed in October 1977. Their untiring struggle to find missing children is internationally recognised, and every Thursday afternoon the Grandmothers march in the Plaza de Mayo outside the Presidency in Buenos Aires. With their heads wrapped in distinctive white embroidered scarves, they hold placards bearing faded photographs of their missing sons and daughters, and the names of the grandchildren they still hope to find. 'We may have lost our children but we must fight for their children and make sure this never happens again,' says 76-year-old Juana, who has never missed a Thursday afternoon in the fifteen years since her son was taken. 'I will never give up asking what has happened to them.'

For Juana, and many like her, the search for missing grandchildren has become their main reason for living. It is exhausting work and for seven years during the military rule they had to operate in secrecy. They were followed constantly, received threatening phone calls and were even taken into detention as they brought the plight of the Disappeared to the world's attention. 'We are all over 60 and mostly just housewives with no political experience or militancy, but we all share the knowledge that we have been robbed, not only of our children but also our grandchildren,' says Estela Barnes de Carlotta, president of the Grandmothers. Their small office is filled with children's toys and photos of the children who have been located. On the wall behind Estela is a photograph of her stunning daughter, Laura, who was two months pregnant when she was abducted, along with her boyfriend, in November 1977. Laura's body turned up in August 1978 riddled with bullets. Estela learnt that she had earlier given birth to a boy named Guido but, so far, she has not been able to trace him.

To find the missing children the Grandmothers rely mostly on anonymous phone calls or letters from people who inform on neighbours acting suspiciously or who move away suddenly. 'There can be all sorts of clues,' says Haydee. 'It could be that they worked in the regime and then appeared with a baby after showing no signs of pregnancy, or that they are dark while the child is fair, or they treat the child badly. They often act shiftily and are usually not liked because of their military connections. Although people are scared of them, they will still denounce them anonymously.'

Estela recalls the time when the Grandmothers first launched their heart-rending search. 'It was real 007 stuff. Imagine, we're looking for children whose names we don't know, nor their appearance, nor even their date of birth.'

With the aid of international fund-raising, the organisation now has an investigating team. Their task was made easier in 1984 when the new civilian President, Raúl Alfonsín, sanctioned the setting up of a National Bank of Genetic Data. Samples of blood from all the grand-parents are registered there, creating a genetic map for each child. Once a child such as Marie Jose is found, the data can then be used as proof to match her up with her legitimate family.

So far the organisation has found 50 of the 215 confirmed *niños desaparecidos*. They believe, however, that there are many more – the estimated total number of 'disappeared' adults is a staggering 45,000. Of the children they have traced, twenty-five have been returned to their legitimate families, thirteen are in contact with their legitimate families but have remained with their adoptive families, who were unaware of their origins, five are currently being fought over in court and seven were found to have been killed.

Haydee had been looking for Marie Jose for eight years, ever since she was told of her granddaughter's birth by a friend of her daughter's.

She says: 'I knew when Monica was taken that she was pregnant and I often imagined there had been a child. But I didn't know how to begin finding her.' Haydee joined the Grandmothers and began what was to be a long and painful struggle. To fund her search she sold her wedding ring and television. Her house was broken into – an act she believes was connected – and everything was stolen, leaving her only memories and one crumpled black and white photo of Monica and Gustavo. The other grandparents, Gustavo's parents, refused to acknowledge that the couple were missing; like many Argentinians they tried to ignore the repression. Disapproving of Haydee's involvement with the Grandmothers, they sought to restrict her access to Monica's other daughter, Marie Laurie, whom they were bringing up. A year older than Marie Jose, she had been abducted as a baby with her parents but was found a few days later abandoned near her paternal grandparents' house, suffering from malnutrition.

When Marie Jose's adoptive parents heard that the Grandmothers were on their trail they moved four times. Marie Jose was scarcely allowed out. Each time the family moved, complaints would come in from suspicious neighbours. Finally Judge Padilla, who was investigating complaints from the local Grandmothers group, discovered that Teresa Gonzalez had worked in the Banfield concentration camp, where many of the missing children were taken, between 1976 and 1978.

At first Gonzalez denied she had taken Marie Jose, but after being detained she openly admitted that the child was not hers and that she had worked in the detention centre where the child was born. In fact she was said to seem almost relieved, 'as if she had discharged a ten-year lie', says Padilla. When Judge Padilla told Haydee about this little girl, she knew the age fitted, but hardly dared hope it was her grandchild. She was lucky – Marie Jose was only the second *niño desaparecido* to be located.

Judge Padilla was unsure of what to do. 'It was all new and I didn't know what was best for the child. It seemed to me a terrible suffering for a child to suddenly discover that the people she assumed were her parents were not. I spoke with psychiatrists and was unconvinced. Finally I talked to my 12-year-old son who said, 'Look, Daddy, truth is truth.' I realised then that it was better for a child to know the truth, however painful, than to be lied to.'

At the same time Marie Jose's sister, Marie Laurie, was coming to terms with her true identity, the fate of her real parents and the knowledge that she had a younger sister.

Marie Jose was silent and withdrawn during counselling sessions with the judge and a psychiatrist. 'At first I thought I'd rather go back to the people who had brought me up because I was frightened. I had always been with them,' she says. Finally she was left alone with her sister, to whom she bears a striking resemblance. After forty minutes of complete silence the judge heard voices, then giggles and finally bursts of laughter. The two came out showing their arms – they had discovered that they each had a moon-shaped birthmark on the same part of the arm. 'As soon as I met my granny and sister I didn't want to go back,' Marie Jose admits. And Marie Laurie adds: 'It seemed as if we had always been together.'

Gonzalez's confession made Marie Jose's case far simpler. Within a week of her discovery, Marie Jose had chosen to live with her grandmother, and Marie Laurie decided to leave her father's parents. Now 72-year-old Haydee is very happy living with her two grand-children in their small Buenos Aires flat. They were both brought up as only children and often have terrible fights, but they are adapting, she says. Through the Grandmothers, Marie Jose and Marie Laurie have access to a team of psychologists to help them readjust.

Marie Jose appreciates that she was brought up in some measure of luxury, almost spoilt. But she says: 'They treated me well and over-protected me, but it was all a lie.' As Haydee says: 'A child can be given beautiful clothes and toys but if she has been robbed of her identity, she has lost the most precious thing. It's worse than being a slave, as at least a slave has a history.'

In fact Marie Jose has bloomed since moving in with her grandmother. Haydee proudly shows a line written by her grand-daughter about her lost years. 'I could not grow, Granny. It was as if a hand was pressing down on my head.'

For many of the other Grandmothers the search goes on, made more difficult as some of the children have been taken to neighbouring

Paraguay. Despite persistent demands, the Grandmothers have been given no access to police records. In 1987, all officers in the junior and middle ranks involved in the repression were pardoned by the government. In December 1990 President Menem pardoned all those senior officers still behind bars, making the Grandmothers' fight even harder, because even when children are found, the courts in today's officially democratic Argentina are not necessarily sympathetic.

Estela hopes that as children who are still living with their foster parents get older, they will start asking questions about their past, become suspicious and approach the Grandmothers. They are already getting lots of inquiries following a publicity campaign, one they hope to take to prime-time television.

There are various theories about why the repressers took the children. Alicia lo Judice, a psychiatrist involved in counselling returned children, says: 'They don't accept they stole the children, they say they adopted them. Maybe they even believe it. But it's not adoption – it's stealing children.'

None of the 'parents' who have had to return children are willing to explain their side of the story, but an acquaintance of Teresa Gonzalez said in her defence: 'She wanted to give Marie Jose a chance of life. Surely it's better that the child was saved and brought up in security than left to die in the camp.'

The grandparents are less sympathetic. Some believe it's a macabre form of war booty; others see it as a form of brainwashing. Estela says, 'It's as though, having killed the parents, the repressers then wanted to control the destiny of their children.'

In summing up the case of Marie Jose, Judge Padilla pointed out that Teresa Gonzalez had deliberately falsified her birth documents and compared the child's condition to that of 'a pet animal which is treated with affection but with the sole objective of giving pleasure to the owner'.

Estela hopes that, as they get older and discover the truth, the children will turn against their adoptive parents, seeing them as captors. Marie Jose repeats: 'They treated me well but now I don't want anything to do with them. What more can you take from a person than their history?'

'My people trust and love me': on the road with the President of Peru

The Spectator, 13 August 1994

Lima

'CAN YOU HEAR ME, CHILDREN?' asks the Japanese man on the platform in the wheedling manner of a pantomime performer. Hundreds of small, dusty faces shake stubbornly, impervious to anxious gestures from rows of mothers and teachers in shiny best dresses and pink make-up, greasy in the midday heat. Black-clad marksmen on the roofs of half-built adobe houses surrounding the new brick school train their guns on the crowd. 'Can you hear me now?' yells the man. This time the playground erupts in a frenzy of red and white flag waving and chants of 'Fuji! Fuji!' led by a long-armed youth in a scarlet tracksuit.

Welcome to the wonderful world of Peru's President, Alberto Fujimori. Born of Japanese parents, he is called the Emperor by his critics. As he rushes round the country smashing bottles of apple champagne to unveil public works and bestow largesse on a bemused public in staccato Spanish, Fujimori's role does seem more imperial than governmental. With his smooth, round face, wire-rimmed glasses and sombre suit, he may look like a Japanese banker but he clearly sees himself as a modern-day Inca bringing prosperity to all four corners of his empire.

The Benito Juarez school is in one of the sprawling slums amid the permanent smog that hangs above the ugly city of Lima. It's the President's second school visit today in a helter-skelter schedule of inaugurating public works that keeps him out of his office all but two days a week. 'This is my style,' he says, in between autographing photo-calendars and kissing blushing teachers. 'Other presidents know the interiors of their own offices. I know the reality of my country.'

Such populist activities are rather surprising for a technocrat who calls himself the ultimate anti-politician and who defeated the novelist Mario Vargas Llosa in the 1990 elections by standing as the outsider not tied to any party. The 55-year-old former rector of the National Agrarian

University prefers to be addressed as Engineer Fujimori rather than as President and never misses an opportunity for politician-bashing.

His public seems to appreciate it. Despite having closed down Congress and the courts and assumed near dictatorial powers in April 1992, in a move which received international condemnation, Fujimori is by far the most popular president in Latin America. In his last year in office he still notches up more than 60 per cent approval ratings, and, having changed the Constitution to be able to stand again, may well be re-elected. Voters in nearby countries such as Brazil and Venezuela regularly place him top of polls of those they believe most capable of solving their problems. A new verb, 'fujimorisation', has entered the lexicon for the process of *auto-golpe*, or self-coup – the seizure of complete control of all branches of government by a civilian head of state.

Although his means may have been dubious, Fujimori's popularity is understandable. The Peru he inherited had been as stripped of wealth by years of misrule as it was back in the sixteenth century by Francisco Pizarro's conquistadors. Between 1985 and 1990, under the populist rule of Alan García, who is now in exile, prices had increased 20,000-fold. Real per capita GDP had fallen to the level of 1960. Sixteen exchange rates were in operation, and the state was bankrupt, with no more foreign exchange reserves, and a pariah of the international community for non-servicing of debt. The proliferation of iron bars, lookout towers and security guards in Lima testifies to the havoc wrought by Shining Path, the Maoist guerrilla movement, which cost the nation $20 billion and 25,000 lives and made life unbearable for citizens with constant car bombs and power cuts caused by attacks on transmission lines. Risk analysis firms rated Peru the most dangerous place in the world to do business.

It took a chess-loving engineer who was told he would become president by a tarot card reader to undo this. Borrowing heavily from the Vargas Llosa programme that he had opposed during the campaign, Fujimori announced on taking office the 'Fujishock' to overturn years of statism and xenophobia. Following the same IMF-prescribed 'miracle recipe' already in place throughout much of Latin America, the plan involved scrapping subsidies, liberalisation of trade and foreign exchange, lifting price and wage controls, freezing public spending, tightening up tax collection and selling off all state assets, from cinemas and tomato-paste producers to the electricity company.

But while his yellow skin won Fujimori support from a largely non-white population who felt exploited by years of white elite rule, his political independence and imperial manner won him few friends in Congress or the judiciary. Frustrated by traditional congressional deal-making slowing his reforms, and by the timidity of the courts towards terrorism, on the night of 5 April 1992 Fujimori sent tanks into the streets to close both institutions. Condemned internationally, the tanks were met locally by cheering crowds. Since then, through an all-out war on the guerrillas, the government has captured Abimael Guzmán, the near-mythical leader of the Shining Path, and most of his lieutenants, and even extracted an apology from him. Fujimori has reduced annual inflation from 8,000 to 10 per cent and set the economy growing again and the stock market booming. All this, he insists, would have been impossible without his *auto-golpe*. Claiming to have inspired Boris Yeltsin's suspension of the Russian parliament last year, Fujimori is angered by the international outcry his own move provoked: 'We were in a state of war and every nation has the right to defend itself in such a situation.'

We had been discussing all this at a long table in the dark-panelled Grau room in the presidential palace when Fujimori suddenly announced: 'The only way you can understand what is happening is to come with me. If you have any appointments cancel them – say the dictator President commanded you!' An aide in dapper army uniform whisked me through the garden into which the Shining Path lobbed grenades just two years ago, past the parking lot where twenty ambulances await calamity, and into a convoy of black Mercedes sedans.

Shining Path may be in terminal decline but it is not yet dead, and the President's activities give his security men nightmares. His schedule is only decided at the last minute, so many schoolchildren wait in vain in hot playgrounds for a presidential appearance. Inside the car Fujimori's pen is constantly at the ready to note down problems to enter into his Toshiba laptop later. 'I'm always looking for things which need doing because often it is little things that are at the root of big problems,' he says. 'But there is so much to do.' We both stare wordlessly at the endless line of massive red-and-white pillars that were supposed to hold up a monorail but were long ago abandoned by a previous government.

As we drive through the streets of Lima, he rolls down the one-inch-thick bulletproof glass and waves to the *ambulantes*, or street-walkers, selling plastic fruit refrigerator magnets and executive toys – strangely inappropriate wares for a country in which two-thirds of the population live below the poverty line. The *ambulantes* appear amazed and then delighted to recognise him and try to catch one of the photo-calendars he keeps permanently on hand. '*El Chinito*' (Little Chinaman) they shout as they try to grasp his hand. Others call '*El Hombre*' (the Man) to signal appreciation for their gutsy President. Tossing out calendars in fast succession, recruiting both myself and the driver to help, he smiles in delight. 'The names they call me show they trust and love me,' he says. I try not to laugh as one of the calendars hits a sheep grazing innocuously on a patch of grass.

Fujimori is not surprised by the adulation. Jabbing his stubby finger at a slum on a hill, he says: 'That slum, San Cristóbal, has been there fifty years. It is right in front of the presidential palace yet it still does not have water or sewerage. That's what politicians do for you.'

Perhaps reflecting his Japanese heritage, the key terms in Fujimori's vocabulary are efficiency and good management. A pragmatist free from the shackles of any ideology, he does not like to waste time and at the Peru-Japan school – our next stop –struggles not to look impatient while a padre sprinkles droplets from a plastic bottle labelled 'Holy Water' and two grubby children dance a clumsy *marinera*, a formal dance from the coastal regions.

Fujimori makes no secret of the fact that he prefers soldiers to civilians. 'I like to get things done, to execute things, and that's why I like working with the military,' he says. He uses the army for everything from carrying out development projects to administering justice. As he announces gifts of computers, school bags and books to each school, it is a general who keeps tally in a notebook. The army is Fujimori's political party, and his main adviser and intelligence chief is Vladimir

Montesinos, a cashiered captain known as Peru's Cardinal Richelieu and so shadowy that he has only twice been caught on film in the last decade*.

Having initially avoided the foreign press, Fujimori now welcomes them as heralds for his message: 'My experience can be an example for the world. Various countries can question democracy as we did in Peru. The most important thing is efficiency. Government has to be efficient or people suffer.'

He told this to his fellow leaders at last month's Ibero-American summit in Cartagena, who not surprisingly were unenthusiastic. Fujimori didn't care: 'It's a new concept and a taboo theme, like that of the armed forces. But here in Peru it is I who control the armed forces, which is not true in some other countries round here.' With these words he throws the last calendar out to an astonished-looking man at a bus stop.

He has less control, it seems, of his domestic affairs. Last week his wife Susanna, a professed admirer of Mrs Hillary Clinton, packed her bags and left him on grounds of 'political differences'. Mr Fujimori had ordered Congress to pass a law preventing the spouse of the president from running for the presidency herself. The First Lady, it seems, had other ideas.

---

* Ironically it was a videotape showing Montesinos bribing opposition Congressmen to back Fujimori that led to both his and Fujimori's downfall in 2000. Montesinos is currently serving a twenty-year prison sentence for supplying weapons to Colombian rebels. Fujimori fled to Japan and then to Chile, from where he was extradited in September 2007 to face trial in Lima for corruption and human rights violations.

The Rise and Fall of
Fernando Collor

Before leaving London for my assignment in Brazil, I had enjoyed a long lunch with the genial Ambassador to Britain, Paulo Tarso Flecha de Lima. His wife was a close confidante of Princess Diana and they had become society figures in London, present at all the best parties. 'My country is neither a threat nor an opportunity to yours,' he said, pointing out how rarely Brazil appeared in British newspapers. 'So the best thing is just to enjoy.'

He was wrong. I was about to witness the demise of yet another head of state. Fernando Collor de Mello, Brazil's first democratically elected President in thirty years, had taken office just before I arrived, promising to shake up the elites. He had come from nowhere, or rather the small poor north-eastern state of Alagoas where his family controlled the local television station. But he had the support of the country's most powerful media mogul, Roberto Marinho, and his TV Globo empire. Marinho wanted to avoid a victory for the main candidate Lula, a left-wing trade unionist who had lost a finger when he was a metal worker in a car factory. With Globo's help, Collor ran a clever campaign appealing to the '*descamisados*' – the shirtless, somewhat ironic for one always so well dressed.

Collor cultivated an action man image. As President, he liked nothing better than being photographed flying supersonic fighter jets, setting fire to great pyres of cocaine, or piloting submarines. In true Latin machismo fashion, he banned women from wearing trousers in the Presidency.

The main dragon he was intent on slaying was hyperinflation, then running at 20 per cent a month. Within days of taking office in March 1990, he had launched an economic plan which froze bank accounts so no one could withdraw more than $150. People jumped off buildings as weddings, holidays and operations were cancelled.

Later we would find out that the $150 figure had been chosen at random by the Finance Minister. It also transpired she was having an affair with the Justice Minister, using the head of the navy to pass *billets-doux* during Cabinet meetings. The pair were caught smooching to '*Bésame mucho*' at a party and the next time the Finance Minister appeared in public, the presidential band struck up the song and watched her blush. The couple fled to Paris where the Justice Minister then abandoned her, claiming he needed urgent dental treatment.

Collor had a nickname – 'Fernandinho do Pó', 'Little Fernando of the Powder'. Every so often he would invite select foreign journalists to breakfast (girls in skirts of course) and we would all comment afterwards on his occasional trips to the bathroom, from which he would emerge strangely focused. The following day we would all be sent commemorative videos showing him greeting us as we trooped in and out of the palace.

In those first two years Brazil revelled in Collormania. First he took on the entrenched business interests that had benefited from years of protectionism, and opened up the country to cheap imports. At last we could buy fax machines, computers and decent wine. He also declared he would save the Amazon – an astonishing turnaround for a country which had remained defiant in the face of worldwide censure for the burning down of its forests in the name of development.

In his new role as defender of the environment, Collor hosted the world's first ever Earth Summit in June 1992. Suddenly everyone was talking about 'sustainable development' and 'biodiversity'. It was to be the biggest ever gathering of heads of state – 103 of them, from John Major to Fidel Castro – and a proud Collor commissioned the world's largest wooden conference table.

Rio had been scrubbed and polished for the occasion and was at its sparkling best. No one knew what the authorities had done with the street children. There was even an alternative conference in a beachside park which attracted everyone from Olivia Newton John to the Grand

Mufti of Syria. At the specially convened Earth Parliament of spiritual leaders, a giggling Dalai Lama turned up to tell everyone he was having 'fun, fun, fun'. Inside the tents, groups discussed diverse topics such as 'Breastfeeding is an Ecological Act', 'Mental Pollution in the Inhabitants of Large Cities' and 'The Culturing of Worms in the Process of Organic Fertilisation'. So moved was the Prime Minister of Barbados that he penned an ode.

But it was all about to go horribly wrong. On day two of the Earth Summit, I got a phone call that I could hardly believe. Collor's younger brother, Pedro, had lodged a video with a bank in New York exposing a web of corruption with the President at the centre. For good measure he also revealed how Collor held black magic sessions in the palace, cutting the heads off chickens and drinking their blood.

His timing was impeccable. The Earth Summit was wiped off the front pages and proceedings set in place for Latin America's first ever impeachment.

An awful lot of trouble in Brazil
The Spectator, 12 September 1992

Brasília

THE TAXI DRIVER in Brazil's futuristic capital releases his Senna-like grip on the wheel, jerks his thumb towards the presidential palace and mutters darkly, 'We've got a thief living in there.' He is referring to the country's dashing young President, Fernando Collor de Mello.

The frequency of such comments illustrates the sad demise of the rich former playboy who swung into office in March 1990 – a political unknown with a mission to modernise the capitalist world's most protected and regulated economy. His daredevil stunts, which ranged from riding jet-skis and piloting supersonic fighter planes to freezing the population's bank accounts, quickly won him record popularity and for a while he seemed set to go down in history as the man who led Brazil into the First World.

Yet only two years on he sits isolated in his office, condemned to be remembered in the history books as the first president to face impeachment, after the publication of a damning congressional report accusing him of raking in millions of dollars from a massive influence-peddling scheme.

Remarkably, Mr Collor's aides say he seems unruffled by the daily demands for his resignation issued by everything from chambers of commerce and the Bar Council to football clubs and bishops. The karate association wants to strip him of his black belt and the usually passive Brazilian populace has taken to the streets en masse clad in black. Amongst the many protest marches was even one entitled 'Babies against Collor'.

The amazing nonchalance of the man at the centre of the Brazilian equivalent of Watergate is attributed by critics to immense arrogance or even illicit substances. Others say the usually temperamental President simply refuses to believe what is happening. In his one television appearance since the report came out on 24 August, he appeared controlled, though with narrowed pupils and blinking eyes, and in his only interview he insisted that he had 'no trouble sleeping at night'.

George Bush once called Mr Collor 'Indiana Jones', impressed by his swashbuckling style and exaggerated promises to 'defeat the inflationary tiger with a single bullet'. The tiger is still alive and kicking, but Mr Collor has never before been so deserving of his nickname as in his current desperate fight to buck the Brazilian tradition of presidents not completing their mandates. The republic's first President, Marshal Deodoro da Fonseca, was forced to resign in 1891; Getúlio Vargas shot himself in 1954; Jânio Quadros resigned abruptly in 1961; in 1985 Tancredo Neves died before he assumed office.

Perhaps the odds were always stacked against Mr Collor. He was the country's first directly elected president for thirty years and his voters were the 'shirtless and shoeless', wanting change, which was the last thing Brazil's ruling elites had in mind. Originating from an inconsequential poor north-eastern state and a party which has only 23 out of 503 seats in Congress, Mr Collor nevertheless took on Brazil's formidable cartels and monopolies, ending thirty years of price controls and protectionism and allowing the import of items such as cars, cement and fax machines.

Humberto Souto, the leader of the government in Congress, believes

it is these 'vested interests' that are now campaigning against Mr
Collor. 'Imagine the money at stake. In the context of Brazil, Fernando
Collor was dangerous. I would compare him to John F. Kennedy,' he says.

His wife Rosane, a buck-toothed Barbie doll, caused her own scandal by favouring her family with contracts to supply the government
charity which she headed. She was sacked. Mr Collor's subsequent two-
stone weight loss caused a reporter to ask him if he was suffering from
Aids.

Yet by May this year, having appointed a new more experienced
Cabinet, things seemed to be looking up. Brazilian business actually
seemed to be learning the art of competition and for the first time ever
there were price wars between petrol stations. But in a *Dallas*-style saga
of fraternal vengeance it was all brought tumbling down by Mr Collor's
younger brother, Pedro. It was he who set 'Collorgate' in motion with
an interview accusing the President of coke-snorting and of using his
position for large-scale personal enrichment through the services of his
friend and former campaign treasurer, Paulo César Farias, known as
PC.*

A congressional inquiry into Mr Farias was set up and, with hearings
televised live, quickly became the hottest thing on the box in the land
of soap where more people have access to television than clean water. It
even took precedence over football, the national sport, though one
channel tried splitting the screen to show the hearing and Brazil v
France simultaneously.

Instead of the expected cover-up, the emergence of key witnesses
enabled the commission to piece together an alleged multi-million-
dollar scam. PC had placed people in ministries and state companies to
secure government contracts for companies, particularly in the area of
construction, which were paying him enormous kickbacks – usually
around 30 per cent of the contract. Most of the proceeds are believed
to have left the country in PC's plane, the Black Bat. However, after
banking secrecy was lifted, the inquiry discovered that a sizeable chunk
had ended up in the accounts of Mr Collor and his family through
phantom account holders.

* PC Farias would later be found murdered in his hotel room in north-east Brazil.

Mr Collor's situation was made worse by the dubious defence given by his former private secretary that the mystery deposits were the remains of a $5 million loan raised in Uruguay to fund his campaign and used to buy gold. After eighty-five days of investigations, the inquiry concluded with a direct accusation. The man who had come to power on an anti-corruption platform had made at least $6.5 million through the PC scheme, it said. Even Rosane's expensive taste in dresses and haircuts had allegedly been funded by PC, to the tune of an average $240,000 a month. One of the most bizarre items was $2.5 million for the landscaping of Mr Collor's private garden. The landscaper said last week that the Collor garden 'made the hanging gardens of Babylon look shabby'.

And so the world's third-largest democracy now has a moral and political crisis to add to its economic and social problems. Thirty years of high inflation have yet to be resolved and for the last year inflation has stuck at more than 20 per cent a month. Partly as a result, Brazil has the world's worst income distribution, according to the World Bank. The effects of this are obvious in the poverty-stricken north-east, parts of which resemble famine-struck Africa, and in the streets of Rio de Janeiro where people live in trees and it is possible to be shot for a pair of sneakers. Not surprising, then, that there should be indignation over the President's millions.

Way behind the rest of Latin America on the road to stabilisation, Brazil is bankrupt. Schools and hospitals are closing daily; 1.2 million are unemployed in the industrial capital, São Paulo; and the private sector is suffering so much that businessmen are already sending out next-year calendars, having given up on 1992.

Such is the weight of the task of resolving these problems that the army has remained securely in its barracks, to which it returned in 1985, showing democracy may be more firmly rooted than in some of Brazil's neighbours. Admiral Flores, the Navy Minister, points out that 'this is the first time in a hundred years that the military has not intervened in a political crisis'. Moreover, if any of the key characters are jailed this could be the end of traditional impunity, leading to cleaner administrations in future.

Whether Mr Collor survives the impeachment process will be

determined in the next few weeks by a congressional vote in which he needs the support of a third of the house or 168 deputies. If he fails he will be tried by the Senate for 'crimes of responsibility'. The Attorney General is studying 40,000-plus documents to decide whether to start a criminal case.

Meanwhile, inside his palace, Brazil's pin-up President straightens his designer tie, sucks on the Cuban cigars sent by Comrade Castro and refuses to listen to the voices outside clamouring for his exit. He ignores the numbers flashing on his computer screen showing the fall in the stock market every time he reaffirms his determination not to quit. Nor does he take notice of the exodus of his supporters now beating a path to the door of his Vice President, Itamar Franco, until recently more of a liability than Dan Quayle, but the man who will take over if Mr Collor succumbs.

In a nation addicted to soap opera, the greatest fascination was why Collor's brother had betrayed him in such a way. It turned out that the President had had an affair with Pedro's glamorous wife, Teresa. That hardly endeared him to his own less glamorous wife, Rosane. Such was the state of animosity between the First Couple that Collor emerged one day from their house, the Casa da Dinda, to wave a ringless finger at TV cameras and reveal that he had thrown his wedding ring in the lake.

Horrified at seeing her sons tear each other apart in public, Dona Leda, the matriarch of the Collor family, flew down from Alagoas in a fury. She demanded that Pedro take a sanity test, which he duly did and passed, brandishing the results at reporters and renewing his charges against his brother.

It was all too much. Dona Leda suffered three heart attacks and ended up on a life-support machine in a Rio hospital. TV cameras outside filmed each son coming and going at different times.

By then the move for impeachment was unstoppable. Collor's attempts to appeal to the public with an emotional TV address were to no avail. Every day there were demonstrations against him.

After he was suspended from office I went to see him in the Casa da Dinda and found him sitting at his desk while his secretary inserted signed photographs into envelopes. Rosane was nowhere to be seen.

A suitable case for treatment
The Spectator, 21 November 1992

Brasília

ON THE TABLE in front of Fernando Collor sits an embossed leather presidential pen-stand and a 'President of Brazil' name plaque from a United Nations conference – the forlorn remains of his former life as head of the world's ninth-largest economy. Suspended from office by a landslide congressional vote six weeks ago amid Brazil's biggest corruption scandal, today Collor faces criminal charges and an impeachment trial.

Now a recluse in his lakeside home in Brasília's 'Mansion Sector', every morning Collor walks the few hundred yards to the rudimentary library where he works without the benefit of air conditioning to relieve the oppressive summer heat. Only the solitary police car outside and the two security men clutching walkie-talkies in the yard suggest this is a man of any importance.

Surrounded by books on his favourite subjects, modern government and mind control, Collor presents a tragic figure. With an ear of wheat placed in front of him for luck next to an empty presidential agenda, he is left with nothing to do but dwell on how in two and a half years he threw away what appeared to be the most promising political career in Latin America.

As I waited in the small anteroom with its scratched terracotta floor tiles and paint-smeared windows, its white walls bare except for a few ship prints – in sharp contrast to the rich oil-painted battle scenes in the plush Presidency – I wondered what to expect. That morning the Brazilian press had carried cartoons of Collor in prison uniform, alongside the news that the Attorney General had recommended criminal charges against him for running a patronage-trafficking scheme with an alleged personal benefit of $55 million.

Would he be a touch repentant? Maybe. Twisted with bitterness over the younger brother who initiated the scandal with his allegations, and the politicians who had taken 'his' money, promising their support, and then betrayed him? Surely.

What I had not expected was what happened: we sat talking for more than two hours, competing with the angry chorus of crickets and swatting the occasional fly, as the conversation wandered into areas such as the size of Einstein's brain and Collor's memories of eating waffles and honey with his grandmother in Rio.

As I listened to these rambles, I recalled with a shock that as recently as June, when Brazil played host to the Earth Summit, Collor had presided successfully over the planet's biggest gathering of heads of state, and seemed on top of the world.

Today there was no one but me at the table; no one outside waiting at the door. Sitting bolt upright, Collor gave a tight little smile, cleared his throat, lit his characteristic Cuban cigar with uncharacteristic shaking hands and began, for the first time since his suspension, to tell of his feelings. 'I have suffered a lot but am resisting to my limits,' he said, his tight hold on himself reminding me of a patient on his deathbed making a ghastly effort not to allow the pain to show through.

He could not, however, hide the signs of distraction such as the occasional glassy stare, the inability to remember words and the tremulous shaking of his shoulders. Only the rare bursts of spirit recalled the rich, self-confident 40-year-old who in March 1990 became Brazil's youngest and first directly elected President for thirty years, on a platform to wipe out corruption and modernise the economy

Evandro Lins e Silva, the prosecution lawyer in the impeachment trial, calls Collor the 'Dorian Gray of the Planalto' (the Brazilian Presidency). 'Behind the public persona of this slender and beautiful youth with active eyes and impressive gestures, the true painting was the disfigured figure of corruption, vice and fraud.'

Despite his pinched cheeks, Collor still has the good looks which won him a mention in *People* magazine in 1990 as 'one of the world's fifty most beautiful people'. Elegant despite the stifling heat, his hair greased back in the manner favoured by Latin leaders, Collor is hard

to visualise as the man at the apex of a vast network of people within his government collecting kickbacks. They even had a computerised corruption manual accessed with the password 'Collor'.

Any talk of why he had become embroiled in such a scheme was soon ruled out of order. 'I'm absolutely convinced of my innocence,' he said. 'In no moment did I do anything beneath the dignity of the President. If I'd done anything wrong I could have put my foot down and stopped the whole inquiry process.'

The corruption scheme is shrugged off as 'a matter for the lawyers'. Of PC Farias, his former campaign treasurer and alleged front man, he says: 'I don't even want to touch upon anything so ugly.'

What he wants to discuss is what he calls his 'summary execution' by the Senate, which has marked his impeachment for 22 December. 'It's completely unacceptable. They've already announced the date of my execution. Well, I won't go to the firing line like they think. Never,

never, never. In any country in the world a fair trial is the basic human right of any citizen and above all for a president. That's all I ask.'

He gets agitated at the mention of resignation. 'To resign is to run away. I don't flee. I fight. I was elected for five years and have a programme which I must carry out.' Adding, through some rather tortuous logic, that he's staying on for the good of the country, he says, 'I am still President. I have simply been suspended from my functions.'

I ignored what seemed to be a hint that I should be addressing him more respectfully as Mr President, and asked how he explained the criminal charges. Laughing bitterly, he exclaimed, 'What did I do to receive such a blow? Was it a crime to modernise the country, to build up reserves to $22 billion, to secure Brazil's re-entry into the international financial community, to defend indigenous people and children?'

The way Collor tells it, he did nothing wrong and the whole 'lamentable episode' (as he calls it) was a campaign against him by those angered by his modernisation programme. 'I was brought down by a combination of business and union elites that had their corporate interests harmed by my actions, and politicians who wanted power all under a false cloak of morality. These people don't care about clean administration.'

Apparently unaware of the irony, he continued, 'I always saw power as an instrument for great social transformation, whereas they saw it as a way to great personal satisfaction.'

Collor seems to believe that this 'great social transformation' is now threatened by his successor, Itamar Franco, whom he refuses to mention by name, referring to him only as 'the Vice President'. 'The Vice President is dragging Brazil into the fifth world,' Collor exclaimed.

Then, like a magician, he pulls out of his briefcase sheaves of documents showing measures passed by his government, decrees over-turned and measures in progress, as well as a calendar marked with what is expected to be done when. 'Look at this,' he crows, picking one at random which turns out to be a rather insignificant measure about trade in tropical plants. I began to wonder what a psychiatrist would make of Fernando Collor.

He refuses to admit the strength of the nationwide street campaign against him demanding his impeachment. 'If a president had to resign every time a few people came out in the streets, then Helmut Kohl and John Major would both be out of office.'

Collor's main interest now is in mind control, a theory he expounds on at length: 'We are all born with the same hardware. Einstein's brain was no bigger than the next man's. The difference is in how we programme it. For this I am avoiding ignoble thoughts like hate and resentment as these are like a virus in the system.'

Armed with his Einstein-sized brain, Collor clings to what straws he can find. Proudly he talks of letters of support from Fidel Castro and Jacques Cousteau. Someone, he said, had told him that President Mitterrand was sympathetic.

But somewhere in that half-crazed mind Fernando Collor must know there is little chance that he can avoid impeachment and eight years' suspension from public office, even if, given Brazil's tradition of impunity, he is unlikely to go to jail. He concluded our interview by stating: 'The world has not seen the end of Fernando Collor.' He may be right. Brazilians have very short memories.

In the end Collor resigned to avoid impeachment and fled to Miami. In the final ignominy, his resignation did not even make the front pages. For in the early hours of that December morning, the body of the star of the country's favourite *novela* or soap opera had been discovered dumped on wasteland in Rio. Daniela Perez had been stabbed eighteen times with a sharp instrument. The principal suspect was her co-star and jealous screen lover, confused it seems between real life and fiction. In an even stranger twist, Daniela's heartbroken mother was the writer of the *novela*. The story had moved on and it was time for me to go too.

Claudio had been transferred to New York and I was supposed to follow. But I couldn't bear the idea of leaving Rio. Then one morning I suddenly panicked. Rio was so seductive. If I didn't move I would be there for ever like thousands of foreigners who had fallen in love with the city or one of its beauties.

I had learnt the Brazilian art of *jeito* or finding a way round things and applied for a fellowship at Harvard, persuading them to take the application despite having missed the deadline. When I left it felt like more than saying goodbye to a country. Brazilians have an expression – *saudade* – that means missing something in a yearning, sailors-lost-at-sea kind of way. Somehow I knew I would never be as happy again.

In New York, Claudio and I soon discovered we had almost nothing in common besides bossa nova, beach and Rio. He liked kung-fu movies on a wide-screen TV and mountain biking; I liked looking at the Matisse dancers in MOMA and off-Broadway theatre. But even today I cannot think of Brazil without a smile. Whenever I hear people speaking that unmistakable sing-song *brasileiro* on the tube in London, I am transported back.

A few years later I went back on holiday. I walked up the tree-lined street in Ipanema where Claudio's grandmother had lived. She had died and somehow I knew what I was going to see. The little house, crammed with mementoes, where she would shout out the names of London sights, was gone. Instead there was yet another glass and concrete apartment block.

The Tarantula Crossing the Street

Amazonia 1990–1993

It was the first time I had seen a tarantula in real life. Spiders had been my one reservation about going to the Amazon. I had no problem with snakes or cockroaches or any kind of beetle or bug. I was sure if it came to it I could eat monkey brains or live caterpillars, particularly if proffered by a head-bashing Indian. But I hated spiders. My skin crawled as I read Amazon travel books that talked of spiders the size of dinner plates, wolf spiders whose bites can leave scars ten inches long, and crab spiders that clamber down the ropes of your hammock while you sleep.

I was not even in the rainforest proper yet but in a town on its edge when I saw the tarantula crossing the street. I had just emerged from my no-star hotel in Rio Branco (summed up by my guidebook as 'the best of a bad bunch: not clean') and was crossing the main road when I noticed it alongside. It was not scurrying like spiders back home but walking quite nonchalantly, one thick hairy leg in front of another.

This first arachnid encounter was not the only thing that made my first experience in the Amazon in December 1990 rather alarming. I knew from the books that the Amazon contains half the fresh water on the planet and its forests provide a tenth of our oxygen. I'd read of a place of great mystery, a vast green cathedral that had led people into crazed schemes such as taking grand pianos up the river or building opera houses in the middle of the jungle. I had imagined being silenced by the majesty of trees thousands of years old and of dizzying height. I had pictured waking gently to the splash of fish, chatter of monkeys and whoop of brightly feathered birds, perhaps peering out from my hammock in the night at a painted Indian with a toucan on his shoulder or into the yellow eyes of some passing jaguar.

Instead Rio Branco was a shabby town where everything smelt of mould and people looked poor and underfed. The buildings shimmered with heat and the humid air felt like thick wet cotton and induced a sullen kind of torpor. Only the river was busy, small canoes jostling for space along the banks of muddy waters to unload slabs of blackened rubber to sell to waiting buyers.

I sat in the central plaza in the shade of the enormous *ceiba* trees and ordered a *chopp*, a draught beer that I wished was ice-cold. I asked for a menu and someone brought me a bowl of *tacaca*, a soup of tiny river prawns and dark green *jambu* leaves that looked like spinach but left my mouth numb.

Soon a man appeared trying to sell me a Chico Mendes T-shirt. At the next table I could hear American accents. I was in the middle of Brazil's nowhere – so far from Rio that the time was two hours behind – but the place was packed with foreigners. Correspondents from everywhere from the *New York Times* to *Asahi Shimbun*, environmentalists and competing Hollywood scriptwriters had turned out for the trial of the killers of the world's first international eco martyr.

The men who assassinated rubber tappers' leader Chico Mendes had undoubtedly expected that the killing would go unpunished and unreported – as had those of hundreds of Brazilians murdered in land conflicts over the previous twenty years. He was the ninetieth rubber tapper to be killed in 1988 alone. But that fatal shotgun blast had reverberated around the world. More than 4,000 people had attended his funeral and the trial seemed set to be the first time a rancher behind such a killing would be convicted and sent to prison.

The year Mendes was murdered had been a scorching hot summer everywhere, from New York to Paris. Suddenly people started listening to scientists who warned that the burning and clearing of the Amazonian rainforest was contributing to a gradual warming of the earth known as the greenhouse effect, altering our climate and melting polar ice caps. Amazon burnings had reached their highest ever level in

1987, with 350,000 fires detected and the loss of 48,000 square miles of virgin rainforest – the equivalent of six football fields every minute. Thirty per cent of the world's plant species were found in the Amazon and scientists argued that a living pharmacy – perhaps containing cures for cancer and Aids – was going up in smoke before even 1 per cent of the Amazon's plants had been studied.

The forest martyr
Financial Times, 8 December 1990

THE SMALL BLUE HOUSE rising on stilts from the Amazonian mud of the sleepy jungle town of Xapuri looks unremarkable. But on its rickety back wall, bloodstains and bullet holes mark the place where, just before Christmas two years ago, a rubber tapper was gunned down for defending the world's largest rainforest. Little known in Brazil, Chico Mendes had achieved international fame even before his assassination.

The remote state of Acre on Brazil's north-west border with Peru and Bolivia is an unlikely location for the world's first ecological martyr. And Mendes, short and pot-bellied with owlish eyes, was not an obvious hero. Yet he, more than any other person, has come to symbolise the plight of the Amazon forest. On Wednesday in Mendes's home town of Xapuri, a father and son will stand trial for his murder amid a ferment of debate about the basic question of Amazonia – can modern man and rainforest co-exist?

Mendes mobilised rubber tappers and Indians in an unlikely alliance against developers who were tearing out the green heart of the region, wanting to turn it into ranches to raise cows to supply the world with hamburgers. In the process he managed to save Acre from the deforestation that disfigured other western Amazonian states.

The Green movement could not have wished for a more harrowing tale to promote its cause. It reads like a movie script: indeed, the film rights to the story of Chico's life were auctioned in Hollywood last year for a reputed $1.76 million and there are already several competing versions in preparation.

On one side, the simple rubber tappers and brazil-nut gatherers fight for their right to use the forest as they have for a hundred years. They are up against landowners who want to bulldoze the rainforest for pasture, foresters who want to sell its wood, and big companies, foreign and Brazilian, which bought parts of Amazonia cheaply for speculative profits.

The tale is set in Xapuri, an Indian word which means 'the place where there didn't used to be a river'. It's a one-horse town where guns settle disputes and tropical storms swallow up the muddy red road for weeks on end. It was during one such storm on 22 December 1988 that Mendes sat in his kitchen, a baby on each arm, restlessly playing dominoes. His young wife, Ilzamar, glanced repeatedly from the stove to the window, alert for the gunmen who they knew were waiting their chance.

Tearfully recalling the moment, she said: 'In all our five years together Chico never spent a whole day with me. He was a man who belonged to everybody. But that day he wouldn't leave me.' When dinner was almost ready, Mendes picked up a towel and rose to take a shower in the outhouse. Ilzamar stopped him from taking their 4-year-old daughter, Elenira, because she was sickening for flu. As Mendes opened the door into the sheeting rain, bullets thudded into his chest. It was the sixth and final attempt on his life. Screaming, Ilzamar ran into the street for help, but the police guards who had been assigned to them after Mendes began receiving death threats had long fled. She showed me the bloodstained towel she has kept as a relic.

If it had not been for a chance encounter in 1962 when he was 18, Mendes might still be alive, scraping a living as a rubber tapper like his father and grandfather before him and as he had been doing since the age of 9. But one sweltering afternoon he was introduced to Euclides Tavóra, a former revolutionary in hiding in the forest and the only person the young Chico had met able to read newspapers.

For three years Mendes would walk three hours through the jungle every day to learn to read and write. It was a political education too. Together they would listen to the BBC and Voice of Moscow, the news interpreted by Euclides, who had taken part in a Brazilian uprising in the 1920s before going into exile as a communist in Bolivia.

From Euclides, Mendes came to understand the oppression of the tappers by rubber barons who had brought them from the poor north-east in the late nineteenth century and kept them as slaves to debt. They did this by holding wages below the cost of subsistence provided by company shops. But after the rubber boom of World War II, international competition from the Far East (caused by Britain smuggling rubber seeds from Amazonia to Malaysia) slashed Brazil's share of the world market from its historic monopoly to the 4 per cent it is today. As the barons went bankrupt the tappers became their own masters, able for the first time to sell directly to buyers and to grow their own food.

Mendes began educating fellow tappers, none of whom had ever seen a school, and organising them to resist the buyers who were paying a third less than the fixed government minimum price. In 1975 he became secretary of the local branch of CONTAG, the state-sponsored union for agricultural workers. He soon encountered a dangerous enemy – the ranchers.

Many were managers working for multinational companies and businessmen in São Paulo, attracted by a new government policy of cheap credits to buy up vast tracts of Amazonia. Tappers were evicted at pistol point by ranchers waving dubious land rights to old rubber estates. According to Dom Moacyr Grecchi, the outspoken Bishop of Acre, 81 per cent of the state is now in the hands of *fazendeiros* or large landowners, mostly holding fraudulent titles.

Terrified of the ranchers with their big cowboy boots and pistol-packing manner, the rubber tappers flocked to the union Mendes set up in Xapuri, drawn by his slogan 'Against Eviction of Men for Cows'. Styling himself the Gandhi of the Forest, the avuncular Chico was backed by the Church and its network of padres across western Amazonia. He persuaded his fellow rubber tappers to join hands with their women and children around each threatened piece of land to prevent its deforestation. At that time the burning of the forest was so heavy that the sun and moon were blocked out and Xapuri was constantly coated with a layer of soot. But Mendes would lead his band of fifty underfed tappers through the smog-filled undergrowth to surround the holding. The presence of women and children meant the police could not fire; the rancher would be forced into court to prove his right to deforest. Mendes claimed he saved 3 million acres by this non-violent tactic known as *empates*, or stand-offs.

But this strategy could only save small pieces of land for temporary periods and many tappers lost their livelihoods. The ranchers meanwhile hired more gunmen than cattle hands and started issuing threats to those who dared rally the landless. The first important assassination, in 1980, was of Wilson Pinheiro, the head of CONTAG. After that, Chico, with the backing of the PT, Brazil's workers' party, urged tappers to fight, not compromise.

A group of tappers, angered by the police's failure to find Pinheiro's murderer and suspecting the culprit was a local ranch manager, ambushed and killed him on a road. More than a hundred tappers were later arrested and tortured. War had been declared.

There was little doubt which side the authorities were backing. The Catholic Church estimates that more than 1,500 rural workers have been killed since 1978 in conflicts over land. Not one of those who ordered the murders has been brought to justice and only two contract killers have been sentenced.

Violence increased after 1985 when the ranchers became worried by the government's reversion to a policy of settling landless families in Amazonia. A new party, the União Democrática Ruralista (UDR), was set up to lobby for agriculture remaining in the hands of big producers. The ranchers also used increasingly well-armed gunmen to protect what they claimed was their territory. As pitched battles raged, tappers were forced out of the forest and the population of Rio Branco, the capital of Acre, doubled.

The tappers responded to the increased violence by forming a national council to demand a legal right for local people to exploit the forest in ways which preserved the trees. In 1987, only two weeks after the Minister for Land Reform signed a new law giving effect to their demands, he was killed in a mysterious air crash. The law, however, survived: it said that land which had been fraudulently expropriated by *fazendeiros* could be turned into reserves.

The ranchers were furious. But João Branco, then UDR leader in Acre, denies that they took up arms in protest. 'If the land in Acre cost the same as that in Japan it would be worth fighting over…this is an artificial conflict created by the press. They have been manipulated, just as Chico was, by the Church and the traditional politicians scared of losing the power they wield through state patronage if we ranchers, who don't depend on them at all, became too powerful.'

Although Mendes was then unknown in Brazil outside Acre, he had begun to receive international recognition and support from leading ecologists. His battle was presented to millions of American television viewers. Yet for Mendes it was still a struggle for survival. The Bishop of Acre explains: 'He was defending the jungle, defending ecology but most of all defending their land.'

But the limelight – and a United Nations prize now resting in the grisly shrine that was once his house – made Mendes the champion of the Amazon and a hero of the international Green movement. Suddenly he was caught in the crossfire between those who wished to fence off the whole forest as a museum and those who wanted to destroy it for profit.

Ranchers still believe deforestation is the only course. The cemetery of charred tree stumps along the road to Xapuri and the squalid huts in Rio Branco inhabited by rubber tappers forced out of the forest make it easy to condemn Brazil for its policy in the past two decades of opening up the Amazon. But many Brazilians argue that the First World has no right to prevent development in a country with the largest debt in the developing world and the worst income distribution, and, in spite of its immense size, 12 million landless poor. João Branco argues: 'In a state with no energy or transport, what economic alternatives are there to cattle raising?'

At the airport bar where he is drinking with fellow ranchers, Branco hardly endears himself by initially demanding $10,000 for an interview. A stocky man with a bushy moustache, he insists that the tappers' claims that the land is not suitable for agriculture or pasture are ludicrous. 'This is good business – we'd hardly be spending $100 a hectare to deforest if it wasn't. The rubber business on the other hand was finished long before 1971 when we moved in. Preserving the forest is just preserving their starvation.'

The international support for Mendes put considerable pressure on the government, as did his achievement of bringing together the traditional enemies, Indians and tappers, in a Forest Peoples Alliance. He used this influence to fight against the clearing of forests in Cachoeira where he had grown up. The area belonged to Darli and Alvoria Alves, two brothers who had fled from Paraná where they were wanted on murder charges. In September 1988, after Mendes staged a sit-in, the government declared the area a reserve.

The Alves brothers were much feared in Xapuri and that May had sent gunmen to break up an occupation of the local forestry office by rubber tappers, seriously wounding two young boys. Mendes knew he would pay heavily for his victory at Cachoeira. Just before Christmas they struck. Mendes's assassination provoked an international outcry and two days later Darcy, one of Darli Alves's sons, gave himself up. Three weeks later Darli confessed, though both men later retracted their confessions.

Since Mendes's assassination the rubber tappers' movement has disintegrated, riven by infighting and the desire to cash in on his death. Many have gone to Bolivia. Acre has become an important cocaine-smuggling route; the Church has been weakened by an explosion of evangelical sects; the PT narrowly lost the presidential elections in 1989 and has all but collapsed.

But his influence remains. More than 15,000 journalists, politicians, union leaders, diplomats and ecologists are expected to descend on Xapuri for the two days the trial is predicted to last.

Mendes's greatest legacy has been the reversal in Brazilian attitudes. Brazil has long been happy to play the role of eco villain, its military drawing up vast plans for the 'defence of Amazonia' and complaining that the rest of the world had cut down their forests so why shouldn't they. Under President Fernando Collor, for the first time Brazil has a government committed to environmental protection. His Environment Minister José Lutzenberger, Brazil's foremost ecological activist, was a great supporter of Chico Mendes. 'We want to preserve as much as possible of the Amazon,' he said on a visit to the Pantanal.

Some landowners are selling up because of the current recession and multinationals have moved out because of the bad publicity. The killings seem to have stopped too, though Francisco Barbosa, the president of the rubber tappers' union in Acre, fears this is a temporary lull by the ranchers so as not to prejudice the trial.

The struggle over the fate of the forest continues. The Bishop of Acre is not hopeful for the future. 'Once this trial is over the issue will be seen by the public to be resolved and attention will move on,' he said. 'The world must realise that there are thousands of Chico Mendes.'

The trial took place in a small courthouse in a dusty street on the edge of Xapuri. The courtroom was packed every day with journalists, foreign observers, local citizens and rubber tappers, some of whom had walked for days. Those who could not get inside gathered at the open windows. Outside, vendors tried to sell flavoured water, chewing gum and paper cones of river prawns.

It was over quickly because of the unexpected confession on the first day by Darcy Pereira da Silva that he had pulled the trigger. After just four days of testimony, the jury ruled him guilty of the killing and his father Darli for ordering it. They were sentenced to nineteen years in jail.

At the time it felt like an important precedent. But in February 1993, the men escaped from the prison in Rio Branco. Police claimed the men had sawed through the bars of their cells; others said they simply walked out, with the apparent complicity of their guards. It was more than two years before they were recaptured. They were later released after serving less than half of their sentences.

Yet Chico Mendes did not die in vain. The international outcry forced the Brazilian authorities to meet some of the demands of the rubber tappers of Acre and set up reserves where local people are allowed to extract forest products like rubber and brazil nuts, and no one can cut down the trees. One of the larger ones, near his home in Xapuri where he was shot, was named the Chico Mendes Reserve and sprawls over 2.4 million acres.

Although the trees from which they tap the milky latex that becomes rubber are now protected, the rubber tappers of Acre eke out a pretty meagre existence. Not only has the world price of rubber dropped, but companies like tyre manufacturers Michelin complain that the rubber produced in places like Xapuri is mixed with too many impurities because of all the twigs and insects that drop into their collecting cups.

Travelling in the Amazon was hard work. From the moment one left the air-conditioned chill of the airport to be slammed with heat and humidity, everything seemed to slow down. The air was busy with biting insects that made you scratch and curse and could give you all manner of horrible diseases it was better not to think about. In the river, which was often the only place to wash, there were bloodsucking piranhas, giant anacondas and tiny candiru, otherwise known as the toothpick fish, which could swim up a penis then emit barbs.

And the distances were huge. Once, the FT foreign desk in London phoned me in Rio to tell me a fax had arrived about a press conference in Manaus that morning. I had to point out it was five hours' direct flight away and in a different time zone.

For all the dire warnings of the destruction of the Amazon, I thought I had never seen so many trees. On and on for hour after hour you could fly over an endless mosaic of trees. I soon learnt that to really appreciate the Amazon it was no good just going to towns with airports like Manaus, Belém or Santarém. That was just the start. From there you needed to get a boat up a tributary then a canoe, or one of the ageing single-engined planes that touch down on tiny mud landing strips.

Only then could you see the waterlilies with flowers the size of pineapples or flocks of screeching red macaws. I'd seen from my own terrace in Rio that Brazil is so fecund that you only need to drop a fruit pip for a tree to start growing. But in the Amazon the plants and flowers seem several times larger than anywhere else on earth. Leaves unfurl to the size of tablecloths, roots swell thick and grainy as elephants' legs, tree trunks spread wide and pleated like dirndl skirts, and flowers pout voluptuously from plants that look as if they belong to the beginnings of time.

It was shocking then to fly north from Santarém along the Tapajós River and suddenly be blinded by thick black smoke which blotted out the sun. Down below as we came in to land, centuries-old trees stood dead and burnt amid bubbling craters of black mud where *garimpeiros* or wildcat gold miners were using mercury to separate and clean gold.

It looked like a war zone and indeed in the early 1990s much of the Amazon was a battlefield. Small wars were under way between ranchers and rubber tappers, miners and Indians, people of the forest and major companies producing paper, soya or iron ore, landowners and the *sem terra* or landless.

It was the misfortune of some of the most vulnerable tribes to be sitting on vast deposits of gold, platinum, magnesium or iron. Nor was it always the case of the small man or native against rich powerful interests. Tales of Amazonian gold had brought thousands of poor from the dry north-east and the *favelas* of Rio and São Paulo to try their luck, as well as desperate young girls working as prostitutes.

Most at risk were the Yanomami Indians, a tribe usually described as Stone Age, whose traditional lands had been invaded by *garimpeiros*. With them came malaria, influenza, to which the Yanomami have no immunity, and sexually transmitted diseases.

A number of celebrities had taken up their cause. The Amazon had become fashionable. In 1991 The Body Shop ran a 'Stop the Burning' campaign, collecting a million signatures on a petition which its founder, Anita Roddick, presented to the Brazilian embassy in London. Sting and his wife, Trudie Styler, had started a Rainforest Foundation and travelled to see the Yanomami. It helped that the tribe were very photogenic.

Extermination in Eden
Financial Times, 20 February 1993

'Those who have already died will have their revenge. They will cut the sky into pieces so that it falls all over the land.'

DAVI KOPENAWA YANOMAMI

THE US AVIATION MAP of the north-western reaches of Roraima, Brazil's most northern state, warns intriguingly that the area is 'largely unknown' and from the air it is easy to see why. Its dense jungle inspired the setting for Sir Arthur Conan Doyle's *Lost World*. Under the pounding glare of the Amazonian sun, a few wispy clouds throw their shadows on to a carpet of green treetops covering mountains and chasms as far as the eye can see. Stencilled through the heart is the flashing ribbon of the Mucajaí River. Along its banks, the occasional clearings for a *maloca* (a conical woven hut) are the only signs of human presence.

Almost 500 years after Pedro Cabral discovered Brazil, this stretch of rainforest remains untouched by the highways, hydroelectric projects, woodcutters and settlements that have devoured much of the Amazon. It is home to an estimated 9,000 members of the world's oldest-surviving isolated Indian tribe – the Yanomami.

The Yanomami are believed to have been there for thousands of years. They do not read or write, and use bows and arrows. Female children are often killed at birth and names must never be spoken. After a death, the body is left in the trees for a week before burning, and the ashes are then eaten with banana paste. They subsist on hunting and fishing and precarious agriculture. The land is poor so the population is sparse and moves often.

The Yanomami reserve is accessible only by small plane after a laborious process of government permissions. The nearest road linking Roraima to the rest of Brazil starts 200 miles away. It was built in 1977 and has yet to be paved. Bulldozers and four-wheel-drive vehicles are unknown. The somnolent day is interrupted only by the shrieks of parrots, unidentifiable whoops and calls from the bushes, and the chatter of monkeys in the trees.

Until 1987, the Yanomami's only contact with whites was the occasional missionary. Five years ago it was discovered that these Stone Age people were sitting on one of the world's richest mineral deposits replete with gold, tin, diamonds and uranium. The result was a flood of 45,000 *garimpeiros*, or wildcat gold miners. They brought guns, rum and diseases which, in three years, wiped out 10 per cent of the Yanomami population in what human rights groups called genocide.

The international outcry prompted three operations to remove the *garimpeiros*. The first official trip by image-conscious President Fernando Collor in 1990 was for the widely televised destruction of eighty-four clandestine airstrips. Last year, amid a blaze of publicity, he awarded the Yanomami a 9.4-million-square-kilometre reserve (the size of Portugal) to win kudos at the Earth Summit and reverse Brazil's environmentally unfriendly reputation. Now Collor is in disgrace, the Earth Summit forgotten and the *garimpeiros* are back – 12,000 since November.

Once more, Yanomami are dying: 200 in the past twelve months. The Homoxi region under the shadow of the Surucucu Mountains has been mutilated by airstrips slashed out of the jungle. The Mucajaí River has been choked with silt, polluted by mercury used to extract gold, and diverted in the frantic search for the precious metal.

From above, you can see tiny figures working Heath Robinson-type wooden sluice contraptions. Fetid water gathers in the craters they have dug, breeding mosquitoes that carry malaria lethal to the Yanomami. Charlotte Sankey from Survival International, a London-based organisation active in the fight to preserve them, says: 'If we don't do something, we will see another people wiped out – for ever.'

Although Brazil's 1988 Constitution guarantees that all its 180 remaining Indian tribes will be granted their traditional lands by this October – a total of 90 million hectares in 510 reserves – powerful interests threaten the extermination of the Yanomami, like so many others before them. Since 1500, Brazil's Indian population has fallen from 5 million to 220,000. The 'noble savage' has been seen as a barrier to development. Fernando Ramos Pereira, then Governor of Roraima, said in 1979: 'We're not going to let half a dozen Indian tribes stop progress.'

That Constitution is to be reviewed this year. Bishops, mining companies, politicians, landowners, the military, environmentalists and *garimpeiros* are battling over the mining of Yanomami land. This would provide work for thousands of poor Brazilians and revenue for the government – but probably destroy the tribe.

In Homoxi, Funai, the national Indian agency, and Médecins Sans Frontières, a medical aid organisation, have a clinic tending to the forty-eight Indians living nearby. At the sound of the plane, several Yanomami emerge from their *maloca*, naked except for small knotted tangas, bodies painted red, and straws protruding from above their upper lips. Like children they come forward, touch and stare, chatter and giggle to themselves. Bored quickly, they go back to their hammocks where they loll listlessly, their stick-thin limbs and distended stomachs no advertisement for the natural life. Suddenly, they begin jabbering. Zelia, the Peruvian nurse, says they want to know if we have come to remove the *garimpeiros*.

At the other end of the short runway, makeshift huts covered with blue plastic sheeting show how close the invaders have come. Eight planes a day unload more, along with such diseases as influenza, malaria, tuberculosis and syphilis. The pollution of the river has killed the fish and the noise of the planes has scared off animals. To appease the Yanomami, the *garimpeiros* gave them flour and rice – but their plantations have been left to wither and die. In their brutal intro-duction to western civilisation, they were given rum and the women were seduced. According to Zelia, two-thirds of the Homoxi Yanomami have had malaria. On the morning of my visit, three more sorry sufferers came in.

The *garimpeiros* may be well armed and sport gold watches or nuggets round their necks, but most have hollow cheeks, dull eyes and dirty shorts. All the ones I met were from the poverty-stricken north-eastern states of Maranhão and Bahia. They had been forced out by drought, and all asked for food. Many have no alternative but to move from place to place, following the latest *fofoca* (rumour about a gold discovery). 'I will only leave dead,' said Vajel, who has been a *garimpeiro* since he was 15. 'On a good day, you can get twenty grams of gold – that's five months' minimum salary,' said Raimundo. 'If they push us out again, we'll come back. We've got no other option.'

Some 5,000 kilometres and what feels like several centuries away in Brasília, a bearded man with furrowed brow paces a government office in heavy hiking boots and khaki shirt. Sidney Possuelo is charged with protecting Brazil's indigenous people as the head of Funai. He is angry. He feels powerless and worried that Brazil's new President, Itamar Franco, will succumb to pleas to open up the reserve for mining. 'I'm a *malandro* [scoundrel], not a politician,' he says as he fires off a letter to the army chief complaining about the arrest of a French nurse in the Yanomami reserve.

At Possuelo's offices the lift is out of order, the phones are often cut off, and few lights are on. The government cash crisis has left Funai with no funds to monitor the 272 existing reserves, or to demarcate the 238 outstanding. Last year, Possuelo received less than 10 per cent of his budget. So far this year, he has received nothing. None of Funai's nine planes is working. The Collor decree, overriding military protests to create the Yanomami reserve, should have been a victory but, without the money to enforce it, Possuelo now suspects it was a mere marketing stunt.

'It's not enough to create a reserve when, inside, you have riches and, outside, marginalised people,' he says. He accuses his opponents of distorting the argument. 'What we're talking about is not maintaining the Yanomami as they are, like some museum piece for the benefit of anthropologists, but of giving them the option of staying as they are or joining the world around with time to adjust.'

Over the road in the capital's flying saucer-shaped Congress building, Senator João Fagundes is having none of this. 'We never felt we needed to keep the Vikings preserved in cages. It's no good saying that the Yanomami's ways are lovely, let's keep them. What was good 200 years ago is not now.'

He favours the solution of the previous government, which demarcated 19 islands each of 2.4 million square kilometres for the Yanomami but gave *garimpeiros* or mining companies access to all the rest. 'The Yanomami land takes up 40 per cent of Roraima. That's ten square kilometres per person – no nation on earth has that amount of land,' says Fagundes.

Davi Kopenawa Yanomami, the tribe's Portuguese-speaking representative, also visited Brasília that day to present a bow and arrow to President Franco. 'I will tell Great White Chief that Omame [a Yanomami god] put minerals beneath the earth because it is cold. When these are taken out, they spread hot air and venom, which causes many illnesses. We have tried to tell the whites but they don't listen.'

To Possuelo's surprise, Franco did listen and agreed to a £1.4 million operation to remove the *garimpeiros*. But in the Funai office in Boa Vista, the capital of Roraima, Wilk Celio, the coordinator of the removal programme, is sceptical. 'It's useless – the *garimpeiros* will keep going back. There are 100 *garimpeiro* planes operating in this area while we don't have a single one. The only answer is constant monitoring and that means funds. Last year, we didn't get a cent.' His colleague, Manuel Reginaldo Tavares, gestures at a wall map of the state showing the location of its 24,970 Indians of eight different tribes, and laughs. 'Our resources are not even enough to run a crèche of 100 children, let alone 25,000 Indians.'

Tensions are high over the issue in Boa Vista. Roraima state depends on federal handouts but would be rich if allowed access to its minerals. The population has tripled to 230,000 in ten years because of the influx of *garimpeiros*, and not just from Brazil. A Londoner has just arrived from Mile End and a Scot, John Boyle, runs the Bay Bar and nightclub after eight years as a *garimpeiro*.

Prices in bars and restaurants are in grams of gold, and everyone seems to have a stake in the struggle between *garimpeiros* and Yanomami. The headlines in the local papers are about murders. People mutter of mafia-like activities and aid workers tell of pet dogs slaughtered in their gardens. Celio gets constant threats and lives between his office and hotel. 'I'm a prisoner,' he says, and talks of going on holiday and not coming back.

An enormous concrete statue of a *garimpeiro* dominates the town's main square. It stands in front of the state assembly, where all twenty-four members are against demarcation for the Yanomami. Next to this is the palace of the Governor whose spokesman, Francisco Netto, says: 'The federal government can keep on spending more and more but will never succeed in taking out the *garimpeiros*. The only answer is to create mining reserves and allow in companies so that we can collect taxes.'

Elton Rohmelt, the head of the state energy department, has no doubt that day will come. He is one of the main *garimpeiro* bosses and owns a fleet of four planes and a helicopter. 'No one knows the Amazon better than me,' he says. He is so fat that his jowls quiver as he speaks and the buttons strain on the patterned shirts he buys in Savile Row. Rohmelt decided to lie low when Collor took office. 'I saw he was mad, so I took up the Governor's invitation to run the state energy department.'

He is using his position to put in place the infrastructure for his future mining operations. Here a hydroelectric project, there a road to Venezuela and the port. His company, Goldmazon, has more than sixty claims in the Yanomami areas.

'Refusing access to this is a crime for a poor country like us,' he says.

'I'm absolutely sure that, within the next few years, mining in Yanomami areas will be allowed – and I'm ready.'

His great rival, the ebullient Zé Altino, a media-loving representative of the *garimpeiros*' union, Usagal, is more careful to play down his personal interest. 'What's the point of blowing up airstrips if, six hours later, they are rebuilt?' he asks. He claims that there are a million *garimpeiros* in Brazil, of which 400,000 are 'professional'. He adds: 'They say *garimpeiros* are illegal, but there are more *garimpeiros* in indigenous areas than there are Indians in Brazil. Don't they have rights, too?'

Haroldo Eurico dos Santos, the State Planning Secretary, is a former professor who used to advise governments to burn down the Amazon. He is busy drawing up mega-plans for Brazil's poorest state. Above the noise from roaring, clanking pipes, he shouts: 'This state is basically unviable. We generate only 16 per cent of our expenditure and our only potential economic base is either demarcated or will be. Ninety-nine per cent of the population is against demarcation. The only ones in favour are the Church, communists and some Indians.'

The most vitriolic opposition is on Rua do Ouro (Gold Street). There, many of the gold shops are boarded up, the stores full of mining

utensils deserted, and *garimpeiros* huddle miserably in the bars, biding their time, comparing how often each has had malaria (one man has had thirty-four bouts). They recall the days when they could make a good living just from the end-of-day sweepings outside the gold shops.

Most of the gold is smuggled out of the state to avoid taxes, so figures for the amount produced are vague. According to Altino, production reached 12 tonnes in the peak year of 1990, as well as 500,000 kilos of diamonds. Even then, few got rich apart from the bosses, the Rohmelts and Altinos, who run airstrips, planes, bars, brothels, and rent machinery at inflated prices.

In Rua do Ouro, the blame for the latest crackdown is laid on everyone from the Americans ('they are scared of Brazil becoming a great power') to the padres for their defence of Indian rights. So unpopular is Dom Aldo, the Bishop, that a petition was mounted last year to get him out. One man told me: 'I'd like to have his kidneys on a barbecue fork.'

After seventeen years in Boa Vista and overseeing a Yanomami mission, the fire seems to have gone out of Dom Aldo. Wearily, he tells me: 'People say we are working for gold or trying to create another nation, but that's a lie. Nor are we trying to convert them [the Indians]. They don't yet have the terminology for catechism, so it's very hard to explain our Christian concepts.

'People get angry because we tell the Indians their rights. It's a war between economic interests and human rights in a country where the powerful always win.'

Among so many voices, the only ones not to be heard are the Yanomami's. Experience from other tribes suggests that Indians are keen to have the badges of progress such as televisions, speedboats and ghetto-blasters. Some of the more acculturated Amazonian tribes, such as the Kayapo and Xingu, have organised and demand royalties for prospecting in their areas. But along the Rio Branco River from Boa Vista, at Fazenda São Marco, a community of Macuxi Indians live in pitiful conditions. White contact has robbed them of their old ways without equipping them to find a substitute. For the primitive Yanomami, the future looks bleak.

Most of my Brazilian friends in Rio could not understand my fascination with the Amazon, regarding the region as a Dante-like cauldron of death and disease.

But I was finding the Amazon was full of stories, not all grim. I spent an unlikely few days with a Japanese community deep in the jungle who had opened a karaoke club. Delighted to find someone English, they made me sing all the Elvis songs in the catalogue then the Beatles until I felt like Tony Last in Evelyn Waugh's *A Handful of Dust* forced to endlessly read Dickens to a mad recluse in the Amazon. I accompanied the Amazon's first Avon ladies selling lipsticks and blushers from canoes up and down the river. There, I saw my first *botos* – the Amazon's famous pink dolphins which are said to turn into men at night and seduce young girls, a handy excuse for inconvenient pregnancies.

I even went to an opera in the jungle – *The Magic Flute*. The accompaniment was provided by an orchestra of sweating Bulgarians who looked somewhat alarmed to find themselves in this sweltering place that rotted their violins. The newly renovated candy-pink opera house with its yellow and blue dome was all that remained to mark the rubber boom that had once made Manaus one of the richest towns on earth, a place where men fed buckets of champagne to their horses and sent their shirts to be laundered in Paris and Lisbon. It may have been in the middle of a malarial swamp but it was the first town in Brazil to have electric streetlights, a telephone system and trams.

It seemed like something out of a novel. After I left Brazil, I would go back again and again.

Love Intervenes

From Boston to Khartoum 1993–1994

We said goodbye at Central Park boathouse. In my bag was the plastic snow globe that had been his first present to me, and in my mind, his words in romantic broken English: 'We fit together like the last pieces in a jigsaw.' I was heading off to my dream job and should have been happy. At Kennedy airport I cried so much that a man asked me if I was scared of flying.

On my application for the Nieman fellowship I had written how I planned to spend my year at Harvard studying environmental policy-making. Secretly, I had thought that at last I would write my novel. I had not expected to fall in love.

I'd noticed Paulo immediately the first day. All twenty-four of us fellows (twelve Americans and twelve from the rest of the world) gathered in the Nieman Foundation's white clapboard house and each gave a small introduction. Paulo came from Portugal and was wearing a suede waistcoat over a white shirt that perfectly set off his olive complexion, dark eyes and black hair. I thought he was dashing and arrogant in roughly equal measure.

Most impressive was Kofi Coomson, the editor of the *Ghanaian Chronicle*, who was resplendent in gold-threaded Ashanti robes and informed us that he was going to be the next president of Ghana. Then there were Jaroslav Weis, a Czech intellectual with a scruffy beard and baggy jumpers who wrote science-fiction books in between political columns, and Ratih Hardjono, an Indonesian of swan-like beauty who battled daily against a dictatorial regime that allowed none of the freedom of the press which the rest of us took for granted.

The Harvard course directory was as thick as a telephone book and the first subject that caught my eye was 'Introduction to Opera 101'. Mondays at 9 a.m. seemed a little brutal yet it was the perfect way to start the week, listening to Professor Lewis Lockwood talk about the leitmotifs in *Don Giovanni* and *Der Rosenkavalier* then play the blissful music which was the reason we were all there. Sometimes he even brought in singers from the Boston Symphony Hall.

Paulo, the dashing Portuguese Nieman, had had the same idea. It would have been rude not to sit next to him, particularly as I spoke Portuguese from my years in Brazil. As we walked across Harvard Yard after class, he made me laugh. Soon, I found I was looking out for him at the twice-weekly opera mornings, disappointed if he did not turn up.

Our mutual passion for *Der Rosenkavalier* quickly developed into something more. Paulo had been to Boston before and our first date was over lobster in the Union Oyster House, America's oldest restaurant, followed by fiery shots of grappa in Caffe Vittoria in the Italian quarter. We laughed at the 'foliage hotline', a local free-phone service that told you the best days to see the autumn colours in all their glory, and rented a car for the day to drive into the New England countryside and look at leaves.

Soon we were seeing each other almost daily. On fine days we went cycling along the Charles River to buy hot melt-in-the-mouth cinnamon buns. Sunday mornings were spent in Harvard Square with a large paper cup of coffee and sticky Danish from Au Bon Pain, wading through the thick wad of the *New York Times* or watching old men play speed chess as minutes ticked by on old-fashioned clocks.

Best of all were visits to the Avenue Victor Hugo bookstore* on Boston's Newbury Street. Housed in a brownstone building, there was a fat cat in the window and the desk was manned by a crotchety old

---

* Sadly it closed in 2004 after thirty years. On their website they posted 'Twelve reasons for the death of small and independent bookstores'. It was a bitter list, blaming everyone from big chains like Barnes & Noble to publishers 'marketing their products like soap or breakfast cereal'; writers; teachers and the public. But the main reason was the Internet – online book sales had cut their income by a third.

man who had started out selling books from a barrow. The books were second hand and crammed into lots of tightly packed shelves in no particular order. In that room I discovered the short stories of Raymond Carver and Flannery O'Connor, John Kennedy Toole's *Confederacy of Dunces,* and rediscovered Tennessee Williams and Jack Kerouac.

Perhaps Paulo and I had watched too many movies but the shop took on another role. Sometimes, tucked between the pages of certain books like Hemingway's letters, Neruda's poems or *Sonnets from the Portuguese* by Elizabeth Barrett Browning, I would find a note. *Cinnamon buns at 5?* one might read or *Meet me at Swan boats lunchtime tomorrow.*

Then the cold came. To start with, we were like small children full of excitement at waking to a world cloaked in white and with all the sounds muffled. Wrapped up in woolly hats and puffy parkas we had bought at bargain prices in Filene's Basement, we ran into Harvard Yard where the statue of John Harvard had become a white hump on which a student had stuck a carrot nose and tied a scarf. Someone found a tray and we took turns tobogganing down the steps of the Widener Library.

But the snow did not stop. That winter Boston had twenty-six snowstorms. The *Boston Globe* ran a daily chart comparing the amount of snow to the height of Larry Bird, a legendary basketball player from the Boston Celtics who stood six feet nine inches. Soon the snow had topped Bird – we'd had over ninety inches, making it Boston's snowiest winter since records began some hundred years earlier. The snow was no longer white and crispy but hard and dirty, piled up in walls along the pavements and stained an unpleasant yellow.

And the cold hurt. It did not matter how many clothes you wore – there was always a bit of earlobe or nose for the chill wind to cut into. Weathermen warned that exposed skin could freeze within thirty minutes.

I began to dream of going somewhere warm. I had never forgotten sitting in the FT office in February 1990 watching the TV showing Nelson Mandela emerge from jail after twenty-seven years, no one knowing how he would look since that one grainy black and white photograph everyone had used for years. I had desperately wished I was there reporting on it. So when the new editor of the *Sunday Times* phoned and asked me if I'd like to be his Africa correspondent based in Johannesburg, I did not have to think twice.

On 15 August 1994, a day after flying back from America, I walked into Fortress Wapping, the News International headquarters, to collect my laptop and press card. It was an inauspicious start. I was surprised to find Britain's biggest quality newspaper housed in what seemed like a Portakabin and everyone glued to their desks. Richard Ellis, the managing editor, had a chart on his wall listing all the reporters, with red dots awarded for each front-page story. The word was that if you did not rack up five in a year, you were out. That evening on the Northern Line back to my parents' house, I was mugged for the first time and had my new laptop stolen by two men with knives.

Within a few days I was on a flight to Khartoum. Carlos the Jackal, then the world's most wanted terrorist, had just been spirited out of Sudan by the French secret service and I was supposed to find out how. Suddenly I had the life which I had longed for, jumping on planes to places I had never been. I was working for the same paper as the correspondents I most admired, Jon Swain and Marie Colvin. But it was Thursday night and I would arrive in Khartoum with only one day to get my story. And half of Fleet Street seemed to be on the same plane.

Stumbling through the airport in the early hours, we were met by Tariq from the Sudanese Information Ministry. He told us he was there to 'facilitate'; in fact he was our minder and determined to ensure we did not get any information or evade a single piece of red tape. Consequently we journalists were by far the last to emerge from Customs.

In most capitals there is one hotel favoured by journalists. In Khartoum this was the Hilton, perched on the confluence of the Blue Nile and the White Nile. It was the wrong side of 4 a.m. by the time check-in was completed, but I felt wide awake as I looked out from my room over the swollen waters from which dark treetops poked. 'The Nile!' If I followed it downriver I would come to the heart of Africa and Lakes Tanganyika and Victoria where Burton and Speke had searched for its source. Along the bank stood an elegant white building. This was the former Governor's Palace where General Gordon was under siege for ten months. I imagined him prowling the flat roof desperately scanning the river for signs of a relief expedition from London against the Mahdi, whose guns were amassing across the river. It did not come and in January 1885 he was gunned down and his head paraded round the city on a spike.

It was my first night in Africa and I had one day to prove myself to my new employers. It was hard to sleep.

The next morning Khartoum's adobe walls and pink minarets were cloaked with dust from one of the *haboob* sandstorms that periodically blast the city. First stop was the Information Ministry to get permission to enter the apartment where Carlos the Jackal had lived. Permits seemed to be needed for everything in Sudan; that morning's newspaper carried the story of an Englishman from the World Food Programme arrested for taking a photograph of the Nile. Precious hours were wasted drinking warm sugary Coke with ministry officials who were as obstructive as they were charming. As in many countries it would have been more aptly named the Disinformation Ministry.

I gave up and escaped to the New Sudan Club where a few florid-complexioned men who seemed to have been there since colonial days were nursing warm gins on the terrace. I was in luck. One of them told me that Carlos had lived just a few streets away and gave me the name of Carlos's neighbour Benedict Fultang, who was recovering from an operation in a nearby hospital.

The Khartoum Clinic was an uninspiring place with no staff in sight and a waiting room dominated by a huge handwritten price list. Hernia operations were available for 30,000 dinars, a hysterectomy for 50,000, and, surely a bargain, just 25,000 for an appendectomy. Despite his imposing name, Benedict Fultang was a slight, sorry-looking figure from Cameroon in a dark room filled with flies and extended family.

He confirmed that he lived in the same small apartment block as the Jackal and had often taken him and his wife drinking at the Diplomatic Club. Although he had known Carlos as Abdallah Barakhat, a businessman of Cuban-Lebanese descent, Mr Fultang had noticed the Magnum bulging from his hip.

With a wad of dinars and an obliging member of the Fultang family as guide, it turned out to be easy to persuade the guards to let me into the dingy ground-floor flat on the corner of Africa Road. This was where the Venezuelan-born killer had ended up, reading his *Cigar Lover* magazine and the FT (there were piles of both in his study). I imagined him there reminiscing of his 'glory days' as a Marxist revolutionary, blowing up trains and shopping centres in France, massacring Israeli athletes at the 1972 Munich Olympics and kidnapping eleven oil ministers at an OPEC conference.

The fridge was still full of food, including some half-eaten pasties and a box of luxury Syrian chocolates. One room had been turned into a liquor store lined with steel shelves bearing cases of Johnnie Walker, Tuborg beer and Rémy Martin cognac, as well as some cartons of Marlboro.

In the wardrobe hung three of the army-surplus waistcoats that Carlos wore to hide his gun and some laundry bags from the Hilton, where he sent everything to be washed. By his bed were photographs of his two very different wives: the hard-faced German revolutionary Magdalene Kopp, and Lana Jarrah, a beautiful young Palestinian whom he and Benedict used to watch belly-dancing at the Armenian Club.

It was his weakness for women that caused the Jackal's downfall. At the Armenian Club, I learnt of another woman in Carlos's life. I was taken to meet Zainab in her jewellery shop, Chez Zed. The sultry widow of a general, Zainab was clearly desperate to confide in someone and broke down in tears as she told me of the brawl in her shop a few months earlier when her grown-up son confronted Carlos over taking his mother as a mistress. As crowds gathered, Carlos's gun had fallen out of his pocket and police had taken him away for questioning. She believed this was what had led to his discovery in the country, though it seemed unlikely the Sudanese regime had not known he was there.

I had my story – and my first red dot on the chart.

Had I but realised, there was an even bigger terrorist in town. Once again I was unknowingly in the same city as Osama bin Laden, who had by then shifted operations from Peshawar.

Before I left Khartoum, I stopped by the many-arched Grand Sudan Hotel where I had heard that my hero, Hemingway, used to stay en route to hunting expeditions. At the reception desk, I asked if this was true. 'Mr Hemingway?' said the concierge. 'We will ring up to him. What room is he in?'

To the City of Gold – via Baghdad

Africa 1994–1996

The locals know it as Jo'burg or Jozi. More poetic is its Zulu name, Egoli or City of Gold – 40 per cent of the world's gold has come from around the city. As the plane descended towards Johannesburg airport, I could see the distinctive city centre skyline of office blocks and TV tower. The strange flat hills beyond were old mine dumps, the remains of mine workings from the days of Cecil Rhodes in the nineteenth century. Most of the houses we were flying over seemed to have swimming pools.

That morning I sat in the News Café in Rosebank over a cappuccino and blueberry muffin and started leafing through *The Star*, the main national newspaper. One of the headlines was 'Couple Collide with Rhino'. Between reading I couldn't help noticing that the only blacks around were carrying trays or wielding mops, as well as one begging for 'transport money'. So much for the new South Africa. Still, we were in the so-called 'Northern Suburbs' and it was only four months since Mandela had taken office as the country's first black President.

Anyway, I was looking for rental ads not news. A yellow bird was singing in the tree and, compared to Pakistan and Brazil, everything seemed incredibly efficient. By the end of my first day I had opened a bank account, tracked down when and where my belongings would arrive, and sorted out my press accreditation.

All I needed was somewhere to live. As I drove around looking at places to rent, I was taken aback by all the electric fences and '24-hour

Armed Response' signs. Having lived in Rio, which at that time had worse crime statistics than Jo'burg, I was determined not to give in to what seemed like paranoia. So I found a house near Zoo Lake with a pool, a sauna and no razor-wire fences or bars on the windows. When visitors to my house shrieked, 'How can you live like this?' I laughed. But within a week of moving in, I came home one evening from Kippies jazz bar to find my terrace door open and a scuffling noise inside. I dialled 10111 and, minutes later, a posse of blond men bearing large guns had arrived: the Parkview police. They found a window forced open but to their evident disappointment the intruders had left. 'Ma'am, this house is very unsafe,' said one of them in thickly Afrikaans-accented English. 'You must get a dog and an alarm system. These *okes* will know you are living alone and they will be back.'

Before I had time to do anything about it, however, a call came from my foreign editor instructing me, 'Get to Baghdad'. Saddam Hussein had sent his troops to the Kuwaiti border. Everyone thought he was planning another invasion like that which four years earlier had led to the Gulf War.

I flew to Jordan where the Intercontinental Amman was packed with journalists from Britain, Germany, Japan, Italy and the US. Every day we would all make our way to the Iraqi embassy in search of visas. 'I'd forgotten how much of this job is spent waiting,' I wrote in my diary. 'Waiting on the pavement outside the Iraqi embassy, waiting in the café across the road from the embassy, waiting in the small anteroom where the guards sit glued to high-pitched movies on Arabsat…'

The person for whom we were all waiting was Adel Ibrahim, the Iraqi Consul, a neat little man with a trim moustache and shiny Italian shoes. One day, to the envy of the other journalists, most of whom were male, I was singled out and summoned inside. But once in Mr Ibrahim's hallowed office, far from stamping the precious visa into my passport, he proceeded to invite me to dinner. Over glasses of liquorice-tasting arak at Amigo Nadeels, he told me how he was looking for love while I told him how much I needed a visa. 'We will see,' he said. The next morning the hotel reception called saying something had arrived for me. I rushed to the door, hoping for a message that my visa was ready. Instead there was an enormous bouquet of salmon-coloured flowers and a note from Mr Ibrahim saying, 'I wish to keep you in Amman for ever.' Fuck. My charm offensive was having the opposite effect to that intended.

Finally I convinced him that the *Sunday Times* would pull me out immediately if I didn't get a visa whereas, if I did, then I would come back to Amman and we would have dinner. I may even have said, many dinners.

The visa was mine and that night I literally fled to Baghdad. The desert was a disappointment. Far from the swirling sands of Lawrence of Arabia, it was grey, gritty and flat. The taxi journey took thirteen hours, a couple of which were spent at Baghdad Customs where I passed through a series of dejected waiting rooms full of flies and broken plastic chairs, paying bribes to various officials, including $50 not to take an Iraqi Aids test. On one of the broken chairs a man in an Arab headdress sat silently, a small bird clasped tightly in his right hand.

Baghdad was not the exotic city of domes and spice markets that I had pictured from those old Orient Express posters. Instead it was a drab place of Stalinist-style cement monuments and shadowy people with grey faces. The great Tigris river flowed brown but nobody fished or boated, scared away I guess by the occasional military patrol. From every corner Saddam's despotic gaze stared out of gigantic multi-coloured billboards. There was Saddam, the stern military commander; Saddam, the wild tribesman with flowing chequered headcloth; Saddam in bowler hat; and there was rosy-cheeked smiling Saddam walking through meadows with his arms round children. I imagined the Saddam artists trying to come up with ever new poses that would please their leader. My personal favourite was Saddam speaking on a pink telephone.

In those days the journalists' hotel was the Al-Rashid. To enter you had to walk across a floor mosaic of a grimacing George Bush under which was written 'Bush is Criminal'. It had taken me so long to get there, what with the journey from South Africa then the wait for the visa, that by the time I stepped across Bush's face, Saddam had already pulled back his troops from the Kuwaiti border. There was not going to be another war; at least not for now.

Those who had managed to get in had left and practically the only journalists still in the Al-Rashid were Angus MacSwan from Reuters, Mark Nicholson, an old friend from the FT, and Peter Arnett from CNN. Peter had a whole floor of the hotel kitted out with microwave oven, video player and stores of American food he'd had sent in, which I sneered at but would later gratefully share. The only supply I had smuggled in was a bottle of gin which Mark and I drank in one session with plum juice, the only mixer we could find, ensuring my first day in Baghdad began with a hangover.

Even with a clear head, reporting in Iraq turned out to be harder still than Sudan. People were scared to talk and I was assigned a minder who was a Benny Hill fanatic but determined to let me speak to no one but regime apparatchiks. My driver Abu Zaid did not even want me to sightsee, constantly reminding me of his ten children who could be left fatherless. 'I want to sleep sound, not with the click-click-click in my ear,' he said, mimicking a gun against his head.

Most Iraqis had not yet found ways round the sanctions and food was in short supply. One night Mark and I went to a restaurant called El Musheef where we were enjoying our meze when suddenly an enormous brown rat appeared down the stairs and sauntered across the room. We told the waiters, who just laughed. The menu offered 'Bird: fried or grilled' and 'Brain in a Pan' so we went for the only other option – chicken tikka. They brought us a plate of chopped unrecognisable meat which we both thought tasted distinctly rat-like.

I managed to get out of town to see Babylon where Saddam was rebuilding King Nebuchadnezzar's palace. The new bricks were inscribed with the words: 'In the era of Saddam Hussein, protector of Iraq, who rebuilt civilisation and rebuilt Babylon.'

Back at the Al-Rashid where the phones hardly ever worked, my Afrikaner landlord in Johannesburg had somehow got a message through, complaining my rent was late. My belongings were waiting at Customs. I was supposed to be Africa correspondent. It was time to get back.

Once more I travelled through the desert by night because it was cooler. Arriving in Jordan in the early hours, I was anxious to avoid spending more time in Amman where the adoring Mr Ibrahim would be waiting in his shiny shoes. Rather than check in to the Intercon, I went to the travel agency and asked the lady if there was any way she could get me to Lisbon in time for dinner then on to Johannesburg. She looked at me as if I were mad. When I explained, she turned out to have a romantic soul and drove me to the airport at speed to catch a departing flight. It was only 4 a.m. in Portugal so she promised to call Paulo who I was not even sure was in town (fortunately, he was).

Back in Jo'burg, the *Sunday Times* was eager for stories about Mandela's 'ineptitude'. This was a problem as I thought Mandela by far the most impressive man I had ever met. The only solution was to get out of Johannesburg and travel round Africa. Having fallen in love with South Asia and Latin America, I had been sceptical of those people who bore on about Africa's wide skies and dream of buying a farm at the foot of the Ngong Hills. But I quickly became one of them. Later when I returned to London to become diplomatic correspondent for the *Sunday Telegraph*, I would go back again and again.

Learning to dance on a Zambian train
Financial Times, 21 February 1998

WHEN WE DECIDED to go by train from Mpika, in northern Zambia, to Dar es Salaam, I did not expect my dancing prowess to be on trial.

But I should have realised it would be no ordinary journey when I telephoned Tazara reservations and a giggling voice answered, 'Here is Beauty.'

When I explained I was calling from Portugal, Beauty was very excited. 'Por-too-gell,' she said in wonder, 'what time is it?' When we established it was the same as in Zambia, Beauty was astonished. Someone called Precious came on the line, equally amazed, then it went dead.

After several conversations, which never got near reserving a compartment, I gave up and decided to try my luck on arrival. The Tazara train goes from Zambia to Tanzania twice a week and, according to my guidebook, is one of Africa's most reliable.

The line was built by the Chinese and the company's motto is 'On Time All the Time'. So on the Friday morning that I arrived with my boyfriend at Mpika station – a concrete monstrosity in the African bush – to buy our tickets and catch the afternoon train, we were confident of soon departing.

Forty hours later, we were still waiting. Now forty hours is a long time, even for those used to the vagaries of England's Connex South Central. It is a very long time in Mpika, where the concrete road from the station peters out after fifty metres into red clay dotted with shacks. Few tourists stop and we were soon the object of fascination.

People popped up from nowhere to tell us about Chinese railway workers breeding dogs to eat for dinner. The one-eyed station master confided his dream of becoming a marketing executive. A group of evangelists with black briefcases tried to convert us, and a man asked Paulo how many cows he had paid for me.

We hung out in Kalolo's bakery, the only café, where we introduced the custom of halving scones and spreading them with butter, and bought the only painting off Kalolo's wall. News spread and we were besieged by people trying to sell us land, baskets and brown pebbles. By the time the train came, at 4 a.m. on the second day, we had many new friends.

We were, however, seriously short of sleep and dreaming of our first-class sleeper compartment, which we had paid to have to ourselves. So when I slid open the door and nine smiling Zambians stared out, my heart sank.

'Come in!' they called, apparently well into their second case of Mosi beer. Sharing a compartment for four with nine other people who are drunk and want to party when you want to sleep is not conducive to international relations. Grumpily clearing people off our bunks, we covered ourselves in Tazara blankets and tried to sleep.

At 6 a.m. the radio came on, blasting out music. One of our new bedfellows opened the blinds and announced it was time for breakfast. Barely conscious, we stumbled along the corridor to the dining car for rubbery omelettes, cold toast and grey tea.

Everyone else seemed to be in their best clothes – men in shiny shoes, spotted bow ties and colourful shirts, women with complicated

headdresses – putting us, the only white passengers, to shame in our dusty jeans and T-shirts.

Back in the compartment, our fellow passengers introduced themselves and apologised for the previous night. I apologised for my bad mood. They handed us beers and we were all friends. They were travelling to Dar es Salaam to buy car parts. In Zambia, they cost five times more because of high import tariffs.

'What about Customs?' I asked Chola John, the leader of the group.

'We have an arrangement with the Customs officer,' he smiled.

The day got hotter and the music louder. More beers were drunk. We stopped at villages of beehive huts and acacia trees.

Suddenly Chola John's wife Joan slid her ample frame off the seat. 'Time to dance,' she shouted.

'Yes, yes, yes!' yelped Chama, a big-bottomed schoolteacher.

Soon everyone but us was dancing.

'Cristineee, you will show us how people dance in London,' commanded Moses.

Never the most elegant of people on the dance floor, I shuffled my feet. My audience was not impressed. 'Cristineee, we will teach you to dance like an African mama.' Soon the whole train had heard about the white woman trying to dance the African way. People came and offered advice, but it was no good – my hips refused to sway like theirs.

Paulo, who is dusky and Portuguese, kept getting mistaken for the Zambian Minister of Agriculture, and was thus excused from dancing. We were both relieved when lunch was announced. In the dining car, everyone we met told us they were off to Tanzania to buy spare car parts.

Having resolved to be late, the train fell further behind schedule. By the second day the water ran out, so we were not only drinking Mosi, but brushing our teeth in it. The stream of visitors to our compartment continued.

On the third and last day, as the train crossed into Tanzania, and the beer switched from Mosi to Safari, we hogged the window seats, pointing at the Masai with their cattle and hoping to see wild animals.

'How is the bush in Portugal?' asked Chola John. 'Do you have giraffes?' Before we could answer, the radio, which had been mercifully silent, started blaring again.

'Time for dancing!' shouted Moses.

Delta blues: Nigeria's poor prepare to fight for the oil riches of their country
Sunday Telegraph, 21 February 1999

CHIEF OGIBO OTODJARERI is holding court in a wattle-and-daub hut decorated with goat skulls on strings and faded black-and-white photographs of his ancestors. He still remembers when oil was first struck in West Africa in 1956. 'We thought we would be rich,' he smiled sadly, recalling the excitement that spread through the tangled jungles of the Niger Delta where it was discovered.

Instead, like most of the region, his village of 5,000 people still has no electricity or running water, no clinic, no school. The bandy-legged children who gather to see the *oyibo,* or strange white woman, have the swollen bellies of the malnourished.

Pointing out the nearby oil pipeline which runs right outside the huts, Otodjareri says: 'We can't understand why our area is producing all this wealth yet when you come to my house I cannot even offer you a cup of porridge.'

The Niger Delta is the world's sixth-largest oil producer, pumping out 2 billion barrels a day, yet most of Nigeria's 108 million people are growing poorer. In Arab countries which produce this much oil, people have living standards beyond most Nigerians' wildest dreams. But in Africa's largest country, billions of pounds in oil wealth are siphoned off by a small clique of politicians and generals like the late General Sani Abacha*, while the average income has plummeted to £160 a year. So skewed is the system that motorists must queue for two days to get petrol.

---

* Between $3 billion–4 billion in overseas accounts was traced to General Abacha after his death.

In the Delta region where more than 90 per cent of the oil comes from, people live in some of the worst poverty in sub-Saharan Africa and they are losing patience. Much of the Delta is in a state of near insurrection, with groups of militant youths turning off oil valves, occupying flow stations and kidnapping foreign oil workers. Yesterday a Chevron boat was attacked and one person killed. The next step, says Oronto Douglas, one of the groups' leaders, is to bring the entire oil industry to a halt.

The government has responded with violence, sending in security forces and turning one of the world's largest wetlands into a battle-ground.

Few believe the current elections – yesterday for parliament, and next Saturday for the presidency – will change anything, despite ending fifteen years of military rule. The candidate expected to win is General Olusegun Obasanjo, a former military dictator, although the only one ever to hand over power to civilians.

'The real problem is the mineral resources are in minority areas, while the government is always run by a majority tribe who don't find it worthwhile to divert funds to develop those areas,' said Robert Azibaola, the president of the Niger Delta Human and Environmental Resources Organisation.

The plight of the Delta first came to world attention in 1993 when the playwright Ken Saro-Wiwa led the Ogoni tribe against General Abacha's military regime to try to force the British-Dutch oil giant Shell out of its region. Thousands of Ogonis were beaten or detained and there was an international outcry when Saro-Wiwa and eight colleagues were hanged in November 1995, particularly after it emerged that Shell had been paying 'field allowances' to the Nigerian troops.

After Abacha's Viagra-fuelled death in the arms of prostitutes last June, the new President, General Abdulsalam Abubakar, reduced repression, freeing political prisoners. Many tribes have been emboldened to follow the Ogonis' example.

A British employee of Shell and his 2-year-old son were kidnapped last week, although they were released within days, and oil workers travel in convoys with armed guards.

A new report by Human Rights Watch catalogues numerous cases of people being 'brutalised' by Nigerian security forces for attempting to raise grievances with the oil companies. The largest is Shell, responsible for almost half the country's oil production, followed by the American companies Chevron and Mobil, Elf of France, and the Italian state-owned Agip.

Most of the protesters are Ijaws, the largest tribe in the Delta with more than 6 million people, presenting a far more serious threat to the regime than the Ogonis, who number fewer than 500,000. Armed mystical cults of the Ijaw god of war, Egbesu, have sprung up, hiding in the mangrove swamps which cover a third of the Delta.

Last month there was a series of killings in the riverside village of Kaiama after troops moved in to end a demonstration calling for foreign oil companies to leave. A week-long gun battle raged, leaving more than thirty people dead. Owonaro Kesiegha, the 26-year-old youth president, gave a warning: 'We are not afraid. We are angry.'

Travelling in the Delta last week, in a car driven by a man named Good News who fancied himself Michael Schumacher*, I hid in the back as foreigners are not allowed. Every couple of miles we screeched to a halt at checkpoints manned by soldiers brandishing machine guns, looking for youths whose backs bear the tattoos of the Egbesu cults. Soldiers have spread terror by looting houses and demanding money to let people pass.

The Ijaw have threatened to bring the oil industry to a halt. This month, leaders of all the Delta tribes gathered for the first time and issued a declaration demanding autonomy and a share of oil royalties.

With disruptions flaring up every week, Shell's production has been cut from 450,000 to 250,000 barrels a day. 'Many of our operations have been closed down and our staff are exposed,' said a senior executive. The foreign oil companies feel unfairly targeted. Since the Ogoni crisis, Shell has conducted a major review and is building hospitals and schools, paying for more than a hundred teachers in the Delta. It says the real blame lies with the state, which receives the royalties and is supposed to distribute a percentage to local people.

The anger of the Ijaw people hangs heavy in the already humid air

* I was pregnant and terrified we would crash.

of the Delta. At the village of Otuegwe, which is only accessible by boat, a strange gloom hangs over the community.

Ijaw youths led the way through the forest, where spiders are the size of rats and everything seems to grow to ten times the normal size. Suddenly the birds stopped singing. As we emerged from a swamp, the damp odour of the jungle was replaced by an overpowering nausea-inducing smell of hydrocarbons, and we entered a place that looked like Armageddon.

A pipeline had burst, spreading black oil over the vegetation and casting a thick film over the pools of water. When it rains, as it does every day, this runs into the creek and pollutes the water used by the villagers, in addition to killing the mudfish which they eat. Many of the palms on which they depend to produce palm oil and alcohol lay brown and dying.

This happened four months ago, yet nobody from Shell has visited the village to clean up or apologise, let alone offer compensation. Scooping up some crude to take home for fuel, Igonibo Ido said: 'We want the world to know our plight.'

The oil companies admit that many pipelines are older than the fifteen-year safe lifespan, but blame the government (which has a 55 per cent stake in Shell's operations and 60 per cent in the others') for not putting up its share of investment. Hundreds of pipeline leaks occur each year, although Shell claims that many result from sabotage.

Last October, word went around the community of Jesse that a pipeline had burst. Thousands of villagers rushed to the leak to collect oil. Among them was Eunice Akamugbe, a 30-year-old mother of two. 'We were all filling buckets when suddenly there was a huge explosion.'

When Eunice regained consciousness, she was covered in horrific burns. She was one of the lucky ones. More than a thousand people died in the blaze. In November, General Abubakar said there would be no compensation, as sabotage was suspected.

The current low price of oil, and the rash of demands which democracy is likely to bring, will make it hard for a new government to meet the needs of the Delta region. Oil earnings, which make up 80 per cent of government revenue, are projected at £4.8 billion for this year, far short of 1997's £9.3 billion.

Some campaigners fear that the Delta people's fight will provide an excuse for the military to retake power. But Fawehinmi Gani, a leading campaigner for democracy, warned: 'You can send in 50 million troops but you cannot cow the people. They have been cheated for so long that they are fighting the battle of their lives.'

Eat, eat, eat if you want to be loved...
In Africa, big is beautiful
Sunday Telegraph, 25 March 2001

Calabar
ARIT ASUQUO IBOK is large. Her thighs wobble like blancmange as she walks, her bottom is as round and squashy as two over-ripe pumpkins, and at least seven chins quiver when she swallows. For the past two months, she has woken at 5 a.m. for a pint of millet in water and a plate piled high with fried plantain, followed by a special body-rounding massage. Then she has spent the day in whale-like recline,

stirring only to stuff herself with glutinous bowls of yam and crayfish, or for the occasional game of ludo.

Worried that, at 35, she is still not married, Arit's family has paid to send her on a three-month programme to make her more desirable to men. Whereas in the West this might mean going to a health farm or gym to lose weight, in the steamy jungle port of Calabar in southern Nigeria, it means going to so-called fattening rooms, where women do nothing but eat.

'I must eat so I'll be fat and people don't laugh at my figure,' explained Arit, as she measured her thickening waist with one of the strings of special beads that she wears in the fattening room. 'It shows that my family has money and can afford to feed me properly and I will make a good bride.'

The fattening room in which she is staying is run by Madam Eke Eden and Madam Elizabeth Eyo, two middle-aged women, both on the corpulent side. They operate out of 42 Iboku Street, a peeling sky-blue and yellow bungalow, under a large mango tree in a dusty suburb of Calabar.

The terrace functions as a beauty salon, with two young girls busily plaiting and crimping hair. Behind the screen door, the two madams hold court in an expansive room with turquoise satin ruched curtains, a ceiling fan that occasionally stirs the thick air at the whim of the Nigerian electricity company, and framed photographs of large women – graduates of the fattening room.

'We can make any woman obese,' boasts Madam Eyo, looking critically at my size-10 figure. 'You might find the odd man who thinks that kind of shape is modern but, sorry to say, you look underfed,' she said. 'If a man were to choose you as his bride, people would feel sorry for him. If you stayed here some months, we could help you.'

Though intrigued by the idea that the way to a man's heart might be through my stomach rather than his, I decided not to take up her offer, which might have been more attractive had it involved bingeing on Belgian chocolates and cream buns rather than pounded yam and millet water. Instead, I ask to know her secrets. It is rare for an outsider to be admitted to a fattening room, because clients are supposed to be kept in seclusion until ready to emerge newly rounded.

The main component of the fattening room experience seems to be total inactivity, combined with as much yam, plantain, millet, and pepper soup as can be stuffed into one person in a day. A special red powder, ground from the bark of a tree, is taken to thin the blood to stop it coagulating with all the fat, and the women are painted with a native chalk that cools the skin, enabling them to eat more. They are also given special massages in which their bodies are kneaded to direct the fat to certain places, specifically the bottom.

'It is a bit tiring eating all the time,' admitted Arit, as she tucked into another large pan of yam and crayfish. 'But I know that when I come out I will be attractive, healthy and beautiful.'

Being fat is a beauty ideal for much of Africa and, in some countries, such as Nigeria, there are beauty contests to be the heaviest, with women eating animal feed and steroids to pile on the pounds. But fattening rooms are peculiar to southern Nigeria and the people of the Efik tribe.

In the Old Residency, a prefabricated house transported from England in 1884 to house the then British Governor and now the Calabar Museum, there is a series of black-and-white photographs of fattened Efik women with enormous, pendulous breasts and large pot bellies.

'Efik men liked their women fat and juicy,' explained Prince E. E. Eyamba, the son of the late Obong of Calabar, the traditional ruler. 'My mother spent seven years in a fattening room, as did most women whose families could afford it, from the age of 12.'

However, tastes are changing. 'Personally, now I like slick waists, but big breasts and bottoms,' said the Prince, tracing a swollen hourglass figure with his hands. 'In the past, we said big hips are good for child-bearing, but we have learnt that sometimes overblown hips are hiding a narrow pelvis, so now we check out the families to see if they have a history of difficult births.'

In fact, fattening rooms have become increasingly controversial since a recent study that links the intensive fattening to diabetes. Although the practice is still common, many have moved underground.

A campaign to stop fattening has been launched by Girl Power Initiative (GPI), a Calabar-based women's rights organisation founded in 1994, long before the Spice Girls adopted the phrase. Ofon Ekpoudeom, a facilitator for GPI, explained: 'We go to schools and villages telling girls to be happy with their bodies and teaching them to be more assertive, so they can reason with parents not to send them to fattening rooms.'

One of the objections of GPI to the fattening rooms is that time between eating is used to give lessons in how to be a good wife, in other words being obedient. Arit recounted: 'I have learnt that, if my husband is annoyed with me, then, even if it is his fault, I am not to react, but to stay quiet and let his temper calm, maybe cook him coconut rice or melon-seed soup.'

In a town with a history as one of the world's biggest slave-trading centres, where down by the riverside thousands of lives would be bartered for gin or gunpowder, the GPI members see such lessons as imparting a slave mentality to women. 'What they are being told is how to be slaves in the homes of their husbands,' said Ms Ekpoudeom.

Fattening rooms, however, have an even more sinister side. Apart from helping brides reach their enormous potential, they are also used to prepare young girls for circumcision, or genital mutilation as it is more commonly referred to in the West.

Sharing a room with Arit is 15-year-old Glory Ita Asuquo, a high-school student, naked apart from a short sarong around her waist, her skin painted with chalk designs. She is preparing to undergo female circumcision.

'They will cut off part of my genitalia with a razor blade,' she said matter-of-factly. 'It's painful, but it's part of our tradition. I feel comfortable about it.'

Asked about cases of local girls who have bled to death or later experienced gynaecological problems, she said: 'It will be done in a hygienic way and they will put a mixture of gin and special herbs on the wound to stop the bleeding. My friends say the pain goes away after two days.'

Glory, a slim, beautiful girl whose ambition is to go to university and become a lawyer, hopes to return to the fattening room when she is older to prepare to be a bride. 'I want to be fat like her,' she said, pointing at Arit admiringly.

Despite the GPI campaign and the changing taste of some Nigerian men in favour of sleeker women, a visit to the town's sprawling Watt Market shows that the desire to be large remains common. Beyond the tables piled high with cassava, yams and snails is an area with stall upon stall offering fattening accoutrements.

Apart from blood thinning bark and massage chalk, they sell special fattening peppers for pepper soup, as well as stomach-turning substances such as dead chameleons to soak in water. When drunk, this supposedly cures bloating and allows the women to keep on eating.

Along the road, one of the many Pentecostal churches is called the Church of Divine Enlargement to attract ladies who long to be fatter. Local pharmacies do a thriving trade in a product called Wate-on, bought by women whose families cannot afford the 5,000 naira (£30) a month, plus the food cost, of the fattening room – a substantial amount in a country where the average wage is £200 a year.

Some younger girls are resisting the pressure to be fat. Mary Adi, a plump, lively 31-year-old who runs a beauty salon where many local girls hang out, said: 'I think fattening rooms are a dreadful idea. I try to dissuade the girls who come here.'

Talking as she painted crimson varnish on the toenails of an enormous woman in royal blue, she added: 'You have to laugh that you in the West, with all your money, are obsessed with losing weight, whereas us poor Africans, with no money for anything, are trying to be fat.'

While the practice may be on the wane in town, families in local villages struggle to send their daughters to fattening rooms in the hope of their winning the most eligible bachelors.

Creek Town, twenty minutes' boat ride along the muddy Calabar River, used to be a European trading post and is today an eerie place full of abandoned, prefabricated two-storey wood chalets with stained-glass windows criss-crossed with thick cobwebs. On the step of a small concrete shack, across from one of these ghostly relics, three sisters sit sorting periwinkles. Each spent two years in fattening rooms and proudly brings out photographs of her fattened self.

'Women who are not fattened are cursed,' explained Glory Ita Eyo, the middle sister. 'If you don't do it, the gods will be angry and terrible things will happen.'

Back at the bungalow under the mango tree, Madam Eden was busy fixing bells round Arit's ankles, elaborate brass combs in her hair, and bracelets of yellow and red pompoms on her newly plumped arms for her coming-out ceremony.

'Any time your man is losing interest, you just come to Auntie,' she told me, clucking sympathetically. 'You'll see how men like fattened women.'

You Never Know When You Might Need a Wailer

Letters from Portugal 1996–1998

When I was living in Johannesburg and Paulo in Lisbon (this being in the days before email), we would keep in touch by sending each other breakfast faxes. One morning my fax machine spurted out a black and white photograph of a pretty cottage with window shutters and geraniums and an open-top car outside. Underneath it read: 'Boy missing girl. When are you coming?'

By late 1995 I had tired of having my body on one continent and my heart on another. And after more than a year of pretending it did not bother me, I was fed up with crime in South Africa's biggest city. Everyone talked about it at every dinner or party; no one would come downtown any more to the Market Theatre or Kippies but only to shopping centres with 'secure parking'; and it seemed a matter of time before I too was carjacked, or raped and tied up in my own home, or murdered.

I weakened and had an alarm fitted. At night I would lock myself in my bedroom and lie in bed staring at its electronic eye blinking red. The next step would be a rape gate, a steel barrier across the bedroom door, based on the idea that intruders could make off with your belongings but not get to you. Even that wasn't enough – the latest dinner-party horror story was of attackers breaking in by abseiling through the roof.

I felt even less safe after an unsavoury episode with a British mercenary who had been involved in fomenting black-on-black violence. The mercenary had been brought back into South Africa by one of my *Sunday Times* colleagues, whom he had befriended, and they set about digging up bodies of people he'd helped to murder. I was so horrified that I told the South African Police and they arrested the man, which led to threats against me from his friends in the white extremist movement.

So my heart leapt when Paulo told me he had found us a cottage in a little village called São Pedro de Sintra. It was on the estate of a *condessa* who had fallen on hard times and his description sounded perfect – whitewashed with yellow windows and a terrace full of flowers overhung by a lemon tree – perfect for gin and tonics.

Before I met Paulo the only time I had been to Portugal was on a cruise with my parents when I was 6. Among their old slides was one of me standing in front of a fountain wearing heart-shaped sunglasses and a pair of hot-pants of which I was clearly extremely proud. The cottage Paulo had rented was round the corner. It had to be fate.

I was planning to write a book on an incredible house I had come across in a remote part of Zambia built by an eccentric British aristocrat and this seemed an ideal place. Sintra after all had been home to Lord Byron, Hans Christian Andersen, William Beckford and the poet Roy Campbell. As a final good omen, England and Portugal were the world's oldest alliance, dating back to 1386, and Sintra was where the treaty had been signed.

Once more I packed up my boxes of books (at the age of 30 I still did not own a stick of furniture) and for the first time moved in permanently with the man I loved. It was odd living in a village after years of noisy cities but wonderful to be somewhere so peaceful that windows and doors could be safely left unlocked. I adored exploring the mystical green Sintra hills that the Romans had known as the Mountains of the Moon. One path led to a psychedelic pink palace built by a mad German king, Ferdinand II, and another to a Moorish castle with proper fairytale turrets, one of which I adopted as my own. I would sit there looking out to the sea in the distance and reading Neruda or writing my diary, and glare at any tourist who dared to approach.

Running with the bulls
New Statesman Diary, 8 August 1997

SUMMERTIME IN PORTUGAL and every day coachloads of lobster-tinted British tourists are deposited in our village. After they've done the castle, palace, and guesthouse where Byron once stayed, they usually end up outside the large yellow house which is home to the Duke of Bragança, the man who would be king were Portugal still a monarchy. As it is not, he whiles away his days inaugurating hospitals, consorting with other displaced European royals and opening fêtes – rather like our royal family really, only without the privy purse. The Duke, a jolly moon-faced fellow, still hopes to be king one day and reclaim the crown jewels that are gathering dust in the vaults of the Bank of Portugal (next to those mysteriously swastika-stamped gold ingots). In the meantime I often see him on the bus.

Last weekend I bumped into the Duke in Cascais, the sea resort to which most of the British tourists return after having their fill of sights. He was there to name a new ambulance, while I had gone to watch the annual 'Running with the Bulls'. It may be a tourist trap but Cascais remains a fishing village at heart and the bull-run is the yearly chance for local fishermen to demonstrate to an admiring female population just how macho they are.

Cascais is not quite Pamplona and the bull-run takes place on the beach so as not to cause chaos in the streets, where people are busy eating fried chicken and ice cream. Even so, there was great confusion among the tourists soaking up their daily dose of UV when hundreds of tanned men in tight shorts leaving little to the imagination suddenly descended on the beach and started gesturing frantically, shouting '*Touro, touro!*' Some of the sun worshippers got the idea and moved; others just lay there looking British and baffled. Finally a truck bearing five fairly menacing bulls drew up on the sands and they got the point and fled, the Germans even removing their towels.

The bull-runners took up position and the first bull was released amid catcalls and whistles from local women gathered on the over-looking walls. The aim of the contest is to seize the bull's horns and risk life and limb to block its path. My money was on a muscled man whose scowl looked enough to deter most large mammals, though I was quite taken by a Gérard Depardieu lookalike tossing his long hair disdain-fully. But the first to grab the horns was a John Cleese beanpole with a droopy moustache and stripy red-and-white bathing shorts, whose name was Senhor Manteiga, Portuguese for Mr Butter.

The next bull was bigger and sent men scattering into the waves as it approached. After a few charges it got bored and headed into the sea where, after some remarkably dolphin-like bobs, it was soon out of its depth. 'It's going to drown,' said a woman standing behind us. 'It happens every year.' The old man next to her shook his head. 'No, it won't,' he said knowledgeably. 'It takes four hours for a bull to drown.' Soon everyone around was joining in, outdoing each other with bovine expertise and elaborate tales of the time when a bull escaped the beach and ran into the front of Hotel Baía where it surprised a British tourist doing her knitting.

I suspected the RSPCA wouldn't approve of these goings-on, but the bull was duly rescued and a third sent into the fray. Mr Butter, who had presumably been dreaming of what he'd do with the giant slab of dried codfish he stood to win, was upstaged by a passing drunk who literally seized the bull by the horns and rode around on it, a surprised grin on his face, before passing out on the sand. By the fourth bull everyone was getting braver. Even Gérard Depardieu drew nearer before flicking his hair and walking away. But the last bull was a massive 1,200-pound beast which no one dared approach, despite the taunts of the female spectators. Several people were trampled and rushed off in the ambulance that had conveniently just been named by the Duke, until finally an old man in a small yellow rowing boat managed to lasso the bull's horns.

Mystified, I asked an important-looking man with a megaphone who had won the codfish. 'The bulls,' he replied angrily. 'The youth of today are too busy chasing English girls to learn how to deal with bulls.' Thus condemned, the young men in question sat around on the seafront, comparing their wounds.

In his cabriolet, Paulo drove me around a Portugal that tourists don't normally see. We went to drive-in castles where locals were drying their laundry, cobble-stoned Alentejan villages where we had to leave the car outside as only donkey-drawn vehicles are allowed, and a fish restaurant with a tree through the roof. We picnicked among Roman ruins about to be submerged by a vast new dam. Frank Sinatra sang out of the car stereo and we filled the back seat with bunches of yellow mimosa.

In the Gothic abbey of Alcobaça, I traced my finger over the inscription 'Até ao fim do mundo' (till the end of the world) on the intricate marble tombs of Pedro and Inês, Portugal's own Romeo and Juliet, as Paulo told me the story. Inês de Castro had been the Spanish lady-in-waiting to the wife of Prince Pedro, who was heir to the Portuguese throne, and they had fallen in love. Pedro's wife then died in childbirth but his father King Afonso IV refused to let him marry Inês, ordering her to be confined to a convent in Coimbra. A stream flowed between the convent and a royal hunting lodge, and the couple would float little wooden boats to each other bearing messages arranging assignations. When word got back to the King, he had Inês killed – her 'heron neck' severed by axe – leaving the stream flowing red and his son devastated. When Dom Pedro became king two years later, he had Inês's body exhumed and made his courtiers kiss her decomposing hand before reburying it in a tomb carved with friezes depicting scenes from their life. On top was her marble body held aloft by angels. Opposite, he had one built for himself, feet facing, so that the first thing they would see on Judgment Day would be each other.

'Where the earth meets the sea', wrote Portugal's most famous poet, Camões, of this land from which explorers had set out to discover two-thirds of the world and brought back untold riches. Now it was a land turned inward and one of the poorest countries in Europe. But as the light took on the almond-pink glow of evening and the storks returned to their nests, their giant wings flapping slowly, we would find a village café in which to stop. Over coffee and *bagaço* (brandy), we always seemed to find a story.

You never know when you might need a wailer
Financial Times, 6 January 1996

I MET A WOMAN recently who wails for a living. At first I thought my Portuguese must have let me down and I had misunderstood. The word she had used was *carpideira* – something to do with carp fishing, I thought, though it seemed an unlikely specialism in one of Portugal's most arid regions. Besides, her behind was so voluminous I found it hard to imagine how she would keep her balance on a river bank.

Then she opened her mouth to demonstrate. What came out of this small middle-aged woman with the neat bun of hair and the big backside was not a moan or a cry but truly a wail, a long shuddering wail of such epic proportions that it had the dogs howling for miles around and sent grown men and women scurrying for cover.

When I had recovered, eardrums still ringing, she presented me with a business card. 'Maria Teixeira, Professional Wailer,' it said in flowery italics. I have come across some strange occupations in my time but this was a new one on me. 'Excuse my ignorance,' I said, 'but why would anyone need a wailer?'

'You never know when you might need a wailer,' she replied, reminding me of a man dressed as Elvis I had met long ago on Sunset Boulevard. He posed for a photo with me then pressed a card into my hand with 'Eddie Powers as Elvis' stamped on it. 'You never know when you might need an Elvis,' he said. I can honestly say I have been in some tough situations when a Harrison Ford or an Arnold Schwarzenegger might have come in handy. But an Elvis?

Meeting an Elvis impersonator is the sort of thing you expect to happen in Los Angeles. You would want your money back otherwise. But Portugal is a more sober place and I found it hard to imagine any circumstance in which a wailer might save the day.

'I do weddings, funerals, graduations,' explained Teixeira. 'Anything where a wail or two might add some authenticity. Usually I find that after the first few wails those gathered take over.' Seeing my continuing bafflement, she added: 'Think of the shame of an occasion' – she pronounced the word with special reverence – 'with no wailing.'

It turns out that just as English towns and villages used to have town criers, in Portugal they have wailers. 'It's an honour to be the town wailer,' stressed Teixeira, who comes from one of those whitewashed and cobble-street villages that the Portuguese do so well. As usual with these towns, hers has a story attached. It was given by a king to his queen after his forces successfully stormed the castle disguised as cherry trees. And I thought the British had invented Monty Python.

Teixeira's wailing career began at an early age when it was discovered she had a particularly strident cry. Her mother was the family black sheep, having come from a long line of wailers and failed to make the grade herself, being unfortunately endowed with a squeaky voice box which no amount of cod-liver oil and tobacco smoke could deepen. Condemned to a life of taking in laundry, she was overjoyed when Maria came into the world with a deep, throaty and unmistakable wail. To encourage its development she took to locking Maria in cupboards or losing her in forests, forcing her to wail for attention.

But there is more to it than just the quality of wail, Teixeira was anxious to point out. Wailers need to be able to blend in with gatherings so that it is not immediately obvious who is emitting the wail. 'We wailers are performers, actresses, just as much as your Hollywood stars.

I modify my wail according to the occasion.' I felt honoured to be in the presence of the Emma Thompson of the wailing world. I risked my eardrums with one last demonstration and took my leave.

Because of its place in modern Europe and its holiday resorts on the Algarve with 'real British breakfasts' and 'tea like mother makes', it is easy to forget how traditional Portugal still is. But behind the medieval walls of its villages, you discover a different world where women yearn to be wailers, and donkeys are the main mode of transport. And, while many young people have left the countryside for the city, they have not forgotten the old ways.

Indeed, they are blending the modern and traditional. Teixeira's daughter, who has moved from the village to Lisbon, is thinking of starting wailing classes for stressed executives. 'It is a great way of letting out tension,' she explained as I wished her luck in finding a sufficiently soundproof room. Next time I need a wailer, I know where to go.

The poet with blood on his apron
Financial Times, 17 February 1996

I STUMBLED ON José Valentim Lourenço, the rhyming butcher, by accident.

It was a wet and windy Saturday, so miserable that only the promise of a hearty Portuguese lunch of roast hog and fulsome red wine could drag me out from beneath the covers. Somehow in the tangle of narrow stone-walled streets between my village and the one famous for its hog lunches, I lost my way and found myself in Gouveia.

At the entrance of the village stood a large sign on which was painted in bold blue strokes 'Welcome to Gouveia, Village in Verse'.

Underneath was the following poem (roughly translated):

> *The roads are free-moving*
> *The air is sweetly calm*
> *The doors are all open*
> *To welcome everyone.*

Driving on, I saw that every street wall bore a tiled plaque on which a poem was painted inside a blue and gold border. There were rhymes about the chapel, the village square, the road to the sea, the wells and even the butcher's shop, encapsulating the history of the area.

Intrigued, I stopped a cherry-cheeked lady weaving baskets by the roadside. 'Ah, you want José, the butcher,' she said, waving an arm up the road. 'Yes, it was quite a day when we all woke up to find the poems on our streets. Of course we're pleased now. They attract a lot of people to the village, taking photographs and buying souvenirs. This place was really run-down, but with all the money coming in we've built a children's playground, restored the wells, the chapel and the town square.'

Sure enough, not far along the road I found José Valentim Lourenço in his glass-fronted shop, hacking away at a large piece of pork. When I explained my interest in his verses, he wiped his knife on his blood-spattered apron and extended a flabby hand in welcome.

Still in his foul-smelling apron, he closed up his shop ('not much custom in the rain') and led me into his house.

To my astonishment, José told me he had left school aged 10. His passion for doggerel was inspired by his grandfather. He used to accompany him into the fields every day to help tend the cows of a local farmer.

'My grandfather couldn't read or write but he could tell stories in verse. People would come from all around – the Peasant Poet they called him.'

Working his way up over the years to owning his own cows and eventually becoming village butcher, José, now 51, was determined to give something back to the place in which he had grown up.

He helped found a local theatre – no mean feat in a poor village of just 200 people – and started producing plays. With the proceeds, he launched a programme of public works and set about putting Gouveia on the map.

For a long time José had been making up poems as he chopped the meat into steaks or slapped it into burgers. 'The rhythm of cutting gives me ideas,' he grins. One day he had a brainwave. 'The streets of Gouveia had no names,' he recalls. 'I decided I'd not only give them names but also verses.' For two years he walked the eighteen streets, compiling verses.

'It's not easy,' he said, 'to put the whole history of a street in four lines.' Secretly he worked with Geraldo, the local tilemaker, to paint the verses on tiles ready to place on the streets.

But they had overlooked one thing. 'The roads had no walls,' laughs José. 'There was nowhere to hang the tiles.' Undeterred, he led a campaign to build street walls of local stone. Finally he and Geraldo crept out late one night and put up the tiled verses.

The first most people in Gouveia knew of all this was waking up one Saturday morning to find that every street had its own plaque painted with a name and verse. That day was spent walking around, staring in wonder at each plaque and reading the verses to themselves and each other.

Not everyone approved. José recalls: 'Some people felt the poems on their streets were not as good as on others. One complained that there were too many verses. Maybe I did go a bit too far giving poems to all the wells, the chapel and the public water fountains.'

That night, it was decided that being the Village of Verse was a real coup for Gouveia. So it has proved. Portuguese villages like to be individual, each with its own yearly festival. By becoming the Village of Verse, Gouveia put tremendous pressure on the surrounding villages.

Emergency meetings were held at village halls all over the area. Fontanelas, next door to Gouveia, even commissioned José to pen some poetry. But, as José admits: 'My heart just wasn't in it. There can only be one village of verse.'

Yes, I Was a Cynic until I Met Her – Diana

Sunday Times, 7 September 1997

LIKE MOST thirty-something women, I grew up with Princess Diana. We were just 16 and discovering the other sex when she glided up the aisle in that Emanuel dress and, though my friends and I shrieked with laughter at the creases when she stepped out of the carriage, in those days we, too, dreamt of finding our fairytale prince as we clutched our commemorative wedding mugs.

Some of us went to the hairdresser afterwards clutching magazine pictures and asking shyly for a 'Lady Di' and our first highlights; others with less pocket money experimented at home with Sun-In. Following in Diana's footsteps, we bought the pedal-pushers and the woolly jumpers patterned with sheep. Like Diana – and quite unlike what our mothers had told us – we gradually discovered that there was more to life than gilded carriages and bridal gowns, and that the best place to feel good might be the local gym.

As we got older, went to university, took jobs and even got married ourselves, most of us formed a love-hate relationship towards Diana, detesting what we saw of her as a control freak, but impressed with her ever-changing image and the way she embraced those with Aids or leprosy.

She made it all right to have eating disorders or need therapy – if someone that beautiful could have an image problem then we had every right to be screwed up. The stick-thin girl in our class whose mysterious absences we were never allowed to talk about, we all remembered with guilt. I was living abroad when the famous 'alone in front of the Taj Mahal' photo appeared of Diana, and a friend who had just broken up with her fiancé faxed it to me with the message: 'And I thought I had problems!'

But in an era when we were striving to become career women as can-do as any male, Diana was just too feminine and emotional. So in January, when the editor of the *Sunday Times* asked me to cover her trip to Angola, I had very mixed feelings.

When I told my friends where I was off to, they laughed, knowing me as someone more used to reporting on wars, with little patience for the media obsession with Di's latest look. Having seen first hand the terrible effect of landmines in Afghanistan and Mozambique, I cared deeply about the issue her trip was intended to publicise, although I feared it would be a vast publicity stunt. At the same time I was intrigued to have a closer look at this woman with just one CSE whose fans were so diverse that they even included my hippie friend Sarina who knits jumpers in Bolivia and always asked me to send pictures, and Tanya, who is so ambitious that when we were students she had written a list of ten things to achieve by the age of 30, including becoming a company director and making her first million.

Standing in the baking sun at Luanda airport waiting for the

Princess to arrive, I remembered the footage of Diana assisting in the heart operation at Harefield in full make-up. I scowled, fearing this was going to be more of the same. I was pleasantly surprised then when she turned up in jeans, white shirt and no make-up, and consoled myself over how good she looked by snidely spotting the Armani label. As she sped off in a Red Cross jeep, forty cameras in hot pursuit, a bemused Angolan selling chewing gum tugged my sleeve and asked who she was. It took me a while to understand that after thirty-five years of armed conflict and civil war which had torn the nation apart, this was one of the few countries in the world where Princess Diana was not an instantly recognisable figure.

It was all the more remarkable then to see her effect on the hundreds of mutilated mine victims we were to come into contact with that week. She'd come, she said, determined to work, and work she did. The Red Cross whisked us from one hospital to the next, each with ever more horrific scenes of skeletal figures with missing arms, missing legs and half-blown-off heads – victims of some of the 16 million landmines scattered around the country. Many of the injuries were so gruesome that I could not look, despite years of Third World reporting. But Diana never turned her head away. Instead, she had something I'd only ever seen before in Nelson Mandela – a kind of aura that made people want to be with her, and a completely natural, straight-from-the-heart sense of how to bring hope to those who seemed to us to have little to live for. As I speak Portuguese, I interpreted for her a few times and felt absurdly pleased to have those familiar blue eyes turned on me, knowing I'd tell my friends they were even bluer than they appeared on television.

It was not an easy trip. Decades of civil war had turned much of Angola into bombed-out ghost towns and its people seemed hard and unforgiving. In summer it is infernally hot and dusty; the streets of Luanda were piled high with stinking rubbish and flies buzzed around us non-stop; every other person seemed to be an amputee, and yet I never once saw Diana express fatigue or ask for a drink. OK, so she had brought her own butler, but I was jealous as hell of her ability to stay cool and neatly pressed – a stark contrast to my own sweaty and dishevelled appearance. Just how remarkable was her adaptation

became evident talking to the royal hacks who sat in the bar of the Hotel Presidente every night, wistfully recalling previous jaunts to Klosters and Barbuda, and longing for the Diana of old who went to balls and banquets and wore Versace instead of flak jackets.

That trip wiped out all my past cynicism about Diana, to my own astonishment as well as that of friends familiar with my views. That Lady-with-the-Lamp performance wasn't just for the benefit of the cameras. Of course, she knew all right when there was a good shot to be had, always gravitated to the woman with twin babies and no legs, or the cute young girl. But I wasn't sure it mattered, if these pictures made people back home aware of the reality of life in this forgotten nation.

Once, at a hospital in Huambo when the photographers had all flown back to their air-conditioned hotel to wire their pictures, I watched Diana, unaware that any journalists were still present, sit and hold the hand of Helena Ussova, a 7-year-old who'd had her intestines blown to pieces by a mine. For what seemed an age the pair just sat, no words needed. When Diana finally left, the small girl struggled through her pain to ask me if the beautiful lady was an angel.

I thought of Helena when I woke up last Sunday to the incomprehensible news that Diana had been killed. At the end of the Angola trip Diana said that the lasting image she'd take away was of that terribly ill young girl. Both of them are dead now and my lasting image will be the two of them just sitting together hand in hand, finding peace. Diana wasn't my friend – I'd only met her that one week – yet I, like so many women, somehow feel that she could have been. At one lunch in Huambo that I'd sneaked into because I had a Red Cross watch, Diana poured me coffee and insisted that I fill my plate from the buffet, saying, 'You're too thin.'

It has been odd this week to be abroad and watch on television my country transformed from the land of stiff upper lip to one where it's more than OK to cry in public. If I lived in England, I don't know if I would have gone to lay flowers among the fields of bouquets outside Kensington Palace and sign the book of condolence at St James's. Most of my friends went and told me how moved they were by the peace of the place and how, instead of just biting their lips, they shed tears – in some cases the first time publicly in their lives, a fact which by itself shows me how much one woman changed a nation. My friend Tanya has blacked out her website on the Internet, turning it into a tribute to Diana; Julie has cancelled her holiday to watch the funeral; Jane is to run the marathon for charity in her name; and Emma has named her newborn daughter Diana.

We don't feel ambiguous about Diana any more – she was a modern woman, always reinventing herself, balancing the demands of being a single mother and having her own life, and looking beautiful at the same time. We grew up with her and now we must grow old alone.

A Zanzibari Wedding

Sunday Telegraph, 13 June 1999

When my husband of all of two minutes was asked to tick on our marriage certificate whether he was monogamous, polygamous, or potentially polygamous, he hesitated and I feared this could be a very short alliance. But he picked the right box, and we emerged into the sweltering Zanzibari heat at the outbreak of the monsoon somewhat sticky, but husband and wife.

Unlike this season's more high-profile wedding couples, we did not commission a coat of arms, nor did we run a marathon en route, and decided against inviting 6,000 members of the public. Our only witnesses were the priest's wife, our taxi driver and a man at the back of the church dusting palm leaves in preparation for Palm Sunday.

Both in our thirties, we had watched friends dedicate more time to

JAMHURI YA MUUNGANO WA TANZANIA   RGM. 8
THE UNITED REPUBLIC OF TANZANIA

SHAHADA YA NDOA—CERTIFICATE OF MARRIAGE   A № 00062470

Steria ya Ndoa 1971—*The Law of Marriage Act 1971*

Ndoa imefungwa.. THE CATHEDRAL CHURCH OF CHRIST-MKUNAZINI ZANZIBAR Mkoa... URBAN UNGUJA   Tanzania
Marriage contracted at   *Region*   *Tanganyika*

Tarehe ya Ndoa *Date of Marriage*	Majina Kamili ya Wafunga Ndoa *Full Names of Parties*	Umri *Age*	Hali *Status*	Mahali wanapoishi *Residence*	Jina la Baba *Father's Name*	Aina ya Ndoa *Kind of Marriage*
27th March 1999	PAULO MARQUES NUNES da SILVA ANUNCIACAO	35	Bachelor	LONDON	MARIO CARLOS DA SILVA ANUNCIACAO	*Ndoa ya Mke Mmoja Monogamous* *Hauada ikawa ya wake wengi Potentially Polygamous*
	CRISTINA ELIZABETH LAMB	35	Spinster	LONDON	KENETH ERNEST EDWARD LAMB	*Wake wengi Polygamous*

Ndoa imefungwa kwa Madhehebu ya... CHRISTIAN FAITH
This Marriage was contracted according to

Mbele ya yangu/Imetolewa na   Rev Canon Thomas Godd. JABROM
Before me/Issued by   Majliti/Kadhi (
     Registrar

Baina Yenu *Between us*   [signatures]

Madadihikili *Witnesses*   Emily Woods

Tarehe 27/3/199?
Date

Tarehe na mahali wa Maelezo ya habari... 17th FEBRUARY 1999
Date and source of Statement of Particulars

Futa isiyotakiwa /Delete whichever is inapplicable.

organising weddings than NATO appeared to have put into its plans for bombing Serbia. This, we decided, was our day: rather than fret over table linen, seating plans and drunken uncles with radical political views, we would do as we pleased.

The idea of being married in Zanzibar came about last summer when Paulo and I holidayed there, captivated by its silver sands, and air redolent with cinnamon, clove and vanilla. Long fascinated by Livingstone, I had been eager to visit the house where he stayed before setting off on expeditions – and dismayed to find it in a state of decay, the garden an evil-smelling sanctuary for giant tortoises. But the Cathedral Church of Christ where he preached against slavery was a different matter. Its crucifix is carved from the tree under which the great explorer was buried in Zambia after his ill-fated last journey in search of the Nile, and we decided it would be perfect for a wedding.

The first problem was finding the priest. Christians keep a low profile on the strongly Islamic island, and Canon Godda turned out to be in hospital in Dar es Salaam, recovering from malaria. By the time he returned, our holiday was ending. He was taken aback by our request, saying, 'This is not Las Vegas,' and pointed out that he would need three weeks for the calling of the banns. But he agreed that if we could provide 'Christian references' he could do the service at some future date.

We returned to England and the distraction of new jobs and house-buying. Only occasionally, when I caught a whiff of clove from the basket of Zanzibari spices in the kitchen cupboard or saw a picture of a coconut palm, did I think wistfully of the far-away island in the Indian Ocean.

Then winter came. After eleven years living in hot countries, January and February seemed months without light or sky, and we found ourselves drawn to windows of travel agents with posters of white beaches and lists of exotic destinations.

Consulting the Zanzibar guidebook, we realised the monsoon was due to start at the end of March, so we would have to act soon. We attended Sunday service at our local church in north London, charmed the vicar into giving us references, finally managed to get through to Canon Godda in Zanzibar, and booked our flights.

To give time for the banns meant having our honeymoon before the wedding, but at least we would be tanned for the wedding photographs. We spent the first few days on safari among Masai who told us when they wish to marry they must kill a lion and present its head to the father of their intended.

Arriving in the Zanzibari capital of Stone Town after a week in a hut on a remote beach, we began wedding preparations. In the narrow lanes of the jewellery bazaar, amid tiny Omani shops selling yellow-gold bangles, we found Mr Suriya to make us rings and inscribe them with the word 'Zanzibar' and the date. Through a wooden doorway I saw a woman having her hair straightened in a room plastered with magazine pages. I wandered in. Communication was problematic as the owner spoke no English, and my Swahili was limited to ordering two beers (*mbili biri*) or asking small children their names. But somehow I emerged with hands and wrists painted in swirling flower designs with black henna and red *mehndi* traditional for a Zanzibari wedding. That night, drinking gin and tonics in the Livingstone Bar, the only real drink for the tropics, we heard a large crack. We ran to the shutters to see the heavens opening with a force that turned stone alleys into rushing rivers. The monsoon had come early and we feared our day would be spoilt.

Wading back to the hotel, I found an urgent message from my news desk at the *Sunday Telegraph*. Having been cut off from news all week, I wondered if something had happened. It had – my foreign editor, Con Coughlin, told me NATO had started bombing Yugoslavia and that the verdict had been given on General Pinochet, both stories I had been covering. Could I make a few calls? 'I'm afraid I'm a bit busy tomorrow,' I replied to his evident shock. 'We're getting married.' Even he thought that was a good excuse.

The wedding day dawned fine and cloudless. Breakfasting on papaya, I watched the dhows sail past and small children shrieking as they washed in the sea. It was hard to imagine that I would soon be a wife. I had always been a free spirit, moving country – and relationships – as the mood took me, priding myself that all my possessions could fit into one suitcase.

Had there been relatives and friends fussing, I might have panicked.

Instead I returned to the beauty salon where, despite our lack of a common language, a garland of white jasmine was waiting for my hair. The owner of the salon abandoned her customer and began weaving my hair into tiny plaits, fixing them with coloured beads. Soon the customer had been enlisted to help, and friends of the owner dropped in to see the *mzungu* – white person – who was marrying in Zanzibar. My hennaed hands were examined critically and my fair hair pulled and twisted. Finally, the garland was placed on top and I was ready. My new friends wanted to make me up as well, but seeing the box of scarlet lipsticks, strawberry pink blusher and thick black kohl, I escaped.

Back at the hotel, I pulled on my ivory linen dress and high-heeled shoes, and jumped into a taxi. Entering the church five minutes late, I was disturbed to find it empty, apart from the man polishing the palm leaves. Then I heard voices. I hid behind the palms as Paulo, the priest and the witness passed by. But there was a problem – the photographer hadn't arrived. Eventually, the taxi driver was dispatched to find another, and both came at once. A friend of the priest appeared with his Instamatic, and we suddenly had more photographers than guests.

With everything finally ready, I strode up the aisle, noticing Canon Godda signalling frantically. His wife, my bridesmaid and witness, was having difficulty keeping up. I slowed down and made my way more serenely to the altar. We exchanged vows and rings engraved with ZBR, which hadn't quite been the idea, and to my surprise tears pricked my eyes. I did not even protest when the priest's sermon included the exhortations, 'Paulo, you have had many women in your life. But now it is over. Christina, Paulo is the head of your household and must be obeyed.'

Clutching the certificate proclaiming us man and wife (and committing Paulo to monogamy), we wandered back through Stone Town. Local men broke off from card games and bottle-top backgammon to congratulate us, asking Paulo, 'How many wives do you have?'

That night we dined on a rooftop overlooking the harbour, lying on cushions like sultans while waiters brought us titbits and Swahili musicians serenaded us. Listening to the muezzin's call, and watching swallows swoop and dive in the setting sun, it seemed the most romantic place in the world.

There was only one cloud on the horizon. How would my mother react when she learnt that she had missed watching her only child walk up the aisle? She wasn't amused. But surprisingly, friends were also miffed. 'You eloped!' they said accusingly. Looking at the bottle of Zanzibari sand on the mantelpiece, I wouldn't have done it any other way.

Tea with Pinochet

New Statesman, 26 July 1999

WHEN I CALLED a cab to take me to Wentworth Golf Estate, the driver expressed surprise that I was carrying no golf clubs, but seemed satisfied with my explanation that I was visiting someone for tea. I told him that I was a journalist from the *Sunday Telegraph*, but it was only when I directed him past one of the estate's dancing fountains to a leafy cul-de-sac guarded by two Scotland Yard officers in a white Portakabin that it dawned on him exactly who I was going to see.

'S'pose you'll be going to interview Milosevic next week,' he growled, as we pulled up at the tall iron gates of 28 Lindale Close, residence of one Mr A. Pinochet since last November. Feeling guilty, I gave him a large tip and was shepherded by another Scotland Yard officer to join my editor, Dominic Lawson, on the general's patio.

It is not every day that one takes elevenses with a dictator – even a retired one. That the encounter took place in a rose-filled Surrey garden on a hot summer's day, at a table overlooking a lawn in the middle of which fluttered a Chilean flag and a colourful plastic windmill, rather than in some sombre wood-panelled room lent an air of improbability. I was high on morphine, too, having only got out of hospital the previous day, after an emergency Caesarean to deliver my first child eleven weeks early, and that added to the surrealism of the situation. Had any of Wentworth's other famous residents such as Bruce Forsyth or Fergie dropped in, I doubt I would have lifted an eyebrow.

Gathered on the patio were several of Pinochet's advisers in smart suits, slicked-back hair and dark glasses: the *Pinochetistas*. Since his arrest last October, I had often met them in the coffee bar of Claridges to hear the latest word from his camp and be delivered outrages such as 'Pinochet denied Midnight Mass'. As we waited for the general to emerge, they shuffled nervously. Pinochet does not like journalists and had only agreed to this encounter after protracted negotiations and in the belief that his situation could not be worse – proceedings to extradite him to Spain to be tried for torture and conspiracy to torture begin in September. The current commander-in-chief of the Chilean Army had been on the phone the day before, they told us, trying to stop the interview.

There was a sudden silence as Pinochet emerged from the French windows, then a chorus of '*Buenos días, mi general*'. I stared at the man I had read so much about, joined protests against at university and written about since his arrest, who now shook my hand, smiling and congratulating me on the birth of my son.

Without his uniform and the sinister dark glasses he used to wear, he didn't look as I expected a dictator to look. Eighty-three last November, he was dressed in a navy suit with a high waistband, a pearl tie-pin on his silk tie. Leaning unsteadily on a crutch, a hearing aid in his right ear and his thin white hair ever so carefully combed, he looked like someone's elderly uncle. Adding to this impression was the pushchair propped against the wall, belonging to the youngest of his twenty-five grandchildren, three-month-old Augusta Victoria, who had just been flown over from Chile with her mother. But the most unexpected thing was the voice. Instead of the military bark that I had anticipated was a high-pitched whisper.

The general took his seat, the Chilean Constitution placed ostentatiously in front of him. This, his extremely polite manner and frequent references to God (there are Catholic icons all over the house) took me back to an encounter eleven years before with the then military dictator of Pakistan. General Zia-ul-Haq had insisted on pouring me tea and serving me yellow iced cakes as he lied through his teeth, constantly justifying his actions with references to the Constitution, a document he had completely emasculated, and to Allah.

'I do not normally authorise such meetings,' Pinochet began, with a smile which did not reach his pale-blue eyes and was not at all reassuring. Dominic presented him with a plastic bottle of holy water from Lourdes, which the general passed to an adviser dismissively. Watching him gesture with liver-spotted hands, I was fascinated by his fingers. They were flat and meaty like those of a butcher. We could, he said, ask him anything.

We started on safe ground with Pinochet's midnight arrest last October while he lay in a private suite at the London Clinic recuperating from an operation on a spinal hernia. He insisted that he had been 'kidnapped', and strangely his main objection seemed to be that no one had had the decency to warn him beforehand. 'The least they could have done is warn me that I was going to be arrested,' he complained. 'I wasn't in England as a common bandit. I was here as a diplomatic figure and had been welcomed as such.'

His arrest, he said, had been particularly hurtful because it had happened here in England, his favourite country, where he liked to shop in Burberry and Fortnum & Mason, visit Madame Tussaud's and take tea with his friend Margaret Thatcher. 'As a child, my teachers and other people who educated me always said that Chile was one of Britain's best friends…I was always happy when I came here because I felt Britain was a place where people really respected one another.'

Speaking so softly that we had to lean forward to catch what he was saying, his words often lost in the whirr of the fan, he reminded me of Marlon Brando in *The Godfather*. 'Britain was famous for its justice system,' he whispered, before complaining with some justification about the farcical nature of the legal proceedings against him which have so far run up millions of pounds in costs and will probably never see him brought to trial. Even if he were tried and convicted in Spain, he is too old to go to jail.

'First there's the ruling. That's appealed; the appeal succeeds; then they appeal against the appeal and so it goes on. It's like being on a wheel.' He waved one of his meaty fingers to illustrate his point. 'They are playing with the life of a person who is very old, giving him hope of being freed, then taking it away again.

'I'm the only political prisoner in Britain,' he added, banging his fist on the patio table. 'Bandits, common criminals, violent people are all pardoned and allowed home.' It was hard not to smile at the image of Pinochet appealing to Amnesty International, who had documented hundreds of cases, during his regime, of victims tossed from helicopters, people herded into sports stadiums and executed by firing squads, or undergoing electric shocks and other tortures in the changing rooms.

Had he committed crimes against humanity such as torture and conspiracy to torture, for which, in their historic judgment in March, the Law Lords ruled that his status as a head of state gave him no immunity from prosecution?

Instead of the argument I had heard many times from his advisers – that the situation in Chile under Salvador Allende had been near civil war and that the country had been in the front line of the war against communism – the general simply denied everything. 'Never!' he replied. 'Not now. Nor do I think I could do something like that in future because, if you read these acts which I drafted, you will see the first thing I said was that we must encourage people's development and provide security to anyone detained.'

Brandishing the Constitution, he jabbed at a section: 'It is forbidden to apply any unlawful force on any person.' I thought of this later in his office, where I saw a shelf of Jean-Claude Van Damme videos.

He implied that, after he had seized power in the 1973 coup, he was too busy to torture anyone. 'I didn't have time to devote myself to controlling the actions of others. To say that would be gross slander!' He added: 'There was so much to sort out. We had inflation of 500 per cent. We had to recuperate agriculture to provide food for the people and we had to build houses because they were living in shacks and huts. It would be too long to list everything...'

This version of events did not really correspond with the report of the Chilean National Commission on Truth and Reconciliation, according to which 3,197 people were murdered or disappeared during his seventeen years in power. Was he saying he had never given orders to torture or kill anyone?

His reply to this – the crux of the case against him – was a Chilean saying. 'One does not erase with the elbow what one writes with the hand,' he said, pointing again to his Constitution.

Yet General Manuel Contreras, head of the DINA, the Chilean secret police, with whom Pinochet breakfasted every morning, claims that he did nothing without Pinochet's authorisation. Recently declassified Pentagon papers include one stating: 'General Contreras reports exclusively to and receives orders from President Pinochet.'

Pressed on who was responsible, Pinochet launched into a complicated discussion about 'how' and 'what'. 'There are many things I ordered him to do but who can say what? You see, as head of the army you always ask "what", not "how" – that's up to the chief of intelligence. Civilians don't understand.'

The July sun was getting hotter and Pinochet's Chilean butler came and served strong coffee in tiny china cups. Clearly not leading anywhere on torture, the conversation moved on to his conditions at Wentworth. 'Would you be happy confined to the same eighty square metres for ten months?' asked Pinochet. 'Always seeing the same place, the same people?'

A tour of the house revealed it is less luxurious than the reported twelve-bedroomed mansion. With some of Pinochet's family visiting for lunch – his favourite lamb stew, which his Chilean cook was making in the kitchen – the living-cum-dining room was crowded. Two of the four bedrooms are taken up by Scotland Yard officers in case Pinochet tries to leg it, as is a small room next to the kitchen full of surveillance screens. There is little space for Pinochet's exercise bike, and he spends most of his time in a cramped office, reading books on his hero Napoleon or surfing the Internet to read the Chilean press. Typical of rented accommodation, the decor has little character – all cream carpets and cream leather chairs – and the only personal touches are the photos on every shelf and mantelpiece of the general, his family and Margaret Thatcher.

Since last month, Pinochet has been allowed to move freely in the garden, though always monitored by Scotland Yard officers and various surveillance cameras and infrared movement detectors. His greatest joy is his grandchildren. 'I'm too old to run around or play ball, but we have a set of remote-control cars and hold races round the lawn,' he said.

With this unlikely image of the dictator and his toy cars, we bade farewell to the old man and left the red-brick house with the roses rambling over the white shutters where we had taken elevenses and chatted about torture.*

* Pinochet was eventually allowed to return home on grounds of ill health. He died in Chile in December 2006, having never been brought to trial.

A Day Trip to Lagos – the Sad Story of Damilola Taylor

'There's something wrong here,' said the woman at the British Airways check-in desk. 'You're booked to arrive in and leave Lagos on the same day.'

'No, it's not wrong,' I replied. 'It's my job.'

The previous day I had been sitting at the foreign desk thinking about lunch when I noticed my editor Dominic Lawson emerge from his glass box and head purposefully towards me. I immediately tried to find something to do. Dominic could be a bully but he was a brilliant editor with wonderful quirky ideas. However, they were just as likely to be something emerging from a dinner party with his posh friends, such as 'no one has dining rooms any more', or involving his pet obsessions of chess and abortion.

In this case it was one of his interesting ideas. Two days earlier, on 27 November 2000, a 10-year-old Nigerian boy called Damilola Taylor had been stabbed in the leg and left to bleed to death in the stairwell of the grim council estate where he lived in Peckham. The photograph of Damilola in his school uniform with his shy smile was all over the papers. Even sadder, Damilola's mother had said they had moved to Britain from Lagos for a better life for their children.

'I want you to go to Peckham then Lagos,' Dominic told me. 'Compare and contrast Damilola's two homes. Cast your foreign correspondent's eye on Peckham. I wouldn't be surprised if, for example, the trains are better in Lagos.' (He was fixated by the inefficiency of British railways, once even asking the transport correspondent to look into what would happen if all the railways were converted to roads.)

But there was a problem. 'I can't,' I replied. 'I'm off this Saturday for my best friend's wedding. It's been down in the book for months. I'm reading the lesson in the church.'

This, it turned out, was no excuse. It was Wednesday and there was a daytime flight on Thursday which would get me into Lagos late that night. I could then fly back overnight on Friday to get home, change and be at the church in Pimlico at eleven on Saturday morning. When I would actually write (or sleep) was not clear.

I knew someone at the Nigerian embassy so managed to get my visa the same afternoon. That evening was spent exploring Peckham and the next day I was on the flight with Justin Sutcliffe, a photographer with whom I often worked, to go and see Damilola's birthplace. The one major flaw was that Lagos was a vast, sprawling city of 14 million people and we had absolutely no idea where the Taylor family had lived. (The news editor, who had clearly never been to Africa, suggested we tried consulting the electoral roll.)

The flight was much delayed and it was the early hours of Friday by the time we checked into the Ekos hotel. When I stumbled into reception a few hours later for breakfast I discovered we were not the only ones. The *Daily Telegraph* and *Sunday Times* had just arrived in the shape of three friends, Peter Foster with photographer Paul Grover, and Tom Walker, having persuaded the embassy it had been unfair only to give a visa to the *Sunday Telegraph*. Worse, Peter was clutching a fax – the ever-resourceful *Daily Mail* had already found the Taylors' home and done a double-page spread that day.

According to the article, Damilola had lived in a suburb called Isahi where he had attended Luciana school. As we were all headed to the same place we decided to join forces in two cars – and, for some reason I don't remember, forgo breakfast, something I rarely do as on the road you never know when you'll find your next meal.

We set off to the nearest primary school to ask if they knew Luciana school. The secretary had never heard of it nor of anywhere called Isahi. I called a friend on the *Nigerian Guardian* and he hadn't heard of it either. We bought a map but there was no district with that name or anything similar.

Peter suggested we look in the phone directory. Finding a phone book in Lagos is easier said than done. We tried the hotel, and various shops, but no one had one. Eventually we went to the headquarters of the telephone company, Nitel. They could only produce a directory from 1990. There was no Luciana school listed. Nor had anyone there heard of Isahi.

I was starting to become suspicious of the *Mail* article. One of the schools had told us all schools must be registered so we decided to go to the Education Ministry to consult the list, even though we knew this probably meant getting dragged into African bureaucracy.

It was worse than I feared. The Lagos traffic meant it took hours to get there, then, when we arrived, the Director of Private Education said we could only have the list if we had the permission of the Deputy Undersecretary. The Deputy Undersecretary said we needed the agreement of the Permanent Undersecretary, a stern woman who said such a request needed letters from our editors and two weeks' notice. We explained we only had that day but to no avail. 'Why are people in Britain so interested in the death of one small boy?' she asked, suspiciously. 'Hundreds of boys die here every day.'

I had spent enough time battling Third World bureaucracy to know we were heading nowhere, so I slipped outside to her assistant and asked who actually had the list of private schools. The Statistics Division on the fifth floor, she replied. I ran up the stairs into the room, clutching a wad of notes and announced, 'I've come to buy a copy of the list of schools, how much is it?' The man quickly got the idea and told me I could have it for 200 naira (about £1). I produced 500, at which point he said he'd just remembered the price had gone up to 1,000. It was still a bargain.

Back downstairs the others were still arguing and trying to arrange faxes from editors. Waving the prized list, I beckoned them out to the car park. So intent was I on scanning it for Luciana school – and so pleased with myself – that I did not look where I was going. There was a sickening crack, so loud that people passing by turned round. I had walked straight into a pothole deep enough for a small child to be lost in, and my ankle had turned right over. Within moments it had swollen to the size of a melon.

The knife-like pain, combined with the sweltering heat and lack of sleep and breakfast, made me feel faint and I had to lean against a parked car. This being Africa, a small crowd gathered. A man in a pinstriped suit pulled off my shoe and from out of his pocket whipped a small tin of Temple of Heaven balm with which he started massaging my ankle. It smelt revolting. Another man somehow produced an ice pack. But the swelling didn't go down and gentlemanly Tom had to half carry me to the car.

We headed off to the nearby International Hotel to discuss strategy. What with the size of my ankle and the sound it had made, we all assumed it was broken. But time was ticking away and the last thing I wanted to do was go to a hospital, particularly in Lagos. The bad news was that, after all that, Luciana school was not even on the list, which left us with precisely no leads.

My contact at the *Nigerian Guardian* thought we should try going to Isoshi, suggesting that perhaps the *Mail* had got the name wrong. This seemed plausible so we set off through another hour of traffic. When we finally got there it looked quite promising, with sandy streets and lots of children coming out of school in neat uniforms as the *Mail* had described. But no one had heard of Luciana school or Damilola Taylor. We had to keep explaining the story to bemused locals who, like the Permanent Undersecretary of Education, could not understand why people in Britain cared about the death of one small African boy.

Isoshi was ruled out so we headed back downtown. Damilola's mother, Gloria, had worked as a clerk for Union Bank of Nigeria. Maybe, just maybe, someone there would know where they lived. Our *Daily Telegraph* colleagues thought we were clutching at straws and decided to go to the BBC bureau to phone their desk. Justin went with them so he could call our office as our UK mobile phones did not work.

Meanwhile, Tom and I braved more traffic to get to the Union Bank tower. By this time my ankle was agony. Tom produced some butterscotch for me to suck as neither of us had any painkillers. I was starving as the only food we'd had was a sugary Coke and a fried banana bought from a stall. I stayed in the taxi while he went in to inquire.

He came back downcast. Gloria Taylor hadn't worked there and nobody knew her. All we could think of was to head off to another suburb where she was rumoured to have worked. I needed to find a phone to let Justin know, so Tom helped me up the steps back into the bank. An enormous lady with her hair pulled back in a small, neat bun was coming out.

'Oh dear, oh dear, what have you done?' she exclaimed.

'I fell in a hole.'

'So sorry,' she said. 'You must come to our clinic.'

We were whisked up to the sixth floor only to find the clinic closed. But the kind lady found some bandage and more magic balm, sat me down and tightly bandaged my foot, which hurt like hell. Grimacing, I hopped back to the lifts. Then the strangest thing happened. Also standing waiting was a woman so pregnant that she looked as if she was about to give birth. In her hand she was holding up a photocopied sheet as if she meant us to see it.

Tom and I both caught sight of it at the same time and looked at each other in astonishment. The paper was a map of a place on which was clearly written Isashi Road, just one letter different from the *Mail*'s Isahi.

'Excuse me,' I asked, 'are you from that place?'

'Yes,' she replied, looking surprised.

'Is it called Isashi?'

'Yes.'

'Does it have a school called Luciana school?'

'Yes, it's just round the corner from my house.'

We couldn't believe it. Discovering that she was about to catch a series of three buses to get back there, we offered her a lift. If she had refused we would have kidnapped her. She insisted on bringing her friend, a banker in a suit, so all four of us squashed into the back of our yellow taxi and set off.

It was about 5.30 p.m. and rush hour but the pregnant lady assured us it was only an hour or so to Isashi. That was African time. The traffic out of the city was barely at walking pace, so packed was the highway. Alongside us were buses so crammed that passengers were crouched on the roof and squeezed out of the windows.

In and out of the traffic weaved hundreds of small boys younger even than Damilola, coming to the car windows offering everything from clothes pegs to shower curtains, garden shears to toilet rolls. You could literally sit in your car and do your shopping, though not buy the one thing I wanted – a wedding card for my friends, Mark and Caroline. My request sent them all scurrying about in search of one.

The sun was setting as we turned off the Benin road and I began looking at my watch. By 7.30 p.m. we were at a complete standstill. Cars had apparently changed their minds about where they were going midway and turned around, blocking traffic in both directions. I'd never seen anything like it. No one seemed to have a clue how to get out. Then we heard gunfire. 'Highway robbers,' said our driver. It was completely dark and, trapped inside our car, Tom and I began to feel rather vulnerable as the only white people in sight.

I couldn't believe that the pregnant lady and the banker did this journey to work and back every day, and by three buses, so it was presumably even slower.

It was almost 9 p.m. when we finally arrived in Isashi. I was nearly in tears, wondering how I was ever going to catch the 11.50 p.m. flight to London to be back in time for the wedding. The area had no electricity so we could not see much. But luck was on our side. Our pregnant passenger guided us up a side street and outside the white walls of Luciana school. A guard appeared and told us the headmistress lived next door.

My foot felt like a ton weight but I hopped out of the car and into the school where the headmistress and her husband agreed to talk. It was a short interview as I had one eye on the clock and was standing on one leg. They were very helpful, however, and told us that the best friend of Damilola's father lived round the corner. We piled into their jeep, still with the pregnant lady and the banker in tow. The friend of the family had the key to the Taylors' house so took us inside. It was a pleasant house, no comparison to the squalid Peckham council flat. I was exhausted so collapsed on the sofa and rather imperiously demanded they bring things over, such as a large framed photo of Damilola and one of his school friends.

I rudely rushed the interviews, neglecting all the usual niceties, and we were out of Isashi by about 10.20 p.m., waving farewell to our baffled friends from the bank. I'd got the story; all I needed was to catch the flight. Once again we quickly got trapped in one of the world's worst traffic jams. The minutes were ticking by and I was losing hope. Eventually, I got the driver to ask one of the many people milling around if they knew a short cut to the airport. A young man jumped in and led us through a warren of dark alleys, the middle of a market and across some farmland. It did occur to me that he could be leading us to some remote spot in order to rob us, but instead he led us on to the airport road. The wad of naira I gave him was well worth it.

We got to the airport at 11.30 p.m., just twenty minutes before the flight. The counters were already closed. I imagined the shocked silence in church the next morning as no one appeared to do the reading. I was lucky to be with Tom, who was one of the nicest correspondents you could hope to meet on the road. Although he was from a rival paper and also needed to file, he had become as determined as I was that I would make the wedding. From somewhere he rustled up Victor, the BA manager. Fortunately the *Sunday Telegraph* had been in touch to warn I'd had an accident. But there was an unforeseen problem. They needed a doctor's certificate to allow me to fly. I couldn't believe it. 'It's only my foot,' I wailed. 'I'm not ill.' Finally, Victor said that if I could get to the gate before the doors closed then I could fly. A wheelchair was summoned. I jumped in.

We'd gone about twenty metres when the lady pushing it stopped. 'Madam, there's a problem,' she said.

'What now?'

'The tyres are flat.'

I got out and started hopping manically, then another wheelchair appeared. This was little better. The lady pushing it was wearing stilettos she could hardly walk in and tottered in tiny steps like a Japanese geisha. Victor appeared and exhorted her to hurry. We got to the door of the aircraft just as it was closing. The stiletto woman made a final push and I was in.

Damilola thought he was coming to a better life in England – how wrong he was
Sunday Telegraph, 3 December 2000

IN THE SMALL community of Isashi village on the dusty western edge of Lagos, life in England is seen as a far-off dream – a green and pleasant land where there is always running water and electricity (Isashi has had none for the past three months), where people are always polite, doff their hats and stop for tea at four in the afternoon, and where there are nice clean trains, and buses driving along tree-lined roads with no traffic jams.

So in August, when 10-year-old Damilola Taylor told his friends and teachers that he was going to London to live, they were envious. 'Sometimes, when we have a generator, we watch TV programmes like *Sesame Street* and see the lives and toys that children have in England and America,' said his friend David Akbapot. 'It is like another world.'

Lucy Ikioda, the headmistress of Luciana school, where Damilola studied, was delighted. 'England is a fantasy land to the children. I thought Dami would have access to so many things that he did not have here, that he could be a doctor or something respected. I told him that one of these days when I get to England you can help me out, look after your old teacher who once looked after you.'

That within four months Damilola would be found bleeding to death in a dingy stairwell of a half-derelict estate which would not be out of place in central Lagos, having been stabbed probably by schoolmates, has horrified the people of Isashi and shattered their rosy vision of England.

'We just don't understand,' said Mrs Ikioda, who wept when her husband told her the news. 'Nigeria is one of the most dangerous countries in the world and England the safest. But such a thing could not happen here. I read that Dami dragged himself a hundred yards bleeding, but no one came to help. Where were his neighbours? Why were his teachers letting him walk dangerous ways home? What are the schools doing there that children do not learn discipline and respect for each other?'

Such questions might seem odd coming from a resident of a city where nothing works, the heat and humidity are relentless, corruption is so endemic that I once had to bribe a bellboy for a bulb to have light in the room of my five-star hotel, and violent death is common.

Friday's newspapers reflected a typical day in the Nigerian capital. Fifty people killed in an oil pipeline explosion that occurred when they were collecting oil for fuel from a leak. Two people killed and scores injured when a minibus ploughed into a crowd and a gang called the Area Boys started shooting. Such incidents – along with diseases such as cholera, malaria and typhoid – mean that life expectancy is less than 50.

However, Nigeria – even Lagos, with its population of 14 million – has a sense of community long lost in England. In Isashi, everyone helps each other when times are hard, dropping over some rice and goat meat for supper, and looking after each other's children. Almost everybody seems to go to church – a growth industry in Nigeria, with numerous Pentecostal churches springing up in every neighbourhood, boasting names such as Feed My Sheep and Operation Naked the Devil.

While foreigners are warned to stay off the roads at night – on the way to Isashi I saw people held up at gunpoint while stuck in their cars in a traffic jam – children play safely in the dark streets. Not with Sony PlayStations or Pokémon cards, but with cars and lorries that they have cleverly crafted from wire and bottle tops.

Benson Owoturu, a builder who constructed the Taylors' bungalow in Isashi and has been the best friend of Damilola's father, Richard, for twenty-five years, recalled: 'It's almost exactly a year since Damilola's tenth birthday party on 7 December. There were hundreds of people, a live band and whole goats on the barbecue. Look, everyone got gifts.' He shows me a pink plastic mug printed: 'Hurray! Damilola Taylor Is 10. Wishing You More Prosperous Years Ahead.'

Mr Owoturu took me next door into the house that the Taylors planned to come back to after receiving medical treatment for the epilepsy of Beme, their eldest daughter, so that she could be married off. This was the reason why Mrs Taylor took her three children to London.

It is a comfortable place, with neatly trimmed conifers in the garden, large rooms with black-and-white tiled floors and ceiling fans to slowly stir the heavy air. On the terracotta painted walls are a selection of framed photographs of the wedding of Richard and Gloria Taylor and of their children, including several of their youngest, Damilola – the boy whom his headmistress remembers as 'lovable' and whose favourite book was *Cinderella*. Even as a baby, he had that shy, beseeching smile that was all over British newspapers last week as the image of what has gone wrong with our society.

From the house, Damilola had only to walk two streets away to enter the green gates of Luciana school, passing its small playground with a Donald Duck slide under a palm tree, to be in morning assembly at 7.45 a.m.

Painted white and Mediterranean blue, the walls are dotted with slogans such as 'Create Time Now to Train Your Children and You Will Have Peace For Ever'. Any child ten minutes late is caned – Mrs Ikioda is a stern disciplinarian. 'All my children are well behaved,' she explains. 'That's the job of a school – to make sure that they are properly trained.'

It is easy to see why the people of Isashi might think that England offers a better life. Luciana school might look nice but, with fees of only 1,500 naira (£10) a term for its 200 pupils, it cannot afford computers, telephones or teaching aids any more sophisticated than a blackboard and a poster of the digestive system.

The local shops consist of one shack selling yams, rice, unrefrigerated meat and condensed milk for treats. The village has no roads, only sandy tracks. The local buses look as if they started life on a scrapheap. Their bodywork is rusted, all the seats torn out, windows broken; radiator grilles hang off, engines clank and they have been painted with slogans such as 'Put Your Faith in God'.

The last train in Lagos ran some fifteen years ago. Despite being the world's sixth-biggest oil producer, Nigeria has constant fuel shortages and there are mile-long queues to buy canfuls on the black market.

The journey to Lagos from Isashi, a trip that Damilola's mother Gloria made every day to reach her job as a manager at the Union Bank, means taking three buses. The day that I made the trip by car, it took four hours because of the 'go-slow', as traffic jams are known locally: cars were attempting to do U-turns, blocking the whole road. For such a commute, people must leave home at 6 a.m., often not returning before 10 p.m.

And, while children are prized in Nigerian society, theirs can be an extremely tough life. The highways are thronged with children as young as 6 selling to captive customers in gridlocked cars everything from Venetian blinds and apples on strings to Michael Bolton CDs.

Even so, when they dream of England, they do not dream of ending up in another hellhole 3,000 miles away.

On the way to Isashi, sitting in what seemed like the Perfect Traffic Jam in which nobody could move, inhaling carbon monoxide and hearing gunshots, the only white woman amid thousands of cars, I felt the same unease that I had experienced two nights earlier.

Yet then I was in south-east London, only a few miles from where I had grown up. North Peckham by night is a menacing place. Few streetlamps work, teenagers in hooded sweatshirts hang about on corners sizing up passers-by, BMWs with blacked-out windows park in dark spots for drug deals, receivers hang uselessly from broken telephone boxes, and everybody avoids eye contact.

It is everyone out for themselves. Even in the brighter lights of Peckham High Street, with its award-winning library, no one is safe. A month ago, there was a shootout at Chicago's nightclub with youths firing Uzi sub-machine-guns across the room.

St Briavels Court, where Damilola's family moved in August, sounds like the sort of place that should have small almshouses with rose-covered trellises. Instead, it is a grim block daubed with graffiti, all the ground-floor windows boarded up. Inside, past the lift that has been out of order for longer than anyone can remember, the corners reeking of urine, the ceilings black with mould, and the slimy walls, four flights of stairs lead to number 32 where the Taylors live.

Each flight ends in a dark walkway, lit by flickering forty-watt bulbs, in which shadowy figures lurk – the squatters who have moved into the abandoned apartments. When one of them, with long, matted hair, suddenly appeared from a door revealing a room with no electricity – only a candle – a figure huddled in a corner and two syringes on the floor, I grasped my bag as tightly as I would in an African city. Down one corridor, firefighters were trying to put out flames caused by a dropped cigarette.

As a foreign correspondent who has spent the past fourteen years reporting mainly on Third World countries and eleven years living in them, I found it hard to believe that such a dismal place existed on my own doorstep. I have been to numerous places such as Damilola's village of Isashi and far worse in Africa almost unblinkingly, yet in England my own middle-class existence had fooled me into thinking that people in my country all lived better.

Was the spacious bungalow in the sandy village of palm trees and daily sunshine, where children and chickens run free, really a worse place to live than this dingy flat with peeling paint and not a green leaf in sight, where Damilola had to sleep on the sofa?

Politicians will say that north Peckham is changing. Built in the 1960s and described by the Bishop of Southwark as one of the worst housing estates in Europe, the five blocks are gradually being demolished in a £260 million project, to be replaced with so-called 'family-friendly' units with a nursery, parks and a youth centre.

But, for Damilola, it is too late. Michelle, the tenants' representative, whose mother lives below the Taylors, showed me the black burn mark round the letter box where someone had thrown in a lighted rag. 'Every evening we collect my mum from here because it is too dangerous to be here at night,' she said. 'You in the media and the politicians will all forget us soon.'

I hope not. It's hard to forget that appealing little face in the photographs. I might complain about commuting and the English rain, but, with the arrogance of most western foreign correspondents, I had always assumed that life in my country was superior to most places that I had reported on. Damilola's death forced me to confront realities about my own country that I never dreamt existed.

I did get to the church just before the bride, the above article written on the plane at speed. There was no time to explain to my friends as I hopped up to the lectern to read the lesson. It was a wonderful wedding with lots of champagne to dull the pain. When I finally got to casualty that evening, at University College Hospital, they told me there was an eight-hour wait. I couldn't help wondering whether it would have been that long in Lagos.

A Short Arrest in the Ivory Coast

It was Easter Monday and I was enjoying a rare day at home with my
husband and baby before flying out the next evening to Pakistan when
the news came in that a ship was sailing round West Africa bearing a
cargo of 'child slaves'. A spokesperson for Unicef was saying that there
were at least 100 children and perhaps as many as 250 on board and
they had been sold by their parents for as little as £10. The ship had left
Benin three weeks before but not been allowed to dock by officials in
Gabon and Cameroon. The crew were thought to be running so short
of food and water that some children may have been thrown over-
board.

It was a horrific image. Worse, the children were thought to have
been bought to work on cocoa plantations harvesting the cocoa beans
that had gone into many of our Easter eggs.

'Forget Pakistan. Find chocolate slaves forthwith' came the message
from Con Coughlin, the *Sunday Telegraph* managing editor.

This was easier said than done. Rounds of phone calls to aid agency
press officers established that Ivory Coast would be the best place to
look as it was the largest exporter of cocoa beans and had the most
children working on cocoa plantations. I phoned the travel office to
cancel Islamabad and book Abidjan. As usual they reacted as if I were
randomly switching continents just to spite them. There was a flight
first thing on Wednesday, which gave me a day to get visas.

I was at the embassy the moment it opened the next morning along
with Justin Sutcliffe, the photographer with whom I had gone to Lagos.
You can tell a lot about a country from its London embassy – the

Russian you cannot get near; at the Nigerian anything is possible with
a spot of 'dash'; the Brazilians have great parties; while the first time I
went to the Afghan embassy the door handle came off in my hand.
The embassy of Côte d'Ivoire was grandly situated in Belgravia but the
paint was peeling and there was an air of Gallic sullenness over all the
staff.

We did not of course say we wanted to report on child slaves but
muttered something about the regional situation. No one was working
in our office on the Tuesday as the day before had been a holiday, so I
had written my own official letter forging the foreign editor's signature
and requesting an immediate visa.

Mrs Tuaré, the visa officer, looked at us in a way that clearly said *zut
alors*. It would, she said, take 'a minimum of a week' to issue a visa.
'Anyway, first you need an invitation from someone in Côte d'Ivoire to
visit,' she said.

'But I don't know anyone there,' I replied.

'Doesn't the *Sunday Telegraph* have an office in Abidjan?' she asked
in apparent astonishment.

Well, no.

We were at an impasse.

After a series of increasingly desperate phone calls to anyone I could
think of who might know someone in the Ivory Coast, I finally got
through to an adviser at the Information Ministry. He agreed to send
an invitation letter as long as my editor sent him an explanatory fax.
There was still no one in the *Sunday Telegraph* office so I called my
long-suffering husband who faxed the ministry from home pretending
to be my editor. The adviser then faxed the promised invitation but that
still didn't satisfy Mrs Tuaré.

'The letter is addressed to the Ambassador, not to me,' she said
triumphantly.

At this point I lost patience. We were booked to fly first thing the
next morning. I made it clear to Mrs Tuaré that we were never going to
leave her office. Finally at 4.30 p.m., just before the embassy closed, she
stamped the visa angrily into our passports.

I rushed home to pack. Paulo had picked Lourenço up from nursery.
'God knows what kind of mum he thinks I am,' I wrote in my diary in

between mashing carrot and chicken for his tea. 'He says "bye bye" every time I walk into the room.'

It was Wednesday evening when Justin and I flew into Abidjan. As usual in West Africa we had to fight our way through a swarming multitude wanting to change our money, carry our cases and find us taxis before we could go through the door into the steamy African night.

I had arranged to meet a priest involved in rescuing child slaves but had not realised how rusty my French was. I was pretty sure I could still write an essay on Marie-Claude and Philippe going shopping, but discussions about child slavery were not on my O-level syllabus. After greeting him with a breezy '*bonsoir*', I was reduced to asking, '*Où sont les enfants du chocolat?*'

All was not lost. By a complete fluke we woke the next morning to find that a conference on child slavery was taking place at our hotel. Mostly this seemed to involve people selling things; I bought a painted wooden picture after the man said the money would be used to buy an oven for orphaned children.

'Shopping the world?' asked Justin, raising his eyebrows. We were interrupted by a helpful man called Ackebo Felix from Unicef. Along with a mass of information, he gave me the number of a Mr Drissa who helped repatriate chocolate slaves brought from Mali and was apparently the key contact.

We did not manage to get through to Mr Drissa but I was anxious to be on the road so we found a car and an interpreter and set off north towards Daloa, in central Ivory Coast, where he was based. The wide highway which had so impressed us quickly petered out into mud.

About four hours later, as darkness was falling, we suddenly found ourselves on another highway – eight lanes wide and lined with hundreds of streetlights, most of which weren't working. The only traffic was us and two other cars. Looming ahead was something that looked like a giant white boiled egg suspended in the sky. We had reached Yamoussoukro, the country's bizarre capital. What we could see was the dome of a vast basilica; there was also a golf course, a revolving restaurant and a massive palace complex surrounded by a moat of man-eating crocodiles.

Kamara, our driver, had got carried away by the highway and when it turned back into mud hit a pothole at such speed that the front tyre exploded. He took so long trying to change it that Justin lost patience and did it himself.

The burst tyre meant it was almost midnight by the time we got to Daloa. Hôtel Les Ambassadeurs was less grand than it sounds. My journal notes: 'Everything is very brown and there are ants everywhere. The staff are sulky and the restaurant very firmly *fermé*. I turned on the shower and the thinnest trickle of brown water came out. I'd just soaped myself when it stopped altogether.' It was at that point that my phone beeped. It was a message from the foreign desk. 'Slave ship docked. Not hundred of kids but twenty-seven. Maybe not slaves at all.'

I thought nothing more could go wrong but, the following morning, Mr Drissa was still not answering his phone. Somehow by the end of that day we needed to have found children in bondage on cocoa plantations and filed the story. I couldn't quite imagine phoning Con and telling him I had gone all that way and not managed to find any. 'Well, it's only Friday,' I said to Justin.

At least there were fresh croissants for breakfast – there is some advantage to being colonised by the French. I had almost given up on the elusive Mr Drissa. Then just after nine, as we were setting off on our own, his phone unexpectedly answered. He told me he was several hours away from us on a plantation and suggested we met up on Monday.

'You don't quite understand…' I replied.

This is Wambi Bakayoko, who is 15. He is a chocolate slave. Last year he was sold to a plantation owner for £37.50 – what the average Briton spends on chocolate in just seven months
Sunday Telegraph, 22 April 2001

HOME FOR 15-year-old Wambi Bakayoko is a small mud-walled cell with no windows. His clothes – a Bayern Munich jersey, a faded blue T-shirt, a pair of yellow trousers, some ragged brown trousers – hang on a wooden beam above the straw pallet on which he sleeps. His only other possessions are half a bar of soap, a towel, an enamel dish and mug, and an almost empty tin of Nescafé.

As with many African children, Wambi, one of a family of fourteen from Mali, has worked since he was 8 and did not have great expectations from life. He expected more than this, however – a year ago, Wambi was tricked into becoming a child slave.

From 6 a.m. to sundown, he labours on a small cocoa plantation in Bediala in central Ivory Coast, hacking weeds with a machete or chopping down cocoa pods, with only a short break for a lunch of yam porridge.

The plantation is more than two hours' drive down a muddy track from the nearest hard road, followed by a mile-long walk through knife-edged grasses which slash at the skin. We are told we must stay quiet because if the owner sees us he may turn violent.

There are more than a hundred children working in this patchwork of plantations but, dwarfed by the cocoa bushes, they are not visible at first. The landscape is stunning: the jungle is lush, the earth rich red, and the green leaves of the cocoa bushes glint in the afternoon sun.

Wambi notices none of this. Pulling back the leaves of the cocoa bushes and disentangling their yellow pods is an endless task. He wears a green woollen hat to keep the swarms of insects from biting his head and the relentless humidity makes his limbs slow and heavy. His hands are swollen and calloused, like those of a labourer three times his age.

Sold to the plantation owner for 37,500 local francs (£37.50) – the amount that the average person in Britain spends on chocolate in seven months – Wambi cannot run away because he has no money, speaks Malenki not the local French patois, and the owner has his identity papers.

Known by campaigners as 'chocolate slaves', the US State Department estimates there are 15,000 child slaves on plantations in Ivory Coast. The country is the world's biggest cocoa grower, producing 48 per cent of the global supply and much of the cocoa that ends up in British chocolate. Aged as young as 8, most of the children come from Burkina Faso and Mali, countries so incredibly poor that they view neighbouring Ivory Coast as a wealthy nation.

Their plight was highlighted last week by the search for a suspected child slave boat heading for Benin. Although the vessel was not carrying the 250 children initially reported to be aboard, around 30 unaccompanied children were taken ashore when it docked.

The horrifying cycle into which the children are locked is particularly shocking in West Africa, a region which saw millions of men, women and children sent from the Slave Coast to the Americas to work on plantations between the sixteenth and nineteenth centuries.

A map produced by the United Nations Children's Fund (Unicef) shows a complex web of arrows depicting child-trafficking routes in the region. Most of those used in slavery or bonded labour come from Mali, Benin, Burkina Faso and Togo; the main destinations are Ivory Coast and Nigeria (both relatively richer) as well as Ghana, which both sells and receives children. Girls as young as 8 are traded to become domestic servants – in Abidjan there is still a slave market – while the boys end up in mines, on plantations and in fishing boats.

Some are lured by false promises, some are sold by parents too poor to feed them, others are kidnapped while playing in the streets. 'The selling of people was a scandal hundreds of years ago,' said Mike Dottridge, president of the UK-based organisation Anti-Slavery International. 'That it's happening today with children, and on an even greater scale, is shocking beyond belief.'

Wambi's story is typical. Born in a poor village near Bamako in southern Mali, he started making bricks at an age when European children would still be doing hand paintings in nursery. At 14, he and some friends travelled for a day by bus to the town of Sikasso to seek better pay. When a Malian man 'in a smart suit with a nice car' approached them with tales of fortunes to be made if they went with him to Ivory Coast, it seemed the answer to their dreams. Instead, it was the start of his current ordeal.

'He lied to us,' said Wambi. 'We believed him because we had heard that Ivory Coast is so rich it has roads as wide as seas and a church the size of a city, and I thought I would make so much money that I could buy clothes for my parents and brothers and sisters and they would be so proud. We paid him 9,000 francs [£9] each so the border police let us through. Then he sold us.'

Once across the border, the children were surprised to discover that

Ivory Coast was also poor. (The figures mean little, but the average annual income there is about £350 a year, double the level in his poverty-stricken homeland.) After travelling for a day and a night, they were split up and Wambi was taken to the town of Daloa where he was handed over to another man, a local trafficker. His next stop was the plantation that is now his home-cum-prison.

'I didn't know what to think,' he recalled. 'I was in the middle of nowhere, couldn't speak the language and was expected to do work I had never done before. The first day I cut my leg badly with the machete, it was hot in the fields and insects fell on my head, and my arms were aching so much I couldn't sleep.'

What initially sustained Wambi was the prospect of the £130 promised as wages for the year. But, at the end of the year, the owner explained that after docking the cost of food, medicine and the amount paid for him, there was nothing left, so he must work another year.

While in some cases the children come from homes so poor that just receiving food and shelter on the plantations makes them better off, that is not the case for Wambi. 'My life in Mali was much better than here. My father has ten cows and some land and we ate better. I miss Mali a lot.'

Asked why he does not simply leave, he explained, 'I can't because then I won't get my money and even if I did manage to escape I have no money to get back and, if I did, how could I face my family?' In any case, there is little chance of him raising the £17 for the bus and bribes to get home. On his Fridays off, he sometimes manages to earn 50p for a day's work on other plantations but he uses that to buy soap and coffee. 'If I have any extra, I buy Pecto candies which we suck as medicine for coughs,' he said.

'Wambi's experience is typical,' said Ackebo Felix, an expert on child trafficking with Unicef in Abidjan. 'The children are in a trap. After the first year, the farmer will say, "I have to recoup my expenses so I can't pay you." Then the second year he'll say, "I got less for the crop than I expected, so you must wait another year"; the third he says, "My wife is ill so I have no money."

'So instead of coming here for a year and going home with maybe £200, the children end up here for five or six years and go back with nothing or stay because they don't know anything else. If they try to flee they are caught and beaten to make them understand they are slaves.'

The use of children has increased in recent years because of the collapse in world cocoa prices which last year hit a 27-year low of £570 a tonne, leaving many plantations in financial crisis. One owner explained: 'Children are easier to discipline than adults. They wait and wait and wait and then, at a certain stage, they get fed up and escape and we get new ones.'

Biarra Drissa, secretary of the Mali community in Daloa, who has helped twenty children escape back to Mali, is trying to get another twelve off a cotton plantation where they labour at gunpoint under the master's son. Some sleep in fields and are left to forage for food.

The Ivory Coast government has so far been what one Unicef official described as 'in denial' over the problem. To be fair it has had its own difficulties, after its first military coup, two army mutinies and a flawed election that led to a popular uprising in which up to 400 people died. Another problem for the authorities is that the plantations are usually small, inaccessible and difficult to regulate. However, last week, after the international outcry over the Benin slave ship, Laurent Gbagbo, the Ivorian President, promised to act.

Campaigners emphasise that child slavery is not restricted to cocoa but also exists on coffee and cotton plantations and in domestic labour. Nor do they want the West's chocolate consumers to boycott the product as this could lower prices further.

Guiltily, I told Wambi that I spend more on chocolate a year than his promised annual wage. 'That's just too big for me to imagine,' he said.

————————

I was starting to find stories like this harder to write. When I met children in dire situations, I imagined my own little boy in their place. I felt guilty about all his Baby Gap clothes and cupboards of toys. I wondered if Wambi had ever had a toy or anything new. Probably not. I'd given him all the money I had on me in the hope he could buy himself out, but I knew that wasn't the answer.

Another thing that had changed since becoming a mother was that

I wanted to rush straight home after finishing stories. But back in Abidjan on Sunday we discovered that Air Afrique had gone on strike. No one knew when there would be a flight. At the airport we met the Arsenal player, Kanu, who was on his way back from the African Cup in Sierra Leone when his plane had engine failure and had to make an emergency landing. He too was stuck in Abidjan. With no fixers around he was looking lost and meekly boarded the courtesy bus to a hotel on a flyover with no air conditioning.

At 6.30 a.m. on Monday morning I was woken by my hotel phone ringing. It was someone from the Ministry of Information whom I couldn't understand. At 8 a.m. when I went down for breakfast there was a man waiting in reception. 'We have seen your story,' he said. 'It is interesting but it is not correct. You must make an appointment to see the Minister of Family Affairs.' He gave me two numbers which I duly phoned. Neither worked.

I tried to think of a story to do while we waited for Air Afrique to restart operations. I wanted to go to Niger to meet the Tuareg, who I had heard were not enjoying being nomads any more, but the foreign editor was not keen. Then I remembered something the priest had told me about on our first evening.

£5 for a slave girl with a nervous smile
Sunday Telegraph, 29 April 2001

FOR A MOMENT, I thought that I had stepped into one of those guilt-inspiring etchings in museums all over Africa of nineteenth-century European slave-traders buying up women and children. Only this time, I was the main character. Ranged in front of me, seated on wooden benches under the baking Ivory Coast sun, were row upon row of young African women for sale, eyes lit up at the sight of a white woman, all pleading to be the one I would choose.

This was Abidjan's *marché de jeunes filles* (Market of Young Girls) and for 5,000 Central African francs – about £5 – I could take one home as my very own servant.

Aged between 14 and 30, the girls were dressed in their Sunday best, tight-waisted, large-bottomed suits in bold printed cotton, hair tweaked and plaited into elaborate arrangements, their eyes beseeching like abandoned puppies as they each stood up to be examined. Some giggled nervously. Others simply looked desperate.

Overseeing their sale were four men, slick characters with gold medallions flashing under open-necked shirts, tight jeans, black-and-white brogues, fake gold watches, and leather-covered mobile telephones on their belts.

The market is in the shadow of a highway in the northern suburb of Adjame, next to the affluent residential district of Cocody, where many of the girls may end up working. Each man has about fifteen girls on his books and claims to sell at least five a week. 'You're lucky, madam,' said one of the men with a simpering smile. 'You're a white woman so they all long to go with you because they think you'll treat them better.'

That a white master or mistress would be preferable seemed a sickening irony. Over the years reporting from Africa, I have visited the slave forts on the Ghana coast and seen the desperate scratchings on the walls of the cells where thousands of men, women and children were jammed before being shipped to the Americas; the steamy jungle port of Calabar, one of the principal trading posts; and the large tree at Zanzibar where the slave market was held which inspired David Livingstone to fight against slavery. You get used to feeling shame. But, until going to this market last week, I think I had never appreciated just how humiliating it is for people to be on sale, and my stomach turned as the girls all tried to catch my eye or touch my hand.

In theory, the women are not slaves. 'We're agencies,' insisted one of the traders. 'You pay us to have them but, once you've taken them home, it's up to you if you pay them.'

How much would a decent wage be, I asked? 'Obviously, you would want an experienced one,' he replied. 'She could do all your washing, cleaning, cooking and look after your baby. If you paid her £20 a month, she would be extremely happy.'

He claimed that he would not take a cut of the wages but anti-slavery campaigners, who would like to see the market closed down, insist that this is not true. 'The traders make the girls believe they are their property and, even if you buy one, they are only on loan and must pay the traders to cover their costs,' explained Desire Kuikui, from the Catholic Children's Fund. 'There is little difference from slave-trading of old.'

The Ivorian authorities are so sensitive about the market amid the current international focus on child slavery in West Africa, after the docking in Benin of a boat suspected to have a cargo of child slaves, that when my colleague Justin Sutcliffe started photographing the girls we were arrested.

Surrounded by shouting and drunken police, we were manhandled into a police car and held for five hours in the nearby 27th Precinct police station, accused of being spies. Sutcliffe's film was confiscated and destroyed, apart from one that he had managed to hide, and we were interrogated by a series of officers who kept demanding: 'What is the tenure of your mission?' Describing what had happened as 'a serious incident', they harangued our poor terrified interpreter for letting us go into 'sensitive areas'.

It was an uncomfortable, if not particularly threatening, experience and, as we sweated it out in the oven-like police station with not even a warm Coca-Cola to quench our parched lips, it was hard to get the picture of all those women on the benches out of my head.

Before our arrest, one of the traders had insisted that 'the girls are free to leave here any time'. That may be true but, according to Apolle, a girl with whom I had a snatched conversation, they have nowhere to go. Claiming to be 17, but looking more like 14, she said she had travelled for several days to get to Abidjan from the east of the country. 'I was told by a man that he would employ me in a big department store and train me, but when I got here he left me,' she said. 'Now I have no money to get home and know no one here. My only hope is some nice lady like you buys me.'

More women end up on display at the market every week, coming from all over the country, as well as neighbouring Mali, to the city that styles itself as the Paris of West Africa. At first sight, particularly by night with the glittering lights of the high-rise buildings reflected in the lagoon, Abidjan does look affluent. But, during the past few years, it has become as riddled with unemployment and crime as any West African city and, in the heat of the day, the lagoon stinks.

'This market is a function of the socio-political situation of the country,' said the youngest of the traders.

And perhaps more than anything that is a function of the megalomania of African leaders. Nowhere illustrates that more vividly than Yamoussoukro, the surreal capital of Ivory Coast, created by the late President Félix Houphouët-Boigny out of his home village and renamed after his mother. This city in the middle of nowhere has eight-lane highways but no cars, and lines of motorway lights which long ago lost their bulbs. Oddest of all, though, is the world's tallest church – 170 metres high with 30-metre foundations.

Built in just three years between 1986 and 1989, compared with more than a century for St Peter's in Rome – on which it is modelled – the Basilica de Notre Dame de la Paix cost £200 million and uses marble from Italy and Spain and stained-glass windows from France, as well as French-made lifts to whizz visitors to the top of the dome. It seats 18,000 people but, on a good Sunday, draws just 500 and has absolutely nothing to do with Africa.

At the Abidjan slave market, I recalled the words of the church guide. 'It is nice to have something stunning in our country,' he said. 'But maybe it would be nicer if we didn't have ugly things, too.'

———————————

I often wonder how long we would have stayed in that police station in Abidjan had it not been for a fortuitous call to my mobile phone. I had telephoned the *Sunday Telegraph* to tell them of our plight once it was clear we were not simply going to be warned and relieved of some dollars. I had also called the British embassy who, as always in these cases, sounded as though they wished we did not exist; how I longed sometimes to be an American. I had recently started house-hunting so my mobile kept ringing with estate agents bursting to tell me of 'highly desirable' properties with 'original features'. Edward from Foxtons was only momentarily fazed when I explained I was in a police station in the Ivory Coast and perhaps this was not a good time. *Monsieur l'inspecteur* was getting very cross and threatening to snatch my phone, when it rang again.

It was Michael Daly from the Margaret Mee Foundation at Kew Gardens, phoning to invite me to a conference on the Amazon.

'Michael, it's not really a very good time,' I replied. 'I am under arrest in Abidjan.'

'Côte d'Ivoire!' he exclaimed in stentorian tones. 'I was our last ambassador there. Put me on to them at once.'

'*C'est monsieur l'ambassadeur de l'Angleterre*,' I told the inspector with a little bit of poetic licence. 'He demands to speak to you.'

The inspector went pale and literally stood to attention as he answered. Moments later we were freed.

9/11 – Back to Where It Started

War in Afghanistan 2001

I was on book leave in Portugal, and it was my first day of writing after several months of research in the Amazon, when my sister-in-law telephoned and told me to switch on the television. A plane had flown into the World Trade Center and a thick plume of smoke was rising from one of the twin towers. I stared in grim fascination as over and over again I watched the second plane come from a clear blue sky, smash into the second tower and turn into a fireball.

'Mummy, Mummy, plane crashing!' shouted my son Lourenço. He was just 2, and I had been thinking about giving up the peripatetic life of a foreign correspondent to write books full time so I could be more of a mother. But, as I stayed glued to the television that afternoon, one pundit after another started linking the attack to the al-Qaeda leader Osama bin Laden. Maps of Afghanistan were produced to show where he was hiding. All those years after the battle for Jalalabad, I felt a familiar shivering in my guts. I knew I had to go back.

The Taliban were not granting visas for Afghanistan so Justin and I decided to go to the Pakistani city of Quetta. Not only was it just the other side of the border from Kandahar, where the Taliban were based, but it was also the home of my old friend Hamid Karzai.

There was only one decent hotel, the Serena, and we managed to get rooms just in time. Within days it would be so packed that they were charging journalists $100 a night to sleep in the laundry room.

Just as in my old Pakistan days, the lobby was full of ISI agents in grey *shalwar kameez* and aviator glasses. Pakistan was once again living under a military dictator – General Pervez Musharraf, who had seized power in 1999. We journalists were not allowed out of the hotel without a policeman 'for your safety' and had to sign a disclaimer accepting 'all life risk'. There was no way my best Afghan contacts were going to talk with a Pakistani policeman present so I was constantly trying to shake mine off. Eventually, I discovered that if I went into the Fuji photo shop just off Jinnah Road, I could escape via a back exit that led on to a market which I could walk through and jump into a friend's waiting car.

The Karzai house was in Satellite Town, the area of Quetta where many Afghan refugees lived, and was always crowded with tribal elders sitting cross-legged on the floor munching at sugared almonds from little bowls. Since 9/11 it had also become the focus of reporters, diplomats and CIA agents. This was extremely galling for Hamid, who had spent years trying to get officials in London and Washington to listen to his warnings that his country was being taken over by terrorists. 'None of this need ever have happened,' he would complain.

Days were spent interviewing tribal leaders and Afghan commanders but curfew meant evenings had to be spent back at the Serena. The manager did his best with a nightly barbecue in the orchard of lamb *saji*, leg of lamb rotating on an enormous skewer, washed down by fresh apple or pomegranate juice. However, sitting under the stars, with the sound of bubbling water in the little channels criss-crossing the orchard, began to lose its charm as the weeks went by waiting for war.

There was already an autumn nip in the air when one night Karzai's nephew, Jamil, joined me in the orchard for dinner. He was accompanied by three men who, it turned out, had defected from the Taliban. One in particular had a horrifying story.

I was one of the Taliban's torturers
Sunday Telegraph, 30 September 2001

'YOU MUST BECOME so notorious for bad things that when you come into an area people will tremble in their sandals. Anyone can do beatings and starve people. I want your unit to find new ways of torture so terrible that the screams will frighten even crows from their nests and if the person survives he will never again have a night's sleep.'

These were the instructions of the commandant of the Taliban secret police to his new recruits. For more than three years one of those recruits, Hafiz Sadiqulla Hassani, ruthlessly carried out his orders. But sickened by the atrocities that he was forced to commit, last week he defected to Pakistan, joining a growing number of Taliban officials who are escaping across the border.

Mr Hassani has the pinched face and restless hands of a man whose night hours are as haunted as any of his victims'. Now aged 30, he does not, however, fit the militant Islamic stereotype usually associated with the Taliban.

Married with a wife and 1-year-old daughter, he holds a degree in business studies, having been educated in Pakistan, where he grew up as a refugee while his father and elder brothers fought in the jihad against the Russians. His family was well-off, owning land and property in Kandahar to which they returned after the war.

'Like many people, I did not become a Talib by choice,' he explained. 'In early 1998 I was working as an accountant here in Quetta when I heard that my grandfather – who was 85 – had been arrested by the Taliban in Kandahar and was being badly beaten. They would only release him if he provided a member of his family as a conscript, so I had to go.'

At first Mr Hassani was impressed by the Taliban. 'It had been a crazy situation after the Russians left; the country was divided by warring groups all fighting each other. In Kandahar warlords were selling everything, kidnapping young girls and boys, robbing people, and the Taliban seemed like good people who brought law and order.'

So he became a Taliban 'volunteer', assigned to the secret police. Many of his friends also joined up, as landowners in Kandahar were threatened that they must either ally themselves with the Taliban or lose their property. Others were bribed to join with money given to the Taliban by drug smugglers, as Afghanistan became the world's largest producer of heroin.

At first, Mr Hassani's job was to patrol the streets at night looking for thieves and signs of subversion. However, as the Taliban leadership began issuing more and more extreme edicts, his duties changed.

Instead of just searching for criminals, the night patrols were instructed to seek out people watching videos, playing cards or, bizarrely, keeping caged birds. Men whose beards were shorter than a clenched fist were to be arrested, as was any woman who dared venture outside her house. Even owning a kite became a criminal offence.

The state of terror spread by the Taliban was so pervasive that it began to seem as if the whole country was spying on each other. 'As we drove around at night with our guns, local people would come to us and say there's someone watching a video in this house or some men playing cards in that house,' he said.

'Basically any form of pleasure was outlawed,' he continued, 'and if we found people doing any of these things we would beat them with staves soaked in water – like a knife cutting through meat – until the room ran with their blood or their spines snapped. Then we would leave them with no food or water in rooms filled with insects until they died.

'We always tried to do different things: we would stand some prisoners on their heads to sleep, hang others upside down with their legs tied together. We would stretch out the arms of others and nail them to posts like crucifixions. Sometimes we would throw bread to them to make them crawl. Then I would write the report to our commanding officer so he could see how innovative we had been.'

Here, in the stillness of an orchard in Quetta, sipping green tea as the sun goes down, Mr Hassani finds it hard to explain how he could have done such things. 'We Afghans have grown too used to violence' is all he can offer. 'We have lost 1.5 million people. All of us have brothers and fathers up there.'

After Kandahar, he was put in charge of secret police cells in the towns of Ghazni and then Herat, a beautiful Persian city in western Afghanistan that had suffered greatly during the Soviet occupation and had been one of the last places to fall to the Taliban. Herat had always been a relatively liberal place where women would dance at weddings and many girls went to school – but the Taliban were determined to end all that. Mr Hassani and his men were told to be particularly cruel to Heratis, who were Persian-speaking, unlike the Pashto-speaking Taliban.

It was his experience there that made Mr Hassani determined to do whatever he could to let the world know what was happening in Afghanistan. 'When I was in Herat, after the capture of Mazar-i-Sharif in August 1998, truckloads of Hazara people were driven into the square,' he said. 'There were 450 prisoners, mostly women and children, herded into three metal trucks. It was baking hot, maybe 50°C, and they had no food or water. They were gasping and many had fainted but we were told not to let them have anything or let them out for the toilet. We kept them in that square for two days.

'Maybe the worst thing I saw,' he said, 'was while on duty in Kandahar jail. There was a man beaten so much, such a pulp of skin and blood, that it was impossible to tell if he was dressed or not. Every time he fell unconscious, we rubbed salt into his wounds.

'Nowhere else in the world has such barbarity and cruelty as in Afghanistan. At that time I swore an oath that I will devote myself to the Afghan people and telling the world what is happening.'

His plans to escape were thwarted when he was appointed as a bodyguard for Mullah Omar because he comes from the same Ghilzai tribe. 'He's medium height, slightly fat, with an artificial green eye which doesn't move, and he'd sit on a bed issuing instructions and handing out dollars from a tin trunk,' said Mr Hassani. 'He doesn't say much, which is just as well as he's a very stupid man. He knows only how to write his name "Omar".'

Mr Hassani's contact with the Taliban leadership made him more and more disillusioned. 'It is the first time in Afghanistan's history that the lower classes are governing and by force. There are no educated people in this administration – they are all totally backward and illiterate. They have no idea of the history of the country and although they call themselves mullahs they have no idea of Islam. Nowhere does it say men must have beards or women cannot be educated; in fact, the Koran says people must seek education.'

He became convinced that the Taliban were not really in control. 'We laughed when we heard the Americans asking Mullah Omar to hand over Osama bin Laden,' he said. 'The Americans are crazy. It is

Osama bin Laden who can hand over Mullah Omar – not the other way round.'

While in Kandahar, he often saw bin Laden in a convoy of Toyota Land Cruisers, all with darkened windows and festooned with radio antennae. 'They would whizz through the town, seven or eight cars at a time. His guards were all Arabs and very tall people, or Sudanese with curly hair.'

He was on guard duty when bin Laden joined Mullah Omar for a bird shoot on his estate. 'They seemed to get on well,' he said. 'They would go fishing – with grenades.'

The Arabs, said Mr Hassani, have taken de facto control of his country. 'In my last days in the Taliban, the Arabs were so in control that even when we were eating they were saying you must eat this amount. All important places in Kandahar are under Arab control – the airport, military courts, tank command.'

Twice he attended Taliban training camps and on both occasions they were run by Arabs as well as Pakistanis. 'The first one I went to lasted ten days in the Yellow Desert in Helmand Province, a place where the Saudi princes used to hunt, so it has its own airport. It was incredibly well guarded and there were many Pakistanis there, both students from religious schools and military instructors. The Taliban is full of Pakistanis.'

He was told that if he died while fighting under the white flag of the Taliban, he and his family would go to paradise. Soldiers were given blank marriage certificates signed by a mullah and encouraged to 'take wives' during battle, basically a licence to rape.

When Mr Hassani was sent to the front line in Bagram, north of Kabul, a few months ago, he saw a chance to escape. 'We were sixty-two friends and our line was attacked by the Northern Alliance and they almost defeated us. Many of my friends were killed and we didn't know who was fighting who; there was killing from behind and in front. Our commanders fled in cars, leaving us behind.

'We left, running all night, but then came to a line of Arabs who arrested us and took us back to the front. One night last month I was on watch and saw a truck full of sheep and goats, so I jumped in and escaped. I got back to Kandahar but Taliban spies saw me and I was arrested. Luckily I have relatives who are high-ranking Taliban members so they helped me get out, and eventually I escaped to Quetta to my wife and daughter.

'I think many in the Taliban would like to escape. The country is starving and joining is the only way to get food and keep your land. Otherwise there is a lot of hatred. I hate both what it does and what it turned me into.'

The following week, on 8 October, the bombing started. It was weird lying on my comfortable bed in the Serena watching CNN show the Pentagon footage of B-52s taking off on their bombing raids. The pictures were green and looked like a video game but the targets they were blowing up were real and just across the border.

The start of the bombing provoked anti-American riots in Quetta. A cinema showing Antonio Banderas in *Desperado* was torched, the city's only cashpoint was ripped out of the wall, and rocks were thrown over the hotel wall into the swimming pool. Police had to use tear gas to disperse the rioters, which gave ISI the excuse to lock us in altogether. Two hundred journalists locked into a hotel with no alcohol is not a good combination. A BBC crew rigged up their satellite so we could listen to Radio 5 Live's commentary on England's crucial World Cup qualifier against Greece. We sat on the floor of a corridor and cheered Beckham's goal but it was not much of a distraction. Some of the photographers were so stir-crazy that they tried to climb out over the walls.

Even when ISI allowed us out of the hotel, it was frustrating trying to report on a war so near but where we could not get in or talk to the people. All we could do was interview refugees fleeing the bombing.

I spent much of my time with my old friends trying to find ways to sneak into Taliban Afghanistan. One of them ran hospitals in Quetta and Kandahar and offered to smuggle me in – my old ambulance trick. Unfortunately, by then, another British journalist, Yvonne Ridley from the *Sunday Express*, had been taken captive and my editor Dominic Lawson overruled the idea.

Jamil Karzai ran a students' organisation and when I first arrived in Quetta I had asked him if he could get an educated young woman inside Kabul to describe what it was really like living under the Taliban. One evening I was over in Satellite Town when he handed me a thin envelope. It was almost curfew so I did not open it till I was back at the hotel. Inside was a torn sheet from an exercise book. It was addressed 'dear kind and beautiful lady' and as I started reading I was soon in tears.

'I hear the bombs drop and I pray that they will end our suffering'
Sunday Telegraph, 14 October 2001

THIS WEEK I LISTEN to the bombs falling on the airport and military command just a few miles away and, though we are scared by the bangs which shake our flat, we believe they will not hurt us and we come out and watch the flashes in the sky and we pray this will be an end to our suffering.

Although Marri is not my real name, please use this as what we are doing is dangerous. I'm 30 years old and live in a three-roomed flat with my family on the outskirts of Kabul. I graduated from high school and speak Dari, Pashto and English as my father was a diplomat and my mother an English teacher.

I know from our friend that you have a kind husband and a beautiful son and you travel the world reporting and meeting people. I dream of a life like that. It's funny we live under the same small sky yet it seems we live 500 years apart.

You see us now in our burqas, like strange insects scurrying in the dust, our heads down, but it wasn't always this way. Women worked as professors and doctors and in government. We went for picnics and parties, wore jeans and short skirts, and I thought I would go to university like my mother and work for my living.

Hidden in our house, behind all the burqas and *shalwar kameez*, is a red silk party dress, my mother's, from the time when the king was in power and my father was in the Foreign Ministry. Sometimes I hold it up against me and imagine dancing but it is a lost world. Now we must wear clothes that make us invisible and cannot even wear high heels. Several of my friends have been beaten because the Taliban could hear their shoes clicking on the pavement.

Life here is very miserable. At night there is no light. We do not have schools; the doors of education are closed on all, especially us. We cannot paint or listen to music. The Taliban ran their tanks over all the televisions. We asked the world, are we not human beings? Can we not have rights as women in other countries?

Many people have left but my family is staying, praying for change. I hope they do not come and bomb, then forget us again. Maybe when you watch the bombs on CNN you will think of me and know we are real feeling people here, a girl who likes to wear red lipstick and dreams of dancing, not just the men of beards and guns.

I do not know what you want me to write to you. If I start writing I will fill all the paper and my eyes will fill with tears because in these seven years of Taliban no one has asked us to write about our lives. In my mind I make a picture of you and your family. I wonder if you drive a car, if you go out with friends to movies and restaurants and dance at parties? Do you play loud music and swim in lakes? One day I would like to show you a beautiful place in my country with mountains and streams, but not now while we must be hidden. Maybe our worlds will always be too far apart.

_____

My past experience in Pakistan and Afghanistan had made me extremely sceptical that ISI would overnight reverse their policy of supporting the Taliban, as Washington and Whitehall seemed to think they had. Of course when the Bush administration gave Pakistan the ultimatum after 9/11 – 'You're either with us or against us, in which case we'll bomb you back to Stone Age' – they had agreed. Musharraf later admitted in his autobiography that he had 'war-gamed the US as an adversary' and concluded that Pakistan could not take them on.

Even if Musharraf was genuine in his support, it seemed naïve to think that ISI would meekly obey. They had made the Taliban what they were and supporting them had been an ideology, not just a policy. When I lived in Peshawar in the late 1980s, ISI had been playing a double game, misleading the CIA over what was going on in Afghanistan and making sure most of the arms and money went to their favourite fundamentalists. I was quite sure they would do the same again.

So I was not surprised to learn that when the ISI chief General Mahmood Ahmed went to see Mullah Omar in Kandahar after 9/11 at America's behest, rather than asking him to hand over Osama bin Laden, he offered him help. Hamid Karzai was certain that ISI was still supplying weapons to the Taliban. I spoke to one of the chiefs of the Achakzai tribe, which was spread across the border, and he confirmed that a number of arms trucks had been crossing. I began investigating.

I knew Hamid was planning to go inside Afghanistan to try to rally Pashtun tribes against the Taliban. I begged him to take me but he would just laugh. One day I arrived at his house to find him gone. His assistant, Malik, told me he was in Karachi. The next time I called, Malik claimed Hamid was in Islamabad. Malik was not a good liar. 'He's gone inside, hasn't he?' I asked.

Eventually Hamid's brother Ahmed Wali arranged for me to speak to him by satellite phone from their home. We had a long conversation on the evening of 8 November in which he told me he'd had a narrow escape (from the US, it later turned out – a pilot had been given the wrong coordinates and bombed them instead of the Taliban).

That night I was fast asleep when, at 2.30 a.m., there was an insistent rapping on the door. I got up and looked through the peephole. The duty manager was standing there with four men in grey *shalwar kameez*. They looked like ISI.

'Madam, there are some guests for you,' he said.

'It's 2.30 in the morning,' I replied indignantly. 'Tell them to come back at 7 a.m.'

As I started walking back towards my bed they snapped the door chain, snatched my mobile phone which was charging at the side, and told me I was under arrest.

Downstairs in reception I was made to pay my bill, then a dazed-looking Justin was brought down to join me.

We spent the next two days detained in an abandoned bungalow that we later discovered had been the railway rest-house in colonial times. Fortunately Justin always carried two mobile phones and had smuggled one out. While I made a loud fuss to distract our captors, he phoned our newspaper from the toilet to alert them to our plight. We later learnt that Dominic called the Foreign Secretary Jack Straw. Three months later, after the abduction and beheading of *Wall Street Journal* reporter, Daniel Pearl, in Karachi, we would wonder what might have happened had we not had that phone. Finally, on the third day we were moved to Islamabad and deported to London accused of being a threat to national security. The Information Ministry released a bizarre story claiming we had tried to buy plane tickets in the name of Osama bin Laden.

As we were marched on to the familiar green and white Pakistan International Airways plane, I decided I'd had it with Pakistan. Then, shortly after take-off, one of the flight attendants brought a message from the pilot inviting us into the cockpit. His name was Johnny Afridi and he had long dark hair tied back into a ponytail, John Lennon spectacles and a refreshing irreverence for his country's authorities. 'Just ignore all those goons,' he said to me as he let this 'threat to national security' sit in the co-pilot's seat for the landing at Heathrow.

Back in London, the head of consular services at the Foreign Office called us in and apologised that they had only been able to get us out of the country rather than be freed to do our jobs. 'You understand it's a very sensitive situation at the moment with the bombing and we need Pakistan as our ally,' he said. I did not understand. It felt like my war had ended before I had even arrived where it was happening.

But it's funny how things work out. Being kicked out of Pakistan forced me to be more imaginative. While little of interest was coming out of Quetta, where our colleagues were again under lockdown, Justin and I went to Rome to interview the elderly ex-King of Afghanistan, a midnight meeting that took place with him in his pyjamas. We then managed to get a visa to Iran from where we could travel into western Afghanistan and the ancient Persian city of Herat, arriving there the day the Taliban fell.

I was still in touch with Ismael Khan, the by then white-bearded old mujahideen commander for the area, and he sent one of his lieutenants to meet us at the border. Ayubi was an impressive man with a long, swirling woollen cape and a giant ruby on a silver ring. 'Welcome my Afghanistan,' he said as he scooped up some earth and kissed it. His theatricality suited my own excitement to finally be back in Afghanistan again after twelve years.

The road to Herat had been completely destroyed and it was a long, dusty journey before the city's leaning minarets came into view. On the way in we drove across a wide plain covered in tents. Ayubi told us it was a refugee camp. Its name was Maslakh, which meant slaughterhouse, and I had never seen one so vast. Eventually, the tents ran out and then there were shelters of plastic sheeting and after that families just huddled on the hard ground with nothing.

'They must freeze at night,' I said to Ayubi.

'Yes, often the children die,' he replied, pointing at rows of grey slates stuck upright into the ground, as is the custom when Afghans bury their dead.

I kept thinking about the camp as we checked into the Mowafaq Hotel. A sweeping staircase suggested the hotel had once been grand but now it was cold and dingy with a manager who looked like Charlie Chaplin in a frayed suit. There was a dead bird in my bathroom and nothing to eat but eggs that came fried and congealed and one of which had a fly trapped in the white. Early the next morning we went back to the camp.

A woman called Bibi Gul was burying a tiny cloth-wrapped bundle, her 2-year-old son Tahir, who had frozen to death the previous night. My little boy was the same age. Everywhere we walked hands clawed at us, begging for 'a tent' or 'a piece of bread'. Justin, who also has a young son, is rarely short of words but we were both silent driving back after a day in Maslakh.

At the hotel we climbed up to the roof to set up the satellite phone to be able to call the office. The old days when it was impossible to file from Afghanistan were long gone. The sat phone was bulky to lug around but once we'd locked on to the Indian Ocean satellite, using the built-in compass, we could connect our laptops and transmit my words and his photographs as we stood there shivering in the bitter cold.

Dominic came on the line, delighted to hear we were finally inside Afghanistan. 'You must be overjoyed,' he said. 'You must celebrate with a drink.' I wondered where he thought we were. The only beverage available in the Mowafaq was green tea.

Wonderful as sat phones are, they do presume some form of power supply. At the Mowafaq, the dining room was lit by pink and green neon strips that flashed on and off as electricity came and went. Most of the time there was no power but when it did come it was often in great surges, far too much for an ordinary surge protector to withstand. Such a surge came just as Justin was in the middle of downloading his powerful photographs of Bibi Gul burying her baby at the Maslakh camp. There was a shower of sparks and a smell of burning as his power supply blew up. All the pictures were lost. Justin was devastated.

To try to cheer him up I suggested we went for a walk. Round the corner from the hotel was a street rather gruesomely called Bloodbank Road. A little way along was a small white building with a sign in Farsi and English saying 'Literary Circle of Herat'. It was impossible to resist.

When Zena Karamzade's dreams of being a doctor ended under the Taliban, she joined a dressmaking circle – or so the regime thought
Sunday Telegraph, 16 December 2001

DOWN A MUD-WALLED alley adjacent to the Flower crossroads in central Herat, where only a few weeks ago the Taliban were still publicly displaying the bodies of those they had hanged, a small blue plaque reads: 'Golden Needle, Ladies' Sewing Classes'.

Three times a week for the past five years, young women, faces and bodies hidden by their Taliban-enforced uniform of sky-blue burqas and flat shoes, would knock at the yellow iron door. In their handbags, concealed under scissors, cottons, sequins and pieces of material, were notebooks and pens. Once inside, they would pull off their burqas, sit on cushions around a blackboard and listen intently as Mohammed Nasir Rahiyab, a 47-year-old literature professor from Herat University, taught forbidden subjects such as literary criticism, aesthetics and poetry.

The innocuous blue sign masks an underground network of writers and poets who became the focus of resistance in this ancient city in Afghanistan's north-west, risking their lives for literature and to educate women during the years of Taliban control.

Under a regime where secret police beat women merely for wearing heels that clicked, the sewing classes of Herat were a venture that could easily have ended in more bodies swinging above Flower crossroads. To safeguard his students, Professor Rahiyab's children were recruited to play in the alley outside while classes were being held. If a stranger came near, the children would warn their father, who would slip into another room with his books while his place was quickly taken by his wife holding up a half-finished garment.

Once, two years ago, the professor's daughter was ill in bed and his son had gone to buy bread, so there was no one to raise the alarm when a black-turbaned Talib rapped at the door. 'Suddenly, he was in the courtyard outside,' said Professor Rahiyab, a shy, soft-spoken man who becomes passionate when he talks about his beloved Russian writers. 'I just got out of the room in time and my wife ran in and the girls hid their books under cushions, but I realised that I had not cleaned the board nor hidden my Pushkin bust, which I always brought out for classes. I sat in the other room, my hand shaking so much my cup was rattling.

'If the authorities had known that we were not only teaching women, but teaching them high levels of literature, we would have been killed. But a lot of fighters sacrificed their lives. Shouldn't a person of letters make that sacrifice, too?'

To lessen suspicion that might be cast his way, Professor Rahiyab never openly criticised the regime, even though the Taliban laid waste to his syllabus for male students at the university, forcing him to replace most literature classes with Islamic culture.

The ruse of using sewing classes as a cover for teaching women was thought up by Ahmed Said Haghighi, the president of Herat's 90-year-old Literary Circle, after the Taliban not only closed all girls' schools, but also began destroying them and using the sites as mosques.

'When it became clear that the Taliban were going to retain control of Herat, we sat around discussing what we could do to stop the culture of the city dying and to help our female members,' he explains. 'The only thing we could think of that women were allowed to do and that would allow comings and goings without suspicion was dressmaking classes.'

Inspired by the Golden Needle, hundreds of similar classes were held all over the city, some writers even dressing in burqas to go to women's houses to teach. Had the Taliban investigated, they would have realised that the pupils never made any clothes. Instead, they were encouraged to write and were introduced to the forbidden works of Persian poets and foreign classics by Shakespeare, James Joyce and Dostoevsky. A Unicef study found that 29,000 girls and women in Herat province received some form of secret education while the city was under Taliban control.

Perhaps it is not surprising that such resistance should have taken place in Herat, which has a history of standing up to oppressors – an uprising against the Russians in 1980 led to 24,000 deaths in a few days, after Moscow sent in helicopter gunships to pound the city. When the Taliban took over in 1995, locals saw them as another occupying force.

The Persian-speaking city, with its large Shia minority, was anathema to the Taliban who were Pashto-speakers and Sunni Muslims. They treated Heratis particularly brutally, referring to them as 'strangers'. The regime closed the city's many shrines of Sufi saints, made Pashto the official language and whitewashed a mural depicting 500 years of the city's history.

Such acts provoked outrage in a city proud of its reputation as the cradle of Afghan civilisation. Herat is a centre of learning and has produced so many poets that the country's inhabitants have a saying: 'If you stretch out your feet in Herat, you kick a poet.'

Professor Rahiyab explains: 'We were poor in everyday life. Why should we be poor in culture, too? If we had not done what we did to keep up the literary spirit of the city, the depth of our tragedy would have been greater.'

One of his students, 23-year-old Zena Karamzade, was in her second term as a medical student when the Taliban ended female education. With her dreams of becoming a doctor in tatters, she was on the verge of suicide when a friend introduced her to the sewing classes. 'We didn't live under the Taliban,' she explains. 'We just stayed in our rooms like cows. If we did go out, we had to be accompanied and wear a burqa, which is like being imprisoned in a closed space. With the carbon dioxide you breathe out and not enough oxygen coming in, after a while your lungs feel like exploding. The only time we felt human was in the sewing classes.'

The friend she went with was Leyla Razeghi, a 24-year-old who has had several stories published in the Literary Circle's journal. Written under male pseudonyms to protect her identity and based on one theme – life for women under the Taliban – her stories use metaphors to criticise the regime. One, called 'The Good News', is the monologue of a girl called Rusa who writes of her frustration at not being able to study because of a sick relative. Others used voices of birds and animals so as not to attract the attention of the censors who vetted all publications. 'The head of censorship was too stupid to realise what I was doing,' said Leyla.

The effects of the Taliban's hatred of literature can be seen at Herat's old public library, a one-storey whitewashed building with tall green-painted windows that look out on to the bare branches of the winter trees. Most shelves are empty apart from a bookcase of gold-engraved Pakistani books on Islamic jurisprudence and a few shelves of tattered paperbacks that include *Moby Dick* and a book called *The Road from Huddersfield*. 'We call it the book graveyard,' said Zena, who took me there.

Zare Hussaini, the white-bearded librarian, explained that, last year, a line of trucks roared up to the door bearing the Governor of Herat, the head of censorship, and twenty-five Taliban soldiers. 'They said all books "contrary to the tastes and beliefs of Sunni" must be confiscated, as well as those with pictures and political books, and they began packing them all up.'

Around 25,000 books were removed and burnt in an enormous pyre outside the city. Pakistani Korans and religious volumes were brought in to replace them. 'Nobody reads them,' said Mr Hussaini. 'They are in Arabic, which no one here speaks, and far too theoretical.'

The only non-religious books saved by the library were a few boxes that members of the Literary Circle had managed to remove earlier and bury under the ruins of an old theatre in the next-door garden, as well as in the lavatories of a youth centre. Last week, these books, including *Moby Dick*, were ceremoniously returned to the library's shelves, which are still mostly empty.

That same day, the Herat Literary Circle held its first open meeting of men and women for seven years, over lamb meatballs and rice. Inside the restaurant, men and women chattered together excitedly. Yet, before leaving, the women without exception disappeared inside burqas. 'Walking around uncovered attracts a lot of attention,' explains Zena. 'The Taliban have gone, but they have altered this city and people won't change their habits overnight.'

From Herat we travelled to Kabul on an Ariana plane which had to be jump-started. The flight over the snowy mountains of Bamian was spectacular if somewhat disturbing when the pilot told us no instruments were working and he was flying 'by vision'. The Afghan capital was almost unrecognisable from the place I had visited in 1989. The shining blue river along which I had sat eating ice cream with girls from the university was now a brown trickle piled high with garbage. The Jadi Maiwand carpet bazaar where I had bought my living-room rug had been almost flattened, leaving row after row of crumbling bullet-spattered ruins. Yet this was not the work of the Russians – the damage had been done by the Afghan mujahideen whom I had known in Peshawar and who had spent much of the 1990s fighting each other.

My old friend Hamid Karzai had been chosen as head of the interim government by a UN-organised meeting of Afghan leaders in Bonn and had moved into the palace where he was waiting for his inauguration. Huddled by a one-bar electric fire, he looked thin after his weeks in the mountains and was wearing a long stripy *chapan* coat someone had given him to keep him warm, as he had not had chance to go back to Quetta to fetch clothes. Later it would become his trademark. It was disturbing to see him there in this palace where so many previous presidents and kings had been horribly murdered. He showed me how the Taliban had knocked the heads off the stone lions on the drive and used white paint to blot out the heads of the peacocks on the wallpaper of the Peacock Room because of their ban on all human and animal images.

I just managed to get back to England for Christmas, arriving on the morning of 25 December. There were no direct flights from Kabul to Europe but, even so, the two-day trip had left little time for acclimatisation. It was a shock to go from this land of dust and hunger to an enormous lunch of turkey with all the trimmings at my parents' house and a mountain of presents under the tree for Lourenço. I couldn't stop myself snapping at him for leaving food on his plate, though I knew he was far too young to understand.

All Roads Lead to Pakistan

Face to face with the Taliban leaders
Sunday Telegraph, 10 February 2002

THE TELEPHONE CALL came shortly after breakfast. 'The carpet has arrived,' said a voice. 'It's a very valuable one and we can't keep it here long for security reasons.'

It was the strangest feeling. For most of the previous five months since September 11, I had been in Pakistan and Afghanistan writing about the evil Taliban regime and meeting one after another of its victims, from Hazara women whose husbands were burnt to death in front of their eyes, to a Kandahar footballer whose hand was cut off in a public amputation at which officials then discussed whether to also chop off a foot. Now this coded telephone message meant that I would soon be meeting some of the regime's key members in their hiding places in Pakistan.

Four hours later I was taken down a rubbish-strewn alley where I entered a house through the women's quarters. Finally a bearded old man in a swan-white turban summoned me through the dividing curtain into a room where two former Taliban ministers were sitting on floor cushions along with our go-between. For a moment I was taken aback. For the past few months the combined might of the American armed forces has been hunting the former leaders of the Taliban regime who presided over a reign of terror in Afghanistan. Any Taliban leaders captured are shipped off to Camp X-Ray in Guantánamo Bay, Cuba, for interrogation about their links with the al-Qaeda network. So far only one high-ranking member has been caught – Mullah Abdul Wakil Muttawakil*, the Taliban's Foreign Minister, who yesterday surrendered to Afghan officials and was turned over to US forces. He is being held in the former Taliban stronghold of Kandahar for questioning that the United States hopes will yield intelligence about fleeing leaders of the Taliban and the allied al-Qaeda guerrilla network.

But a large number of Taliban leaders have managed to escape and are now hiding out in the Pakistani province of Baluchistan, apparently unhindered by the attentions of the Pakistani security authorities.

It took me a few moments to come to terms with the fact that I was sitting cross-legged in front of some of the world's most wanted men. With their beards trimmed short, they looked surprisingly young. I knew the Taliban leaders were mostly in their thirties, but somehow I had thought of them as bigger and older – and more malevolent.

One of the two men, Maulana Abdullah Sahadi, the former Deputy Defence Minister, was only 28 and looked vulnerable and slightly scared, greeting me with a wonky Johnny Depp-like smile. It was the first time he had ventured out of his hiding place since escaping Afghanistan after the fall of Kandahar two months ago.

The other minister, a burly man in his mid-thirties who agreed to meet only on condition of anonymity and is responsible for some of the acts that have most horrified the western world, looked defiant. Later that day I would also meet the director-general of the passport office, who had issued Afghan visas to some of the Arab fighters who are now on America's most-wanted list.

My interviews took place in Baluchistan, a vast smugglers' land of desert, mountains and earth tremors, much of which is governed by tribal law, where women are kept locked away and federal government officials fear to tread. It was here in the madrasas, or religious schools, that the Taliban originated and, perhaps not surprisingly, it is where they have taken refuge after surrendering their last stronghold of Kandahar on 7 December.

---

* Muttawakil was later released to live in a government guesthouse in Kabul as part of a reconciliation programme to try to win over so-called 'moderate Taliban'.

'We shaved off our beards, changed our turbans from white Taliban to Kandahari [green or black with thin white stripes], got in cars and drove on the road across the border,' says Maulana Sahadi, adding, 'My beard was as long as this.' He gestured down to his chest.

The Pakistani authorities, he claims, turned a blind eye. While US Special Forces based in Kandahar continue to go on daily operations in the Afghan mountains searching for al-Qaeda and Taliban, just across the border it is an open secret that senior Taliban ministers are sheltering in madrasas and houses. Among those are Mullah Turabi, the Justice Minister; Abdul Razzak, the Interior Minister; Qadratullah Jamal, the Culture Minister; and Mullah Obaidullah Akhund, the Defence Minister.

According to Sahadi, bin Laden was still in Afghanistan when the Taliban fell at the end of last year, and he laughed at the Americans' failure to catch him. 'I spoke to him on the telephone the day we surrendered Kandahar and he was in Paktia and he was fine. I briefed him and he wished me Godspeed. Now we think he is in Saudi or Yemen.

'The last time I actually met him was in November during the bombing in Herat. We met there to talk about finances. He was helping us to buy cars. He may have gone to Iran at that time.

'He seemed well. A couple of years ago, he had some health problems linked to his kidney but now he seemed better. The Americans were bombing the military installations while we had lunch in the Mowafaq Hotel. He was taking anti-anxiety pills, some kind of sedatives, but he was not hiding.'

Mr Sahadi said that bin Laden spent much of his time in Afghanistan travelling around in Toyota Land Cruisers with darkened windows like those favoured by Afghan warlords, with just one other car of armed Arab bodyguards from his elite 55 Brigade accompanying him.

He suggests that bin Laden might have fled through the tribal areas of Pakistan. 'I have had no direct contact with him since December but my information is that he is definitely alive.'

I was able to arrange this extraordinary meeting because thirteen years ago, during the jihad they waged to drive the Russians out of

Afghanistan, I had travelled on the back of motorcycles in Kandahar for three weeks with a group of young fighters known as the Mullahs' Front. These had later helped found the Taliban.

'You see, we don't have two horns,' said one of the ministers with a smile as he poured me tea and offered me boiled sweets in place of sugar. 'Now anyone can say anything about us and the world will believe it. People have been saying we skinned their husbands alive and ate babies and you people print it.'

We started off talking about how they had joined the Taliban. Maulana Sahadi's story is typical. When he was 5, his family moved to a refugee camp in Quetta after his father, a mujahid with Hezb-i-Islami, was killed fighting the Russians. They were very poor, surviving largely on bread begged or bought with money from sewing carpets, and were pleased when he got a place at a madrasa at the age of 8. His food, board and books were all provided. At some point, he learnt to use a Kalashnikov, though he would not say at what age, claiming, 'A gun is such a thing, one day you use it, the next day you master it.'

In mid-1994, a delegation of elders and *ulema*, or religious scholars, from Pakistan came to the madrasa. 'They issued a fatwa telling us we must join the Taliban and fight jihad. I joined with a group of friends from the madrasa so we were there right at the very beginning in the first attack on Spin Boldak [a town just over the Afghan border on the way to Kandahar] that October. At that time, we were only about a hundred people.

'We were killing men and many of our companions were martyred, but we were happy because we were doing it for Islam. We were the soldiers of God.'

Sahadi went on to fight in battles all over Afghanistan, including Herat, Mazar-i-Sharif, Kunduz and Bamian, commanding 500 people, then 2,500 people, then becoming director of defence. 'I would motivate my troops before fighting by telling them that if they were martyred they would go to paradise and could take with them seventy-two of their family members.'

He got on well with Mullah Omar, whom he describes as 'a very nice, good-natured person with good morals. He treated me like a son. Whoever came to him, he treated with respect.'

Two years ago, Sahadi became Deputy Defence Minister and as such says he had frequent personal contact with Osama bin Laden, though he insisted that 'the Arabs were not controlling things'. 'Anyone who supports Islam was welcome in our country – we had British, Americans, Australians,' he adds.

Sahadi admits that, during the American bombing offensive, he and his colleagues were required continually to change houses in Kandahar to avoid being hit. But he says the Taliban never contemplated handing over bin Laden to save themselves. 'He was a guest in our country and we gave him refuge because hospitality is an important part of our code of behaviour. Besides, he was supporting us, giving us money, when no one else was.

'The Taliban leadership do not believe the Twin Towers attack was carried out by al-Qaeda,' he continued. 'According to my own opinion, the attack was wrong. It is not Islamic to kill innocent people like that.'

How did they explain the videos in which bin Laden talks of the attack. 'They were fake,' he replied.

The other minister interjected. 'What this war really is about is a clash between Islam and infidels. America wants to implement its own *kafir* religion in Afghanistan. We are the real defenders of Islam, not people like Gul Agha [the Governor of Kandahar] and Hamid Karzai. They are puppets of America.'

But why, then, did the Taliban collapse so easily? 'We're not broken, we're whole,' insists Sahadi. 'We weren't defeated, we agreed to hand over rather than fight and spill blood. Our people went back to their tribes or left the country. Now we are just waiting. The fighting for power has begun in Gardez, Mazar, and different provinces. Karzai cannot even trust his own people to guard the presidential palace but has to have American troops. We are regrouping. We still have arms and many supporters inside, and when the time is right we will be back.

'Thank God this war happened because now we really know who is with us and who is against us,' Sahadi adds. 'Karzai went to the other camp. Once he pretended he was with us, but now we see he just wanted power. They will all be brought before justice and punished according to Islamic law.'

Sahadi insists that the 'Americans have failed'. He said: 'They have not caught bin Laden or Mullah Omar. All they have done is oust our government. We never did anything to them. Mullah Omar is still in Afghanistan and will stay there making contact with those commanders unhappy with the new government. You will see Islam will win out and we will break the Americans into pieces as we did with the Russians and bring back the name of the Taliban.'

As early as February 2002, it was already clear that the US had not won the so-called war on terror. The B-52s may have driven the Taliban out of Afghanistan in less than sixty days but Mullah Omar's zealots had lost the battle not the war. Far from being wiped out, they had simply fled over the border into Pakistan, finding safe haven back where they started.

It was unnerving being back in Quetta, alone this time. I had entered Pakistan by land over the Bolan Pass from Kandahar but I knew that ISI received the names of all foreigners arriving in the city. There was no point checking in anywhere other than the Serena but while I was there I hardly slept, tossing and turning in expectation of that midnight knock on the door.

Yet, again and again, I found myself being drawn back. This was where the real story was. As the British would later discover in Helmand, the West could send as many troops as they liked into Afghanistan but if they could not staunch the supply of Taliban fighters from madrasas in Pakistan, they would never resolve the problem. One American colonel fighting in eastern Afghanistan told me that defeating Taliban who come across the porous 1,470-mile border is 'like trying to drain a swamp when you can't shut off the streams feeding it'.

And in March 2003, western foreign policy, namely the war in Iraq, was about to provide them with a whole lot more recruits.

Hail, the mini bin Ladens
New Statesman, 24 March 2003

THE NEW MUSLIM Speeches Music Shop in Quetta does a fine line in posters and stickers depicting grenades, hand-held rocket launchers and other jihadi weapons of choice imprinted with slogans calling for youth to rise up against the West. It is a shack really, rather than a shop, part of a crowded bazaar just along from the bus station where a man stands with a muddy pelican on a string. Any stranger who lingers long outside is quickly warned to move on in whispers, for this is the gathering place every Thursday of a group of men with the silky black turbans and kohl-rimmed eyes that mark them out as Taliban.

The dust-covered, earthquake-prone town of Quetta amid the fudge-coloured rifts of the Baluchistan Desert is known as Taliban Central these days. Several former Taliban ministers and commanders live there and have formed the Quetta Shura, a war council guiding operations inside Afghanistan. In this they are helped by their former backers in Pakistan's military intelligence, ISI, according to close advisers of the Afghan President Hamid Karzai, who believes Islamabad has not given up its long-held designs on its neighbour.

'The Taliban were defeated but they were not eliminated,' warns Yahya Massoud, sitting in his Kabul house beneath a picture of his dead younger brother Commander Ahmed Shah Massoud, the leader of the Northern Alliance who for years led the fight against the Taliban. Massoud was assassinated by al-Qaeda two days before 11 September 2001, apparently as a favour to Mullah Omar in return for protecting Osama bin Laden. 'ISI continues to support them and al-Qaeda while paying lip-service to helping the West.'

As the West's key ally in the war on terrorism, Pakistan might be expected to support its aims. After all, ISI has been crowing about its recent string of successes in capturing senior al-Qaeda members such as the operations chief Khalid Sheikh Mohammed. Earlier this month, it even held a bizarre press conference at which spymasters drew flow charts of the organisation while waiters in white gloves and astrakhan hats

served tuna sandwiches and tea in china cups. But such arrests also raise
the question of how so many terrorists have been able to seek refuge in
Pakistani cities; it suggests considerable local support for their objectives.

The most high-profile of those captured were Khalid Sheikh
Mohammed, known by western intelligence as 'the Brain', and Mustafa
Ahmed al-Hawsawi, known as 'the Paymaster', arrested together in a
smart suburb of Rawalpindi on 1 March. Yassir al-Jazeeri, a communications specialist, was found in the posh Gulberg district of Lahore
on 17 March. Ramzi Binalshibh, the suspected twentieth hijacker, was
captured after a six-hour shootout in an affluent part of Karachi last
September. Others have been arrested in Peshawar, Quetta and
Faisalabad, often in the houses of doctors.

The past year has seen a string of attacks in Pakistan on western and
Christian targets such as churches, the American consulate and the
Sheraton Hotel in Karachi. In elections last October, 20 per cent of
the seats went to religious parties campaigning on an anti-American
platform. In the North-West Frontier Province, now governed by an
alliance of mullahs, Taliban-style measures such as the banning of
music and satellite television have already been introduced.

No one doubts that an American attack on Iraq will intensify
antipathy towards the West. Already Saddam Hussein's picture has
joined that of Osama bin Laden on the barrows of street vendors
selling pistachio nuts and sugar-cane juice. Neither man is in any way
representative of Islam, a religion which preaches tolerance. One is a
suit-and-tie-wearing secular dictator of unspeakable brutality and the
other a long-beard from the extreme Wahhabi sect, which rejects
modernity. Yet the two have become icons for Muslim youth.

'By making them such objects of hate, the West has turned them
into heroes,' complains Mehmood Shaam, editor of the *Daily Jang*,
Pakistan's biggest-selling newspaper, sitting in his office in Karachi not
far from some of the recent bomb blasts.

After the suicide bomb attacks on the US consulate and the Sheraton
in Karachi last year, Shaam wrote an article entitled 'Letter to a Suicide
Bomber', urging the nation's youth to reject militancy and instead
follow the peaceful way of the poet Iqbal, Muhammad Ali Jinnah, the
founder of Pakistan, and Gamal Abdel Nasser, the late President of

Egypt known for his Arab nationalism. 'I got hundreds of threatening letters saying: "We are on the right track, who are you to question us?"' he says, shaking his head. 'Even political leaders contacted me saying you should not discourage this tendency.'

Such sentiment is likely to be exacerbated by a war in Iraq. 'I'm afraid war in Iraq will create lots of mini bin Ladens,' warns General Rashid Qureshi, spokesman for President Musharraf.

A country where a third of children are educated in madrasas, many of which espouse an extreme Deobandi version of Islam similar to Wahhabism, is fertile ground for breeding terrorists. A recent report by the Brussels-based International Crisis Group entitled 'Pakistan: madrasas, extremism and the military' accused President Musharraf of failing to integrate or reform the madrasas as promised after 11 September, and warned that 'their constrained world view, lack of modern civic education, and poverty make them a destabilising factor in Pakistani society. For all these reasons they are also susceptible to romantic notions of sectarian and international jihads which promise instant salvation.'

'It's a very dangerous situation,' echoes Yahya Massoud. 'If you take the official figure of 10,000 madrasas and say each has 200 militants, that's 2 million. Then, if a quarter of these get military training, that's a potential army of 500,000.'

Even in Pakistan's ordinary schools, the standard textbooks contain numerous examples of distorted history and the preaching of intolerance and hatred. 'Minorities are described as inferior entities or second-class citizens,' says Mohammed Shehzad, author of a survey on textbooks for the Future Youth Group of Liberal Forum. 'It's basically state-sponsored terrorism.'

Pakistani youth are not the only ones in the Islamic world who increasingly reject the West and all it represents. From Cairo to Jeddah, the plumpest and sweetest dates on sale are sold as Bin Laden Dates. In the soft drink wars, Muslim Up has joined Mecca Cola to take on Seven Up and Coca-Cola. Started by a group of French Tunisians, the company states its aim on its Internet site as being 'to thumb our noses at the "Made in USA" superpower and the arrogance it demonstrates in wanting to manage world peace'.

Top of the Arab charts is 'The Attack on Iraq' by Shaaban Abdel-Rahim, an Egyptian folk singer. The chorus goes: 'Chechnya, Afghanistan, Palestine, South Lebanon, Golan Heights and now Iraq, too. / It's too much for people, shame on you!'

————————————

Eventually Pakistan got wise and started stamping on journalist visas 'Not valid for Quetta'. Once I even got one marked 'Islamabad only'. Friends of mine from *L'Express* who ventured there in December 2003 were arrested. Later a *New York Times* correspondent, Carlotta Gall, was beaten in her hotel room (the Serena again) as was her fixer, and her computer and notes were seized.

But Quetta was not the only problem. There were madrasas all over the country that espoused a Taliban version of Islam. I knew if I were a destitute mother in Karachi given the choice between a madrasa where my children would receive free board, lodging and education, however warped, and a government school where I had to pay, I would have little choice but to opt for the former. I thought about all those billions of American dollars that had flowed into the country in the 1980s to arm the Afghan resistance – if only some of that had been used to fund secular education.

In addition to the madrasas, the other problem was the militant jihadi groups such as Lashkar-i-Toiba, Jaish-e-Mohammad and Sipah-e-Sahaba. Since the 1980s, under a policy begun by General Zia, these had been encouraged by Pakistan's military to fight their war for Kashmir against India, so the government could deny responsibility. Now these groups were out of control. Pushed by Washington, Musharraf would periodically announce a ban on these jihadi organisations, only for them to re-form under new names. 'We've created a Frankenstein,' admitted one former ISI officer.

The official line remains that General Musharraf is the West's staunchest ally in the war on terror (even if the US did give him $5 billion of aid for his troubles and millions of dollars of CIA bounties for the arrests of al-Qaeda suspects). Pakistan's President has after all narrowly escaped three assassination attempts because of this support.

His ministers point out that, by the start of 2007, Pakistan had lost over 700 of its own soldiers looking for al-Qaeda in tribal areas like Waziristan– more than the entire coalition fighting in Afghanistan.

Until early 2007 not a single senior Taliban official had been arrested by Pakistan despite operating so openly that journalists like me could find them*. When Musharraf was confronted by US military officials with video evidence of armed Taliban freely passing Pakistani border guards, he finally conceded that some 'retired ISI officers' might still be helping the Taliban. But what if they were not really retired? And what if some of that American aid to Pakistan was going to fund the very people western troops were fighting in Afghanistan?** Back in the 1980s the Pakistani military had not had any qualms in siphoning off CIA money destined for the mujahideen and using it for their own purposes such as funding the nuclear programme.

The West's abandoning of Afghanistan after the Russians had gone had left a legacy of mistrust. Like the Afghans, many Pakistani officials thought the Americans were not really in it for the long term, so were hedging their bets.

---

* Mullah Obaidullah, the former Taliban Defence Minister, was arrested in Quetta in February 2007, just as US Vice President Dick Cheney was visiting Pakistan.
** Another unanswered question in the 9/11 Commission report was just who wired $100,000 from two Pakistan banks to Mohammad Atta, the ringleader of the 9/11 pilots, in the run-up to the attack.

War in Iraq with a Dolphin-tamer

January–April 2003

News editors love wars. Male news editors love wars, to be exact. It is always said that wars sell newspapers but that isn't why they love them and that hasn't been true of the war in Iraq anyway. They stick up maps with coloured pins in for their 'troops' – us correspondents. Some collect caps from different regiments or armies as booty. At one paper where I worked, they even got out tin hats when a war started.

At the beginning of 2003, I had just rejoined the *Sunday Times* from its rival *Sunday Telegraph*. There were already 60,000 American troops in the Gulf – the biggest military build-up since Operation Desert Shield in 1990 – and it was clearly only a matter of months until Bush and Blair launched the invasion.

My first meeting with my new colleagues was at a war summit in Clapham at the house of fellow reporter, Hala Jaber, and her photographer husband Steve Bent. Over one of Hala's mouth-watering Lebanese spreads, we stared at a map of Iraq to decide who would go where. None of us wanted to be embedded with US or British troops, feeling this would compromise our independence. Matthew Campbell was to be in Baghdad along with Hala and Steve; Jon Swain in the south where the British troops would be; Marie Colvin, entering from Jordan, and I would be in the north, the Kurdish areas where I imagined Turkey might try to invade in search of lost Mesopotamian ambitions once Iraq became a free-for-all.

I found it difficult to be enthusiastic about covering the war. From my experience of reporting in Pakistan, Saudi Arabia and the West Bank, I worried that the impending war would provoke anti-western sentiment across the region and a wave of support for bin Laden and other militants. I had not liked Iraq on my only previous visit in 1994. The creation of Iraq – like so many African borders and the Durand Line between Pakistan and Afghanistan – seemed another of Britain's historical time bombs. I'd read about the British capture of Baghdad from the Turks in 1917 and warnings from the time of the impossibility of creating a nation from three communities – the Shia majority and Sunni and Kurd minorities – who hated each other. When I met Iraqi exile groups in London, it appeared not much had changed.

In January 2003, while we waited uneasily for war, I was sent on my first Hostile Environment course. Almost all the other participants were from CNN, which appeared to be sending its entire staff. Among them was the presenter of their weekly golf show, one of those stretched-smile women who came down to breakfast every day in full make-up. As by then I'd spent much of the previous fifteen years in hostile environments, while most of my course fellows had never been anywhere near a bullet, it was difficult to take seriously simulations of ambushes in rural Wales. It wasn't helped when a woman we were supposed to rescue urged us in a thick Welsh accent to 'get a move on, will you' as she had to collect her children from school.

Bush and Blair's assertions about Saddam's weapons of mass destruction – the infamous 'forty-five minutes from doom' – meant we all had to attend a one-day course in a country house to learn how to protect ourselves from NBC – nuclear, biological and chemical weapons. Basically, we learnt that if any of these were unleashed, we'd had it. Even if by some miracle we managed to get into the cumbersome protection suits without being contaminated, we then, somehow, had to find an evacuation chamber within twenty-four hours. Along with the suit came a little book of touchpapers which would change colour to tell us which gas we were being poisoned by, though by then we would probably be undergoing a horrible death by blistering, vomiting or choking. I decided then and there that I would not take the kit. The self-injecting vial of atropine against nerve gas sat in our fridge among the milk and eggs, an unpleasant reminder of what was to come.

Since my previous trip to Iraq, all I'd had to do with the country was binning the faxes of uncheckable 'information' that would arrive on the *Sunday Telegraph* foreign desk every Friday afternoon. These were from exile groups in London, all of whom seemed to hate each other. Most active was the Iraqi National Alliance (INA), led by Ayad Allawi, a genial former Ba'athist who had once tried to stage a coup against Saddam from his exile in Wimbledon. Not surprisingly it did not work and he remained in SW19, where we met for lunch one day at Cannizaro House Hotel. Over salmon in béarnaise sauce in the silk-curtained dining room, he offered me interviews with defectors who could reveal all about opponents to Saddam's regime being killed in baths of acid or having their bodies chopped in paper shredders. None of these things seemed verifiable. He smoked a large cigar and when I tried to pay the bill, he refused, pulling out a thick wad of notes and saying, 'It's your taxpayers' money anyway.'

Despite our war summit, we all ended up in different places. On the eve of war, in March 2003, I found myself in Pakistan reporting the capture of the 9/11 mastermind Khalid Sheikh Mohammed. From there it was a mad dash across the border to Afghanistan, hoping to get an Iranian visa to enter northern Iraq, as both the Syrians and Turks had closed off their borders. It was the Shia holiday of Moharrum, however, and the Iranian embassy was closed.

By then Matthew had left Baghdad amid rumours that Saddam planned to use foreign journalists as human shields and the foreign editor called to see if I'd like to go there. 'No,' I said, thinking, I'm a mother for God's sake. He was replaced by Jon, and Marie had gone north, so I was instructed to head south. On Wednesday, 19 March, I departed Kabul at the crack of dawn to fly via Sharjah and Dubai to Kuwait where I would arrive in the early hours of Thursday the 20th then drive into southern Iraq. Before going, I had tea with Hamid Karzai at the presidential palace. Jokingly, he threatened to close the airport so I couldn't leave, then added sadly, 'Everyone will forget us again now.'

The Kuwait Hilton was so full of hacks that people were calling it Groucho's-on-Sea, though unlike its Soho namesake it offered nothing

more potent to drink than alcohol-free Budweiser. Some of the correspondents had been there since January. Forced into teetotalism and
with little to write about, most filled their time waiting for the war in
the blissfully chilled air of Kuwait City's shopping malls. What they
were buying was gadgets: GPS, walkie-talkies, solar panels to charge
satellite phones, inverters to run off laptops from a car battery, mini-
generators and portable DVD players. A weird kind of gadget envy had
developed and over breakfast in the hotel café overlooking the Arabian
Gulf, reporters would boast of having acquired software of street maps
of Baghdad for their GPS or trek towels 'that absorb eight times their
own weight in water'. Some of the most enthusiastic gadget-shoppers
would end up spending their entire war in the Kuwait Hilton.

I couldn't help thinking of veteran journalist Bill Deedes's
description of being dispatched to Abyssinia at the age of 22 to cover
Mussolini's impending war for the *Morning Post*. Before setting off he
was taken by the foreign editor to buy a quarter-ton of luggage,
including solar topees, a camp bed, three tropical suits from Austin
Reed, and jodhpurs and riding boots even though he did not ride. All
this was packed in a cedar-wood trunk lined with zinc to repel ants, and
was mostly useless, inspiring Evelyn Waugh – in Addis Ababa for the
Daily Mail – to create William Boot, the hero of his comic novel *Scoop*.

For all my mockery, I did have to do some shopping. Southern Iraq
was scorching desert unlike the mountainous north where I'd expected
to be, so the sweaters, mountain boots, and arctic sleeping bag I had
with me were all redundant. At the Sultan Centre I acquired a pop-up
pod tent and a stock of self-heating cappuccinos that I knew would be
the envy of the breakfast crowd. At an army-surplus store I bought
military overalls; later I discovered that the *Daily Mail* had ordered
copies of US uniforms complete with embroidered name badges for its
correspondents. Marc from *L'Express* introduced me to Ikea from
where I emerged laden with coloured pens for children, hundreds of
yellow batteries, plastic boxes to put things in, and some picnic chairs.
My colleagues laughed at the latter, but later, when we found ourselves
living out of our car in the desert for three weeks, we would be grateful
we did not have to sit and write copy on the scorpion-infested sands.

The foreign editor kept interrupting my shopping with excited emails entitled 'War Scoops' and requests for memos on how I planned to cover the fall of Basra. The war hadn't even started. I was quite sure it wasn't going to fall that quickly. Not having to file copy like my colleagues on dailies, I thought of another way to kill the nervous waiting time. The previous year I'd covered the war between Ethiopia and Eritrea with photographer Karen Davies who impressed me by heading to the front with long crimson-painted nails. So I headed for the hotel beauty salon where a bored Filipina girl eagerly attended to me, unperturbed by the gas mask by my side. Chip Cummins from the *Wall Street Journal* walked past and banged on the window in disbelief.

'The war's about to start and you're having your nails done!' he shouted.

'What else am I going to do?' I laughed.

The war did indeed start that night – Thursday, 20 March – with a rocket attack on a bunker in Baghdad said to harbour Saddam and his two sons. This was followed up the next day with 'Shock-and-Awe'. On TV I watched the tremendous explosions sending up red fire into the skies of Baghdad and was glad I wasn't there.

That night my colleague Jonathan Calvert and I packed up our jeep with all the supplies we had bought, as well as jerry cans of petrol and crates of bottled water. Sleep was interrupted by endless air-raid warnings. Short sirens signified missiles like Scuds, while a long whining signal meant a gas attack, in which case we were supposed to put on gas masks and run to a basement shelter by the kitchens. The first time I complied, but my room was in a villa a long walk from the main hotel so, by the time I got to the shelter, the warning was over. The second time I started running then turned back. The printed notice in the villa said, 'Find a basement or ground room with no windows' but my room was on an upper floor reached by an outside staircase with no access to the ground floor. The third time, I just stayed in bed. Mostly I watched TV – the coalition was claiming that they had already captured the southern port of Umm Qasr.

It was hard to drag myself away from the Hilton's crisp white cotton sheets. But at 4 a.m. on Saturday morning we set off towards the border, clad in our military overalls and followed by the car of some Portuguese friends, Candida Pinto and José Cyrne from TV channel SIC. We had timed our departure so that we would be going through the main checkpoints at prayer time when the Kuwaiti guards would be occupied.

The dawn was grey and the highway through the desert bleak and windblown. Soon we were out of sight of the modern buildings and refineries of Kuwait City and on Mutla Ridge, a low escarpment of drifting sands and wire fences where several of our colleagues had been turned back. It was an eerie place that had become known as the Highway of Death during the first Gulf War when fleeing Iraqi troops were trapped on it in February 1991 and left at the mercy of US warplanes. Hundreds were killed and reporters described seeing the road littered with wreckage frozen mid-battle.

At the border our luck ran out. We were turned back by US marines and joined the many other cars of journalists who'd been holed up in the car park all night, some for days. I was not sure how we were going to cross – others said they were going to try driving along the border fence as there were rumoured to be some holes. Candida and José set up their camping stove and started brewing coffee. I envied their insouciance.

Suddenly I noticed a huge American convoy approaching. Amongst the hundreds of tanks, trucks and armoured personnel carriers (APCs), some painted with skulls and crossbones and names such as 'Road to Paradise' and 'Size Matters', there were also a few dark-blue Land Cruisers like ours, probably carrying Special Forces. This was our chance. 'Quick!' I shouted.

The Portuguese wanted to drink their coffee so we left them behind and drove off, managing to insert ourselves between a tank and an APC. The gunner in the tank in front looked a bit surprised but we stuck close, figuring they were hardly likely to bring the entire convoy to a halt at that point.

Where were the flowers, or the jubilant cheers?
New Statesman, 31 March 2003

DRESSED IN MILITARY overalls and a camouflage hat from an army-surplus store in downtown Kuwait City, I had sneaked on to the back of an American military convoy entering southern Iraq. As we crossed the border into the dusty flyblown town of Safwan, I looked for the crowds of joyful 'liberated' Iraqis rushing forward, waving flags and bearing flowers.

Instead, some sullen-looking men standing by the roadside gestured angrily with their thumbs down. A few children threw stones at the tanks and one person after another held out their hands in cupping gestures, begging for water. The Stars and Stripes that the marines had taken out on the border so they could fly it from an armoured vehicle was quickly put away.

Perhaps it is understandable why the people of Safwan might be less than enamoured with their liberators. Every day for the past week, thousands of tanks, armoured vehicles, heavy-artillery batteries and troop-carriers have thundered along its main street, bearing the insignia of the best of British and American fighting machines. It is an awesome sight, and just watching such a display of military might for a few hours made it seem astonishing that even the most fanatical Saddam loyalist could begin to imagine holding it off. Yet no one stopped to give the people any food or water. A local doctor called Ali explained that the town's supplies of water had been cut off because of air raids on Basra that had disabled the area's water and sanitation system.

The convoy I had slipped into was heading for Baghdad as part of the relentless push north-west, so I turned off the road and on to the highway to Basra. The strategic port, which is much dirtier and less romantic than the image one might have of the place from where Sinbad the Sailor set sail, lies just forty miles from the Kuwaiti border. Back in London and Washington, it was being reported that the Pentagon had declared the city was 'about to fall'; the vital 51st Division had agreed to defect.

There seemed no reason not to head that way. Not far along under a bridge, a few British military police were guarding two groups of Iraqi prisoners, huddled in makeshift camps of concertina-wire under the hot sun. There were six officers, glaring at us, and roughly thirty soldiers, some of whom were conscripts, judging by their white vests rather than uniforms, their underfed appearance and lack of shoes.

Across the road their AK-47s lay destroyed, having been driven over by the British troops then smashed with a sledgehammer.

I was looking at all this and sharing ginger snaps with the military police when there was the distinct crack of a rifle being fired. 'Get down!' shouted the sergeant, pulling me behind the car. I vaguely remembered from my hostile-environment course that engine blocks provide no protection from gunfire.

We managed to scramble into a nearby pit in the sand and for the next hour there was a tense exchange of fire, soldiers running forward and back, trying to identify the gunman. Dressed in civilian clothes, he and a few others disappeared into the grey dust of the desert. A little later two pick-ups of Iraqis drew up, one bearing a man who had been shot in the back and another with a woman badly wounded in the leg. She said her husband and brother had been killed.

Yet this was only a few miles along from Umm Qasr, the small border port that we were originally told had been captured on the first night of the war, on 20 March, and at least nine more times since. Deciding the Basra road was too risky, I tried to head that way but was stopped by US marines, who said it was 'very dangerous'. There was the sound of heavy firing up ahead.

'I thought Umm Qasr had been taken,' I said.

'Ma'am, it has been secured, but it's not safe,' replied the marine.

That the small port proved so hard to capture, finally being taken after a six-day struggle, did not seem to augur well. Back in Kuwait City – where many locals have a text-messaging service on their mobile phones that alerts them to the latest developments – each time the message came through that Umm Qasr had fallen, people laughed. They laughed too when Geoff Hoon, the Defence Secretary, described the town of 40,000 people as 'the Southampton of Iraq'.

This was supposed to be the easy bit. The population of southern Iraq is mainly Shia; the Shias hate Saddam and his Sunni-dominated Ba'ath Party, and rose up against him in 1991 after the last Gulf War, only to be brutally repressed and their leaders executed. It is also the land of Wilfred Thesiger's Marsh Arabs, whose marshes have been systematically drained by Baghdad.

'Umm Qasr was a bit of a shock,' admitted Colonel Chris Vernon, spokesman for the British military, whose tanned face, swept-back hair and phrases such as 'I'm just in from the battlefield' are making him a star of the airwaves (female fans even sending him their knickers). 'Intelligence is never 100 per cent, and we underestimated their resolve.'

In fact, the failure of local people to rise up against the regime this time round was not surprising given how they were abandoned by the West last time. Moreover, while the Ba'ath regime is still in power, even if in its dying days, people are scared to make their feelings known for fear of reprisals.

The coalition forces were caught unawares by the emergence of the 'irregulars', people in civilian dress who may or may not be army, armed with AK-47s, pistols or rocket-propelled grenades, wandering about taking pot shots at western troops or journalists. Some are *fedayeen*, 'the men of sacrifice', a band of paramilitaries founded and led by Saddam's elder son, Uday. Others seem to be ordinary people. Baghdad has been making much of an old man in an Arab headdress who apparently used his ancient Czech rifle to down an Apache helicopter.

The troops on the road to Baghdad may have had the fastest advance of any force in history but no one in Washington or London had bargained for local hostility in places like Safwan, where the coalition troops are clearly seen as an invading rather than a liberating force. The idea that Saddam might be removed only to be replaced by an American general, or even some cigar-chomping, paunchy Iraqi exile who hasn't seen his country in thirty years, has not gone down well in southern Iraq.

This is not the view you get on television where, in their scramble to fill 24-hour rolling news, channels such as Sky News have been putting out everything unfiltered. On 21 March, for example, they reported that 20 per cent of the Republican Guard had defected, and that Basra would fall imminently, causing many of us reporters on the ground to be asked by our news desks why we weren't there.

A distorted – if fascinating – view of the war has also come from the 500-odd reporters 'embedded' with military units. Criticised for not giving journalists access during the 1990–91 Gulf War, the military sees the embedding idea as a great success. It has provided compelling television, with viewers able to watch real-time battles live on TV.

But the embeds are restricted in what they can report and, having spent weeks with their units, they so identify with them that it is common to hear TV reporters say: '*we* are advancing on...' or '*we* have just taken...' – which is just what the military hoped would happen. 'Of course we will use the embeds,' said Vernon. 'It's war, and in war you use everything at your disposal*.'

As for the so-called 'unilaterals' – those of us who wanted to be able to see both sides of the war – we sit in our cars in the desert, staring out at the sandstorm, wondering when the south will come under the control of the 26,000 British troops struggling to secure it, and what (if anything) we could believe from military briefings. 'Hell is a very small place,' said a colleague from Reuters, recalling shades of Vietnam.

I was having a bad war. Basra was taking much longer to fall than expected and being a 'unilateral' was more complicated than I had imagined. Because we were not attached to any side, we had no access to information and no idea where was safe and where not.

On my first day in Iraq, the US convoy had veered left on the Baghdad road and Jonathan and I had continued straight towards Basra. When it was a decent hour back in London, I set up the satellite dish and phoned in to my foreign editor, Sean. He was gung-ho, telling me that reports were coming in that Basra was about to fall and the 51st Division of the Republican Guard had all defected. This was not borne out by what we were seeing and, as we drove on, there were no signs of British or American troops.

We were in sight of the first bridge over the canal to Basra when I

---

* They did not exaggerate. Perhaps the most spectacular piece of news management was the 'rescue' of Private Jessica Lynch, a 19-year-old army clerk captured when her company was ambushed after taking a wrong turning near Nasiriya and nine were killed. Lynch was said to have emptied her weapon before being caught and taken to the local hospital. This was stormed eight days later by US Special Forces firing guns, all filmed on night-vision cameras. The dramatic rescue made headlines and Hollywood bought up the rights. It later transpired that there had been no militia in the hospital and the whole rescue had been a staged operation. Nor had Lynch shot at the militia. She later accused the Pentagon of using her as a propaganda tool.

called in again and Sean read me some wire copy describing 'US jets pounding the bridges of Basra'.

'We're by the bridge,' I replied, 'and nothing's pounding anything.'

'Are you sure you're on the right road?' he asked.

I was furious. To me the first law of war reporting is to trust your correspondent on the ground. After years travelling in strange places you develop instincts that are hard to explain but you know that you have survived for all this time because of them. I told Jonathan we should turn back.

Some way back we passed a car with masking tape stuck across the bonnet and sides spelling out the letters 'TV'. Inside was the ITN reporter Terry Lloyd, whom I had met in various other hell-holes around the world and liked very much. We stopped and told him we'd seen nothing.

Eventually, we arrived back at the cloverleaf where the roads split for Baghdad, Basra and Umm Qasr and where the British military police were guarding their Iraqi prisoners. 'What were you doing up there?' they asked us. 'You were way ahead of the front line!'

Not really knowing what else to do, we headed up the Baghdad road for a while, following another US convoy. However, that seemed pointless as we were supposed to be covering Basra, so we turned back, ending up once again with the military police. They were having an urgent discussion.

'Hey, just as well you guys came back from Basra before,' said one. 'Some of your colleagues were not so lucky.'

They told us that a car of British TV journalists had been shelled (by US marines, it later transpired) and the reporter and two others killed. I looked at them in horror. It could only be Terry Lloyd.

By that time it was afternoon and my foreign desk was demanding their 'battle for Basra'. Just then a cloud of dust on the horizon turned into a long British military column. It was the 7th Armoured Division, otherwise known as the Desert Rats, heading in the Basra direction. I had my 'top line' but I couldn't stop thinking about Terry and imagining his family getting that terrible call. I also wondered what would have happened if we had not turned back. I hammered out some copy then found it almost impossible to file as a sandstorm had started and the satellite dish kept blowing over in the desert wind.

في هذه المرة سوف نبقى معكم .

لنتعاون مع
بعضنا للنصر .

This time we won't
abandon you.

Be patient
together we will win.

People of Al Basrah
we are here to liberate the people of Iraq
Our enemy is the regime and not the people.
We need your help.
To identify the enemy.

To rebuild Iraq.

English speakers please come forward.

We will stay as long as it takes.

Listen to Radio Nahrain 100.4 fm (94.6 in the evenings)
for important news and information

After a few more days it was clear that Basra was not about to fall any time soon. The expected uprising of Shi'ites inside the city had not happened and the British airdropped leaflets beseeching locals to trust them. In a tent on the old airfield, they set up something called Two Rivers Radio – the soldiers called it 'We Love You Radio' – broadcasting a mix of music and propaganda encouraging the people of Basra to rise up against Saddam.

Meanwhile, Nick Cornish, the photographer with whom I was supposed to be working, had arrived in Kuwait City after visa problems

and was waiting to be collected. It was also clear we needed an interpreter and a Thuraya – a mobile satellite phone – so we did not have to
keep stopping to set up the dish by the roadside where we were easy
targets for snipers. We headed back to Kuwait.

A new lot of British hacks had just arrived at the Hilton from Jordan
where the expected floods of refugees from the war had not materialised
and they had been left with nothing to report. But at the going rate of
$300 a day, there was no shortage of people wanting to work as inter-
preters, despite the danger. Kuwaitis were ruled out because we'd been
warned that the people of Basra did not like them. I was immediately
taken with a chubby Armenian called Edward, who told a romantic
story of rescuing his girlfriend from Baghdad during the first Gulf War.

Romantic stories are not good reasons for hiring interpreters.
Edward's usual job was running a show of performing dolphins in
Kuwait. Once we had crossed back inside Iraq he would be constantly
phoning Kuwait to check on their well-being, making sure that they
were being fed enough fish and practising jumping through hoops. In
between covering the war, I learnt that the best performers are bottle-
nose dolphins, particularly those trained in Ukraine.

There were now four of us and, with nowhere safe to camp, we
mostly slept in the car. The back was loaded with boxes of Mars Bars
and biscuits and all night long I could hear Edward munching away or
rustling chocolate wrappers. After a while, the car reeked of stale food
and sweaty bodies. We began to feel like refugees, driving around trying
to find somewhere safe to stop before dark. For a couple of nights we
parked on the ground opposite a British POW camp on the road to
Umm Qasr, going over to chat to the British guards and letting them
borrow our Thurayas to call home, in the hope they would protect us
if we got attacked in the night.

But then the MOD in London called in our editors, warning them
to withdraw all unilateral reporters because they couldn't guarantee
our safety in the wake of Terry's death and we were getting in the way.
The guards told us that they'd been ordered to escort us from Iraq if we
came near.

One night we managed to get into the old Basra airfield where
the Desert Rats had set up camp south of the city. We had one blissful

day using their solar-powered showers, eating a cooked breakfast and watching Sky TV, sleeping in the ruins of a building. It came to an abrupt end when we were shopped to the commander by an embedded journalist and kicked out.

Finally we retreated to where most unilaterals had gathered – a dusty tanker park behind a gas station where an enterprising Iraqi was charging $50 a night per head for parking space, and guaranteed dysentery. We called it the Republic of Umm Qasr and it was very sociable, full of journalists from everywhere from Holland to Romania, many of whom I'd last seen during the war in Afghanistan just over a year before. It was also filthy. The only bathroom was a hole in the ground that was foul and overflowing, and on our first morning a German correspondent vomited over the bonnet of our car.

Not having expected Basra to take so long to fall, we were getting fed up with our tinned Tuna Surprises and baked beans heated on a tiny gas stove that kept blowing over. Only about one in four of the self-heating cappuccinos worked. Parked next to us was a group of French journalists who had come equipped with a proper two-ring stove, frying pans and labelled boxes of condiments, olive oil and onions. Every evening delicious smells of garlic and herbs would waft over us while we Brits watched sullenly. They had French flags on their car so people would know they were from a nation that did not support the war.

There was dust everywhere, grey powdery stuff that got into computers, nails, eyes and ears, and several people developed horrible eye infections. The pop-up tents turned out to be child-sized so I could only fit in if I curled in a ball, and they kept blowing over in the wind. It was starting to get unbearably hot, bringing out swarms of mosquitoes, and what with the pounding of artillery it was hard to sleep.

Life wouldn't have been so bad if we had been getting to do good reporting, but all we were doing was waiting for Basra to fall. As we listened to reports on our shortwave radio of the rescue of Private Jessica Lynch and the American push towards Baghdad, sometimes it felt as if we were missing the real war.

One day the temperature hit 42°C and we drove around in search of shade. Finally, we found a tree by a derelict farm. The farm turned out to be inhabited but the family were friendly and brought us small glasses of sweet tea. Then some of their friends arrived and began demanding Panadol. When we said we hadn't got any they turned hostile. 'Iraqis all seem to see liberation as their chance to demand things from foreigners,' I wrote in my diary. 'Everyone we meet bangs on our jeep demanding water, but this is going on so long our own supplies are running low.'

We were starting to get a sense of the task facing the allies.

Colonel Cox has a whole town to build
Sunday Times, 6 April 2003

IT LOOKS LIKE a scene from the Governor's office in some far-flung corner of the British Empire. From dawn to dusk people come to the gates of the old Umm Qasr Hotel in their hundreds, clutching slips of paper scribbled with Arabic names.

Some are looking for husbands and sons lost in the bombing, perhaps being held in the prisoner-of-war camp along the road. Some are hoping for jobs. One man wants insulin for his diabetic wife. Another man with a waxy complexion, leaning heavily on a friend, has not been on his dialysis machine since the war started two weeks ago because the hospital has no power. Most plead for water.

Inside, behind the small grove of palm trees, the man they all want to see is Colonel Stephen Cox, deputy commander of 3 Commando Brigade of the Royal Marines. Known as the Mayor of Umm Qasr, he is charged with establishing an administration in the only town in Iraq so far under complete control of the allied forces.

'Our strategic plan for taking over Iraq was that we'd take towns, the Ba'ath Party people would disappear and there would be local councillors or people there to take over the running of the place,' said Cox. 'In fact, they've all scarpered. Everything in town from the port to the factories was controlled by the Ba'ath Party and they've all gone. Every single dollar came from Baghdad. There's no police force, no administration, no one to manage or pay wages. It's like setting up a virgin town.'

As Iraq's only deep port, Umm Qasr was a key military objective that proved far harder to capture than expected. Its market sells little other than rotting tomatoes and its nights are filled with the howls of stray dogs and the occasional gunshot. But as the war rages around the edges of Baghdad, this flyblown town of 48,000 souls finds itself at the forefront of the battle for hearts and minds.

Winning the trust of the locals has proved no easy task, partly because the US marines who fought for the town acted as invaders rather than liberators, erecting the Stars and Stripes at the fort and scrawling 'Property of the US government' over the entrance to the old port.

Najaf, a local poet who has not published a line for thirty years because only poems praising Saddam were allowed, warned: 'We hate Saddam and want to get rid of him but we all have guns and if you don't go we will turn our guns on you.'

Still harder to break through is the fear of a people who have spent twenty-four years under Saddam's rule and see the Iraqi leader still in power in Baghdad. 'We have no prison in Umm Qasr,' said Hasan, a local cook. Tapping his head, he explained: 'That's because everyone has a prison here inside.'

When Cox recruited eighty local men last week to work in the port he was astonished when none of them turned up the next day. 'It turned out they had been phoned by the port manager in Basra who said you mustn't go and work with the dirty British or you'll be killed. I said, "Hang on a minute, you are in free Iraq, that man's in occupied Iraq. Why listen to him?" But they are hedging their bets and I don't blame them at all.'

This is starting to change. 'A week ago I went to see the head of the hospital and he was still sitting in front of a picture of Saddam. I asked him why and he said, "We don't believe you're going to stay." Two days ago I went to see him again and the picture had gone. He hadn't thrown it away, it was in a cupboard. Hopefully, next time it will be gone altogether.'

To help win confidence, the men of 40 and 42 Commando who are guarding Umm Qasr have switched from hard helmets to berets. 'We all have experience from Northern Ireland,' said Cox. 'Lots of talking to locals to win their confidence, an overt presence, an occasional patrol so they know we mean business.'

As a result, for the first time local people are starting to come forward and help. 'We know there has been infiltration back into the area from Basra and Baghdad but locals are giving us scraps of paper with names and addresses,' said Cox. Acting on such a tip led to the arrest of six Ba'ath Party officials on Wednesday morning.

The real difficulties of Cox's task of re-establishing order in Umm Qasr become apparent just along the road at the pipe factory. There is a constant line of people emerging, pushing carts laden with doors, chairs, pieces of wood and machinery. Since the collapse of the regime, looting has become the main industry. 'This is our property now,' said one man, wheeling out an air conditioner ripped from a wall.

Another problem is corruption. 'One of the most astonishing things is how people are used to handing over bribes for everything,' said Cox. 'They keep trying to slip money to my men. There were forty agents in town to distribute aid under the United Nations Oil-for-Food Programme, all extorting money for handing over the aid.'

Umm Qasr will be the gateway for future humanitarian operations and Cox complains that he has already been swamped with aid agencies. 'I had eleven today and sent ten of them packing,' he said. 'The people here don't need food. They have plenty. The big thing they want is to be treated with dignity.'

Yet everywhere there are scavengers and the few aid convoys that have arrived have degenerated into riots. 'The state of law and order in Umm Qasr is like the Wild West,' complained Patrick Nicholson of the Catholic Agency for Overseas Development. 'If the allies can't organise aid for 40,000 people in Umm Qasr, we're worried about them doing it for more than 1 million in Basra and more than 22 million in Iraq.'

A few days ago British engineers repaired the power plant so that lights came back on in most of the town, though not the hotel that Cox has made his headquarters and where he sleeps on the roof.

'I see us as a kind of sticking plaster until this can be handed over to the UN and then back to the Iraqis,' he said. 'In the meantime, I would say 50 per cent think we're doing a good job and 50 per cent are complaining we didn't flick a magic switch and open a McDonald's.'

After two weeks, with the US forces advancing relentlessly on the Iraqi capital, it was beginning to look as if Baghdad would fall before Basra. From a distance Basra was an apocalyptic sight. By day a vast canopy of black smoke hung over the city from burning oil trenches. At night British artillery lit up the sky.

Anxious to avoid heavy casualties from bombing, the British strategy was to encircle the city and hope it would fall from within. A company of Irish Guards had set up positions just south of the first Basra bridge from which they would make forays towards the city in their Warrior APCs or Challenger II tanks to draw fire so as to establish the position of the Iraqi fighters. They called the road they drove up 'Mortar Mile' and it was a dangerous cat-and-mouse game. On one occasion a rocket-propelled grenade (RPG) left two jagged holes in the side of the Warrior of an engaging Irish Guards captain called Jimmy Moulton. He became known as Captain Courageous for his bravado talk of going in to 'zap the enemy'.

In between their forays, Captain Moulton and his men would check the cars of people coming in and out of the city for weapons. We would hang around and interview the people about life inside. No one said much. Most of them were transporting crates of tomatoes.

One afternoon a long convoy of US supply trucks appeared, about to head over the bridge straight into Basra.

'Hey, what the fuck do you think you're doing?!' screeched Captain Moulton, waving them down. 'Basra isn't in our hands yet!'

'We're on our way to free Baghdad,' replied the lead driver confidently.

'This isn't the road to Baghdad,' said Captain Moulton. 'Don't you guys have maps?'

As the days went on, the British edged slightly closer to the city but it was slow going. I started referring to myself as Basra Bridge correspondent.

One day a taxi driver called Abu Rasoul stopped and asked us if we knew where the BBC people were. He opened his boot to reveal cans of Efes, Turkish beer. We had no idea where the BBC were but said we would be extremely happy to buy it – after three weeks without a drink, $20 for a box seemed an incredible bargain. We got talking about the situation inside Basra and he offered to drive me in to see. He seemed trustworthy and we negotiated a fee that would only be paid on my safe return. I wrapped my black shawl over my head and got in. Jonathan told me I was mad and stayed behind.

It was strange to go inside this besieged city that we had watched from afar for so long. On every corner Saddam's face in various guises stared out from billboards just as I remembered from my previous visit. Homes and shops had been bricked up against the bombing and it felt as if the city was just watching and waiting. A couple of goats were nosing in a pool of fetid water. There was a bombed-out building which Abu Rasoul said had been the radio and TV station, but otherwise the city seemed to have suffered little damage. We drove through one area of block after block of apartments, inside one of which I could see faces pressed against the window. The whole street seemed to have been taken over by young men in dark clothing, the *fedayeen* militia.

At the end of the road, the entrance to the port was marked by a copper statue of a soldier on a plinth, one arm pointing east towards nearby Iran. More than sixty of these stand along the Shatt al Arab Promenade, each representing a soldier killed in the Iran-Iraq War. 'I am 35 and I have seen nothing but wars,' said Abu Rasoul. 'Iran-Iraq, the Gulf War, the intifada in Basra, now this war…'

He had assured me that he knew where all the Iraqi Army roadblocks were and could avoid them. But as we rounded a corner near the university, we suddenly saw one straight ahead. My heart sank and I bowed my head and drew my shawl around me. Seven Italian journalists and two Australians had been arrested the previous week at the edge of the city. Abu Rasoul was cool, however. The soldiers were busy inspecting another car and he simply drove alongside and waved, then went straight on.

A few days later, on Saturday, 5 April, we were woken early by a series of deafening blasts. The British had received a tip-off that a meeting was under way of senior Ba'ath officials, including their main target, Ali Hassan al-Majid, better known as Chemical Ali for his role in gassing the Kurds in 1988. Saddam's cousin, Chemical Ali was hated in Basra where he had led the brutal suppression of the 1991 uprising.

They told us they had got him, which later turned out to be untrue.

We hoped they had because we were dreaming of the Basra Sheraton and hot baths and proper beds. Our little stove had stopped working altogether so we could not even make tea, my hair was dry as straw and thick with dust, and we had only two bottles of water left.

After nineteen days of war, Basra finally fell on 7 April, a Monday, which could not be worse for a Sunday newspaper. Unfairly for the Irish Guards who had done all the groundwork, men from the 3rd Parachute Regiment led the way into the city. There was no fighting – the *fedayeen* I had seen had all drifted away.

As we followed the soldiers in, I could not believe my eyes. Almost immediately people began looting. Computers, chandeliers, desks, pipes…anything that could be removed. Inside the university laboratories, I watched people grabbing microscopes and centrifuges, smashing many things in their rush. Electric sockets were ripped from the walls. What they couldn't steal, they set ablaze.

'Why are you doing this?' I asked a man. 'This was for the education of your children.'

'It's all ours now,' he laughed.

Much of the stuff was useless. Soon the bridges out of the city were crowded with people carrying airconditioner units and office chairs back to their farms.

Along the Shatt al Arab, we found the Basra Sheraton but it was on fire. Nearby, looters had left the Natural History Museum a smoul-dering shell with just the odd stuffed lion paw or fish fin trampled underfoot amid the wild hollyhocks in the garden. As we were walking around, a gang of young men appeared with crowbars and a pistol. We left hastily only to drive straight into a gun battle outside a bank which people were trying to loot. Two of our tyres were shot out.

When we really needed him, Edward disappeared – telling us he wanted to look up someone in the Armenian community. Later we discovered he was selling contracts for satellite TV.

At the hospitals, people were literally tipping patients out of beds and grabbing medicines and bandages. I went to the Technical College where the British had set up base and asked an officer why they weren't doing anything. 'Do I look like a policeman?' came the reply.

The same orgy of looting was to happen in Baghdad when it fell two days later. It was the failure of the British and Americans to deal with this that convinced many Iraqis that they did not really care.

All of us *Sunday Times* reporters in Iraq had been instructed to look for incriminating documents that might reveal secret weapons programmes or link the regime with al-Qaeda, so I headed for the headquarters of Saddam's secret police. There was a large crater at the front where a British bomb had struck, and crowds of people had gathered, searching through the debris. Among them I met a man called Ismael Samoi whose left cheek twitched nervously as he spoke.

Torture cells that kept a people in fear
Sunday Times, 13 April 2003

THEY CALLED IT the Black Hole, for it was the room from which no prisoner ever emerged alive. The walls and ceiling were coated with treacly black paint and there were no windows so it was impossible to tell night from day.

The floor was several inches deep in charred remains and faeces, and there was the scuffling sound of something rat-sized in the dark. Whatever had happened in there was so unspeakable that, seven years after being freed from Basra's most feared interrogation centre, Ismael Samoi could not bring himself to look inside.

'They would go into your mind and whatever was your worst horror they would find it,' he said, as he used his cigarette lighter to guide the way down the crumbling stairs under the headquarters of the Amn al-Amm, most hated of all Saddam's secret police.

The building was struck by a British shell in the battle that led to the fall of Basra but the detention blocks for political prisoners remained intact, as did the underground jail where Samoi spent what he describes as 'a 22-month living nightmare'.

Last week, as the news reached Basra that US marines had entered the heart of Baghdad, he summoned up the courage to return. He was not the only one. The secret police headquarters was full of former political prisoners returning – terrified to be back there and at the same time astonished to be wandering around freely – and families searching for the missing.

'Ismael!' shouted a thickset man in his forties, crushing Samoi in a bear hug. For a moment they held each other in silence, too choked with emotion to speak.

The two men had been in the cell together, along with fifteen to twenty others. It was often so crowded that Samoi and his friend, a boxing champion who asked to be identified as Fala, often slept standing.

They had helped keep each other's spirits up over long months, but had lost touch when Samoi was transferred to Baghdad. Neither had known whether the other had survived.

'Look,' said Fala, the older man, pointing to two faded marks on the wall. 'This is where we wrote our names in blood so people would one day know we had been here.'

'Are you still strong, Fala?' asked Samoi with a mischievous grin. Fala immediately knelt on the ground, allowing his old cell mate to climb on to his shoulders so that Samoi's fingertips just reached a small grille high on the wall. 'This was how we dreamt of freedom, just to touch the free air.'

The story was typical among those returning last week. 'I was 23 years old and just married when they came for me,' said Samoi. 'I had been sending information to the Shi'ite opposition based in Iran and someone reported me. I knew the regime was looking for me but I had to go to my job because my wife was pregnant and we needed the money. I was imprisoned for speaking the truth.'

His hands were shaking as he led the way to a series of small, stone-walled rooms. Pointing out the meat hooks in the ceiling from which he had been suspended by a rope tied round his ankles or hands, Samoi showed raised burn marks on his wrist.

'They would beat us with rubber hosepipes while we were hanging until we dripped blood,' he said.

In another of the torture cells, bare wires dangled from the ceiling. 'They would pour water on our heads then attach the wires to our skulls to electrocute us. Other times they brought in a machine for generating electricity and would put a wire in each ear to give us electric shocks of 125 volts. Sometimes they would run it from the nail of my little finger to that of my friend. They had plenty of methods. This corridor would echo with the screams of grown men.'

In the next corridor was a row of even smaller cells, with barely room for one person, where torture by scorpion was carried out. 'We called these the lonely cells,' he said. 'My 15-year-old cousin died here in the dirt and dust. Many died here. They would put you in alone with these big ugly creatures that get on your clothes so you can't get them off and they sting.'

Samoi never had to endure the scorpion rooms. For him, the hardest thing to deal with was the hunger. 'We were fed old bread so hard it hurt our mouths, and sometimes soup with insects. When I left I weighed thirty kilos [four stone ten pounds]. I was like a skeleton.'

When he was released, Samoi was so malnourished that he spent three months in hospital. Although he recovered, the mental scars remain, as they do for much of Iraqi society. 'All that time in prison my wife had no idea if I was alive or dead and had to give birth to our son all alone and in hiding,' said Samoi. 'I hate Saddam for causing that anguish and for stealing the first eighteen months of my son Basil's life from me. And we have never been able to have another baby.'

The lack of information about Samoi's fate was a typical tool of the regime to demonstrate what would happen to anyone who stepped out of line. Wives would sometimes even remarry, only for their husbands to reappear. Mothers cried every day for missing sons.

But it was not just men who were taken prisoner. When Fala was arrested for 'praying too much', because of his regular attendance at the local Shi'ite mosque, his wife was seized too. 'My wife was in a different block at the back and held for four months. They shaved their heads and made them run naked.'

'I don't know how he survived that,' said Samoi. 'At least I could reassure myself that my wife was safely outside.'

'You don't know how much your friendship helped me,' replied Fala. 'I am a simple man, a poor man of no education, whereas you are a man of books; you taught yourself English, you write your memories. In all this, when we were treated like animals, your friendship made me feel I was a person of value.'

After thirty-five years of Ba'athist repression, old fears take a long while to die. The next day, Fala whispered that he had something to show me and we arranged to meet later on a bridge where nobody might 'report back' on him.

'I've found my cousin, Abu Nathan,' he said. He held out a photograph of a dead man, his body spattered with blood from multiple gunshot wounds inflicted after the 1991 uprising. 'At least we know,' he said. 'The world should note all this and not forget, because none of this should be repeated.'

By the time I got home from the war I had been away for two months, first in Pakistan and Afghanistan, then Kuwait and southern Iraq. Baghdad had fallen just in time for me to make it back the day before Paulo's fortieth birthday and my mum agreed to look after Lourenço so we could go to Marrakesh for the weekend. We flew on Friday evening via Casablanca where we noticed the airport staff seemed tense, but didn't think any more of it and arrived so late in Marrakesh that we went straight to bed. The next morning I was woken at dawn by my mobile ringing. It was my foreign editor telling me he knew I was on a weekend off and I'd already been away for months but there had been an al-Qaeda attack on a series of hotels and clubs in Casablanca and as I was in the country already would I mind just going there for the day.

One of the most important qualities for a foreign correspondent is managing to be in the right place at the right time, but now I was a wife and mother I was starting to wish events wouldn't keep following me around. Fortunately we were staying in a beautiful old riad and Paulo felt he could survive a day alone lounging in the courtyard by the turquoise pool, reading and sipping gin and tonics, while I drove to Casablanca at top speed to wander round shattered nightclubs and hotels and interview bloodied survivors. Not quite the romantic weekend I had pictured...

The Last Summer in Baghdad

Just thirty-two prize items still missing as treasures flood back to Iraq Museum

Sunday Times, 15 June 2003

THE RED TOYOTA spluttered to a halt in front of the Baghdad Museum and three men in their early twenties jumped out. As they struggled to lift a large object wrapped in a blanket out of the boot, the American guards on the gate raised their weapons.

For a moment, a priceless 5,000-year-old vase thought lost in looting after the fall of Baghdad seemed about to meet its end. But one of the men peeled back the blanket to reveal carved alabaster pieces that were clearly something extraordinary.

Three feet high and weighing 600 pounds, this was the Sacred Vase of Warka, regarded by experts as one of the most precious of all the treasures taken during looting that shocked the world in the chaos following the fall of Baghdad. Broken in antiquity and stuck together, it was once again in pieces.

Having handed it over, the men jumped back into their car and drove off into the heat of the afternoon.

'Every day people are bringing things back,' said Dr Donny George, the museum's director of research. Only an hour before the return of the Warka vase on Thursday, he had bemoaned its loss, calling it 'one of the real masterpieces of the world'.

The failure of American troops to stop the plundering of priceless antiquities from one of the world's most important museums, while at the same time sending tanks to guard the Oil Ministry, was seen as one of the scandals of the war. Some 170,000 items were reported stolen from the museum and Iraqi scholars were filmed in tears while western archaeologists fell over each other to condemn it as 'cultural genocide'. One Oxford academic compared it to the destruction of the great library of Alexandria in the fifth century.

However, the recovery of the Warka vase means that the number of prized exhibits missing from the museum is in fact only thirty-two. About 3,000 minor artefacts are believed to have been taken from the storerooms – a fraction of the widely reported earlier estimates.

'The museum is a classic example of how you can say anything bad about the Americans and people will believe it,' said a spokesman for the US-led Iraq administration.

Every Baghdadi has stories of how soldiers' night-vision goggles are actually X-ray glasses to enable them to see through women's clothes. Last week a Baghdad newspaper published an article about US troops raping Iraqi women. It was later forced to retract.

A campaign for looters to return the museum's treasures and promising an amnesty has resulted in the return of 1,500 items in the past two months.

Last week alone, ten of the top exhibits were returned. One group of men brought back nine items from the Assyrian galleries. Among them was a statue of King Shalmaneser III – who ruled in the ninth century BC – on a pedestal inscribed with deeds and conquests from the ancient city of Nimrud. The items also included a large inscribed tablet from the sumptuous palace of King Ashurnasirpal II.

A locked room in the museum, guarded by a sullen-faced woman in a black veil, acts as a repository for the returned items. Ivory pieces and figures that decorated thrones in Nimrud dating from the eighth century BC lie scattered on a table, along with beads, ancient silver bangles, swords and pieces of broken pots.

'Everyone said the Iraqis are thieves, but they are bringing all this back and asking for nothing,' said Dr Ahmad Kamil, deputy director of the museum. On one table is a list of the names of people requesting rewards for returning ancient bangles and vessels. 'We still don't really know what we've lost,' he added. 'It's going to take a long time to check all the catalogues and items.'

Founded in 1923 by Gertrude Bell, the British archaeologist and Arabist who was known as 'the uncrowned queen of Iraq', the museum is renowned for the world's greatest collection of Mesopotamian art. Not only is Iraq the home of the Sumerian culture, which produced the world's oldest literary work, the Epic of Gilgamesh, but it is also home to the Assyrian and Babylonian cultures, to Ur, the birthplace of Abraham, and to the hanging gardens of Babylon.

It was the contrast between this 'cradle of civilisation' and American soldiers in full body armour and tanks apparently ignoring its pillage that so incensed public opinion.

An emergency summit of international archaeologists held at the British Museum at the end of April denounced the coalition troops. Neil MacGregor, director of the British Museum, described the looting as 'the greatest catastrophe to afflict any major institution since the Second World War'.

However, it is now clear that the original reports were highly exaggerated. Photographs of distraught museum officials among shards of ancient tablets and smashed glass in the entrance hall gave the impression of mass looting. In fact the main galleries had long before been emptied of their exhibits, which were moved to bank vaults following plans for their protection first drawn up during the Iran-Iraq War.

Coalition troops last weekend entered a vault under the central bank where 179 boxes containing the Treasures of Nimrud – gold and ivory figurines from four royal tombs near Nineveh – had been hidden since before the first Gulf War.

But MacGregor stuck to his comments. 'I can't think of another great museum that has had thirty to forty of its top pieces removed,' he said.

George, who was the source of the original number of items said to be missing, blamed shoddy reporting: 'Someone asked me the volume of items in the museum and I said more than 170,000. It was immediately taken that more than 170,000 had been lost, which is not true.'

He also pointed out: 'I went to the headquarters of the US marines on Sunday, 13 April, after we had already had three days of looting and begged them for help, yet it was only the following Wednesday that they sent troops and tanks.'

As the museum staff returned to work and began sweeping away the debris, many unanswered questions remained. Thieves seemed to know what to take and were able to break into three of the museum's five locked storerooms. 'The keys were in the director's safe, which is an old-fashioned one – easy to break into,' said George.

There was suspicion, too, at the initial reluctance of museum officials to let experts from Unesco into certain rooms. Their explanation was that they had taken an oath on the Koran not to allow infidels into the vaults.

The return of the Warka vase might help to resolve some of these questions, said MacGregor. 'Who had it and how did they come to give it back?' he asked. 'Was it just an opportunist looter? Was it a professional thief?'

Back in Iraq in late May 2003, six weeks after the fall of Baghdad, I experienced some looting of my own.

Like many western journalists I was staying at the al-Hamra hotel in the Jadriyah district of eastern Baghdad. Its windows still had large crosses of masking tape that had been stuck up as rather ineffectual precautions against the US bombing raids. In those early post-Saddam days Baghdad had a gold-rush atmosphere, people talking of a property boom, and contractors and security consultants piling in, hoping for a slice of the reconstruction pie. The hotel lobby bustled with new arrivals as well as Iraqis hanging around wanting to pick up work as interpreters, and a large easel was pinned with notices announcing press briefings and offering shared rides back across the desert to Amman for $500 a time.

My room was on the second floor of the back annexe and looked directly on to an apartment block just across the street. Often its residents would wave at me while I was making calls on the balcony where I had set up my satellite dish. One afternoon I came back from doing some interviews to find that the dish had disappeared. A strong hot wind was blowing from the desert so at first I thought it had fallen into the garden below. When I went down to look, a group of children gathered. They soon realised what I was searching for. 'Ali Baba! Ali Baba!' they shouted, pointing over at the apartments. One led me over and, sure enough, my satellite dish had been purloined by a family in a ground-floor flat. If I paid $200 I could have it back.

I didn't have much choice. Without the dish I could neither file copy, nor call my office or home. I went back to my room to fetch some dollars. On the way out of the hotel I met some young US soldiers whom I had got to know as they patrolled Jadriyah. A couple of times they had used my laptop and sat phone to send emails home. They were only 18 or 19 and it was disconcerting to realise I was old enough to be their mother. One of them had read me out a message from his father saying, 'Son, I'm proud of you, you're doing God's work out there.'

I told them about the fate of my dish and they offered to accompany me to retrieve it. This seemed a good idea as it might mean I had to pay less. But I was completely unprepared for what happened. When we got back to the courtyard of the apartment building, a crowd had gathered. The young soldiers panicked, pulled out their rifles and pointed them at the people, most of whom were women and children.

'You people are all friggin' thieves,' shouted one of the soldiers, poking the butt of his rifle under a woman's chin. 'Give her back her satellite dish or we'll friggin' shoot you!'

I was stunned. The Americans' faces were twisted with hatred. Then I remembered once hearing them refer to people 'speaking in Muslim language'. I thought about the checkpoints where my colleagues shouted at me to poke my blonde head out so the soldiers would know we were not Iraqis and not shoot. If this was how American soldiers dealt with ordinary Iraqis, they were going to create a lot of resentment.

The man in charge of all this was L. Paul Bremer III, commonly referred to as 'the Viceroy'. He had arrived in May to head the Coalition Provisional Authority or CPA, the new name for the occupation administration. A short, smug man who wore a blue suit and cowboy boots even as the heat crept up towards 50°C, Bremer was a workaholic who liked to tell everyone he started his day at 4 a.m. and finished after midnight. He did not appear to know anything about Iraq. His young US advisers, who ran about importantly with clipboards, were almost all Republicans and talked of 'the mission' and 'Free Iraq'. Their headquarters lay inside the high walls of Saddam's old Republican Palace complex in the so-called Green Zone (the outside, where we lived, was referred to as the Red Zone). Each time I went to the CPA they were erecting more barriers, adding razor wire, rows of Hescos (steel-mesh baskets filled with ballast) and tanks. Nor did they seem to speak to real Iraqis. They were not allowed out without two vehicles and four armed guards. One of them confessed to me that they had just 17 Arabic-speakers for 6,000 staff. So cut off were they that after one press conference we were asked if any of us knew any educated Iraqi women who might be interested in being part of the new Iraq.

To start with I dutifully went to the Green Zone every Friday for the weekly CPA briefing. These took place inside the vast convention centre across the road from the Al-Rashid hotel where I had stayed in 1994 and which had now been commandeered by the Americans. The briefings were such blatant propaganda they inevitably became known as the five o'clock follies. At my first one, I noted verbatim the following points made by Bremer.

The regime of fear and oppression is gone.

The Shia of Iraq have been able to honour their religious traditions for the first time in decades.

Town councils and local politicians are starting to meet, and openly and freely select their leaders.

Water quality is better in Basra than it has been for years.

More Iraqis now have access to electricity than ever before.

By the last three I put exclamation marks (today of course it would be next to all five). All the Iraqis I met complained about the lack of water and power supply. There were enormous queues for petrol, and traffic was often at a Lagos-like standstill because of the American checkpoints. It seemed to be taking awfully long for repairs to begin on the damage caused by the bombing and everything was very chaotic. I remembered how at Foreign Office briefings before the war, I had asked about the plans for afterwards and had been palmed off. It had never occurred to me that there was no plan.

When we asked Bremer about the fighting going on in Fallujah, not far from Baghdad, he would bristle and dismiss the insurgents as 'those who refuse to embrace the new Iraq'. The military Sit Rep (situation report) would always refer to 'foreign fighters', part of the constant attempt to try to link Iraq to 9/11.

One of the most amusing announcements was that of the arrival of a consignment of baseball caps for the Iraqi police. In charge of the police was Bernard Kerik who had sprung to network fame as New York police chief during 9/11. He stayed in Baghdad three months – just enough time, said cynics, for the extension to be built on his house back home. Anyway, it turned out there weren't many police to command.

On 16 May 2003, four days after flying into Baghdad, Bremer had announced CPA Order Number One. This decreed the deba'athi-fication of Iraqi society to purge all former senior members of the Ba'ath Party and dissolve the entire army. He compared the measure to the Allies purging the Nazis after World War II. It would prove to be one of the US administration's biggest mistakes.

Ba'ath Party purge leaves Iraq without army or surgeons
4 June 2003 (Unpublished)

INSIDE A BAGHDAD hospital guarded from looters by American tanks, Dr Osama Saleh had just completed his twentieth operation of the week. It was complicated, reconstructing the shattered foot of a farmer called Ismael injured during the American bombing. He had to reuse wire previously used in other patients because of the shortages of supplies left by thirteen years of sanctions. But the doctor's pained expression as he peeled off his gloves had nothing to do with the tricky surgery.

'Look at my hands,' he said angrily. 'They are skilled hands with twenty-five years' experience of healing people but apparently that doesn't matter any more.' Although Dr Saleh is one of only 200 orthopaedic surgeons in Iraq, a decree by the country's American and British occupiers means he is about to lose his job.

Dr Saleh has been a member of the Ba'ath Party since 1972 when he joined as a 17-year-old student before Saddam became president, rising through its ranks over the years. The party which Saddam turned into his own personal tool has now been outlawed by L. Paul Bremer, the US administrator of Iraq brought in last month to replace the retired General Jay Garner. All senior Ba'ath members are banned from holding state jobs.

Under this so-called deba'athification programme, an estimated 30,000 people will be sacked. Many are doctors, professors, school principals, engineers and architects. Aid agencies say they are desperately needed for the reconstruction of Iraq, which, two months after the collapse of the regime, is proving much harder than anticipated with many areas still without power and water. At the same time the entire 450,000-strong army has been disbanded, leaving thousands of families with no income as its planned replacement will have only 40,000 members. Many blame disgruntled former military for the growing lawlessness and carjackings in Baghdad.

'Mr Bremer is not taking into account that, just like the communist parties of Russia and Eastern Europe fifteen years ago, you had to be a member of the Ba'ath Party to get a job or do anything,' said Veronique Taveau, spokeswoman for the United Nations Humanitarian Coordinator in Iraq. 'It didn't necessarily mean you were steeped in blood.'

Dr Saleh says he was astonished when he heard the news that as a result of liberation he would lose his beloved post as head of the orthopaedic department at Al Kindy hospital in one of Baghdad's poor eastern suburbs.

'They are not differentiating between the Ba'ath Party and the Saddam regime which is something completely different,' he complained. 'If I am to be sacked I should be investigated, then if they find something wrong excluded. In the last Gulf War I even treated a British soldier from Middlesex who had been shot in the foot. Is treating the sick for twenty years an act of terrorism?'

Officials say they do not have the time for such investigations. 'Of course there is a risk that some people will be denounced unfairly,' said Charles Heatley, spokesman for the US-led administration, the Coalition Provisional Authority. 'But the risks of doing this are less than the risks of not doing this. The Ba'ath Party was the structure and basis for the terrible crimes and oppression of the Saddam regime and no Iraqi wants it to continue to exist.'

Such explanations cut little ice with Dr Saleh. 'We were told this war was about freedom,' he said. 'I understood that the Americans were liberal, democratic, that they believed in human rights and freedom of speech and thought. Yet now I am being punished because of what I think.'

His views are echoed by Major Haider Ali Said Khusan, 39, who is furious at the disbanding of the army, which he joined in 1985. After fighting in three wars, he now finds himself jobless. Two months ago he was manning air defences south of Baghdad, promised huge rewards for shooting down an American plane, something he says they knew was hopeless; today he mans a roadside stall selling cigarettes and cold drinks to earn a few dinars to support his wife and three pretty young daughters.

'Saddam was a bad man and he betrayed us but now the Americans have betrayed us too,' he complained. 'We are the Iraqi Army, not Saddam's army. Like armies all over the world we followed the orders of our commander. I joined during the Iran-Iraq War when the British and Americans were our friends. And once inside it, it was impossible to get out.'

Dr Saleh has a private clinic apart from his hospital work so is unlikely to end up hawking nicotine to support his four children, but he has no intention of meekly walking away from his job. The director of Al Kindy has pleaded his case to the Bremer administration and Dr Saleh has gathered a petition signed by 461 of the hospital's 700 employees which states: 'Dr Osama is loved by his patients...He has been appointed to posts in hospitals he has worked in due to his efficiency, keenness in carrying out his duties and good personality ...We never felt he was part of the previous regime.'

Although he admits that he chaired weekly Ba'ath Party meetings at the medical faculty of Baghdad University, he insists he received no benefits. Pointing out that the Ba'ath or Resurrection Party was originally based on principles of pan-Arab secular socialism, he said, 'I joined a party thirty years ago whose aims were freedom, unity and socialism. These are not bad aims. Yes, it was hijacked by Saddam but you must understand that once inside it was very hard to leave. I would have been sacked or jailed. I am a surgeon, not a war criminal.'

President Bush had officially declared the war over on 1 May 2003. But there was still no sign of Saddam's weapons of mass destruction (WMD) which had supposedly posed such an imminent threat to the West that it had been necessary to go to war.

Tony Blair insisted in Parliament that they would be found. A 1,400-member team called the Iraq Survey Group had been sent out to look for them. When I met some of them I discovered they were reduced to revisiting sites already checked out by UN weapons inspectors or sitting around in bombed-out palaces watching DVDs. Satellite pictures showing suspect sites had led them to a cupboard of butane cylinders for cooking. Once they burst into a locked room only to find a store of vacuum cleaners. Sensitive documents they seized turned out to be someone's high-school biology project. I took to teasing them: 'Found any WMD today?'

By contrast, it was not hard to find weapons scientists. Every morning they gathered outside the looted offices of the National Monitoring Directorate, the agency set up by Saddam's regime to work with the UN inspectors. They were hoping to be paid. Inside were teams of interrogators – the Americans led by 'Mr John' and the British by 'Miss Rebecca'. One morning I went there with my friend Bob Drogin from the *Los Angeles Times*. Among those waiting we found one of the country's top weapons scientists. He agreed to take us on a fascinating if macabre tour.

Iraq 'destroyed weapons by 1994'
Sunday Times, 8 June 2003

HE ALMOST ENDED up as an estate agent in Brighton. Instead, as he explained last week amid the broken concrete slabs and twisted metal pipes of what was once Iraq's production plant for lethal VX gas, Brigadier-General Ala Saeed became head of quality control for some of the deadliest nerve agents on the planet.

The bombed-out remains of Iraq's main chemical-warfare complex are a gritty desolate place, eighty miles north-west of Baghdad. An acrid smell hangs in the air and only a handful of thin, lonely trees survive the 50°C heat. With one of Saddam's top weapons scientists as a guide, the Al-Muthanna State Establishment bears testimony to evils that chill the blood, even in the furnace-like desert wind.

For it was this plant, ostensibly manufacturing pesticides, that produced the chemical agents Saddam Hussein used on the Iranians, then the Kurds – and which Tony Blair and President George Bush insist are hidden somewhere in Iraq, despite the inability of inspection teams to find any.

Although it was bombed in 1991 during the Gulf War and the remnants destroyed or sealed by United Nations weapons inspectors, it is still possible to pick out individual laboratories spread far apart in the vast complex.

'Here is P7, the production plant for sarin and tabun, and on the right is P8, where we made mustard gas,' said Saeed. All three were used on the Kurds at Halabja in 1988, killing 5,000 people in a single March morning.

A small man in a neat short-sleeved shirt and belted rayon trousers, Saeed, 51, and a father of three, holds a doctorate in analytical chemistry from Sussex University and still has a bank account at NatWest in Brighton, although it has been frozen. As we drove around, he spoke with disconcerting matter-of-factness about agents that paralyse the nervous system and blister the skin. 'It wasn't our responsibility to think about how they might be used,' he said. 'We just produced it.'

He pointed out the building where animals were kept for testing – donkeys, rabbits, dogs and guinea pigs. 'We tied them up in inhalation chambers and released the agents,' he said. 'Blood would run from their eyes, noses and mouths and they would convulse.'

The complex is dotted with earth mounds – dummy bunkers of the same dimensions as the six real chambers concealing the production facilities. Of all the agents brewed at Muthanna, the most horrible was VX. A nerve agent invented by British scientists at Porton Down, it is ten times stronger than sarin. Just a teaspoonful on the skin is enough to kill a person.

For several years after the Gulf War, Iraq insisted it had not made VX. 'My boss, General Amin [General Hussam Mohammad Amin, head of Iraq's National Monitoring Directorate, now in US custody], said there was no point admitting it as it was low-grade and not stable,' said Saeed with what seemed like regret. 'It deteriorated within a week. To be useful it should have a shelf life of two years.'

He said they had produced the last two batches in 1990 and insisted it was not weaponised, although UN inspectors found traces in warheads.

An intensive new hunt for weapons of mass destruction is currently under way amid allegations that Blair and Bush exaggerated the threat to justify going to war.

But Saeed has already told agents from MI6 and the US Defense Department, who grilled him last week, that they will find nothing. 'Between 1991 and 1994 we destroyed everything – all the chemical weapons and bulk agents,' he said.

As author of all three of Iraq's reports on chemical weapons to the UN Security Council, including the chemical weapons section of a 12,000-page document handed over last December, Saeed might be expected to deny that the country retained any banned weapons. But he insists: 'Why should I lie? We are free now.'

Yet Saeed does not look like a free man and admits he does not believe Saddam has gone. His right leg twitched nervously when we first met at a secret rendezvous and he told his story – of how he got caught up in one of the Iraqi dictator's most deadly projects.

After finishing a chemistry degree at Baghdad University in 1972, he joined the army chemical corps, dealing with the protection and training of troops against chemical warfare. When the war with Iran started in 1980, he was selected as one of six officers to run Project 922, developing chemical weapons.

'If any of us had said no, we would have been transferred to the front line of the war with Iran, which was certain death,' he said.

As head of quality control at the Muthanna complex, he began producing sarin, VX and CS riot-control gas in different facilities.

After five years he was sent to Sussex for his doctorate. None of his fellow students had a clue that he was there to pick up as much information as possible on chemical warfare. 'I told them I was from the Ministry of Higher Education,' he said. 'That's what I'd been told to say.'

Saeed loved Brighton, where he lived with his family near the sea and his first son Ziad was born. He was winding up his doctorate in 1988 when he saw the news about Halabja.

'We had already used the same mixture of tabun, sarin and mustard gas on Iranian troops to great effect, but that was different as we knew they had tried to use mustard gas on us. I didn't like to think of it being used on our people.'

It was then he got the offer to become a Brighton estate agent. 'There was another Iraqi living in the same block running an estate agency and he tried to persuade me to stay and said he would train me,' he said. 'I was very tempted but I have a big family – two sisters and six brothers – and they [the regime] told my parents if your son doesn't come back we'll kill you. I was trapped.'

So he returned to Muthanna, importing materials from the UK, Japan and Germany.

After the Gulf War, Iraq was forced to comply with UN weapons inspections and Saeed was made liaison officer.

He admitted there had been confusion over amounts of chemical agents produced but explained: 'At the end of 1991, the SSO [Special Security Organisation] gave orders to our programme as well as the biological and nuclear people to hand over all documents. We handed over fifteen wooden crates.'

Saeed said that in 1994, when UN inspectors required a complete disclosure report, he had asked the intelligence service for the documents. 'They said it was all destroyed, so we had to do it all from memory. It took six months working day and night and maybe some numbers were not right.'

After the 1995 defection of Hussein Kamel, Saddam's son-in-law and Minister of Military Industrialisation, Saeed said: 'They found 150 wooden boxes on his chicken farm, including all our documents.'

Given his insistence that Iraq is free of banned weapons, he is at a loss to explain its cat-and-mouse game with the inspectors. 'We had lied to them from 1991–5 over the VX programme, which they only found out about when Kamel defected so they didn't trust us,' he said.

'More than twenty times I said to General Amin, "Please let my inspectors go everywhere freely without all these agents so we can build confidence and finish this issue." But he always replied, "It's not your decision. It's Iraqi policy."'

Explaining the climate of fear, Saeed said: 'When the inspectors were in town I was terrified of bumping into them shopping on al-Rashid Street, because even if I said hello the security agencies would make a report on me.'

He added that when the UN asked to interview scientists in Cyprus, 'The Vice President called us all into a meeting and told us we were forbidden to go to Larnaca. They made clear our families would be killed if we went.'

So why would Saddam have led his country into a war if Iraq was free of weapons of mass destruction? 'Maybe Saddam just wanted to look big or maybe there were things going on I did not know about,' he said. 'We were completely away from the forbidden programme.'

Pushed on what he meant by 'the forbidden programme', his voice dropped to a whisper. 'We knew the Mukhabarat had small laboratories around Baghdad, but not where or what they were doing. They couldn't have been producing anything, as I know all the top scientists and we would have known.'

An Iraqi general involved with the procurement of supplies for this programme told me that there were secret laboratories in the basements of houses in Baghdad. 'The programme completely changed after Kamel's defection. Whereas in the 1980s there were large production facilities, after 1996–7 the personnel were changed and we had small teams of just three or four people.'

Consulting his Saddam watch, he added: 'Even in the 1980s we never had as much as people thought. The scientists were terrified of Saddam so would never admit if they had failed to produce anything.'

Though Saeed denies that any of his teams cooked the books, he admitted that if the UN had declared Iraq free of weapons and had lifted sanctions, he thought it '95 per cent likely' the regime would have resumed production of chemical weapons 'in six months'.

Fearful of what the British and Americans will do with him, he says he dreams of returning to Brighton. 'I wish I'd taken the estate agent job,' he said. 'I understand the property market has done very well.'

The summer of 2003 in Baghdad was about the last time one could still safely travel around, interview anyone, and go out for meze, wine and kebabs in the evenings in restaurants like Nabil's in Arasat Street. One Sunday I took a rare day off to go with Bob Drogin and another good friend, my former colleague Philip Sherwell from the *Sunday Telegraph*, for a picnic in the ancient city of Samarra right in the middle of what would soon become known as the Sunni triangle. We visited the gold-domed Askariya mosque, one of Iraq's holiest Shia shrines, which contains the tombs of the tenth and eleventh imams, and then climbed the amazing spiral minaret, more than a thousand years old and fifty-two metres high, and phoned home from the top.

Saddam was still on the run then so as we were not far from his home town of Tikrit, we looked for him in the cellars of the old Caliph's Palace on the bank of the Tigris. Four months later, in December 2003, he was indeed found in a cellar not far from there, that of a farmhouse about ten miles south of Tikrit.

By then Samarra would be a no-go area, succeeding Fallujah as the centre of what was by then a full-blown insurgency. When the US eventually took control, they built an eight-foot-high wall round the city. They used the spiral minaret we had climbed as a lookout point, and in April 2005 its top was blown off. In February 2006 insurgents targeted the Askariya shrine, blowing up the shining dome that had dominated Samarra's skyline.

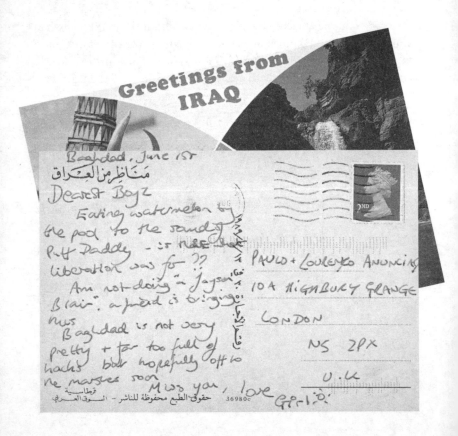

Before I left Baghdad, Bob gave me a souvenir brass plate with a kitsch painting of the spiral minaret against a pink sky. Sometimes, listening to the daily news of bombs in Iraq, I look at it on my shelf and wonder if we really did picnic there that day.

Saddam Stole Our Water

Sunday Times Magazine, 27 July 2003

HALIMA HASHIM has a face wrinkled as a walnut from a life under the sun, and black olive pits of eyes. Her *abaya*, the long black robe covering her head and body, flaps around her in the hot sand blast of a desert wind, the anonymous costume of the Arab village woman. But standing in a canoe re-enacting her wedding day, she commands all the attention of an Oscar-winning actress. 'So, we were here,' she said, hauling on board her husband Jaseem, a small man in *dishdash*, the long Arabic dress, chequered headcloth and thick bifocals from which he peered out with a bewildered expression. 'Then behind us were forty, maybe fifty boats full of people clapping and singing. Come on, children!'

Her seven children and an assortment of neighbours obediently start singing and clapping, for, at 61, Halima has a glint to her eye that no one turns down. 'We rowed to our house for a feast of slaughtered sheep and there was entertainment from gypsy singers, a brother and sister who were famous in those days, and the man who danced like a chimpanzee. Then after seven days we were rowed out to bring bunches of reeds back.'

Halima's exuberance makes it easy to picture the scene, but for one thing. 'Of course those were the days before Saddam stole our water,' she says, suddenly turning serious. For the boat in which she is performing is on dry land and there is no sign of water for as far as the eye can see.

Once set on reed islands amid the legendary Mesopotamian

marshes, the village of al Turaba in southern Iraq is today a desolate place, a cluster of scruffy mud and reed shacks on salt-encrusted ground which crunches underfoot. In the distance a single donkey moves slowly along a ridge, ridden by a man with a cloth wrapped round his head against the fierce 50°C sun. Instead of the soothing rustle of reeds that Halima grew up with, the only sound is the creaking of a toy car made of thick wire and bottle caps pushed by a small boy.

One of the most persecuted of all minorities under a regime that turned persecution into an art form, the Marsh Arabs were victims of an insidious campaign of building canals and dykes to drain the marshes and thus destroy a unique culture and ecosystem that dates back to Sumerian times.

'The destruction of Iraq's marshes involved a genocide,' says Baroness Emma Nicholson, the Liberal Democrat MEP, as she tours the area, visible from far off in her fluorescent pink headscarf. 'The best way I could describe it is as an open-air Auschwitz.'

The biggest wetlands in the Middle East, the marshes extended for 20,000 square kilometres (about the size of Wales) from Iraq to Iran. A paradise in green and blue near the confluence of the Tigris and the Euphrates, it was believed by biblical scholars to have been the Garden of Eden. Its inhabitants, the Madan or Marsh Arabs, lived on small reed islands, fished, grew rice and kept water buffalo in what was regarded by ecologists as a perfectly balanced harmony of man and beast. Millions of birds, including storks, herons and flamingos, lived there or migrated through on their way between Asia and Africa.

In his classic account *The Marsh Arabs*, Wilfred Thesiger described his impressions from his first visit in 1951: 'A naked man in a canoe with a trident in his hand, reed houses built upon water, black, dripping buffaloes that looked as if they had calved from the swamp with the first dry land...Before the first palaces were built at Ur, men had stepped out into the dawn from such a house, launched a canoe like this and gone hunting here. Five thousand years of history were here and the pattern was still unchanged.'

Saddam Hussein was no respecter of such history. To him the marshes represented a threat, a refuge for bandits, smugglers and rebels disdainful of external control, their winding canals and ten-foot-high reeds used by Shia resistance groups as cover. Having drained some of the marshes on the Iranian border to build roads during the eight-year war with Iran, his main assault on the Marsh Arabs began after the first Gulf War. His motivation was the Shi'ite uprising which started in Basra on 28 February 1991 when the commander of a tank retreating from Kuwait stopped his vehicle on Sa'ad Square in front of the ruling Ba'ath Party headquarters and fired shells at one of the ubiquitous giant portraits of Saddam.

The uprising was the most serious internal threat ever faced by the regime and for a while control hung in the balance with fourteen of the country's eighteen provinces in revolt. Thousands of members of the Badr Brigade, a pro-Iranian militia of Iraqi refugees, swarmed through the marshes to Basra where they declared an Islamic Republic.

Once the rebellion had been brutally brought under control with mass executions and bulldozing of bodies, the Marsh Arabs found themselves singled out. The official Ba'ath Party newspaper, al-Thawra, carried six long articles attacking the marsh dwellers as 'monkey-faced people' who were not real Iraqis but the descendants of black slaves brought to the south in the Middle Ages; their women were branded sluttish and immodest.

At the same time Saddam launched his 'Plan of Action for the Marshes'. Crews of workers were hired to dig the 350-mile-long Third River (later to become known as Saddam River), originally started by the British to drain saline water from farmland and carry the waters of the Euphrates directly into the Persian Gulf rather than the marshes. To stop the rivers seeping into the marshes, an elaborate system of dykes and canals was built such as the forty-mile-long Mother of Battles River, which funnelled the waters of the Tigris into the sea.

In case there was any doubt about what Saddam was trying to do, troops were sent in to burn villages and papyrus and set up military bases. What remained of the marshes was allegedly filled with toxic chemicals. Many Marsh Arabs fled across the border to Iran. This is where Emma Nicholson first saw them. 'There were thousands upon thousands coming across, maybe 80,000, this seething mass of humanity full of anguish, many of them sick,' she recalls. 'It was a bitter experience that I will never forget.'

Using her imperious manner to immediately recruit some doctors and commandeer medicines, Nicholson set up the charity Assisting Marsh Arabs and Refugees (AMAR). For years it was a lonely crusade. Few in the outside world realised what was going on for it was almost impossible for westerners to enter the area. Only now, with Saddam gone, are the Marsh Arabs who stayed in Iraq free to tell their stories.

'First the troops would come warning us to move, then the helicopters would come in and bomb, then they would set fire to our houses and the soldiers would move in,' said Mukhtar, one of a group of Marsh Arabs living in shacks near Basra airport. 'We were moved again and again until they broke us apart. My father had been killed, we had lost all our buffalo and in the end my mother just got tired and we moved to town.'

'They took three of my sons,' said Jabbar Minshed. 'One of them they shot in the marshes and two they took away. Now I can't see from crying. They didn't want us to have water. They didn't want us to live.'

A 2001 study by the United Nations Environment Program using satellite imagery found 93 per cent of the marshland had been bled dry since 1991. Of the three main marsh areas, the Hammar and Qurna had completely dried up, villages left to crumble into the sand like ghost towns. The Huwaiza marsh, which borders Iran, was left largely desiccated. According to a report by Human Rights Watch released earlier this year, the population living in the marshes has fallen from 250,000 to less than 40,000.

The buffalo and fish of the Marsh Arabs once supplied two-thirds of the fish and dairy needs of the entire country. Today those who are left are forced to depend on handouts from the United Nations. The number of buffalo in the central Hammar marsh had fallen from 170,000 in 1985 to just 2,000 sorry-looking specimens. Beached on dry desert, families like Halima's became wheat farmers, poor ones. The wheat sits in sacks waiting to be collected by a government that no longer exists. In one of the shacks, a mother fans the stained bottom of a baby boy with dysentery. Their children are malnourished and, with no fresh water, diarrhoea and cholera are a constant presence.

As the women work, along the road the men gather in the *mudhif*, the traditional village meeting house. The only tangible reminder of their ancient culture, the *mudhif* is exquisite – a long straw-coloured shelter fashioned from latticed reed walls with a cathedral-like ceiling held up by nine arches of dried twisted-together reeds. There are always an odd number apparently, though no one could explain why. Once the *mudhif* would have been on a reed island surrounded by water; now it sits stranded on the dusty roadside. A plastic clock hangs incongruously on the outside.

Inside, the sheikh or tribal leader, an old bearded man with a worn brown shawl on his shoulders and the carved wise face of Abraham, holds court as the villagers sit cross-legged on rugs woven in geometric designs by Bedouin. The compulsory portrait of Saddam has been torn down and replaced by one of the white-bearded Shia leader Ayatollah Hakim. A ceiling fan stutters on and off, barely stirring the hot air as the men lean against pillows, sipping endless small glasses of tea, half filled with sugar, poured by a small boy. The Marsh Arabs are stocky people with light skins darkened by years in the sun and many have ammunition belts slung round their waists.

There is an important discussion going on today. The collapse of the regime and consequent breakdown in law and order has led to old feuds resurfacing between the nine main tribes of the marshes. Only the previous week, three of their men were killed in a battle with the Abu Ghaman tribe. Their deaths must now be avenged but the tribesmen are worried that British and US forces will try to disarm them. It was just down the road from here that six British military police were killed last month.

Once that has been discussed, the men do what they always do and reminisce about the olden days, telling me of how in summer they would send people to the desert to collect grass chewed by camels and weave it into the latticed reed walls of the *mudhif* then sprinkle it with water to cool the air. 'Now we have no water,' said a wiry man in his thirties called Khalid Hathiel, taking a shell that looked like a white mussel from his pocket. 'We call it a Baba's nose,' he said. 'I always carry it. We are like fish, we cannot survive without water.'

As a young man Khalid was conscripted into the army and taken to Baghdad. 'I couldn't stand it, I felt like I couldn't breathe being away from the marshes. So after two months I ran away and hid.' He ended up in hiding for twelve years, until the fall of Saddam in April, getting food once a week from his family and living with other men in hiding from the regime. 'During that time my family were moved three times between 1994 and 1996, their village burnt each time.'

He slotted his pistol into his belt and summoned his friend Faisal, the sheikh's son, who appeared equipped with a Kalashnikov, 'in case of other tribes', to accompany us on a tour of the area. 'Look!' he said, pointing at the saltpans shimmering in the white afternoon heat. 'You can almost imagine it is water.'

Khalid and his newly freed friends may soon need to imagine no longer. The Marsh Arabs have suddenly found themselves fashionable and hotels in the southern city of Basra are booked solid with aid workers, European politicians and American ecologists who have come to bring back the marshes. Both the UN and USAID are carrying out surveys.

Some of the Marsh Arabs have already taken things into their own hands quite literally and started tearing down dykes, cheering as the water comes gushing back into their lands. Satellite pictures show that 15,000 hectares have been flooded since the fall of Baghdad. But ecologists warn that such self-help schemes may be risky and could create saline lakes.

Khalid takes me to part of the newly reclaimed marsh on Al Huwaiza where fishermen have already returned, gliding through the water in their long flat-bottomed canoes. One of them, Karim Jasim, paddles over to let me board as Khalid waves me off with a cheerful warning to beware 'snakes and landmines'.

'The water came back a month ago,' said Karim. 'Before we had to dig ten metres to find water and there were military everywhere; we would have been killed if we came out here.'

Out on the marshes it is another world. White herons pick up their long legs daintily, dragonflies pause on the boat to show off gossamer wings. Karim in the front and a friend in the back paddle through the water to lift out their 200-metre-long net, which is full of tiny silvery fishes. Surviving on a bag of flat Arabic bread, they will stay out for two days and nights until they have filled the icebox with fish then take it to the nearby town of Qalat Saleh to sell it for about 2,000–3,000 dinars, between £1 and £1.50.

'We used to catch fish so big one man alone could not carry them,' said Karim, drawing a picture in my notebook of himself in a boat triumphantly holding up a large fish on a trident. 'Now they are just small, but the big ones will come, *Hamdullah* [praise God]. And even if they don't, just to be out here one night and not be scared is worth the world.'

As he speaks he swats with annoyance at the mosquitoes they call 'little Saddams' – one of the unintended effects of liberation. Normally the area is sprayed with insecticide before the mosquito season but this year with the collapse of the regime there was no one to order it.

We drift for a while in silence and Karim tells me in his soft voice of the turtles that used to swim in the waters. 'Now we have water will the animals come back?' he asks. Most marsh species such as the grey wolf, smooth-coated otter and honey badger have died out. But the crack of a rifle on the way back to the village turns out to be that of a hunter, looking pleased with himself as he waves a marbled duck shot with his old Lee-Enfield, one of many British weapons picked up after the First World War, recently modified with the addition of a looted water pipe tied to the barrel.

Another happy man is Haji Mokhdar Mohammed, once the most famous boat maker in the marshes, now old and shaky, his face a spider's web of wrinkles. He smiles as he watches his son Mohammed Jasim hammering a lattice of planks together in the village of Al Huwaira. 'We used to sell one a day but when they took the water from the marshes our business collapsed and we would sell just two or three a month,' he says. 'But now business is good again.'

Leaning heavily on his stick, he takes me through the village, followed Pied Piper-like by a line of children. The mosque has a black banner along its wall listing 138 names of the disappeared. 'Everyone in this village lost someone,' he says. Eventually we come to the edge of a canal where three men are dipping wooden rolling pins into a steaming vat of bitumen to coat his newly made boats in traditional manner.

Yet even if the marshes can be restored, many of the younger Marsh Arabs say they have no desire to return to the life of fishing and buffaloes but would rather live in cities in houses with all the trappings of the modern world. 'The old type of life was good,' said Khalid, taking me to his uncle's house where his mother shyly feeds us buffalo yoghurt and water followed by delicious fresh buffalo curd from two strangely blue-eyed buffalo lying in a small ditch. 'But now we want electricity and phones and running water and PlayStations and satellite TV. Not all that marsh stuff.'

Rather like the Amazonian Indians who have been exposed to what passes for civilisation and then do not want to be kept as some kind of museum for the outside world to look upon, some Marsh Arabs are already starting to tire of the foreign aid workers rhapsodising about their ancient lifestyle.

'Look, I'm delighted Saddam has gone,' said Lefta Saleh, whose hut sits in front of a small pond of foul-smelling green-rimmed water where some of his seven children splash. 'The day he fell it rained and rained like it never had. But that doesn't mean I want to just be sitting in the water with buffaloes and being bitten by mosquitoes. I hate buffalo. If I could, I'd live in Baghdad and have a house and electricity and send my children to school.'

'As an organic farmer this integration between crops and livestock and man is wonderful,' said Andrew Friend, a Devon farmer working as a consultant to the UN Food and Agricultural Organisation in Basra. 'The projects are very sexy. Everyone wants to go floating around with the Marsh Arabs but how much of a dream it is for most Marsh Arabs to go back to that life remains to be seen. We found a lot of young people not too keen on going back and milking buffaloes. They're more into cars and the Iraqi equivalent of the Spice Girls.'

At the end of the day whatever the Marsh Arabs and their powerful new friends in Washington want, their destiny does not lie in their own hands. Oil companies are already eyeing the oil under the marshes while Turkey controls the headwaters of both the Euphrates and the Tigris and is in the middle of its own dam building, the South East Anatolia Project. The line of twenty-two dams, which received British funding, could choke off the two ancient rivers. In 1990 Turkish officials literally shut off the flow of the Euphrates for twenty-nine days.

On my last day in the marshes Khalid gathered some more friends with guns to risk crossing a couple of tribal boundaries, asking them first, 'Are you wanted men?' which seems to be a standard greeting among Marsh Arabs. We drove to Al-Qurnah at the confluence of the Euphrates and the Tigris. In a small walled garden by a shabby hotel, which like most of post-Saddam Iraq has been looted of everything from beds to window frames, stands an ancient tree. 'Adam's tree,' he said. Believed to be the Tree of Knowledge, like everything in this mythical Garden of Eden it appeared to be dead. 'Don't be sad,' smiles Khalid, beckoning me round the back. From the ground a very tiny green shoot is poking its way through.

An Afghan Asks Why

Diary entry, 28 September 2003

KABUL, FIRST CRISP BITE of the forthcoming winter in the air. Stood on the roof of the Mustafa to make calls with the sat phone and saw the sky was full of kites and the old walls of Kabul picked out in relief on the top of the mountain across the way. Ismael, the baker, has promised me hot naan bread for lunch.

God knows why this crumbling city makes me so happy. Down below, the women are still swishing figures in blue burqas. My mouth is already full of dust and it's hard to hear on the phone amid all the jangling horns and that discordant Bollywood music. Freedom seems to mean more noise and traffic.

Happy not to be in Iraq any more, though as usual left a mess in London, my taxes going to miss the deadline (again), still got to find a school for Lourenço, need to find a house, sort out a mortgage, buy a hard drive in case my laptop blows up again…

Happy to be alive maybe: the Ariana flight from Dubai landed with the usual bump and a round of applause (which might have been louder if we'd all known about the previous day's flight losing its front wheel, circling round and round to offload fuel, then making an emergency landing on its belly).

Once we'd touched down a grey-suited man of about 50 stood on his seat and started declaiming, tears streaming down his face as he repeated, '*Wahdat? Wahdat?*' – Why? Why?

Turns out he was returning from Canada after fifteen years in exile and was saying, 'Look what we've done to our country, how we've destroyed it. While other countries were developing we were destroying ours. Why? Why?' Everyone on the plane fell silent.

The Madness of Mugabe

Zimbabwe 1994–2007

Down to the wire
Sunday Telegraph, 11 August 2002

LATER, EVERYONE BUT farmer Chris Shepherd would admit that they had been scared. Not jibbering-wreck scared but tight-chest, senses-super-alert, not-knowing-what-might-happen scared. The kind of fear that comes with being locked inside a compound on the darkest of African nights when all your neighbours have fled overseas, even the moon has retreated behind clouds, and you are alone in a country that has suddenly turned hostile.

It was Friday evening and the sun had just set over the Shepherds' farm in the tobacco region of Karoi in northern Zimbabwe, night falling quickly as always in Africa. Mr Shepherd and his wife, Eleanor, were drinking pre-dinner cocktails in the lounge with his parents, Mike and Lynn, while in the television room their four young children were lying on cushions amid their many cats and dogs, watching Walt Disney's *White Fang*.

Suddenly the radio transmitter in the next room crackled into life and a panicked voice gabbled in Shona. Mr Shepherd rushed to answer, returning grim-faced. 'It's started,' he said. Neighbouring farmer William Dardigan had been surrounded by about thirty land invaders, demanding to know why he had not left his farm.

Like the Shepherds, Mr Dardigan had stayed on his farm in defiance of a government order for 2,900 white farmers to be off their land by midnight on Thursday or 'face the consequences'.

No one knew what those consequences might be. But the deadline followed a two-and-a-half-year campaign of violent land invasions in which twelve white farmers had been killed and hundreds more beaten and kicked off their farms, so most feared the worst. The perpetrators call themselves war vets, though many are too young to have fought in the liberation war and are probably just unemployed youths.

The façade of normality crumbled instantly as the Shepherds began discussing strategy if invaders came or police arrived to arrest them for breaking the law.

'They're trying to break us down mentally,' said Mrs Shepherd, holding back the tears as she cuddled her youngest child, Graham, 4, ready for bed in his pyjamas. 'This whole D-Day was psychological warfare.'

Peering outside, it was easy to understand why the family might break. The only light visible for miles was the fire of the war vets who covet the Shepherd home and have taken to killing the cattle and removing just one leg, leaving the three-legged carcasses to be found the next morning. Although there were thirteen guards out patrolling the lands, no one knew whose side they might be on any more in a society running out of food and rule of law.

'Even our own labour is turning against us,' said Mr Shepherd. 'They stole half my maize crop. My manager is stealing my diesel. But I don't blame them. They are desperate. They know we might soon be gone. That's the cunning of Mugabe.'

Such fear left Zimbabwe's white farmers in a terrible dilemma this weekend. Stay and risk arrest, or leave and perhaps lose everything. Many decided not to take the risk, particularly as today is Heroes' Day, the annual military holiday to commemorate the war of liberation from white rule. Jenni Williams of the farmers' organisation Justice for Agriculture said that at least 30 per cent have left the country, while another 15 per cent went away for the weekend.

The Shepherd family is among those who decided to defy the order and stay, fearing that otherwise they would lose all they had worked for.

Yet for Mr Shepherd, 36, it was a greater risk than for most. An out-spoken critic of Mugabe's so-called land reform, he had already been arrested last month, and was recently warned by war veterans that he would be killed.

'We don't have a conscience about being here,' he insists. 'We're as much African as any black. We were born here, bred here and what we have we've worked for. We're not just going to walk away.'

Until the radio alert on Friday evening, the Shepherds had begun to hope that the weekend might pass uneventfully. They had been buoyed by a High Court decision on Wednesday declaring illegal the Land Acquisition Act which set the eviction deadline.

Thursday started off badly with the vicious beating of another Karoi farmer, Kevin Smith, accused by invaders on his land of trying to poison them after he put gypsum in his dam to increase the alkalinity for his tobacco seed.

The Shepherds, on hearing the news, decided to leave their four children aged between 4 and 10 in Harare. Dinner that evening was a strange mix of forced jollity punctuated with long silences and edgy laughter as people tried not to think about the impending midnight deadline.

But the night passed uneventfully, even if everyone appeared at breakfast the next morning with dark circles under their eyes. I guessed they had lain awake as I had, listening to the distant drumming and imagining men with machetes creeping up to the windows.

With all calm on Friday the children were brought back, happy to be reunited with their nine dogs and seven ponies. As the house filled with noise and laughter it almost seemed like an ordinary weekend.

The radio message changed all that. 'It's the grandchildren I worry about,' says Mr Shepherd's mother, Lynn. 'Chris and Eleanor have this daring in them, but what about the children? It's already affecting them.'

The local Rydings School where the children study has seen the number of pupils fall from 320 to fewer than 200 over the past year.

The Shepherds' second daughter, Terrileigh, 9, has found it particularly hard. The school psychologist gave her a *Homes and Gardens* magazine and told her to cut out pictures of a house and a garden to stick on a sheet of paper. Asked why she had chosen the most luxurious, she said: 'This is like our house and I am scared war vets will come and destroy it.'

Even 4-year-old Graham, whom they have not told that they might lose their home, has been affected. Mr Shepherd said: 'He begs me, "Don't play with the war vets, Dad, because they will cut your head off."'

The tension has caused some marriages to collapse, particularly where one partner wants to leave and the other to stay. Driving around the Karoi area yesterday with Mr Shepherd, I saw that one farm after another lay abandoned or taken over by war vets, the owners fleeing to Australia, New Zealand and South Africa, often to manual jobs.

One of the Shepherds' former neighbours now drives a council digger in Australia, his vast gum plantation and bougainvillea-covered house abandoned. Coffee beans lie rotting on bushes, fields of wheat have been turned to burnt stubble, and fences have been torn from game parks and the wildlife poached. As Mr Shepherd gives me a tour around the tobacco sheds and pigsties, the stables and pony jumps of his 800-hectare farm and what had clearly been an idyllic life, he says: 'It's very hard to abandon all this knowing we'll probably never be compensated. When we got married, all we owned was a car. But we worked hard managing farms, then leasing them until we could afford our own. We bought this in 1995, building it up from nothing, and had just got to a point where we thought we were getting somewhere when the war vets arrived two years ago.'

To leave would mean financial ruin. 'We borrowed money to build the dam, the animal sheds, new tobacco sheds at 26 per cent and within a year the interest rate had gone up to 46 per cent,' said Mrs Shepherd.

Her mother-in-law shakes her head. 'We whites have outstayed our welcome in this country and it's time we realised,' she says. 'Both our daughters and their families have already moved to New Zealand. Mike and I are just waiting to see Chris and Eleanor safe then we will join them. The most important thing is your life. I wish they would just leave.'

But her son replies: 'We can't let Mugabe get away with such a large-scale heist of farms.'

Yet while no one wants to give in to a dictator, many are deciding it is not worth the struggle. The Shepherd family spent yesterday at yet another farewell party for a neighbour moving to America. One of the farmers took children up for joyrides in his small plane, attesting to the lifestyle they had all once enjoyed. Then it was back for another night of tension, expecting police or war vets to arrive at any moment.

As the radio crackled into life again, with a message from a guard reporting a gun missing, Mrs Shepherd looks exhausted. 'I am frightened to let the children go riding on their own in case they get raped or their throats slashed. And I live in fear of Chris being arrested or killed, or a petrol bomb being thrown through the window. I long for a life without fear.'

For all the Shepherds' hospitality, after three days I have rarely been so glad to leave anywhere. Mugabe's prolonged use of violence to keep himself in power is turning one of the friendliest countries in the world into a land of fear where even the fields have eyes.

As I watched a war vet hammer a white-painted window frame clearly purloined from a farmer's house on to the thatched hut he was building in the middle of a corn plantation, another man waves his thumb at me. A thumbs-up is the symbol of Mugabe's ruling party. 'You whites came with nothing,' he spits. 'You should leave with nothing.'

The Shepherds were driven off by war vets a few months after I stayed with them. Their farm was occupied by Francis Nhema, Zimbabwe's Minister of Environment, who was chosen by other African nations to become chairman of the United Nations Commission on Sustainable Development in May 2007 amid international outrage.

When the invasions started in 2000, I, like many, could not believe that Mugabe was serious about seizing all the white-owned farms. Zimbabwe's land distribution was undoubtedly unfair, with most of the productive land still in white hands more than twenty years on from independence. But the 5,000 commercial farms produced most of the food for the nation, were the country's biggest employer and brought in 40 per cent of its export earnings.

I underestimated Mugabe. By 2007, less than 200 white farmers remained on their farms and evictions were continuing. Yet it was never really a racial issue. We in the western media played into Mugabe's hands by initially portraying the land seizures as such, focusing on white farmers like the Shepherds, perhaps because they seemed people like us. But the real victims were the hundreds of thousands of black farm workers who lost their homes and jobs. With nowhere else to go, they fled to the rural areas where they struggle to survive on baobab pods, wild fruits and fried termites. Many were beaten by marauding youth brigades who accused them of supporting the opposition Movement for Democratic Change (MDC). In August 2002, on a journey that took me from the Zambezi Valley in the north-west to Manicaland in the east, I discovered something even more horrific.

For four hours Dora, aged 12, was gang-raped by Mugabe's men
Sunday Telegraph, 25 August 2002

'THE GAME WE are about to play needs music,' the Zimbabwean police constable said to the 12-year-old girl. But as he tossed a mattress on to the ground it was clear that it was no game that he was planning. For the next four hours the girl's mother and younger sisters, aged 9 and 7, were forced to chant praises to Robert Mugabe and watch Dora* being gang-raped by five 'war veterans' and the policeman.

'Every time they stopped singing the policeman and war vets beat them with shamboks and sticks,' said Dora, crying and clenching her hands repeatedly as she recalled the ordeal which took place behind her family hut in a village in the dark shadow of the Vumba mountains of Manicaland, in eastern Zimbabwe. 'They kept thrusting themselves into me over and over again, saying: "This is the punishment for you who want to sell this country to Tony Blair and the whites." When they had finished it hurt so much I couldn't walk.'

Now in hiding, she spends most nights in frightened wakefulness,

----

* The names of the rape victims have been changed for their protection.

remembering the rough breath on her face, the hands forcing apart her thighs, and 'that animal thing' as she calls it slamming into her underfed body. Dora was raped because her father is a supporter of the opposition Movement for Democratic Change (MDC). He is not a candidate, not a party official, just a carpenter who had mistakenly believed that he lived in a country where he could vote for whom he liked.

Dora's story, as she tells it, started with a Land Rover full of war veterans drawing up at the door of the hut around 10 p.m. one evening in June, while her father was away, and ended with her left bruised and bleeding at 2.30 a.m. 'There had been a bad luck owl in the msasa tree that day,' she said. But the real beginning of the horror can be traced back to March when her village voted against Mugabe in the presidential elections. For rape has become the latest weapon in Mugabe's war on his own population. Dora's echoing screams on the African night were a warning to all the other villagers as to what might happen to those who even think of defying the President again.

Dora is one of hundreds of young girls who are being raped in the fields and mountains of rural Zimbabwe every month as part of what human rights workers are calling a 'systematic political cleansing of the population'.

Many of the girls are taken to camps run by Mugabe's youth militia, the Green Bombers, a sinister parallel to the rape camps of Bosnian Muslim women established by Serb forces in the early 1990s. And with half the country facing starvation, more and more youths are being lured to join the militia by the prospect of food.

In Zimbabwe, though, there is an extra dimension to the ordeals that the women endure: with 38 per cent of the population HIV positive, rape is often the start of a death sentence.

'We're seeing an enormous prevalence of rape and enough cases to say it's being used by the state as a political tool with women and girls being raped because they are wives, girlfriends or daughters of political activists,' said Tony Reeler, clinical director of the Amani Trust, a Harare-based organisation that monitors and treats torture victims. 'There are also horrific cases of girls as young as 12 or 13 being taken off to militia camps, used and abused and kept in forced concubinage.

But I suspect the real extent of what is happening is going to take a long time to come out.'

Rape goes unreported in many countries but more so in Africa, particularly in rural areas where a raped daughter is seen as bringing shame on the family and hard to marry off. The pressure to remain silent is even stronger in a police state where the police are often the perpetrators. Dora's family did go to the police station only to be laughed at with the words: 'We're not fools to arrest one of our colleagues.'

Nor do many rape victims receive medical treatment. In Dora's case the local clinic had no drugs and her family did not have money to take her to hospital, so she is being treated with traditional herbs.

Her story is far from unique. In a harrowing month-long investigation, photographer Justin Sutcliffe and I interviewed rape victims in villages throughout the Zambezi Valley, Matabeleland and Manicaland.

Among those we met were a teacher beaten so badly that she had lost her baby, and a former militia member who had participated in the raping and pillaging intended to pacify the countryside. We found a population living in terror, some towns completely 'cleansed' of all opposition.

We spent an uneasy night ourselves when we underestimated the time it would take to reach a safe house in the Zambezi Valley and broke down on sandy tracks in the dark, forty miles from the nearest telephone. Not far away we could hear drums and chants of '*Pasi ne murungu*' ('Down with the white man') and other slogans of Mugabe's ruling Zanu-PF party coming from a group around a fire. In the end we were towed out by men who turned out to be war vets.

Fear and hunger are what passes for life in much of Mugabe's Zimbabwe. In the capital Harare there is a façade of normality – workmen repaint the blue trolley shelter in the gleaming new airport terminal, the traffic lights work, and pavement cafés serve the best cappuccino in Africa. The roads are full of gleaming new BMWs, known as 'Girlfriends of Ministers' cars', bought by government officials profiting from privileged access to foreign exchange at subsidised rates.

The only signs of anything amiss are the long snaking queues for bread, sugar and fuel, the absence of maize (previously the country's staple food) from all shops, and the number of people simply hanging around. Unemployment has now reached 70 per cent of the working population.

In the rural areas that Zimbabwe's Marxist President regards as his stronghold it is a different story. Furious that so many of 'his' people voted against him in elections – which he knows he did not really win – and incensed by calls such as that from the Bush administration demanding a rerun, he has unleashed his forces to wreak revenge in the most horrible manner.

When he was sworn back in as president in April, the 78-year-old, who has ruled the country since independence in 1980, warned the opposition: 'We'll make them run if they haven't run before.' Assuming that his declaration of victory would bring an end to the violence which had dogged the campaign, no one then realised the lengths to which he was prepared to go.

Officials now speak of 'taking the system back to zero' and reducing the country's 12 million population. It's a chilling echo of what the Khmer Rouge did in Cambodia in the 1970s and they seem to be employing similar tactics of emptying cities and targeting teachers. 'We would be better off with only 6 million people, with our own people who support the liberation struggle,' said Didymus Mutasa, the Organisation Secretary of Zanu-PF.

The situation is particularly bad in Manicaland, or the Eastern Highlands as the settlers called it, its misty mountains reminding them of Scotland. In almost every village where people were known to have voted against Mugabe, we pieced together the same story of beatings of teachers and wanton destruction of property. Everywhere we saw the charred skeletons of burnt bicycles, the main mode of transport of rural MDC workers.

'The Black Boots [police] burnt my house,' said 47-year-old George, an MDC campaigner forced to flee Buhera two weeks ago. 'We don't own much but they smashed all we had in front of my children then urinated in the small amounts of sugar and flour we had left.'

The villagers' greatest fear is being taken to one of the camps. Set up before the elections to train the youth militia to harass the MDC and funded from the Food for Work programme, under which youths are supposed to receive food aid for work such as road building, they form the centres for Mugabe's terror campaign.

One of the most notorious is at Bazeley River in Manicaland. There was a police roadblock on the main road outside, clearly designed to stop anyone getting near. With the Corrs blaring from our car stereo, however, they believed our story of being tourists lost in search of a particular mountain and, incredibly, let us through.

We reached the camp by crossing a narrow bridge and driving up a dirt track. The series of tents around a trestle table at which young men were helping themselves to breakfast looked unnervingly like a scout camp apart from the 'Do Not Enter' sign painted angrily on the gate, the surly red-eyed men hanging around wearing T-shirts bearing the legend 'The Third Chimurenga', after the liberation war, and pictures of Osama bin Laden.

It was here that 15-year-old Priscilla, whom I had interviewed in a safe house in Harare, was raped repeatedly for three days then had her genitals burnt with a poker. It was here, too, that Benjamin, a 32-year-old teacher, was badly beaten after having his house burnt down. 'They accused me of repeating the word *chinja* [change – the opposition MDC election slogan] in lessons.

'They took me into one of the tents and forced me to lie on my stomach and said they would keep beating me until I defecated. I told them I had already defecated in my pants but they said: "No, you must defecate your whole intestines." Finally they stopped and made me crawl in the mud. When they let me go, they said this is only a taste of what will happen to you.'

A former member of the youth militia, who fled because he was so appalled at what he was being ordered to do and is now in hiding, agreed to talk about what went on in the camp. 'I was desperate,' he said. 'I had lost my job in a fried-chicken takeaway last November and have a wife and 13-month-old baby girl to support. So when Zanu-PF people came around our houses I joined. They said we would get Z$50,000 [about £600] but we didn't get any money, just food and beer.

'There were about 200 of us in the camp and we called ourselves "the Taliban". We were told if we saw anyone with an MDC T-shirt we must assault them with whips, catapults, steel bars. The idea was to instil fear in people so they would be frightened to vote and to take revenge against those who had.

'Then a couple of months ago they said it is the women who are behind this campaign to bring back white rule. They told us to take them to the bush, that they are daughters of dogs and coconuts [blacks with white centres], and to bring young ones back to the camp to service us. When I said we can't do this, that these are our sisters, they accused me of being a "sell-out" and beat me.'

Zimbabwe is the most heartbreaking story I have ever covered. I first went there in 1994 when I was living in neighbouring South Africa. I was so taken with its friendly people and landscape of green hills and strange balancing rocks that a few months later I went back on holiday with Paulo. In those days, it was one of the most prosperous countries in Africa. We got giggling-drenched in the spray from Victoria Falls, sipped gin and tonics as the sun set over the Zambezi, laughed at road signs warning 'Elephants Crossing'. We sat awed by the silent grandeur of the Matopo Hills, burial place of Cecil Rhodes, the empire builder after whom the country was originally named.

We also marvelled at an African nation with traffic lights that worked (even if they did call them robots), pothole-free roads, neat brick schools everywhere, and book cafés. The roads on which we travelled passed through a patchwork of lush green fields of tobacco, cotton and maize. They looked like model farms with combine harvesters gathering up neat bundles, long greenhouses full of neatly spaced roses, and rainbows playing through the water sprinkling from sophisticated irrigation systems.

Ten years on, Mugabe's campaign of violent land invasions had left Zimbabwe looking as if a terrible scourge had swept through. Some of the most advanced farms in the world had been reduced to slash and burn. The fields were charred and spiked with dead maize stalks or overgrown with weeds and elephant grass; the equipment plundered and stripped; and what little ploughing was still going on was by oxen or donkey.

The war vets had been used and moved on. Just as in the Shepherds' case, most farms ended up in the hands of Mugabe's cronies, used as patronage to keep his allies onside, whether party officials, army and police commanders, High Court judges, even the Anglican Bishop of Harare, Nolbert Kunonga.

By 2004, production of maize, the staple crop, had fallen by 74 per cent and the national cow herd shrunk by 90 per cent. On his farm Mr Shepherd had grown 80 hectares of high-grade tobacco and 200 hectares of maize. Its new 'owner', Mr Nhema, managed three hectares of tobacco and ten hectares of maize.

Zimbabwe has gone from a country which used to export large amounts of food to one dependent on food aid, with half of its 12 million population on the edge of starvation. By August 2007, its inflation was around 10,000 per cent, by far the highest in the world, with money so worthless that the country was returning to a barter economy. Average per capita income had plummeted to 1953 levels. No country has ever experienced such a decline in its economy in peacetime.

A few years ago, I spent an afternoon with James Chikerema, Mugabe's one-time ally in the freedom struggle, who grew up with him at Kutama mission. He insisted that the Zimbabwean President would stay in power until he brought the whole country tumbling down around him. 'Mugabe's behaving like a captain who wants to go down with his ship,' he said. 'He forgets that Zimbabwe is not a ship but a country.'

As a reporter it has been incredibly frustrating going back again and again reporting on more and more unthinkable things – the beatings of the opposition; the series of rigged parliamentary and presidential elections; the households headed by 7-year-olds because their parents had died of Aids; the pensioners living on the equivalent of just 13p a month, not even enough for one toilet roll. All the time it seemed the rest of the world sat by, attention distracted by 9/11, then the war in Iraq. And so cleverly had Mugabe presented what he was doing as a stand against colonialism that other African leaders gave him standing ovations at international forums.

Those Zimbabweans who could leave, left. These tended to be the middle classes – doctors, nurses, accountants, teachers and professors. Each time I go back I find a population weaker and sicker –and thus less likely to rise up.

It has also become an increasingly risky story to cover. Only once did I feel physically threatened – at Lake Kariba during the 2000 elections when I was surrounded by a crowd of Mugabe's thugs late one night and taken into the Zambezi Valley Motel where earlier that week they had tortured, raped and killed opposition activists. That evening Mugabe had been on television railing against his favourite bogeyman, the Blair government. 'Why are the British stealing the fish from the lake?' my captors demanded, ranting for four hours before finally releasing me.

Then the regime banned foreign journalists altogether, or rather made it illegal for them to operate without a licence, which was impossible to get if you were British and had ever written anything remotely critical of Mugabe. In January 2005 they introduced a penalty of a two-year prison sentence for any foreign correspondent caught illegally in the country.

So-called snooping laws were passed enabling the government to monitor emails and phone calls; one in five people are thought to be informers for the Central Intelligence Organisation (CIO). To criticise the government has been made a crime and passengers on buses have been arrested for complaining about the price of tomatoes. Anyone I interview I am putting at risk. One day in Bulawayo, I spent a morning in Emganwini township in which every shack seemed to have someone fading away from Aids on a mattress in the corner. That evening I got a call from the local councillor telling me that everyone I had interviewed had subsequently been visited by CIO agents.

In April 2005 I was at Johannesburg airport boarding a plane to Zimbabwe when a friend called to warn me that Mugabe's spokesman George Charamba had declared me an enemy of the state. Somewhat quaintly, Charamba had added that I had a 'penchant for writing about corpses on golf courses', a subject on which I had never written.

I decided to get on the flight. But I did not sleep easy on that trip. One evening in Harare I was driving out of the house where I was staying. The power was off so the road was dark and, as the gate opened, I was surrounded by blue flashing lights. I froze, thinking Mugabe's men had found me. Then I realised that they were fire engines.

A month later, in late May 2005, I was in neighbouring Botswana researching an article and decided to try crossing the border. I arrived in Bulawayo and drove to my usual money changers. There was an uneasy atmosphere in town, not many people around, and, passing the street of the old Fifth Avenue market, I caught sight of a whole lot of twisted wire and smashed wood. When I asked the money changer what had happened, he looked terrified and whispered that police had broken up the market.

Early the next morning I flew north to Harare. As my taxi neared the city we passed thousands of people streaming along the road with a few possessions tied in bundles on their heads or in wheelbarrows. They looked like refugees fleeing a war.

Mugabe had switched his attention to the cities, targeting the urban population who had dared vote against him in successive elections. That day I watched in horror as police bulldozers demolished thousands of homes, market stalls and small businesses. Worst hit was Mbare, a district on the outskirts of Harare that had housed Zimbabwe's largest market. Street after street had been turned into a battleground of twisted wreckage, torn wood and piles of broken bricks. Sirens wailed and plumes of smoke rose from smouldering ground, in the midst of which stood the occasional wardrobe or iron bed frame – all that remained of family homes. A few figures were picking among the smoking debris like vultures while others huddled in small dazed groups at the sides. Every so often one of Zimbabwe's new Chinese warplanes roared across the sky.

Operation Murambatsvina or 'Drive Out the Filth' had begun with no warning when trucks of police and youth militia clad in riot-protection gear arrived at Hatcliff, a shantytown alongside a large orphanage. From there they swept through the city, smashing dwellings and ordering people to go back to the rural areas. One man showed me a swamp of rotting vegetables stamped and trodden by laughing militia. From Mutare to Victoria Falls, no one was safe – even the colourful women flower-sellers who had operated in Harare's Africa Unity Square for decades. Flowers and carved wooden animals were thrown on to bonfires as their owners watched in disbelief.

'This is Pol Pot-style depopulation of cities,' said David Coltart, legal affairs spokesman for the MDC. 'It's a sinister pre-emptive strike designed to remove the maximum possible number of people from urban areas to rural areas where they are easier to control.'

Back in London I kept waking in the night seeing those blank faces as everything they had ever worked for was destroyed in front of them. The UN estimated that 700,000 people had lost their homes yet only one had protested. I had even watched people meekly burn their own belongings at the behest of the police.

In our garden is a curious giraffe made of scrap metal that I had bought at Harare's Enterprise Road market. Mugabe's 22-vehicle motorcade had passed as I was about to pay, causing everyone to freeze (it's illegal to move the upper body when it goes by). It was a terrifying sight with wailing sirens, ambulances, blacked-out saloon cars and army trucks bearing men with orange-painted faces and Kalashnikovs trained on the roadside. The young man who made the giraffe was shaking. Afterwards, we chatted for a while and, as he laid the animal on my back seat, he asked me to name it Elvis after him 'so you won't forget me'. When I returned during Operation Murambatsvina, Elvis's entire iron menagerie lay crushed and twisted among the rubble. I wondered what had happened to him.

All the time it is getting harder and harder for people to survive. Harare has had a cholera outbreak; doctors tell of a dramatic increase in child malnutrition; hospitals have nothing left but aspirins – not even saline solution for drips. In June 2007 the Minister for Economic Development told me that he thought half the population would be dead were it not for remittances from Zimbabweans who have left the country.

Saddest of all is seeing mothers no longer able to send their children to school. Zimbabwe once had the best-educated population in Africa. I remember on my first visit being impressed by all those neat buildings and lines of children with freshly washed uniforms and rucksacks of books.

And who could forget the television pictures of Robert Mugabe and a young Prince Charles removing the British flag on 18 April 1980 and raising that of the new Zimbabwe – the last colony in Africa to become independent.

How could today's monster be the same man who so impressed the world that day with his talk of reconciliation. 'I urge you, whether you are black or white, to join me in a new pledge to forget our grim past, forgive others and join hands in a new amity,' he said.

But under the lectern while he spoke his fist was clenched.

Zimbabwe's silent genocide
Sunday Times, 8 July 2007

GRANDMOTHER NDLOLO DUBE sits on the dusty ground outside her mud-and-pole hut and looks out on a land that has never seemed so dry and unforgiving. The field that was supposed to feed her and her four orphaned grandchildren is littered with dead, broken maize stalks.

'No rain,' she says, as she shows the half-full fifty-kilo bag of maize that is all the family has harvested this year. It is the third year running that the harvest has failed, but this time is by far the worst. 'It's just enough to last two or three weeks then I don't know what we'll do.'

At every hut, every village, it is the same story. Plumtree and Figtree sound as if they should be verdant places but severe drought has left the area, like much of southern Zimbabwe, with 95 per cent crop failure. People sit with dazed expressions, fuddled with hunger. The United Nations World Food Programme estimates that 4 million people will need food aid.

Shortages are no longer new in this country where President Robert Mugabe's violent land seizures have seen the destruction of commercial farms that once provided work for millions and food for the whole region. But this year they come amid inflation estimated to have reached 10,000–15,000 per cent.

By the end of June prices were doubling daily. Last week the government sent in police and militia youths to force shopkeepers to lower prices. Many responded by locking their doors and suspending business. The police responded by arresting them.

Dube has no idea how she and her family will survive for the rest of the year. 'I have no cow, no goats, nothing,' she says.

When I ask how often they eat, she replies: 'Morning and evening.' Surprised, I ask what they ate that morning. 'Nothing,' she says. And the previous evening? 'Nothing.' It turns out that they often go for days without eating.

Sometimes the children get so hungry they chew green fruits from a tree known as African chewing gum, even though they know they will end up with stomach ache.

Two of Dube's grandchildren – 10-year-old twins Kwenza Kele and Flatter – take me with them to collect water. They are smaller than my 7-year-old back home. The water hole has a fence of twisted logs to prevent cows defecating but it is green and putrid water, topped with scum.

This year's maize harvest is expected to be 500,000 tonnes, compared with the 1.4 million tonnes needed. But Pius Ncube, the outspoken Catholic Archbishop of Bulawayo, believes the shortages will help Mugabe in the run-up to elections next March. 'The government is very happy about the food situation as they know they can use food to make people vote for them again,' he says. 'They use every advantage.'

At the next village, grandmother Dedi Ndlovu is complaining about pain in her legs. She harvested just twenty kilos of maize for her nine grandchildren, eight of whom are orphans. 'Not even half a bag,' she says. 'In the past we would get six or seven bags. Sometimes I think, what if I get sick and die? What will happen to these children?'

It is a while before I notice something even more eerie than the impending famine. These are villages of grandparents and grand-children. There is nobody of my age. In a whole day we meet only one person between the ages of 20 and 50. 'All the young people have either died or gone,' explains Pastor Raymond, the local clergyman.

Many have fallen victim to the lethal combination of Aids and hunger. Others are part of an exodus of 4 million Zimbabweans forced for economic and political reasons to leave their country.

In the towns I have noticed fewer people on the streets, but it is only in these villages that the figures are brought home. This is a country that has lost an entire generation.

Amid the breakdown of society – twenty-hour power cuts, water shortages, collapse of the phone system – nobody I ask, whether government official, diplomat or aid worker, has any idea what the population of Zimbabwe is any more. 'That's the $25 million question,' says a US diplomat, suggesting the figure may be as low as 8 million, instead of the 12 million usually cited.

In fifteen years, life expectancy has fallen from 62 to 34 years for women and 37 for men, by far the lowest in the world. What some call a silent genocide has left Zimbabwe with more orphans than anywhere else in the world – 1.4 million according to Unicef.

At Bulawayo's vast West Park cemetery, it is easy to spot the recent arrivals – a large plot, freshly dug, with row after row of graves, barely a plank's width between them. The gravestones tell their own story. All were born in the 1960s, 1970s and 1980s. Over on the other side in the children's section is a line of tiny earth mounds, the graves of babies who have died in the past week.

At the edges of the graveyard are odd areas of tossed earth. 'People come in at night and bury their relatives secretly at the margins because they cannot afford proper burials,' explains Pastor Useni Sibanda, who leads a church in Bulawayo and speaks for the Save Zimbabwe Campaign, an umbrella grouping of church groups and other civic organisations.

Those who can, join burial clubs – macabre savings groups based on Christmas clubs, only instead of hampers people in a street or a workplace join together to pay for each other's dead. Others register sick relatives under false names at hospitals, knowing they cannot afford a funeral.

Nobody knows how many have died of hunger. But doctors in Zimbabwe say the population's chronic malnutrition, combined with HIV, leads to the onset of full-blown Aids far faster than anywhere else in Africa.

Father Oskar Wermter, a German Jesuit priest working in Mbare,

Harare's oldest township, has spent thirty-seven years in Zimbabwe and says he has never seen things so bad, even during the liberation war. 'How do people survive in this situation?' he asks. 'The answer is many just don't but you don't see them.'

Tears in his eyes, he tells the story of Chipo Kurewa, a lively teacher in her forties whose home was bulldozed during Operation Murambatsvina. 'After that, she was in constant trouble, struggling to find work and accommodation and then diagnosed HIV positive,' says Wermter. He took Kurewa to a centre to get anti-retroviral drugs, but then she disappeared. 'One day I got a phone call from Botswana. It was her – she'd gone to find work. About six weeks later she arrived in a terrible state. A kind lady in Gaborone had put her on a bus. But she had meningitis. Three days later she was dead.'

I ask after Stella, one of his parishioners, who had taken me round Mbare eighteen months ago to see those who lost their homes in Murambatsvina. I remembered her flamboyant clothes and vivacious manner, despite the horror we were seeing and the risks we were taking. 'Dead,' he replies bluntly. 'This is becoming a land of the elderly and very young, the unqualified and underqualified – in other words, the most vulnerable.'

There are other effects too. All the children I speak to are much older than their size would suggest, and a recent study found that more than one in three people in Harare suffers mental disorders. The main reasons were inability to find food and having belongings taken away by the authorities.

Zimbabwe is not yielding photographs of children with stick limbs and flies on their mouths, the images we usually associate with famine in Africa. Something more sinister is under way, almost as if life were just draining out of the country.

At a shack selling firewood in Emakhandeni township, just outside Bulawayo, Sibanda stops to load up and says: 'If the middle classes have been so pauperised that teachers are forced to become prostitutes to feed their family and use firewood because there's no more power, imagine what's happening to the most marginalised.'

Inside the shack, a girl of 15 lies dying on a bed, her blankets soiled and life fading away. Her lips are parched and her eyes flicker weakly at us. The family do not even ask for help. They know it is the same in every shack in every township. Besides, even if we got her to hospital, there would be no drugs.

At Mpilo hospital in Bulawayo, the Japanese-funded paediatric unit was opened in 2004 and is remarkably clean and modern. Inside there are numerous empty beds. Few can afford the bus fare to the hospital.

The only medicines have been donated by a foreign aid agency. On the babies' ward, none is connected to a monitor and only two have drips, even in the malnutrition room. By one cot sit a couple whose 7-month-old daughter desperately needs intestinal surgery, but who have been told they must buy a drip, which they cannot afford. 'We had to borrow to pay the bus fare to get here,' says the father as he watches his wife cradle the sick child.

There are only two young nurses to staff the ward of forty-five seriously ill babies, treating, cleaning and feeding them. 'Anyone that can go has left the country,' says one of the nurses, pointing out that her monthly salary of Z$3.2 million (£4.50) barely covers her bus fares of Z$120,000 a day. 'I eat nothing during my shift as I can't afford it.'

The only reason she and her colleague are still here, she says, is they are newly qualified and the government is withholding their diplomas. 'They're doing it deliberately to stop us going.'

There is no sign of any doctors. According to a Unicef official, 50 per cent of all health posts in Zimbabwe are vacant and there are more Zimbabwean nurses in Manchester than in Bulawayo.

It is not just doctors who are leaving. Over the past few years, the University of Zimbabwe has seen its number of lecturers fall from more than 1,200 to just over 600. According to the Progressive Teachers Union of Zimbabwe, more than 5,000 teachers left between January and April this year.

The magnitude of the exodus becomes starkly clear across the border in South Africa, to which the majority of people flee. At the Central Methodist Church in central Johannesburg, Zimbabwean refugees are literally spilling out on to the road.

More than 3,000 sleep there every night, cramming the corridors and steps, each with a zipped bag containing all they could carry. Yet every person I talk to is a professional: accountants, bankers, headmasters.

One was the clerk of the High Court – forced to flee, he says, because he witnessed the secret police interfering with ballot boxes during a legal challenge by the opposition to presidential elections.

Most have left because the alternative was to starve. 'We just couldn't afford to feed our families,' says a group of teachers recently arrived from a school in Masvingo.

They have to leave the church by 7 a.m. every day and wander the streets hoping to pick up work as labourers or gardeners, or just begging. One man earns more in a day's gardening than he did in a month of teaching science in Zimbabwe.

Most of the refugees are men looking for money to send back to their families. But on the ground floor is a room packed with women and children. One woman, Joyce, sits watching her 2-year-old son and 4-year-old daughter scrape leftovers from someone's pan of *sadza* (grain meal). 'My husband passed away and I couldn't get work in Bulawayo,' she says. 'I thought if we came to South Africa we might still have hope of a life.'

It was a hazardous journey, crossing the crocodile-infested Limpopo river with the two toddlers on her back. 'I was very frightened both of crocodiles and border guards,' she said. 'But I kept thinking there is nothing left for us in Zimbabwe.'

'The numbers have been going up dramatically this year,' says Bishop Paul Verryn, who has fought off parishioners' protests to shelter the Zimbabweans. 'We used to see five or ten arriving a day but for the last few months it has been twenty or more. It's a cataclysmic collapse of a country.'

Where's bin Laden?

Sunday Times Magazine, 18 March 2007

'YOU'RE A GREAT GUY, Crazy, but you ain't that clean,' says the American, spraying his hands with anti-bacterial sanitiser after slipping a $100 note into the palm of one of his local informants.

The American is dressed in long baggy *shalwar kameez* and sporting a beard. But he will never be taken for a local here in the frontier town of Peshawar. We have met before, two years ago in the bar of the Mustafa hotel in Kabul, where such characters hung out amid its pink-marbled walls and mirrored ceilings, pulling out knives and guns to see whose weapon was the largest.

His name is 'Dave' and he works in 'private security' and maybe it is and maybe he does. But what he is really is a bounty hunter in search of the $25 million pay day – Osama bin Laden.

On one thigh is strapped a Glock pistol and out of his pocket he pulls a packet of Cipro (a powerful antibiotic used by the military), a couple of which he swallows after a visit to the bathroom. 'Occupational hazard,' he grimaces.

Over time most of his fellow bounty hunters have given up despite the high prize. But 'Dave' has ended up here in Greens Hotel where last night in bed a cockroach crawled across his face and the windows look out on to the jagged mountains of the Khyber Pass. 'This is the place,' he says. 'Not Afghan-land.'

His eyes bulge as he speaks and I can almost see the $$ signs flashing up in front of them. He talks conspiratorially of the valleys of Dir and Tirah. 'That's where the big guy's holed up,' he says. But he is yet to go. According to the fixer he calls Crazy, any who have tried have been tortured, stripped and castrated. Their eyeballs have been plucked from their sockets; their ears hacked off; and their tongues ripped from their mouths. Dollars have been stuffed in their pockets and notes pinned to their groins declaring: 'This is what happens to agents of the USA.'

Some 7,500 miles away the last CIA agent to come close to killing Osama bin Laden digs his spoon into a thick slab of strawberry cheesecake in a Manhattan diner and smiles coldly.

'He killed 3,000 Americans, here in my city, and I wanted him dead,' says Gary Berntsen. 'I wasn't going to ask permission because I knew I wouldn't get it.'

A large-framed man with pale-blue eyes, he tells me that he will be 50 this year, the same age as bin Laden. The diner is packed with harassed Christmas shoppers, squashing into the melamine booths with armfuls of shopping bags. It seems an odd place to ask if he has ever previously killed anyone.

It is a world away from the mountains of Tora Bora in eastern Afghanistan into which Berntsen's team of four agents and ten Afghans ventured to try to kill history's most wanted terrorist.

They failed, as Berntsen has been regularly taunted through bin Laden's subsequent release of more than seventeen videos and audio tapes. The attempt – code-named Operation Jawbreaker – is to be given the Hollywood treatment by Oliver Stone. But it has left Berntsen, who has since divorced and retired from the agency, a haunted man. He insists that if President George Bush had not refused his request to send troops into Tora Bora to block his escape, the al-Qaeda leader would be dead. 'There isn't a day when I don't think, if only,' he says.

Astonishingly that was the last positive sighting of bin Laden, more than five years ago, despite the most extensive manhunt in history, and the biggest-ever reward.

The trail has gone stone cold. 'It's not just we've no trace, but we don't even know which zone he is in,' admits one US intelligence officer. Agents have taken to referring to him as Elvis.

Although bin Laden has released no new video since October 2004, hardly anyone believes he is dead.* On the contrary, US counter-terrorism officials, admit he is very much in control of a resurgent al-Qaeda. So embarrassing is the failure to find him that George Bush, who once demanded, 'We want him dead or alive,' now rarely mentions him.

To piece together how it was that the combined efforts of the CIA, FBI, National Security Agency, Special Forces, Navy Seals, Interpol, MI6 and SAS managed to lose bin Laden, it makes sense to start where they lost him in Tora Bora.

Following the route taken by bin Laden in mid-November 2001 when the US bombing of Afghanistan sent the Taliban fleeing the capital, I drove from Kabul to Jalalabad in a battered white pick-up between two Afghans.

That evening I went for dinner at the palace of the Governor. A warlord turned administrator, Gul Agha Sherzai looms like a bear with a bushy dyed black beard, missing front teeth and an elaborate turban. I found him presiding over a long table of tribesmen chewing and slurping food which included a bowl of mutton soup he told me he made himself. He insisted I sit next to him and began tearing off hunks of fatty meat, which he plonked on my plate in between sucking the flesh off a large bone then wiping his mouth on the end of his turban. I remembered a British official telling me how Jack Straw lunched with Gul Agha then was incapacitated for days afterwards.

I asked him why he thought the Americans cannot find Osama and he laughed so much his big shoulders shook. 'Poor Americans scurrying here and there, not knowing who to believe,' he said, puffing on a Marlboro Light. 'They think they can solve everything with dollars.' He should know. Gul Agha received millions from the CIA for helping oust the Taliban and al-Qaeda.

After dinner, he took me on a tour of the palace he had just renovated. In the audience room was a painting of the man who built

* He eventually released another video in September 2007.

it, King Abdur Rahman. 'My grandfather,' announced Gul Agha. They may both hail from the Barakzai tribe but I know Gul Agha is the son of a champion dogfighter, not a prince. However, this was not the time to quibble over ancestry. He wanted to show me the basement where the Russians used to kill people, leaving the walls stained with blood. Gul Agha has turned it into a disco. The tour ends outside with a final flourish of warlord kitsch – a display of coloured lights round the fountain and swimming pool.

Early the next morning as promised Gul Agha sends some guards to accompany me to Tora Bora – a police vehicle and two trucks of men with Kalashnikovs, one of whom introduces himself as Commander Lalalai, a famous old mujahid. We speed through the streets scattering donkey carts and men on bicycles. Eventually we turn on to an unmade road towards the White Mountains. 'Tora Bora,' points the driver Mahmood.

Every so often, Mahmood puts on a terrifying burst of speed, throwing up so much dust that we can see nothing as we hurtle along the narrow track and I grip the side of the door. 'Al-Qaeda, al-Qaeda!' he explains. Occasionally the truck in front would screech to a halt and Commander Lalalai would jump out and start berating Mahmood for not going fast enough, saying we could be killed by 'bad guys'.

After two hours we stop at a schoolhouse that was used by the CIA as their base camp during the battle for Tora Bora and collect two more vehicles of guards. Now we have twenty-six gunmen. The road has turned from dust to stones, making the journey even more bone-shaking. But the scenery is spectacular, swirled toffee mountains as far as the eye can see, rising to black rock, under a deep-blue sky. On the other side lie the passes to Parachinar and the tribal areas of Pakistan.

Eventually our convoy pulls up under a tree and everyone piles out. 'Now we walk ten minutes,' says Mahmood. In Afghan time that means at least double but I take the risk of leaving food and water in the vehicle. It is a decision I will regret.

An hour later we are still climbing the stony track along a dry river bed, breathless from the thinning oxygen. But the guards are happy. They hold hands, pose for photographs and pick me some lavender.

Every so often we pass people with donkeys or small children bearing bundles of wood – the slopes all around have been denuded of trees. The women hurriedly pull their shawls over their faces.

Finally we stop and they point across the gorge, shouting, 'Osama house, Osama house.' At first I can see nothing, then I can just make out a few holes and ruins on the terraced slopes. We clamber across past a burnt-out tank and over some large bomb craters and come to a series of mud-walled ruins.

I realise that the reason I did not see it is that it is not what I am expecting. Where are the James Bond-style hi-tech cave systems with internal hydroelectric power plants from mountain streams, elevators, ventilation ducts, loading bays, caverns big enough for tank and truck, and brick-lined walls that were portrayed in newspapers at the time? What about the vast network of tunnels that led to Pakistan?

First used by mujahideen fighting the Soviets in the 1980s, Tora Bora is really just a natural stronghold of caves made by rainwater dissolving the limestone. When bin Laden took them over, he used dynamite to extend them and built some mud-brick houses. Among the ruins is a circular hole around three feet high that seems to be the entrance to a tunnel.

A combination of Afghan scavengers and US and British intelligence have scoured the caves and nothing remains to suggest their past purpose. In one an SAS team found plans for al-Qaeda's next attack in Singapore. Berntsen told me that US agents even scraped the sides of the cave for DNA in the hope of finding they had killed bin Laden.

It was clear from the craters that one hell of a battle had gone on. One of the trees along the bluff must have been where Gary Berntsen's team of four CIA agents crept into position. From there they could observe the encampment unseen and used laser guns to mark out bombing targets.

Their instructions were clear. 'I don't want bin Laden and his thugs captured. I want them dead,' said Cofer Black, head of the CIA's Counter Terrorism Center. 'I want bin Laden's head shipped back in a box filled with dry ice,' he continued as he handed over a large black suitcase containing $5 million. 'I want to be able to show bin Laden's head to the President.'

Berntsen had set up CIA operations in a Kabul guesthouse after the fall of the Afghan capital on 13 November 2001. As soon as he picked up reporting that bin Laden and as many as a thousand of his followers were massed at Tora Bora, he knew they had to act. He went to the US Special Forces commander at Bagram and asked for an SF team to go down there together with some of his agents but was refused. 'He said it's too disorganised, too dangerous, too this, too that.'

'I knew if I didn't do anything bin Laden would escape the country with his entire force so I just improvised. I sent four guys into those mountains alone to look for a thousand people – it was a very, very large risk. If they'd been found they would have been tortured and killed and I would probably have been fired.'

His small team with their Afghan guides left in late November 2001, scaling the 10,000-foot mountains. After two days they spotted bin Laden's camp, complete with trucks, command posts and machine-gun nests. They estimated there were between 600 and 700 gunmen with bin Laden.

'We got them,' they radioed Berntsen, who punched the air in delight. 'One word kept pounding in my head,' he said. 'Revenge! Let's do this right and finish them off in the mountains.'

The agents mounted their laser marking devices on tripods and began lighting up targets. To be double sure one of them punched coordinates into a device which looks like a gigantic Palm Pilot. For the next fifty-six hours they directed strike after strike by B-1 and B-2 bombers and F-14 Tomcats on to the al-Qaeda encampment. The battle of Tora Bora had begun.

Following the bombardment, bin Laden and his men fled further into the mountains. A twelve-man Special Forces team was sent in – as well as some crack SAS operatives – to pin the al-Qaeda fighters against the mountains, using Afghan forces to trap them in a 'kill-box' between three promontories.

Three rival commanders who between them controlled most of Jalalabad were hired – Hazrat Ali, Haji Zahir and Haji Zaman – and a day rate agreed of $100–150 per soldier.

'I raised an army with a couple of million dollars,' says Berntsen.

He sent in an urgent request to US Army Central Command in

Tampa, Florida, for a battalion of 600 US Army rangers to be dropped behind al-Qaeda positions to block their escape to Pakistan.

Berntsen was certain bin Laden was there because a second CIA team he sent in had a stroke of luck. One of the dead bodies they found was clutching a cheap Japanese walkie-talkie. Through it they could hear bin Laden exhorting his troops to keep fighting.

'We were listening to bin Laden praying, talking and giving instructions for a couple of days,' said Berntsen. 'I had the CIA's number one native Arabist who'd been listening to bin Laden's voice for five years down here listening. Anyone who says he wasn't there is a damn fool.'

Over and over he kept urging high command: 'We need rangers now! The opportunity to get bin Laden and his men is slipping away!'

But the answer came back no, it should be left to the Afghans. 'The generals were afraid of casualties!' says Berntsen, still incredulous.

Only on the eleventh day of the sixteen-day battle did Delta Force soldiers arrive and the military take control from the CIA. Yet they numbered just forty – and to Berntsen's amused disgust had to pay bribes to their Afghan allies to be allowed through. Despite the lack of troops, he estimates that between the bombing and the Afghans they killed about 70 per cent of bin Laden's force.

A couple of times he thought they had got bin Laden. Through the walkie-talkie they knew the al-Qaeda fighters were running short of food and water so they let them be resupplied by some local Afghans. 'We delivered food and water to them so we could get a GPS on bin Laden's position then we dropped a 15,000-pound bomb the size of a car and killed a whole lot.'

But on 15 December they heard him on the radio again. The following day the al-Qaeda leader is believed to have split his men into two and left with his group of 200 Saudis and Yemenis over the mountains to Parachinar.

That same day Berntsen also left Afghanistan, full of frustration. Back with his wife and two children for Christmas, he was horrified to switch on his television on Boxing Day and see the bearded face of his tormentor. Bin Laden had released a video to show the world he was still alive. 'I just kept thinking we could have had him.'

'It came out later that the President had been briefed and had turned down my request for soldiers,' he said. 'I found that heartbreaking.'

The evening after my own trip to Tora Bora, I went to see one of the commanders the Americans had contracted, to hear his version of events.

Haji Abdul Zahir is the closest Afghanistan has to mujahideen aristocracy. His uncle was the great commander Abdul Haq, who was killed by the Taliban when he tried to raise a movement against them in November 2001. His father Haji Qadir was Vice President of Afghanistan and assassinated in Kabul in 2002.

The vehicle he sends to pick me up is equipped both with Sat Nav – useless in Jalalabad but Afghans love gadgets – and men with guns. The house we drive into is a vision in warlord chic. A golden chandelier dominates the marble entrance hall and a sweeping staircase leads up to a balcony with a billiards table. The walls are covered with blown-up photographs of himself and his late father and uncle. Haji Zahir himself is lounging on cushions on a raised platform.

A servant brings glasses of fresh pomegranate juice and small bowls of almonds and Zahir's personal camera crew appears to record the interview. But the warlord's words are drowned out by what I first think is screaming.

'I keep hundreds of birds,' he explains. 'I love birds.' I presume he means fighting birds, a tradition in a country where most hobbies involve fighting, but he looks pained at the suggestion. 'Not fighting birds,' he says. 'I like songbirds. They're very sweet.'

The servant is dispatched to take out the birds and he begins to tell the story of Tora Bora, using floor cushions to illustrate the topography.

'From the beginning the mission was not strong enough and the plan was weak,' he says. 'If you have enemies on this pillow and you don't surround it then they will run away. The planes were flying and bombing but the ways were open so of course they ran away.'

Like Berntsen, he has no doubt that bin Laden was there. 'I myself caught twenty-one al-Qaeda prisoners, some from Yemen, Kuwait, Saudi and Chechnya. One was a boy called Abu Bakr who told me that ten days earlier bin Laden had come to his checkpoint and sat with them for twenty minutes and drunk tea.'

The plan had been to attack al-Qaeda from the Wazir Valley to trap them as the Special Forces wanted. The evening the attack was due, one of the commanders, Haji Zaman, said al-Qaeda had sent a radio message asking to be given till 8 a.m. the following morning and they would surrender. 'I didn't agree,' said Zahir. 'I said if they want to surrender why not today? They're the enemy – why are we giving them twelve to fourteen hours to run away?'

But Zaman called off his troops which were supposed to block off the routes to Pakistan. The Americans were outraged. 'Just for the record,' said General Richard Myers, the Chairman of the Joint Chiefs of Staff, 'our military mission remains to destroy the al-Qaeda and the Taliban networks. So our operation from the air and the ground will continue until our mission is accomplished.'

The bombing continued through the night. Sure enough, the next day, the surrendering al-Qaeda troops had vanished. Zahir claims Haji Zaman had been paid off; Zaman says they left because the Americans broke the ceasefire.

Far from Berntsen's estimate of killing 70 per cent, Zahir thinks the majority escaped. 'Supposedly there were 600 to 800 people,' he said. 'I captured twenty-one. Ali and Zaman got nine. Dead bodies were not easy to count but around 150. That means at least 400 got away. For all that money spent and energy and bombing, only thirty were caught.'

To this day he remains mystified by the Americans. 'It would have been easy to get bin Laden there,' he says. 'I don't know why there was no plan to block the passes. And why weren't there more Americans? Believe me there were more journalists than soldiers.'

Mike Scheuer, who headed the CIA's Osama bin Laden Unit from 1996 to 1999, then was its special adviser from 2001 to November 2004, probably knows more about bin Laden than any other westerner alive. He was on the receiving end in Washington of many of the cables from Tora Bora. 'It's like many things in your life,' he says. 'If you don't do something when you have the chance, sometimes that chance doesn't come back.'

According to Scheuer, by the time of Tora Bora the US had already squandered ten different opportunities to get their man (eight with cruise missiles and two using CIA assets) back in 1998 and 1999.

President Clinton had signed a secret presidential directive in 1998 authorising the CIA to kill bin Laden after al-Qaeda bombed the American embassies in Kenya and Tanzania, killing more than 200 people. But when it came to it, says Scheuer, the President did not have the necessary resolve. 'Clinton was worried about European opinion. He didn't want to shoot and miss and have to explain a lot of innocent deaths.

'Yet the very same day we turned down one opportunity to kill bin Laden, our planes were dropping thousands of bombs on the Serbs from 20,000 feet.'

On one occasion in 1999, they had live video pictures of bin Laden from a Predator spy plane. 'But the drone wasn't armed at that time because the fools in Washington were arguing over which agency should fund the $2 million installation of the Hellfire missile.

'It's a very upsetting business. I got into a slanging match with Clinton on TV because he claimed that he never turned down the opportunity to kill bin Laden. That's a very clear lie and we're all paying the price.

'Similarly at Tora Bora, our generals didn't want to lose a lot of our soldiers going after him. They had seen what had happened to the Russians, who lost 15,000 men in Afghanistan. So it was easier to sub-contract to Afghans. I warned them they would be a day late and a dollar short.'

We now know from American journalist Bob Woodward's book *Plan of Attack* that there was another reason for Washington's reluctance to commit troops on the ground. As early as 21 November 2001, when the Taliban had yet to be driven out of southern Afghanistan and bin Laden's men were amassing at Tora Bora, Bush took Rumsfeld aside after a National Security Meeting and asked, 'What kind of a war plan do you have for Iraq?'

According to Woodward's account, when General Tommy Franks got the top-secret message asking for a new Iraq war plan within a week, he was incredulous. 'They were in the midst of one war in

Afghanistan, and now they wanted detailed planning for another? "Goddamn," Franks said, "what the fuck are they talking about?"'

On paper it shouldn't be so difficult to find bin Laden. The FBI Most Wanted poster describes him as between six foot four and six foot six tall, about 160 pounds, olive-complexioned, left-handed and walks with a cane. Few in the world would not recognise his bony bearded face and gaunt frame.

He is also said to be ill, though both his former doctor in Lahore, Dr Amer Aziz, and Mike Scheuer dispute the persistent rumour that he has kidney disease and needs dialysis. 'I came to the conclusion that that was disinformation,' says Scheuer. 'You would have laughed if you'd seen how, whenever a video came out, the agency would get it and have US government doctors and specialists pore over it. No one ever found any evidence. If you have serious kidney disease, you have a certain pallor and a way you move that betrays it and bin Laden never showed any sign. We spent more time studying that than listening to what bin Laden said.'

There have been many rumours of his death. Some had him among the 73,000 victims of the Pakistan earthquake in 2005. A paper in southern France claimed to have seen a French intelligence report that bin Laden had died on 23 August 2006 of typhoid fever in Pakistan.

But still the tapes keep coming. There have been no videos now since 2004 but plenty of audio tapes – three in the last year alone.

So why with electronic surveillance so sophisticated that unmanned Predator drones can provide live video pictures from 26,000 feet, and satellites can spot a goat on a hillside, has he managed to slip so easily off the radar?

'We have become blinded by our own electronic cleverness,' complained a Special Forces colonel involved in the hunt.

'We don't know what to do when there are no telephone lines to tap or fibre-optic cables to tap into,' adds Scheuer.

All the intelligence officers I have spoken to over the last five years, US, Pakistani, Afghan and British, as well as Special Forces involved in the search, agree – the problem is lack of what the Americans call 'humint' – human intelligence.

Says Berntsen, 'You need human resources to penetrate these groups and there's not enough of that going on, nowhere near enough.'

He blames cuts in the CIA staff, particularly during the Clinton years. 'When you get rid of large numbers of people you reduce your humint capacity. You can't just suddenly hire top-level people. To build a capable operations officer is a seven-year process. Hiring, training, language, two tours in field, that's just to get them to journeyman level.'

It is well known that when 9/11 happened the CIA did not have a single agent inside Afghanistan. But just as shocking is the lack of relevant language skills. Berntsen says of the 33,000-strong FBI, 'Only six are proficient in Arabic. That's five years after 9/11.'

The White House belatedly seems to have come to the same conclusion. During the swearing in of his new intelligence chief Mike McConnell in February, President Bush instructed him to develop more recruits with the language skills and background to infiltrate al-Qaeda.

One source the US did have close to both bin Laden and Mullah Omar who agreed to cooperate is now languishing in jail in Manhattan. The story of the arrest of Haji Bashar Noorzai is a salutary tale of inter-agency rivalry.

Perhaps the kingpin among Afghanistan's drug lords, Noorzai was arrested by the Americans in Kandahar after the fall of the Taliban but subsequently released for reasons that are unclear. But as the main financier of Mullah Omar and well connected to bin Laden, he was clearly a key figure. In 2004 he was tracked down to Dubai and approached to be a source given protection in the US rather than re-arrested. After a long period of negotiations he agreed.

In April 2005 he was taken to the Embassy Suites Hotel in Lower Manhattan and grilled by US agents. But after about ten days, when he tried to leave, one of the agents from the Drug Enforcement Administration placed a shocked Noorzai under arrest for conspiring to smuggle narcotics to the US. DEA officials trumpeted his 'capture' on that evening's news. The bin Laden hunters who had helped win him over to be a source were outraged. 'He should have been utilised as a source to get to Mullah Omar and/or bin Laden. I would rather have a reliable source than a squad of marines any day. No satellite will locate bin Laden, it will be a slip of the tongue or somebody in need of dollars who will give up his location.'

So where do the hunters think that bin Laden is hiding? Israeli intelligence has put him in Iran or among the Weiga people of northern Afghanistan, bordering China and Tajikistan. But the main search has focused on two areas – the wooded mountain valleys of Kunar/Nuristan in north-eastern Afghanistan and the wild tribal areas bordering Pakistan and Afghanistan, particularly North Waziristan. Pakistan's President General Musharraf insists the al-Qaeda leader is in Afghanistan, probably Kunar. Afghan President Hamid Karzai insists he is in Pakistan, probably in a city such as Lahore or Karachi.

'I think now he lives in an area where the topography is extremely difficult and where he is a long-term guest of those like Pashtuns who would defend him with their lives,' says Scheuer. 'That could be either the upper part of the tribal areas or in Kunar.'

The only reporter to interview bin Laden after 9/11 was Hamid Mir, a Pakistani journalist who has interviewed him three times and wears a black Casio watch that was a present from the al-Qaeda leader. He claims to have met one of bin Laden's commanders, Abu Daud, in the eastern Afghan city of Ghazni last September. 'I asked why isn't he coming on al Jazeera any more; there's been no video message from him for the last two years. He replied, "We don't want to provide the Americans fresh pictures because they can find him on their Predator planes."'

Like Scheuer, Mir believes that the invasion of Iraq in March 2003 distracted those who had been searching for bin Laden. At a key time, Taskforce 121, the shadowy group of Delta Force and Navy Seals, found themselves shipped off to Baghdad to hunt down Saddam and sons.

'In 2002, bin Laden was facing lots of problems,' says Mir. 'His people were scattered, short of money, and running between the mountains of Pakistan, Khost and Waziristan.' He believes they finally found refuge in the Pech valley in Kunar. 'It was here in the last week of March 2003 that bin Laden held his first meeting of all his commanders since 9/11, taking advantage of the distraction of Iraq. He was very happy. He said the bad patch is over and we'll have a new breeding ground in Iraq. He assigned Saif-ul Adel to go to Iran and meet Abu Zarqawi then establish training camps. Within a few months camps had been set up in Khost, North Waziristan and Iran.'

US officials have also focused attention on Kunar. The remote mountainous area is one of the few forested parts of Afghanistan, with plenty of trails across the border into Pakistan. It is also a long-time stronghold of the anti-coalition warlord Gulbuddin Hekmatyar where much of the population adheres to bin Laden's brand of Wahhabism. A video given to al Jazeera in September 2003 showed bin Laden and his deputy Ayman al-Zawahiri scrambling down slopes similar to those found in Kunar and Nuristan. There were persistent reports too of Arabs coming down the mountains to buy supplies in the bordering Pakistani province of Chitral.

US Special Forces established a series of small bases in the region and in 2005 launched Operation Red Wing to sweep the area of militants. But on 28 June a four-man team of Navy Seals was ambushed and trapped on a 10,000-foot mountain ridge above the Pech valley. Only one survived. When they called in for help, one of the two Chinooks was shot down, killing all sixteen Special Forces soldiers aboard, the biggest blow against US forces in Afghanistan since 2001.

Convinced that the attack must have been to defend a senior al-Qaeda figure, the Americans responded with an intense campaign in late 2005 followed by an assault last spring called Operation Mountain Lion. But the militants are believed to have just fled deeper into the mountains.

It seemed a good place to continue my own search.

It is a long journey to Naray, America's most remote camp in Afghanistan, five hours by helicopter along the Kunar River, through narrow gorges. The Chinooks fly in pairs with a Black Hawk attack helicopter alongside and their gunners scour the rocky hillsides for enemies. It was not reassuring to see that the Chinook's cargo included boxes marked 'Human Blood for Naray'.

We are put down inside a small encampment enclosed by razor wire and sandbags and surrounded by jagged 15,000-foot mountains. To the east is Pakistan and ahead, up amid the snowy peaks, is Nuristan, the land of light, a region so remote that many of its valleys have never seen a westerner.

'It's beautiful until you realise there are dudes up there trying to kill you,' says Captain Todd Polk, the company commander, as he sees me looking up. Then he points out the 'OPs' – US observation posts on top of the surrounding mountains.

Until six months ago, only Special Forces ventured this far north but now there are neat rows of tents along gravel paths that house the men from 10th Mountain Division, some of America's most experienced conventional forces in Afghanistan. Even so, many of the camp's activities are top secret – we must not photograph anything.

Every night, howitzer guns pound away at the enemy in the hills, sending shudders through the whole camp. 'We interact with the enemy on a regular basis,' says First Lieutenant Joe Lang, who heads the Information Operations Cell. 'The camp gets rocketed a lot. You'll probably get rocketed. Who knows if it's something bin Laden is directly involved in?'

'We all want to get Osama to make the world a safer place for our children,' says Private Zak Schultz, of Charlie Company. 'But I gotta tell you, ma'am, it's like chasing shadows up there.'

Fighters disappear across mountains into what the American soldiers refer to as 'Paksville'. 'If we could go just ten miles the other side we could finish this,' he complained.

The US military has been increasingly losing patience with attacks from across the border. Last year they carried out several bombing raids inside Pakistani territory, particularly in Bajaur Agency which borders Kunar. Last January a US drone dropped a bomb on a house in Bajaur where it was believed bin Laden's deputy al-Zawahiri was hiding, just a few miles from Naray. He was not there; US officials suspect he was tipped off. Then in October a madrasa in Bajaur was bombed, killing eighty-two allegedly training to be suicide bombers.

General Dan McNeill, the new US commander, flew to Islamabad before assuming command in February, to confront General Musharraf with video surveillance showing fighters openly crossing into Afghanistan in front of Pakistani border guards.

Having got nowhere through force and searches, American

commanders have changed their strategy in Kunar and hunting militants is now only one part. 'Initially we came here to hunt and destroy the enemy,' said Lieutenant Lang. 'But now we realise we're fighting an insurgency and the cornerstone of fighting an insurgency is securing the population. We're no longer breaking people's doors down – that was a mistake,' he added.

To win over local support they have begun an aggressive programme of building roads which not only make travel much easier for locals but also are harder for the enemy to mine. The commander Colonel Michael Howard has $50,000 a month to use at his discretion on anything from school classrooms to micro-hydro projects.

'This is a very neglected area so what we can do is show we have something to offer – roads, schools, clinics, etc – whereas all the enemy is bringing is fighting,' explains Lieutenant Lang.

But the resurgence of the Taliban and deterioration of the security situation in Afghanistan has meant that many of those who were looking for bin Laden are now engaged in trying to prevent the Taliban retaking southern Afghanistan.

'I think we're just about out of luck,' says Mike Scheuer. 'We still have SF and CIA officers chasing bin Laden but I understand it's a pretty cold trail and as long as we don't go into Pakistan…'

While the US has 22,000 troops inside Afghanistan charged with trying to hunt down bin Laden, most people involved have long believed him to be over the border in Pakistan where they cannot officially look.

It might seem odd to suggest that America's ally in the war on terror could be harbouring its deadliest enemy. After all, as Pakistani officials are quick to point out, they have 80,000 soldiers on the border while President Musharraf has narrowly escaped two assassination attempts. But at the same time this is where al-Qaeda was born and it seems more than coincidence that all six of the most senior al-Qaeda people to be arrested since 9/11 were living in Pakistani cities – Karachi, Faisalabad and Rawalpindi.

'I keep telling our American and British friends, please be patient with us,' says Tariq Asis, General Musharraf's national security adviser and closest friend. 'It's not that we're being hypocrites but there are certain things we can and can't do. You have to remember that Pakistan had twenty-two years of Islamisation after General Zia took over in 1977. It was state policy to support the Taliban. We can't turn this round overnight.'

Others put it more bluntly. 'No one here is interested in finding Osama,' says Shujaat Hussein, president of Pakistan's ruling Muslim League. 'Here he is far more popular than President Bush.'

However, some suggest it is more sinister. Senior UN officials in Afghanistan believe that Pakistan is playing a double game so that while its military intelligence (ISI) officially cooperates with the hunt for bin Laden, there is a shadow ISI making sure no one gets near him. This is after all a country where government ministers I go to interview turn up the television volume because they believe their offices are bugged. Its national hero is nuclear scientist Dr Abdul Qadeer Khan, a man who ran his own black market in nuclear weaponry. Until he was exposed by western intelligence two years ago, he was smuggling weapons technology to pariah states such as Iran and North Korea.

US intelligence is convinced that ISI tipped off al-Zawahiri the few times they got near.

The theory that bin Laden is in a Pakistani city is something an increasing number of US officials now consider possible. Could it be as the Afghan government argues that he is being protected by Pakistan's military?

For the time being the spotlight has been on the seven tribal agencies that run along the 1,500-mile border with Afghanistan, a dirt-poor land where almost everyone is armed and lives on smuggling and kidnapping. So fierce are these tribes that when this area was part of the British Empire in India, colonial officers gave up trying to control them. Instead they put in political agents who acted as go-betweens for central government and the tribes, basically paying off *maliks*, or tribal leaders. When Pakistan was created in 1947, these so-called Tribal Areas were left semi-autonomous.

In these wild lands where mountains rise out of barren plains like scales from a dragon's back, tribes live by the Pashtunwali honour code. Under this, retribution is an eye for an eye, so people live inside forts with walls three feet thick and watchtowers to protect themselves from those with whom they have feuds. They are highly conservative with women kept in purdah and literacy is only about 10 per cent. Pashtunwali also requires that guests must be protected whatever they may have done, all of which suggests this could be a safe haven for al-Qaeda fighters, particularly as many are said to have married local women.

The Waziris are said to be the fiercest of them all and it was in Waziristan that the British met most resistance. One political agent was murdered in his sleep for lying with his feet towards Mecca. In 1936 a mysterious leader known as the Fakir of Ippi led an armed revolt against the *farangi*, or foreigners, in North Waziristan. At one point there were 40,000 British and Indian troops searching for him yet he was never found and died in his own bed in 1960.

'Remember the Fakir of Ippi,' says a friend from the Afridi tribe when I ask him why no one can find bin Laden.

I would like to go to Ippi but there is a problem. My visa is stamped 'Islamabad only'. Local journalists who have tried have ended up dead or badly beaten. I go to the frontier town of Peshawar where friends warn me off.

'Where is Osama?' sighs Lieutenant General Ali Jan Aurakzai, the blue-eyed Governor of the Frontier who is himself from the tribal areas and commanded Pakistan's troops when they entered those areas in 2003 for the first time. 'I'm fed up with this question.

'The Afghans say that the Taliban are being trained in Pakistan and bin Laden is in a Pakistani military base. I would say why would they come to our tribal areas infested with troops and intelligence agencies rather than Afghanistan where the writ of the government barely extends beyond a few cities, and foreign troops are only in a few bases and daren't venture out?'

The embarrassing failure to find bin Laden has led the Bush administration to try to downplay his significance and insist that the al-Qaeda leader and his deputy are fatally weakened, detached from their followers and unable to plan any new operations.

'Al-Qaeda is on the run,' declared President Bush just before last year's mid-term election. The US Army's highest-ranking officer said in February that he believed there was 'not that great a return' in capturing or killing bin Laden.

'So we get him, and then what?' asked General Peter J. Schoomaker, the outgoing Army Chief of Staff. 'There's a temporary feeling of good-ness, but in the long run, we may make him bigger than he is today. He's hiding, and he knows we're looking for him. We know he's not particularly effective.'

As I talk to officials in Washington, many look pained when I raise the subject. 'To be honest I am relatively relaxed about the situation with bin Laden,' says Dr David Kilcullen, chief strategist on counter-terrorism for the US State Department. 'I think he's largely irrelevant. Five years ago the guy killed 3,000 people in New York City. Now he makes videos.'

Kilcullen insists that bin Laden's command and control abilities over al-Qaeda have been damaged. 'You guys want to grant him the kind of rock star status that he's seeking. But the guy is not ten feet tall. He has lots of problems.'

But others say that al-Qaeda has regrouped and is training for new attacks. Those involved say the hunt is now 'confused and unfocused'.

'The President likes to believe bin Laden is running from rock to rock but I don't think he's in a cave – that's the Hollywood version,' says Scheuer. 'I think he's probably in a pretty comfortable compound. He's certainly beaten us at the moment.'

Back in Manhattan, the man who could have got bin Laden, looks at a souvenir postcard that I have just bought that still shows the twin towers.

'We will get him in the end,' insists Gary Berntsen. 'One really good officer can make a difference and one lucky break. I've captured people who have been on the run for sixteen years. They make mistakes. You only have to be right once to be able to pull the trigger and it's all over.'

'Have You Ever Used a Pistol?'

Sunday Times, 2 July 2006

Zumbelay, Afghanistan

'Have you ever used a pistol?' yelled Sergeant-Major Mick Bolton amid the Kalashnikov fire and bursts from a machine gun as we ran across a baked-mud field and dived for cover. 'If it comes down to it, everyone's going to have to fight.'

Round after round fizzed past our ears, sending up clouds of dust. My heart was thudding crazily against my flak jacket, my breath coming in short, rasping pants like an animal. The whoosh of a rocket-propelled grenade (RPG) close enough to lift the hairs on the back of my neck was followed by an orange blaze of flame as it landed nearby.

I hurled myself into an irrigation ditch and crouched amid the tall reeds, the soil just above me flying up as bullets landed all around. Then firing started coming from behind too. The Taliban had us from three sides.

Justin Sutcliffe, the photographer, and I were with the elite of the British Army, forty-eight men of C company, the 3rd Battalion the Parachute Regiment – with an attachment of airborne troops of the Royal Irish Regiment – facing a bunch of Afghans in rubber sandals.

We could not see them, but we knew they were less than a hundred yards away.

The silver-haired sergeant-major had kept us amused for days with his wisecracks, behind which was a touching concern for his soldiers and adoration for the girlfriend, Lizzie, he was due to marry in November, whose photograph he had shown me.

Now this veteran of two tours in Iraq and six in Northern Ireland was telling us we were the closest he had ever come to being 'rolled up'.

'If we get overrun I'll save the last bullet for myself,' said Private Kyle Deerans, a handsome South African of 23. With his black floppy hair, I was sure he had broken a string of hearts.

As I stared at them in horror, it dawned on me what had been wrong about Zumbelay, the village we had just visited on a hearts-and-minds mission with soft hats and offers of development projects. I should have noticed there were no children around.

There was no time to think about that as a mortar landed nearby. 'Get out of the ditch!' screamed someone. I wanted to stay in hiding. 'No, no, it's not safe,' shouted Leigh Carpenter, a military policeman attached to the unit, tugging me away.

I clawed my way up the slippery bank, oblivious to the thorns ripping my hands. I felt terrifyingly exposed as I climbed over the mound and rolled down the other side. 'Keep down! Keep down!' came another shout. As I flattened myself, a mortar landed just where I had been crouching.

For the next two hours we were trapped under such relentless fire we thought we would be killed. The ambush of our lightly armed patrol was not only unexpected but also brought into question the entire strategy being pursued by the British in Helmand, the huge province they have taken on.

The paras had been in lively mood earlier that day when we left Camp Price, the British base at Gereshk, a sprawling town of walled compounds, two bridges and a bazaar. C company is a close-knit group and the trip was the furthest east they had ventured since arriving in Gereshk two months ago.

The plan was to go to Zumbelay, meet villagers, then camp before stopping at another village on the way back.

Some of the soldiers had not been out of the camp before and none had experienced a 'contact' with Taliban, unlike their fellow paras in A company who have had what they describe as a 'fruity' time and were engaged alongside British Special Forces further north. To keep the men occupied, Major Paul Blair, C company's wiry Irish commander, had organised an 'Iron Man' contest the day before involving ordeals such as flipping a giant tyre and sprinting round the camp weighed down with boxes of ammunition.

As we set off with cold drinks and Pringles, we joked about going on a picnic. 'Aggressive camping is what I call it,' said Colour Sergeant Michael Whordley. They laughed at me in my local dress of *shalwar kameez* worn with desert boots and a flak jacket.

We were in a convoy of fifteen vehicles, an assortment of Snatches – the lightly armoured Land Rovers that have caused such controversy over their vulnerability to roadside bombs in Iraq – open troop-carriers and WMIKs (weapon-mounted installation kits), open Land Rovers that look a bit like safari vehicles except for the machine gun on the front and heavy guns mounted on top. Their firepower would save us.

As we drove out of Gereshk we noticed a man in a black turban pull out on a motorbike and follow alongside for a while. But we could hardly hide our intentions, sending up clouds of dust visible for miles as we travelled east through the desert.

Long ago, when the Russians occupied Afghanistan, I travelled around on the backs of motorbikes of anti-Soviet mujahideen who went on to become Taliban. Even back in 1989 they regarded them as the best transport against a fixed army.

The journey east took about ninety minutes through a landscape of undulating sand and gullies in temperatures close to 55°C. We were close to Zumbelay by late afternoon – that special time of day when fingers of fading sunlight trap the dust being churned up by men returning to the village with herds of goats.

Much of Helmand is scorched brown desert but Zumbelay seemed a small oasis. Bedouin tents and mud-walled houses, some with court-yards of flowers, were scattered amid a patchwork of fields of tall green grass and dried poppy stalks. A wide canal ran through one side, with deep irrigation ditches leading off between fields.

The convoy stopped about a mile from Zumbelay. A fire support group (FSG) drove off in the WMIKs with a mortar team to take up a secure position beyond a ridge to protect us in the event of trouble.

The rest of us downed helmets and walked in, crossing a field where a few scrawny camels gazed at us. I caused hilarity by falling into a ditch and emerging covered in mud. Everyone commented how quiet and bucolic the village seemed. 'All it needs is a nice pub where we could enjoy a cold pint,' joked Major Blair as we watched a kingfisher swoop low over the water in a flash of bright green.

Even the name had a nice ring to it: Zumbelay made me think of Manderley from Daphne du Maurier's *Rebecca*. Of course Manderley had a sinister secret and in retrospect the quiet of Zumbelay was suspicious. The one thing we should have noticed was the lack of children, who usually come running up demanding candy or baksheesh.

We sat on a raised bank at the edge of the field under a mulberry tree along with a few other men, one of whom seemed to be glaring at us from under his sparkly prayer cap. 'We are British not Americans,' explained the major through an interpreter. 'We come at the invitation of your government as friends and brothers to help you and find out what you need.'

An old man with a white beard said the other elders were at the mosque for prayers. (Later we would realise it was not prayer time.) He said the village had no problems and suggested we come back for tea two days later on Thursday at 10 a.m. when everyone would be around. As we took our leave, he pointed in the opposite direction to the way we had come. 'If you go that way there is a bridge,' he said.

Afghans are the most hospitable people on earth, offering everything when they have nothing. I was thinking it was unlike them not to offer tea to visitors, but Major Blair seemed happy. 'I think that went well – they seemed quite friendly,' he said to me as we walked away.

Almost immediately a burst of gunfire rang out from the ridge to the left where the FSG was deployed. 'We've had a contact,' crackled the message over the radio.

They had spotted a gathering of twelve to fourteen men dressed in black and armed. Two of the support group's vehicles had peeled off to try to intercept them, but as they did so RPGs started to rain in on the support base – followed by small-arms fire.

For a moment we stood staring up at the ridge listening to the gunfire and explosions. Then we started walking again through a field, looking for the bridge.

Within seconds we heard the staccato crack of Kalashnikovs. I threw myself into a ditch as bullets whizzed overhead. 'Helmets on!' shouted someone. 'Put your fucking helmets on!' I followed the paratroopers, as we ran for our lives across the fields. The ground had been ploughed weeks before and had baked hard into dry, treacherous ridges. We stumbled over the furrows, with bullets and loud explosions all around us. I wished I was wearing camouflage instead of the blue press flak jacket and helmet that made me so visible.

I did not see Justin fall as we ran. 'I lost my footing and managed to turn on to my back as I ploughed into the ground,' he said later. 'As I looked up, a rocket-propelled grenade flew over our heads about ten feet above, bursting in the field near a group of paras who had made the sprint in better time.

'I struggled back to my knees in time to see the first mortar round land exactly where we had been only half a minute earlier. The troops returned fire. A prolonged burst of rapid machine-gun and rifle fire. Then, using white phosphorus grenades as cover, they moved left to take up firing positions behind the ridge.

'Again we were diving to the ground to avoid incoming fire, but this time it was to our left flank as well as the original direction. Feeling very exposed, we returned fire and ran back to a ridge along the field at right angles to our position.

'Once again we took incoming fire, this time from behind us. Their mortars were mercifully slow at retargeting and they fell where we had just left.'

All around me was shouting and screaming. The two platoons had been scattered by the ferocity of the ambush. In the deep ditches their radios were not working. The soldiers were releasing canisters of red or green smoke to show each other their positions, even though this would reveal them to the Taliban too.

The firing came again and again, wave after wave of it, with hardly any break between. The eight-foot-deep irrigation ditches which crisscrossed the fields had turned into trenches. In and out of them we climbed, slipping and falling in the muddy water as the paras tried to regroup, yelling instructions I did not understand like 'Go firm!' which means stay still.

'When we shout "rapid fire", run!' yelled Corporal Matt D'Arcy as we crouched in yet another ditch. 'Rapid fire!' he screamed and, ears ringing amid a clatter of heavy fire that I could not identify as ours or theirs, I forced myself to climb out of the trench.

One of the Afghan interpreters stayed praying and moaning in the ditch until Private Deerans, the handsome South African, grabbed him by the collar and kicked him out.

I thought about my husband Paulo and our six-year-old son Lourenço back home in East Sheen, south-west London; of the World Cup birthday party Lourenço was due to have on Sunday afternoon; and how stupid it would be to die in this Helmand field from a Taliban bullet.

In my belt purse were some of Lourenço's toy cars and pens he had given me for the 'poor children of Afghanistan'. I had taken them to the village but never got a chance to give them out. I had to survive and the image of my son's face kept me running and jumping into yet another trench.

Frantically, I looked around for Justin. We have worked together on and off for years, surviving everything from arrest in West Africa to abduction by military intelligence in Pakistan and regard each other as a kind of talisman. In the confusion we had split up and I had no idea if he was all right.

In fact he was with Major Blair, a usually charming man, who was very angry indeed.

'Where's the fucking air support?' the major was yelling on the radio to British headquarters at Camp Bastion, reading off a GPS position.

'Two A-10s ten minutes away can be with you for twenty minutes,' came the reply. Nothing arrived.

'We need air support. Where's the air support?' Major Blair radioed again after sliding on his back in another trench, pulled down on to the mud by the weight of the kit.

The message came back that the A-10s had been called off to Sangin, a village to the north where two British Special Forces soldiers had been killed. No other planes were available because fighting was still going on. Why they were more important than us was unclear.

'We're going to have to get out of this alone,' Blair said. He checked the grenades on his belt. Later he explained: 'I was counting them because I thought the fight would get down to twenty-five yards.'

I was in a group led by Corporal D'Arcy. At one point we ran back towards the village only to be fired on from that direction.

'They're playing with us like chess pieces,' shouted the corporal. The Taliban clearly had someone on the ridge to the right of us directing movements, for they were constantly changing position.

I ran again and found myself in a trench with the platoon snipers, including Private Deerans. Some used .338 Magnum rifles, which sounded like cannon. Others were armed with Minimi 5.56s, the army's lightweight machine gun.

'Look, two over there behind that white mound!' shouted Sergeant Whordley, who at 39 is in his last year in the army.

Known as the Buzzard, the sergeant usually controls the helicopters

in and out of camp, but he had begged to go along on the patrol. 'In twenty-two years of service I've never been in anything like that,' he said later.

'Got him!' shouted Private Deerans as a man in a blue *shalwar kameez* with a short beard popped out from behind the mound and straight into his sights to be hit in the chest. 'I fucking killed him!'

The day before I had learnt that a private like him earns just over £1,000 a month, and that the British Army is the only one in the world whose soldiers pay tax while overseas.

'Happy days!' someone shouted back. I looked at him incredulously. This was the worst day of my life by an awfully long way.

In the nineteenth century thousands of Englishmen spilt their blood on fields like this and I didn't want to join them. I thought about John Reid, the former Defence Secretary, glibly saying he hoped to complete the three-year British mission to Helmand without a shot being fired.

Why were we there? Why had we thought the Afghans would not fight – they defeated the Russians after all. And why did everyone in Kabul and London keep insisting nobody in Helmand really wanted to support the Taliban but were being forced to?

What if they were wrong? After all, almost everyone in the province now depends on growing poppies. Whatever the British commanders might say, villagers must see the presence of British troops as threatening the opium trade.

I thought back to a conversation with Captain Alex McKenzie, commander of the FSG, before the patrol began. 'We've never been out to these villages and want to see what kind of reaction we get,' he had said, adding that, according to US intelligence, there were between six and eight medium-level Taliban commanders in the valley less than a mile to the north.

'If you ask me, what we get is a Taliban attack,' I had said to Justin.

'How much ammo have you got left?' Corporal D'Arcy called to his snipers. Were we running out? And where was the promised air support? What about Britain's new Apache helicopters that we had all heard so much about?

'Targets at ten o'clock! Targets at ten o'clock!' shouted someone.

'No, don't shoot, they're civvies!' yelled Corporal D'Arcy.

'How can we fucking tell?' screamed someone else.

The firing had been going on for almost two hours and I was finding it harder and harder to run. I had thrown off everything, even dropping my notebook – something I have never done in nineteen years as a foreign reporter – and, less wisely in Helmand's infernal heat, my water bottle.

I was gasping from thirst. Leigh, the military policeman, saw my plight, thrusting the straw from his camel pack into my mouth and urging 'Drink!' before pushing me to run again. My helmet was almost falling off because of the broken strap I had never got round to fixing.

I have been in some hairy situations, not least in Afghanistan, a country that I love, where at the age of 22 I was trapped in trenches by Russian tanks with a group of mujahideen. But this was the first time in my life that I thought I would not survive. Worse, I looked at the taut faces around me and could see the soldiers thought that too.

I thought about all the things left undone in my life, words left unsaid or unwritten, but most of all, I thought about my little boy's big blue eyes and curly hair, and I just wanted it to stop.

We were under relentless fire from AK-47s, RPGs, mortars and a Dushka, a Russian-made heavy machine gun.

Justin – separated in a trench with a group led by Major Blair – was under attack from all sides, but witnessed the turning of the battle.

'We were ordered out of the ditch and, under heavy covering fire, scrambled up the sides. Breaking towards the river, we came under fire again. This time there was a massive burst of fire from the FSG on the ridge directed at the Taliban.'

The paras had managed to regroup impressively. The men of the FSG beat off their own ambushers, drove their vehicles to the south where they were more secure and then moved back along the ridge to our aid – with devastating effect.

'We could see the group of ten to fifteen men who engaged us moving towards the houses down below,' said Captain McKenzie later, 'so we let rip with the four 50-cal heavy guns. The force of the blast from those guns is so powerful it can rip off your arm without even hitting you. All that was left of those guys was a pink mist.'

Down below we managed to get away from the fields of trenches and on to open hillside where I felt terribly exposed but the paras were much happier because they could see. 'Single file with good spaces between! Single file!' barked Sergeant-Major Bolton. 'This is not Club Med!'

By that time it was 8.30 p.m. and the light was fading. Only then came the reassuring rumble of the Apaches, two hours after they had been requested. With those overhead, we reached the vehicles and withdrew.

The battle was not over. There was only one way back to Camp Price and only one bridge back over the Helmand River. Major Blair was convinced the Taliban would lay an improvised explosive device (IED) or ambush us there. We could not go back.

Instead we drove south through the desert. At last we had air support. I was in Major Blair's Land Rover and all the time his radio operator was in touch with the planes overhead.

On and on we drove through the bumpy sand until the pilots assured us there were no ACMs (anti-coalition militia) within a mile or so and we pulled the vehicles into a herringbone formation, where we would stay for the next few hours.

We all tumbled out of the vehicles and started talking, pumped up with adrenaline at having survived. Veterans of conflicts all over the world said they had never experienced such a battle, and none of us could believe we had escaped unscathed.

'I've never been in anything as intense as that,' said Major Blair. 'That was a 360-degree battle.'

Everyone was stunned at how quickly the Taliban had organised themselves and how coordinated they had been. From the time we had walked into the village to the start of the ambush was less than an hour and they had been undeterred by our array of hardware.

'That's as bold as it comes,' said Captain McKenzie, shaking his head in awe. 'The Taliban are quite ingenious but they've probably got twenty-five dead blokes and we've got none, and that speaks volumes.'

Private Deerans said: 'We don't tend to think the Taliban can fight as well as us, but they're fighting for something they really believe in and they have the advantage of local terrain. They're world class at getting rounds down but fortunately their shooting was crap. Still, it was close enough for me. They had the advantage from the beginning and I don't know how none of us got shot.'

Some of the men realised they had forgotten to wear their wedding rings that day. 'I have my fiancée's ring on a string and it's the first time I've gone on an operation without it,' said Sergeant-Major Bolton.

I looked at my own bare finger, remembering how while checking in for my flight at Heathrow three weeks earlier I had realised the two rings I always wear were in an oyster shell by the side of my bed.

The big question was whether the villagers were in on the ambush. It seemed clear to me they had directed us straight into it, and there must have been locals fighting for them to organise so quickly.

'Maybe they were coerced by the Taliban,' said Major Blair. The official British line is that 80 per cent of the population of Helmand are 'floating voters' stuck between a rock and a hard place of an evil Taliban and a government in Kabul that does nothing for them. It seemed more likely to me that they feared the British had come to take away their source of income, the poppy.

While we were discussing this, another burst of gunfire rang out. Surely we were not under attack again? 'Hush,' warned the sergeant-major. 'Everyone still and quiet. It's not over yet.'

We still had to get back across the bridge into Gereshk, and we needed air support.

I lay on the warm sand staring up at the stars that covered the sky. In the distance were flashes I first thought were shooting stars until someone told me it was from the fighting at Sangin.

I looked at my watch. It was after midnight Afghan time, mid-evening in Britain. I realised that had I been in England I would have been at a summer party on the roof of New Zealand House in Haymarket, central London.

For the next two hours Camp Bastion kept telling us that 'all assets' were tied up in Sangin where the snatch raid on four Taliban commanders had succeeded in getting two of them before descending into a bloody firefight where Harriers, Apaches and A-10s had all been called in. Surely they weren't going to leave us to go back on our own?

In between his radio pleas for air support, Captain McKenzie and I discovered we grew up near each other, although I had done so a good ten years before him, and knew the same pubs.

It was after 1.30 a.m. when we finally got the nod for air support – only to find three of our Snatches had got bogged down in the sand. Amid all the stars we could just see the lights of two American A-10s, anti-tank aircraft of awesome firepower.

'How long have we got air for?' asked Major Blair as spades were used to dig the vehicles out.

'Forty more minutes,' came back the pilot's American accent. After that they would have to refuel.

Major Blair checked his watch. It was going to take a good half-hour to get to the bridge and some of the Snatches were still stuck.

I remembered Corporal Robert Jones, an American Humvee driver I had met, who had expressed horror at how exposed the British vehicles were. He had told me that if any American vehicles got bogged down for more than five minutes in Helmand they abandoned them.

'We just hate going west from Kandahar,' he said. 'It's all IEDs, RPGS, Taliban, al-Qaeda. We call it Hell-land.'

Eventually the vehicles were pulled out and we were on the road to the bridge. We reached it just before the planes had to refuel.

'Please don't let there be an IED,' I prayed.

'Do you want me to give a show of force?' came the pilot's American drawl over the radio. 'Could drop to 5,000 feet and drop some flares.'

'Many thanks,' replied our controller and we laughed in relief at his very British reply as we crossed the bridge safely, white flares dropping all around.

It was first light as we drove into Camp Price to be met by those who had been left behind, half anxious and half envious. It was clear there was now a big question mark over the British hearts-and-minds operation.

'I'm going to have to review our approach to villages,' said Major Blair. 'We're going to have to go in with far more security. It's very annoying to think we were sitting there offering things and having a laugh and a joke with villagers who knew that five minutes later we'd be attacked.'

More and more senior military officers are saying it has been an enormous mistake for British troops to move out of the main urban centres of Lashkar Gah and Gereshk and into outlying areas.

They blame the Americans – and some over-enthusiastic British generals – for dragging British forces into Operation Mountain Thrust, a large offensive against the Taliban in which some 500 people have died across the south, creating much local resentment.

What some have described as 'military and developmental anarchy' may change when Lieutenant General David Richards, NATO commander in Afghanistan, takes control of the Helmand operation at the end of this month.

On the military front, the general wants more fixed-wing aircraft and helicopters, and the British government is seeking more military support from its European allies. But General Richards has also been bashing heads together on the need to make some improvements in the lives of the Afghans.

Five years after the fall of the Taliban, Afghanistan still remains bottom of the list for almost every significant indicator from infant mortality to lack of access to water or electricity. 'We've got to stop talking and start doing,' he said last week. 'Otherwise we're in danger of losing this.'

Camp commanders are frustrated that despite being in place for two months they are yet to offer any help to the local community. 'Our credibility is at stake here,' said Major Blair. 'After a while people are going to start saying you came and promised to help us but what have you actually done?'

The main problem is that the British mission is led by a so-called triumvirate of military, Foreign Office and Department for International Development (DFID). The latter is insisting any development must come through its auspices and NGOs rather than the military. Thus Major Blair has been prevented from renovating Gereshk hospital or repairing water pumps. Yet most aid agencies are terrified of going south of Kabul, let alone to Helmand.

'The other problem is when I ask locals what they need they don't come up with projects,' he said. 'Either they are very vague or they ask for things like mobile phones, laptops and motorbikes.' He added that it took the local head of education just ten minutes to remind him of Maiwand, the battle on the borders of Helmand where British forces suffered one of their worst ever defeats back in 1880, losing half a force of 2,600.

Three days before the ambush, I had watched the triumvirate in action at a school in Gereshk. Colonel Charlie Knaggs, the British task-force commander for Helmand, Susan Cronby from the Foreign Office and Wendy Phillips from DFID had all flown in for a *shura*, a meeting with local elders.

After Colonel Knaggs had given his spiel about coming as friends and wanting to help the people of Helmand, the two women made speeches to the shock of the men in this very conservative society. Several men jiggled worry beads noisily while they spoke and one cleaned out his ear with a cotton bud. Afterwards an old man in white with a long white beard got up and accused the women of being spies. 'If your government was really serious about ending insecurity here, it would do something about Pakistan where the terrorists all come from,' he said.

The elders were then shown into another room where a projector had been set up. In a stunning indication of the chasm between thinking in London and the reality on the ground, someone has come up with the idea of making a film to show locals which comprises five minutes of the underwater BBC series *Blue Planet*, followed by a message from the Governor of Helmand and the coalition forces, followed by five more minutes of *Blue Planet*. The tribal leaders of Gereshk sat in utter bafflement, matched only by my own, as images of whales and dolphins were projected on the wall. 'Let's turn this off, shall we?' said Major Blair, looking embarrassed.

Even if the British do start development, it may be just too late. Disillusion with the government of President Hamid Karzai has never been so high. The Taliban have reorganised, possibly with the help of both the Pakistani military intelligence and al-Qaeda, to use the sophisticated tactics I experienced first hand in Zumbelay.

No longer are they just a few dozen ragtag fighters here and there. Now groups often include hundreds of heavily armed men equipped with motorbikes, cars and radios. All over the south they have set up shadow administrations and kill any Afghan who is even indirectly associated with the government, such as teachers. About 1,500 Afghan security guards and civilians were killed by the Taliban last year and some 900 already this year.

The Taliban are also winning the propaganda game. Within hours of our return to Camp Price, the Afghan Islamic Press in Peshawar had put out a statement claiming the Taliban had killed seven British soldiers in Zumbelay.

Far from losing any men, the brave paras from C company had

killed about twenty Taliban. Yet the Ministry of Defence put out nothing. If Justin and I had not been there, you would probably never have read about it.

Two weeks after the Zumbelay ambush the MOD announced it was increasing troop numbers from 3,600 to 4,500 and sending more helicopters.

Major Blair was awarded the DSO for his leadership at Zumbelay.

Sergeant-Major Bolton, Captain Alan McKenzie and Lance Corporal Luke McCulloch of the Irish Guards all received Mentions in Dispatches. Tragically Luke was killed in fighting with Taliban two months later. He was 21.

'It was what we feared, but dared not to happen'

Sunday Times, 21 October 2007

THE SOUND CAME FIRST. A low, ominous bang, like the sound of a large metal door clanging shut.

I was standing in the middle of Benazir Bhutto's open-top bus, talking to Aitzaz Ahsan, her long-time legal adviser. We stared at each other in horror. This was what we had all feared but somehow, crazily, dared to hope wouldn't happen.

Someone shouted: 'Down!' But there was no need. A wall of orange flame came over the left side of the bus and blasted us all to the floor.

The twanging music that for nine hours had been blaring out, welcoming Bhutto home after eight years in exile, stopped. For a moment there was ghastly silence.

'It's okay, it's okay – it's a burst tyre,' said Agha Siraj Durrani, an amiable giant of a man who, as the closest friend of Bhutto's husband, had spent the whole journey scanning the crowds for potential threats. But we all knew what it really was.

Then the sirens and screams started. I was sure there would be another one and that it would be worse. Within a minute, it came.

Again the bang, much louder and nearer this time, and once more from the left. Orange flames shot up all around us, rocking the bus and sending pieces of shrapnel raining down.

In the left-hand corner at the back of the bus, I could see two young men lying dead in pools of blood.

There were probably twenty of us on the bus when the attack

happened in Karachi on Thursday night. Around me were some of Bhutto's closest lieutenants. She had told them not to come, not wanting to place all the party's leadership at risk. But there were also relatives and friends.

Bhutto herself had gone downstairs fifteen minutes earlier to a bulletproof compartment to relax her feet, swollen from standing for so many hours. We had no idea if she was still alive.

'We have to get off the bus,' I shouted. We knew we were the targets. Everything was lit up as if it was day instead of six minutes past midnight, and there seemed to be bodies strewn everywhere. A nearby tree was on fire, as were a police van and a car. Flames were coming from the side of the bus. I was terrified the fuel tank would explode. I climbed over a body and made for the ladder, where people had started clambering down. Someone yelled: 'Don't – it's too exposed.'

There was the sound of pistol fire. One man jumped off the side. I was about to do the same when Victoria Schofield, Bhutto's friend from her Oxford days, pulled me to a chute. She jumped down to be caught by a guard at the bottom, and I followed her, not caring about the fourteen-foot drop.

All about us, the road was littered with body parts and plastic sandals. The nearest bodies had to be those of some of the boys in white Bhutto T-shirts – the so-called Martyrs for Benazir – who had made a human shield around the bus, holding a rope and linking hands so nobody could get through. They had been waving and smiling at us through the nine hours.

I thought about all the people who had travelled for days to see their returning leader and who had been dancing and waving flags and hoisting up children, who would beam with delight when we waved from the bus.

Trying not to look at a severed arm with its palm facing upward, I ran down a side street, just wanting to get away from the carnage.

A crying woman in a pink *shalwar kameez* grabbed me and tried to lead me to an ambulance. Only then did I notice there were great splashes of blood all over my left shoulder and arm and spattered across my trousers. It was somebody else's.

'I'm fine. I'm not hurt,' I said, shaking her away. Not till later would

I realise there were bits of burnt flesh in my hair; and I would stand in the shower for hours under scalding water, trying to wash them – and that awful night – away.

A man with a moustache stopped me running and took me into his house, where I was soon joined by Rehman Malik, Bhutto's frizzy-haired security chief, Farooq Naik, her lawyer, and Makhdoom Amin Fahim, who has led the Pakistan People's Party (PPP) during her years in exile. All three were spattered with blood.

Bhutto was fine, they said, and had been driven to Bilawal House, her fortified family home in Karachi. I wanted to phone my husband and son in London, wishing fervently I had not called home so excitedly earlier to say I was on Bhutto's bus. But the batteries on all of our mobile phones were flat after so many hours in the convoy.

The man with a moustache giving us sanctuary turned out to be an army colonel, a bizarre twist in this land where politicians and the military have rarely worked together. He produced a battery charger, which we all fought over, and made us milky tea. He then drove us to Bilawal House.

Other survivors from the bus had gathered there, and we all hugged one another, crying with relief. Among them was Bhutto's cousin Tariq, who had told me on the bus how his wife had begged him not to get on board and that he had always stayed in farming and avoided politics.

'Our family is cursed,' he had said. 'All the Bhuttos who get involved end up dead: Benazir's father, both her brothers...'

The military hanged her father, Zulfikar Ali Bhutto, in 1979; her brother Shahnawaz was poisoned in 1985; and her brother Murtaza was shot in 1996.

Benazir Bhutto, the survivor of this 'cursed' dynasty, was now sitting, pale but composed, in Bilawal House, watching BBC World's live reports from the scene of the bomb attacks.

I sat on the arm of her chair and she told me how she had survived this attempt on her life.

Nursing her sore feet inside her compartment, she had been working on a speech she was due to deliver when the bus reached the mausoleum of Pakistan's founder, Muhammad Ali Jinnah. With her was her political secretary, Naheed Khan.

'I had been reading it to Naheed, and we'd just finished, but then I thought there were a few more points to add. I was saying we should add the point that I would ask the supreme court to allow political parties in the tribal areas – and as I said "tribal areas", the first bomb went off.'

Both women were thrown to the floor. 'First the sound, then the light, then the glass smashing,' Bhutto said. 'I knew it was a suicide bomb. My first thought was, it's actually happened.'

As she spoke to me, we watched the death toll rise on the television screen. First, they said fifteen. We knew it was far more than that, for the street had been packed with tens of thousands of supporters. Suddenly, it shot up to eighty-nine, then more than a hundred. It was Pakistan's most deadly bombing.

She told me she had not wanted to come back to Bilawal House. 'I thought they would target this, too, and would be waiting, knowing if I escaped I would come here. But my security insisted.'

After a while, Bhutto went upstairs to wash her face. It was her first time back in the house for eight and a half years, and her old toothbrush was still in its glass in the bathroom. As she came back down, she stopped at the group of black-and-white photographs on the wall of her and her three children.

She touched them with her hand.

Bhutto's journey home had begun about sixteen hours earlier at Dubai airport. Journalists and supporters of her party had flown there from London, and spirits were so high that the Emirates airline staff struggled to contain them on the flight. One PPP activist from Canada had ended up rolling round the aisle, drunk.

Bhutto arrived at the airport from the villa where she has been living in exile since fleeing Pakistan amid a welter of corruption charges.

She looked stunning, dressed in an emerald green and white *shalwar kameez*, the colours of the Pakistani flag, to symbolise national unity. Her jacket was finished with tiny white pearl buttons, and over her head was a trademark floaty white *dupatta*, which as usual rarely stayed on.

As she said goodbye to her two daughters and her husband, Asif, in the VIP lounge, she announced: 'This is the beginning of a long journey for Pakistan back to democracy, and I hope my going back is a catalyst for change. We must believe that miracles do happen.'

Already, however, the warnings were coming in. General Pervez Musharraf, Pakistan's president, had publicly told her not to come because of security threats. Bhutto said she had prior warning that suicide squads would try to kill her on her return. She said the telephone numbers of suicide bombers had been given to her by a 'brotherly country' and she had alerted Musharraf in a letter last Tuesday.

As her plane landed at Karachi airport, a message came from the government to her security adviser, Malik.

'They told us it wasn't safe and they would take her in a helicopter direct to Bilawal House,' he said later.

Bhutto is nothing if not brave, and she was defiant in the face of what her supporters thought was a government attempt to stop her triumphant homecoming.

'By then we knew that more than 1 million people, maybe 2 million, were on the streets,' she said. 'They had come from all over the country, taking days and spending what little money they have. How could I disappoint them, sneaking in the back door?'

The excitement among her supporters on the aircraft had reached near-hysteria, and the pilot was refusing to taxi off the runway and open the doors until they quietened. Bhutto herself had to broadcast a message from the cockpit.

Finally we came to a stop, the doors were opened and members of the media were allowed off first. Then came Bhutto. As she reached the bottom of the steps, surrounded by a phalanx of photographers, tears spilt from her eyes and she almost stumbled.

'I was just so emotional to be home,' she told me later. 'It felt like this huge burden off my shoulders after so many years.'

Her wedding in Karachi in December 1987 was my introduction to Pakistan and led me to move there as a freelance foreign correspondent.

Over the next two years, I covered her fight against Pakistan's last dictator, General Zia-ul-Haq, and her struggle to become the country's first female prime minister at 35, campaigning even though pregnant with her first child. Within twenty months of being elected, she was deposed.

Since then I have been back and forth, following her ups and downs as she became prime minister for a second time, only to be thrown out once more amid charges of corruption against her and her husband that were never proved.

Because of this, I know her closest aides. When they saw me among the hundreds of journalists at Karachi airport covering her return, they hauled me on to her bus, one of only two foreigners on board, getting groped by the crowds as I pushed my way to the steps.

Bhutto had always been a crowd-puller, particularly in her home province of Sindh, but I wondered if she would still have the kind of support I had witnessed twenty years ago.

Then she was untainted, a fresh-faced girl not long out of Harvard and Oxford and daughter of a man who had been seen as the first Pakistani to give a voice to the poor before Zia deposed and hanged him.

This time she was coming back as part of a deal with another dictator, Musharraf, even if she refused to call it that.

She insisted it was an 'understanding for a transition towards democracy'. But everyone knew that as a result of the deal the government's corruption cases against her had been dropped, allowing her to return and contest elections due to be held by January.

Moreover, this was a US-brokered deal that had involved frequent meetings with Richard Boucher, the US Assistant Secretary of State for south and central Asia, as well as 2 a.m. phone calls from Condoleezza Rice, the Secretary of State, to break deadlocks.

Britain had also played its part, and Jack Straw was credited with bringing Bhutto in from the cold when he was foreign secretary.

'As long as Washington and Whitehall are wedded to keeping Musharraf in power for their war on terror, she had no choice but to come back like this,' said Malik, who led the negotiations on her side.

Polls commissioned by the US State Department, which showed that Bhutto commands never less than 30 per cent of public support, led America to see that the way forward in an increasingly unstable

Pakistan might be to bring her back as the democratic face of a beleaguered Musharraf.

'Each time military rule has failed, they have turned to a Bhutto to save the situation,' says Husain Haqqani, director of the Center for International Relations at Boston University and a former adviser to Bhutto and the military.

'Her father in 1971, then her in 1988. This time, at least, there is a Benazir Bhutto available to save the situation. If the military and intelligence agencies don't stop meddling in politics, next time maybe there won't be.'

In a country where Osama bin Laden commands far higher popularity ratings than US President George W. Bush, would America's role in her return work against her? It seemed not: her supporters came out in their hundreds of thousands to welcome her home.

From the top of the bus, it was an amazing spectacle: red, black and green PPP flags waving and people cheering, dancing and holding banners showing pictures of Bhutto and her father. Car horns blared.

'Only she can do this,' said her mother-in-law, Mrs Zardari, as she looked out on the crowds from the top of the bus. 'It makes me cry.'

The sun was already setting as we reached Star Gate, at the end of the airport road, and turned right onto the main Shar-e-Faisal highway towards the city. For the first time, we could get an idea of the size of the crowds packing the road, which stretched as far as we could see into the distance.

As we all looked out, there was a flutter of feathers above our heads. Somebody had released a clutch of white doves, which circled above us amid 'oohs' and 'aahs'.

One bird fell to the floor of the bus and hurt its foot. Bhutto cradled it and put it on her shoulder, where it perched for hours as she waved indefatigably to the crowds.

One thing was clear, however. The bus might have bulletproof sides, but we were standing in the open on top. We were travelling at a snail's pace, and, with people all around – on the streets, up trees and lampposts, on top of buildings – it felt very exposed.

'How can you possibly secure this?' I asked one of the police officers on the top of the bus.

He looked up at the heavens. 'It's in God's hands,' he said.

Bhutto herself stood right at the front, not behind the bulletproof screen that had been constructed to withstand even a shot from a Dragunov high-velocity rifle ('available as easily as sweets in the bazaar,' according to Zulfikar Ali Mirza, who designed the bus).

Durrani, the best friend of Bhutto's husband, was getting increasingly worried about how he could protect her.

The route of the convoy took it not only past a number of tall buildings but also under a series of footbridges and flyovers, which we had to duck to pass underneath. The crowds on top were so close that their hands brushed ours. Fortunately, nobody threw anything more harmful than petals and rosebuds.

Durrani told me another fear was that someone might use a remote-controlled toy plane loaded with explosives to land a bomb on the bus. He was constantly on his mobile phone.

'The government promised to provide us with jammers so we could intercept any remote-controlled explosive device within 200 metres,' he explained. 'But the man in the car in front of the bus with the jammer keeps telling me it isn't working and that we should do something.'

Desperately, he tried to phone Tariq Aziz – the national security adviser and Musharraf's point man in the negotiations with the Bhutto camp – but to no avail. Then Asif, Bhutto's husband, called.

'He asked me what was going on. "I can see you all on mobile phones, and they shouldn't work if the jammer is working." I told him it wasn't. [He said:] "For God's sake, get Benazir behind the bulletproof screen." I asked her but she said, "No, I must be at the front and greet my people."' It was not only bombers that they were concerned about. As darkness fell, I stood at the front with Bhutto.

'Have you noticed the streetlights?' she asked me. 'Each one we approach goes off so the road is in darkness and my guards can't see anything. Someone is doing this. We've had information they might try a shooting.'

She was right. Illuminated by the bus's lights, we passed along like a bright bubble while the crowd on either side was in darkness.

I remembered back to when I lived in Pakistan. Whenever there was a mystery attack in Karachi, usually taking out somebody the intelligence agencies did not like, the shootings would be preceded by the streetlights going off.

Suddenly there was a crack of what sounded like gunfire. I threw myself on the floor before realising with embarrassment that it was fireworks.

'I don't like the firecrackers,' Bhutto said. 'Anyone could use it as cover for shooting.'

Her security people used searchlights to sweep the darkened crowds, looking out for anyone with a gun or a suspicious backpack.

'There's no technique to identify a suicide bomber in an open street like this until it's too late,' Durrani admitted. 'That's why we decided on a human shield.'

He said they had trained 5,000 young men, volunteers for the so-called *jan israin na Benazir Bhutto* – the Martyrs for Benazir. Of those, 3,000 were sent on to the bridges and tall buildings and into the crowd, while 2,000 stayed around the bus.

Unarmed, they were identifiable by their white or black T-shirts. Bravest of all – and many of them doomed – were those who formed a human chain around the bus. Others formed an outer cordon around the bus's police escort, holding a rope to stop the crowds coming too near.

At about 10 p.m. we suddenly lurched to a halt. There was a moment of panic until someone explained that the bus had a flat tyre. Some local activists were told to disembark as the load was too heavy. I was allowed to stay.

We sat stationary, crowds surrounding us and the vans of bored-looking police officers with Kalashnikovs forming a cordon on either side. Somebody brought Pepsis and burgers, which we gobbled hungrily. Pizzas also arrived.

Seven hours after leaving the airport, we weren't even halfway along the fifteen kilometre route to the Jinnah memorial, where Bhutto planned to make her speech.

'If we keep going at this rate I'll have to order in breakfast on the bus,' Malik joked.

Eventually the bus started moving again. As it got later, the security fears began to be forgotten and the mood became euphoric.

There were even women in the crowd, which till then had been almost exclusively male. Many had brought their children, dressed in their best and excited to see such a spectacle.

Bhutto rested in an armchair inside the bulletproof shield on top of the bus, the wounded dove still perched on her shoulder, her face animated. I sat on the arm of the chair and we chatted.

'Aren't you tired?' I asked. 'Not at all,' she laughed. 'It's incredible, far more people than in 1986. How must Musharraf be feeling seeing this?' She continued: 'This is the real Pakistan, not the militants or the military. We are giving a voice to the moderates that don't want to see their country taken over by terrorists.'

For a moment she grew sombre. 'I just hope I can meet all these expectations ... but also that I am allowed to.'

Abida Hussein, one of Pakistan's best-known women MPs and a former critic of Bhutto who recently switched sides, got on the bus. The two women went downstairs to the safe compartment. Perhaps twenty minutes remained before the bombs would shatter the euphoria.

Karachi's police chief said yesterday the first bomb was a grenade or car bomb to make space, while the second blast was the work of a suicide bomber. His body – or body parts – has not yet been identified.

Although three people died on top of the bus, the only reason that Bhutto and the rest of us were not killed, it seems, is that the human shield worked – the young volunteers around the bus stopped the suicide bomber getting closer, paying for our protection with their own lives.

So, who did it? The awful thing about Pakistan today is that it could be any one of a number of people or organisations, from militants to the military.

Potential suspects include ethnic groups such as the Muttahida Quami Movement, the organisation that vies with the PPP for rule of Karachi, Taliban sympathisers and even old-guard politicians in deadly opposition to Bhutto.

'Far from bringing stability, Bhutto's return has threatened everybody,' said a member of Jamaat-e-Islami, the country's largest religious party.

Bhutto has pointed the finger at remnants in the intelligence and political elite from the Zia regime that executed her father. Some of them, she says, are still in power – although she is keen to make it clear that she is not implicating the president.

'We have confidence in some elements of the current regime, such as General Musharraf and the foreign minister, but it is the wild cards that give us concern, and those wild cards are usually the old cards,' she said.

Musharraf had telephoned her the morning after the attack, she said. 'He told me he had warned me not to come back, that there were security risks and he himself had faced two assassination attempts. But he said this shows we moderates must stand together.'

Senior members of her party were not so sure. 'My fear is they will use this as an excuse to declare martial law and not go ahead with the elections,' said Malik.

Would the army really relinquish power? It has run the show for thirty-three of the country's sixty years of existence and pulled the strings from behind for much of the rest of the time. During Bhutto's two stints as prime minister she often complained: 'I am in office but not in power.' She later admitted she had been forced to leave both the nuclear programme and Afghan policy in the hands of the military.

Since Musharraf seized power in 1999, the military has markedly increased its role in the public and private sectors. Retired generals and brigadiers run the tax authority, the postal system and the housing department. Two of Pakistan's four provinces have generals as governors. According to *Military Inc.*, a recent book by the defence analyst Ayesha Siddiqa, the army also controls large parts of the economy, and is involved in everything from banks to cornflake factories.

For Bhutto, the assassination attempt was a brutal awakening to how much the country has changed since she packed her bags and fled to London in 1998.

The evening after the attack, I sat with Bhutto in her small, book-lined study. She had just held her first press conference since her return, a bravura performance during which she had railed against 'those who turned triumph into tragedy' and insisted she would not be deterred from her fight to bring back democracy, even if it cost her her life.

Dressed in sombre grey silk with a black armband, she told me she had had just less than four hours' sleep after the attack, from 6 a.m. to

10 a.m. She had woken up with blood in her ears from the effect of the blast.

'I haven't felt weepy yet, but it suddenly hit me about 5.30 a.m. that maybe I wouldn't have made it,' she said. 'I kept thinking of the noise, the light and the place littered with dead bodies. Everything seemed lit up.

'Also I kept thinking of the boys, the human shields. Do you know more than fifty of them lost their lives?'

On the wall of the study was an old spelling certificate for her youngest daughter, Aseefa, who is 14, a reminder that Bhutto may be a politician but is also a devoted mother.

Her eldest, Bilawal, 19, started at Oxford earlier this month, while Aseefa and her other daughter, Bakhtwar, 17, have remained in Dubai with their father and 'a house full of dogs', as both have important exams coming up.

The first thing she thought of after the bomb went off was the children, and she admitted it had been hard speaking to them that morning.

'They kept saying, "Mummy, are you okay? Mummy, are you okay?" They had been desperately keen to come with me, and I said, "That's why I didn't want you to come."' She added: 'The worst thing is hurting them, making them fearful. I feel children need their parents. Losing my father was the worst thing that ever happened to me, and I was 25 – they are still much smaller. I worry about the effect on them.'

She insisted, however, that they understood that she had to return to Pakistan. 'My mother comes from Iran, and many of her relatives and friends never went back home, so I used to think I didn't want to be one of those people who'd lost their country.'

She said that after the attack her husband had been about to jump on the next plane from Dubai to be with her. 'I said: "Don't come back, because what if they don't let you out? Then the girls will be on their own."' Although she vows to continue, she is having to rethink her strategy. Today she had planned to return in procession to her ancestral home in Larkana, but that has been put on hold.

'Originally I was planning to be on the road the whole time, but now that's clearly impossible,' she said. 'We can't be intimidated by them but we can't take reckless risks. We know they won't give up.

'The problem is, in Pakistan people want to see their leaders,' she added. 'Our power base is the poor and dispossessed. They don't have TVs or computers we can reach them through.'

Yesterday the usually cacophonous city of Karachi was subdued. Relatives of those who never came home on Friday morning crowded city hospitals and morgues, waving pictures of the missing. Others brought them to Bhutto's house.

A survivor, Nadir Ali Magsi, a 25-year-old peasant farmer from a village close to Larkana, lay in the neurosurgery ward at Jinnah hospital. He had shrapnel embedded in his head and legs. One eye was bandaged up, and he had difficulty hearing, but he managed to speak. '*Benazir zindabad*,' he repeatedly said. Long live Benazir.

PS In Memoriam

Fonz of Kabul, hotelier and fast-talking fixer, found dead
Sunday Times, 31 December 2006

MOST WAR-TORN CAPITALS have a hotel adopted by foreign correspondents where they can gather gossip and information or blot out the horrors of the day.

In Kabul that hotel is the Mustafa, not because of the place – it was never very comfortable – but because of Wais Faizi, its larger-than-life manager. He was known as the Fonz of Kabul, fast-talking king of fix-it men and owner of the only convertible in Afghanistan. Inside his hotel he opened the first post-Taliban bar, which soon became the gathering point for journalists, mercenaries, bounty hunters and security consultants.

Last Wednesday evening, Wais, 36, was found dead in a hotel bathroom in unexplained circumstances. Within hours my inbox had filled with emails from those of us from different lands and different walks of life he had brought together. Not only were we devastated at losing a friend but his tragic death seemed to symbolise Afghanistan's downward spiral.

I got to know Wais, pronounced Wise, in November 2001, shortly after the fall of the Taliban, when I was among the Mustafa's first guests. Wais had returned that summer after twenty-one years of exile in America. Presuming that with the Taliban in power Kabul would hardly attract tourists, he decided to turn the family hotel into a bazaar for moneychangers and gem dealers.

He had just finished replacing the walls between rooms with glass partitions and iron bars when 9/11 happened. Two months, and many B-52 raids later, the Taliban were gone and journalists and aid workers were streaming into the city looking for somewhere to stay.

With no time to rebuild, Wais simply painted the glass partitions white and reopened as a hotel. The glass boxes were bitterly cold and you could hear everything in the next room, horrible if like me you were between a snoring Australian and a Japanese journalist who had high-pitched conversations with his office in the early hours of the morning.

In truth the Mustafa was not much of a hotel but what it lacked in comfort Wais made up for in personality. Short but powerfully built, he was a former bodybuilding champion with a fondness for Al Pacino movies and Frank Sinatra songs and a puppyish desire to be liked. He talked like the New Jersey car dealer he once was.

The 9 p.m. curfew meant we spent a lot of time in the guesthouse. Wais acquired a television powered by a car battery, which we would watch by candlelight wrapped in blankets as the electricity went on and off. When I was shivering on the roof using the satellite phone to file my copy, he would send out cups of green tea.

One day he asked me to follow him, barely able to contain his excitement. In the garage was a 1968 open-top Chevrolet Camaro that had once belonged to an Afghan prince. We drove through the ruins of western Kabul, laughing and waving like royals as children pointed and old men almost fell off their bikes, and bobbing blue burqas came to an abrupt stop.

Wais was always full of schemes. He held Thursday-night barbecues on the roof terrace where you could sit in the seats of an old Soviet MiG and look at the stars over the Hindu Kush mountains. He located someone raising turkeys in the Panjshir valley so we could have Christmas dinner.

In 2002 he opened Kabul's first bar. Entered through a heavy safe door with a combination lock, it was a marble and mirror extravaganza. A sculpture of the four horsemen of the apocalypse protruded from one wall and a dancing Osama bin Laden doll presided over the bar. Heinekens were known as Green Grenades and its signature cocktail was the Tora Bora Sunrise.

For a while there was a bearded barman whose neck was tattooed with a dotted line and the words 'Cut Here'. Bullet holes in the ceiling testified to the gunfights, and once, when everyone was bored, a macaque monkey was hired from the zoo to stand on the bar bearing a Kalashnikov.

Every time I came back Wais would excitedly show off his latest innovations, whether it was carpets and curtains in the rooms, showers instead of buckets, the courtyard of white doves or the imported espresso machine. I had one cappuccino before the machine exploded due to Kabul's erratic power supply.

As his schemes failed, Wais grew depressed, moaning about the deteriorating security and growing demands for protection money. A Pashtun, he became convinced the Panjshiris from the Northern Alliance were trying to kill him. His desk was covered in pots of vitamin pills, and sleeping often consisted of passing out after an excess of one stimulant or another.

Few of his fellow young Afghan-Americans returned. 'What's here?' Wais would ask. 'Just rubbish and ruins. Back in Ridgefield I was clearing $40,000–50,000 easy after tax and you could pick up a pizza on the way home or take in a movie and when you turned on the shower the hot water came out like "pow!" Here nothing works.'

I felt the same about the Mustafa. I was fed up with the constant power cuts because of his refusal to pay bribes and feared the hotel had become a target because of all the dodgy Defense Department types it attracted. A couple of years ago I switched to a different guesthouse with a generator, feeling horribly guilty, particularly after Wais told me he regarded me as his sister.

Despite all the setbacks, Wais was endlessly generous, throwing surprise birthday parties for those stranded in Kabul, far from home. He remained the first stop for information and the Mustafa was the natural venue for the founding of the Afghan Foreign Press Association.

Last time I went to the bar, in July, a group of men in dark glasses with pistols strapped on their thighs were watching *Apocalypse Now* as if straight out of central casting.

I cannot imagine Kabul without Wais. He was buried at the foot of TV Mountain overlooking the city which he loved and loathed. It is often said, 'You can rent an Afghan but never buy one.' In a land of shifting loyalties Wais was that rare precious thing – a true friend.

Acknowledgements

Being a foreign correspondent largely involves descending on people in faraway lands or tough situations and expecting them to drop everything for you and your notebook. It's a job that would be impossible without the kindness of strangers along the way, from Afghanistan to Zimbabwe.

Twenty years of reporting from four continents is an awful lot of places and people. If I started writing a list of all those who have helped me it would be as long again as this book.

Some who have helped me most prefer not to be mentioned because of the sensitivities of the areas or regimes where they live. Of those I can name, I would particularly like to thank Bashir Riaz and Benazir Bhutto for literally changing my life; Umer for some very interesting introductions; Akbar Ahmed for always patiently sharing his great knowledge of Islam; Hamid Karzai and Zia Mojadeddi for teaching me about the Pashtun tribes; the Arbab family for their hospitality and insights on Pakistan's tribal areas; Kabul Bob for wine and wisdom; Mike and Brian for incredible adventures; Fredi and Rita Ruf for their kindness in Zimbabwe; and Major Paul Blair and C Company of 3 Para for keeping me alive.

I have been very lucky to work for editors who have let me disappear to 'hunt elephants' in remote places – in particular John Witherow and Dominic Lawson, and foreign editors Sean Ryan, Con Coughlin, Bob Tyrer and Andrew Gowers. Those who encouraged me in my early days were Robin Pauley, Jurek Martin, JDF Jones, Peter Bruce, Stewart Dalby, John Ellison and Max Wilkinson.

Mostly I travel on my own. But life on the road – and in grim places such as the Umm Qasr trailer park – would have been much less fun without friends like Philip Sherwell, Dominic Medley, Lucrecia Franco, Mac Margolis, Husain Haqqani, and Paul Salopek, not to mention exchanging late night texts and satellite phone calls with my colleague Hala Jaber.

I very much enjoyed working with photographers Paul Hackett in Zimbabwe and Leticia Valverdes in the Amazon (the wonderful photograph on page 140 is hers) and Zimbabwe.

I'd particularly like to thank the photographer Justin Sutcliffe who seems to have been present in many a scrape. The amazing photographs of the fattening rooms in Calabar (pages 161 and 166) and the ambush in Helmand (pages 355 and 358) are his, as is that on page 193.

I would also like to thank my editor Annabel Wright for her ever-ready smile and good-natured patience in helping distil twenty years on the road into a few hundred pages, and my wonderful agent David Godwin

It would of course be impossible for me to do my job if it weren't for a very supportive Mum and Dad and friends like Ronke and Tanya, and above all my gorgeous husband Paulo and son Lourenço. To them I say: I may be a Mum with a terrible secret in my wardrobe – a flak jacket. But one day I will swap it for a little black dress, I promise…

The articles which appear in this book are reproduced with the kind permission of the publications in which they first appeared. 'Oh for a hero!' © *Financial Times* / 9 July 1988; 'A beast of a contest' © *Financial Times* / 6 May 1989; 'Westernised women dread return to veiled existence' © *Financial Times* / 23 June 1989; 'Where medieval ways die hard' © *Financial Times* / 5 August 1989; 'Pakistan asks FT journalist to leave' © *Financial Times* / 21 September 1989; 'The forest martyr' © *Financial Times* / 8 December 1990; 'The beach is the bottom line – Copacabana beach' © *Financial Times* / 18 July 1992; 'Extermination in Eden' © *Financial Times* / 20 February 1993; 'Carnival: a dance to the music of crime' © *Financial Times* / 13 March 1993; 'The strange case of the Bolivian Navy' © *Financial Times* / 11 September 1993. 'Bhutto the bride' / 19 December 1987; 'Smuggler's paradise' / 3 September 1988; 'Jihad on stale bread and mud crabs' / 17 September 1988; 'You never know when you might need a wailer' / 6 January 1996; 'The poet with blood on his apron' / 17 February 1996; 'Dances in a Carriage – with Zambian Smugglers' / 21 February 1996 © Christina Lamb, though these articles originally appeared in the *Financial Times*. 'War on Top of the World' and 'I run the gauntlet of fear to siege city' reprinted with kind permission of the Express Newspapers. 'Psst…Wanna buy a tank?' © 2007 Time Inc. All Rights Reserved. Reprinted from *Time Magazine*® with permission. 'Why Rio is Murdering its street children' / June 1991 / *Marie Claire*; 'The missing children of Argentina' / May 1992 / *Marie Claire* © Christina Lamb. 'Delta blues: Nigeria's poor prepare to fight for the oil riches of their country'; 'To Zanzibar to be wed'; 'Damilola thought he was coming to a better life in England – how wrong he was'; 'Eat, eat, eat if you want to be loved… In Africa, big is beautiful'; 'This is Wambi Bakayoko, who is 15. He is a chocolate slave. Last year he was sold to a plantation owner for £37.50 – what the average Briton spends on chocolate in just seven months'; '£5 for a slave girl with a nervous smile'; 'I was one of the Taliban's torturers'; '"I hear the bombs drop and I pray that they will end our suffering"'; 'When Zena Karamzade's dreams of being a doctor ended under the Taliban, she joined a dress-making circle – or so the regime thought'; 'Face to face with the Taliban leaders'; 'Down to the Wire'; 'For four hours Dora, aged 12, was gang-raped by Mugabe's men' © Christina Lamb / *Sunday Telegraph*. 'Yes, I was a cynic until I met her – Diana' / 7 September 1997; 'Colonel Cox has a whole town to build'/ 6 April 2003; 'Torture cells that kept a people in fear'/ 13 April 2003; 'Iraq "destroyed weapons by 1994"'/ 8 June 2003; 'Just thirty-two prize items still missing as treasures flood back to Iraq Museum' / 15 June 2003; '"Have you ever used a pistol?"' / 2 July 2006; 'Fonz of Kabul, hotelier and fast-talking fixer, found dead' / 31 December 2006; 'Where's Bin Laden?' / 18 March 2007; 'Zimbabwe's silent genocide' / 8 July 2007; 'It was what we feared, but dared not to happen' / 21 October 2007 © *Sunday Times*. 'Saddam stole our water' / 27 July 2003 © *Sunday Times Magazine*. 'Running with the bulls'; 'Tea with Pinochet'; 'Hail, the mini Bin Ladens'; 'Where were the flowers, or the jubilant cheers?' are taken from articles which first appeared in the *New Statesman*. 'An awful lot of trouble in Brazil'; 'A suitable case for treatment'; '"My People Trust and Love Me": on the road with the President of Peru' © *The Spectator* (1828 Ltd.).

Index of Articles

Financial Times
Bhutto the bride 19 December 1987   9
Oh for a hero! 9 July 1988   27
Smuggler's paradise 3 September 1988   19
Jihad on stale bread and mud crabs 17 September 1988   36
A beast of a contest 6 May 1989   55
Where medieval ways die hard 5 August 1989   22
Westernised women dread return to veiled existence
      23 June 1989   46
Pakistan asks *FT* journalists to leave 21 September 1989   65
The forest martyr 8 December 1990   123
The beach is the bottom line – Copacabana beach 18 July 1992   77
Extermination in Eden 20 February 1993   132
Carnival – a dance to the music of crime 13 March 1993   67
The strange case of the Bolivian Navy 11 September 1993   93
You never know when you might need a wailer 6 January 1996   174
The poet with blood on his apron 17 February 1996   176
Learning to dance on a Zambian train 21 February 1998   153

Daily Express
War on Top of the World 29 August 1989   58
I run the gauntlet of fear to siege city 17 March 1989   41

Time magazine
Psst…Wanna buy a tank? 9 January 1989   31

Marie Claire

Why Rio is murdering its children June 1991 82
The missing children of Argentina May 1992 96

Sunday Telegraph

Delta blues: Nigeria's poor prepare to fight for the oil riches
of their country 21 February 1999 157
To Zanzibar to be wed (A Zanzibari Wedding) 13 June 1999 185
Damilola thought he was coming to a better life in
England – how wrong he was 3 December 2000 204
Eat, eat, eat if you want to be loved… In Africa, big is
beautiful 25 March 2001 161
This is Wambi Bakayoko, who is 15. He is a chocolate slave.
22 April 2001 212
£5 for a slave girl with a nervous smile 29 April 2001 217
I was one of the Taliban's torturers 30 September 2001 224
'I hear the bombs drop and I pray that they will end our
suffering' 14 October 2001 230
When Zena Karamzade's dreams of being a doctor ended
under the Taliban, she joined a dressmaking circle – or so
the regime thought 16 December 2001 236
Face to face with the Taliban leaders 10 February 2002 243
Down to the wire 11 August 2002 309
For four hours Dora, aged 12, was gang-raped by Mugabe's
men 25 August 2002 314

Sunday Times

Yes, I was a cynic until I met her – Diana 7 September 1997 179
Colonel Cox has a whole town to build 6 April 2003 269
Torture cells that kept a people in fear 13 April 2003 275
Iraq 'destroyed weapons by 1994' 8 June 2003 288
Just thirty-two prize items still missing as treasures flood
back to Iraq Museum 15 June 2003 279
Saddam stole our water (magazine) 27 July 2003 297
'Have you ever used a pistol?' 2 July 2006 351

Fonz of Kabul, hotelier and fast-talking fixer, found dead
    31 December 2006   381
Where's bin Laden? (magazine) 18 March 2007   331
Zimbabwe's silent genocide 8 July 2007   324
'It was what we feared, but dared not to happen'
    21 October 2007   367

New Statesman
Running with the bulls 8 August 1997   171
Tea with Pinochet 26 July 1999   191
Hail, the mini bin Ladens 24 March 2003   249
Where were the flowers, or the jubilant cheers? 31 March 2003   260

The Spectator
An awful lot of trouble in Brazil 12 September 1992   109
A suitable case for treatment 21 November 1992   114
'My People Trust and Love Me': on the road with the
    President of Peru 13 August 1994   102